Studies in Talmudic Logic
Volume 10

Principles of Talmudic Logic

Volume 1
Non-Deductive Inferences in the Talmud
Michael Abraham, Dov Gabbay and Uri Schild

Volume 2
The Textual Inference Rules Klal uPrat. How the Talmud Defines Sets
Michael Abraham, Dov Gabbay, Gabriel Hazut, Yosef E. Maruvka, and Uri Schild

Volume 3
Talmudic Deontic Logic
Michael Abraham, Dov Gabbay and Uri Schild

Volume 4
Temporal Logic in the Talmud
Michael Abraham, Israel Belfer, Dov Gabbay and Uri Schild

Volume 5
Resolution of Conflicts and Normative Loops in the Talmud
Michael Abraham, Dov Gabbay and Uri Schild

Volume 6
Talmudic Logic
Andrew Schumann

Volume 7
Delegation in Talmudic Logic
Michael Abraham, Israel Belfer, Dov Gabbay and Uri Schild

Volume 8
Synthesis of Concepts in Talmudic Logic
Michael Abraham, Israel Belfer, Dov Gabbay and Uri Schild

Volume 9
Analysis of Concepts and States in Talmudic Logic
M. Abraham, Dov Gabbay, and Uri Schild

Volume 10
Principles of Talmudic Logic
M. Abraham, Dov Gabbay, and Uri Schild

Studies in Talmudic Logic
Series Editors
Michael Abraham, Dov Gabbay, and Uri Schild   dov.gabbay@kcl.ac.uk

Principles of Talmudic Logic

M. Abraham, Dov M. Gabbay,
and Uri Schild

© Individual author and College Publications 2013. All rights reserved.

ISBN 978-1-84890-093-6

College Publications
Scientific Director: Dov Gabbay
Managing Director: Jane Spurr
Department of Computer Science
King's College London, Strand, London WC2R 2LS, UK

http://www.collegepublications.co.uk

Printed by Lightning Source, Milton Keynes, UK

All rights reserved. No part of this publication may be reproduced, stored in a retrieval system or transmitted in any form, or by any means, electronic, mechanical, photocopying, recording or otherwise without prior permission, in writing, from the publisher.

CONTENTS

CHAPTER 1 INTRODUCTION   1

CHAPTER 2 ANALYSIS OF THE TALMUDIC ARGUMENTUM A FORTIORI INFERENCE RULE (KAL VACHOMER) USING MATRIX ABDUCTION 25
1   Introduction and Motivation   25
1.1   Matrix Abduction in AI   25
1.2   The Talmudic Kal-Vachomer[1]   29
1.3   Preview of the model   30
1.4   Qiyas and Kaimutika Nyaya   32
2   Motivating the matrix model   33
3   Superiority relation on partial orders   35
4   Case study: Sentences for traffic offences   61
5   Analysis of the Talmudic Kal-Vachomer from Kidushin 5a–5b . . .   64
6   Conclusion and discussion   77
Appendices

CHAPTER 3 LOGICAL ANALYSIS OF THE TALMUDIC RULES OF GENERAL AND SPECIFIC (KLALIM-U-PRATIM) 99
     1   Introduction   99
            1.1   General discussion   99
     2   How to define a set of elements 100
     3   The Talmudic options 107
     4   Concluding discussion 114

CHAPTER 4 OBLIGATIONS AND PROHIBITIONS IN TALMUDIC DEONTIC LOGIC 117
     1   Motivating Talmudic deontic logic TDL 117
     2   Contrary to Duties 127
     3   Discussion: Talmudic deontic logic? 130
     4   Intuitionistic standard deontic logic 137
     5   Concluding remarks 145
            5.1   Reward and punishment 145
            5.2   Why 613 Talmudic operators? 146
            5.3   Comparison with legislation in law 147
            5.4   Comparison with preference based models 148

CHAPTER 5 CONTRARY TO TIME CONDITIONALS IN TALMUDIC LOGIC   151
    1   Introduction: orientation and motivation 151
    2   Language for contrary to time with examples 157
         2.1   Choice of language 157
         2.2   Sample uses of the language 161
    3   Introducing temporal Talmudic logic (TTL) 164
    4   Talmudic temporal logic 177
    5   Comparison with the literature 181
    6   Conclusion 185

CHAPTER 6 FUTURE DETERMINATION OF ENTITIES IN TALMUDIC PUBLIC ANNOUNCEMENT LOGIC   187
    1   Introduction and orientation 188
    2   Introducing Talmudic classical models 199
    3   Talmudic public announcement models 202
    4   Propositional Talmudic public announcement logic **TPK** . . . 209
         4.1   Motivation 209
         4.2   Preliminary formal discussion 212
         4.3   Formal **TPK** 216
    5   Discussion and Comparison with traditional public announcement logic 219
    Appendices

CHAPTER 7 THE HANDLING OF LOOPS IN TALMUDIC LOGIC, WITH APPLICATION TO ODD AND EVEN LOOPS IN ARGUMENTATION   233
    1   Background 233
    2   Shkop extensions 235
    3   Caminada counter examples: A discussion 250
    4   Conclusion 253
    5   Appendix A: Tableaux for Caminada Socratic discussion 254
    6   Appendix B: Shkop principle in temporal context 257

CHAPTER 8 UNCERTAINTY RULES IN TALMUDIC REASONING   261

CHAPTER 9 DELEGATION, COUNT AS, AND SECURITY IN TALMUDIC LOGIC   269
    1   Background and orientation 270
    2   Motivating the Talmudic system 271
    3   Technical definitions of the logical model 275
         3.1   Preliminary discussion 275
         3.2   The reactive switch model for the *long arm* view of Tur   286
    4   Comparison with modern literature 288
    5   Conclusion and discussion 290
    References

CHAPTER 1

INTRODUCTION

The topics addressed in this book deal with the logic of Halacha — Jewish law, and in particular with the logic of the Talmud. In this preface we intend to analyse the nature and characteristics of the Talmud, and determine its place within the Halachic context. Next, we shall attempt to define our research aims with respect to these topics, as expressed in the chapters in this book.

A General Survey of the Halachic Tradition: From the Creation of the World until the Giving of the Torah

According to Jewish tradition the origin of the Jewish people is in the ancient East, where Abraham the son of Terach was born and lived. Abraham was the first monotheist. According to the usual time-scale of Jewish tradition he was born in 1812 BCE. Abraham communicated with the Creator, but did not yet know the specifics of the Torah (the Pentateuch) to be given on Mount Sinai several hundred years after his death. Talmudic Midrashim (homiletic teachings on the Bible) state that Abraham fulfilled commands of the Torah, perhaps even all the commands. Formally, however, it is assumed that the Halacha, in its traditional significance as a set of norms that each Jew must obey, did not exist yet in his time.

Nevertheless, first concepts of Halacha existed even before that. The Halachic era began two thousand years earlier, when Adam was given six commandments, and a little later when Noah was given a seventh commandment. These are seven universal obligations for all human beings, whether of the Jewish faith or not, and they are denoted in the Halachic jargon: "The seven commandments of Noah's sons".

The beginning of Jewish Halacha is with Abraham, who received the command of circumcision. After him, the process continues with the Egyptian Diaspora, where Amram, the father of Moses, receives some further early commandments. The process continues at Marah, during the wanderings of the Jews in the desert towards the land of Israel. At Marah the Israelites received an additional three commandments from God. (There are different traditions identifying these three commandments). The giving of the Torah by God takes place at Mount Sinai, where Moses receives the Torah from God and passes it to his disciples and on to the Children of Israel in all generations.

This is how Maimonides[1] describes it (The Book of Judges, Kings and Wars,

---

[1] Moses ben-Maimon, called Maimonides and also known as Rambam (Hebrew acronym for "Rabbi Moshe ben Maimon"), was a preeminent medieval Jewish philosopher and one of the greatest Torah scholars and physicians of the Middle Ages. He was born in Córdoba, Spain, 1135, and died in Egypt (or Tiberias) on December 12, 1204. He was a rabbi, physician and philosopher in Morocco and Egypt.

chapter IX, 1):[2]

> Six precepts were given to Adam: prohibition of idolatry, of blasphemy, of murder, of robbery, and the command to establish courts of justice. Although there is a tradition to this effect-a tradition dating back to Moses, our teacher, and human reason approves of those precepts-it is evident from the general tenor of the Scriptures that he (Adam) was bidden to observe these commandments./ An additional commandment was give to |Noah: prohibition of (eating) a limb from a living animal, as it is said: *Only flesh with the life thereof, which is the blood thereof, shall ye not eat* (Gen. 9:4). Thus we have seven commandments. So it was until Abraham appeared who, in addition to the aforementioned commandments, was charged to practice circumcision. Moreover, Abraham instituted the Morning Service, Isaac set apart tithes and instituted the Afternoon Service, Jacob added to the preceding law (prohibiting) the sinew that shrank, and inaugurated the Evening Service. In Egypt Amram was charged to observe other precepts, until Moses came and the Law was completed through him.

Moses led the Children of Israel out of Egypt, and fifty days after the Exodus the people arrived at Mount Sinai and received the Torah from Moses.

It is important to understand that despite the above description of stepwise receipt of the Halacha, the customary Halachic assumption is that the Sinaitic revelation gives the validity and creates the Halachic obligation. This is what Maimonides writes (The Book of Judges, Kings and Wars, chapter VIII, 11):[3]

> A heathen who accepts the seven commandments and observes them scrupulously is a "righteous heathen", and will have a portion in the world to come, provided he accepts them and performs them because the Holy One, blessed be He, commanded them in the Law and made known through Moses, our teacher, that the observance thereof had been enjoined upon the descendants of Noah even before the Law was given. But if his observance thereof is based upon a reasoned conclusion he is not deemed a resident alien, or one of the pious of the Gentiles, but one of their wise men.

Maimonides states that even a Ger Toshav (a resident alien), i.e. an alien who observes the seven commandments of Noah's sons, must do that as part of the Sinaitic tradition. Observance of commandments through logical acceptance of their importance and truth is not of religious merit, but only of moral value. The commentators at that place explain that this principle also holds for Jews, with respect to the observance of commandments in general.

Maimonides (Commentaries on the Mishna[4], Chulin 7:6) states what at first

---

[2] The Code of Maimonides, Book Fourteen, The Book of Judges, Yale Judaica Series, Yale University Press, 1949

[3] As above.

[4] The Mishna or Mishnah (Hebrew: "repetition", from the verb shanah, "to study and review", also "secondary") is the first major written redaction of the Jewish oral traditions called the "Oral Torah"

sight seems to be a similar principle':[5]

> You must know that whatever we do or refrain from doing today, we do only because of God's command by way of Moshe, and not because of God's command to the prophets that preceded him. For example, we refrain from eating a limb removed from a living animal not because God forbade this to the descendants of Noah, but because God forbade it to us when He commanded us at Sinai that a limb removed from a living animal continues to be forbidden... You see that [the Sages] said (Makkot 23b): "Six hundred and thirteen mitzvot were told to Moshe at Sinai," and all these are included among the mitzvot.

Here Maimonides states that the commandments including the ones from before the Sinaitic revelation should also be obeyed because of the renewed obligation at that point. Thus Maimonides seems to repeat what he said in the Book of Judges, Kings and Wars quoted above, but a closer observation shows that these are really two different statements.

In order to understand this we must mention a concept coined by Hans Kelsen, a jurist and legal philosopher: Positivism. Kelsen, the positivist, saw the legal system as a logical system of hierarchical norms. Each norm depends on a norm higher in the hierarchy. At the top of the normative pyramid stands the "basic norm" which gives validity to the entire system. In the context of national laws the basic norm can be the obligation to obey the legislating body, or carry out the wishes of the electors as expressed by the legislation, etc. In the Halachic context the basic norm may be taken as the Halachic obligation that Jews took upon themselves at Mount Sinai. The Sages expressed it as follows (Tractate Nedarim 8a and similar places[6]): "As if we all swore at Mount Sinai to obey the Torah".

The words of Maimonides in the Commentaries on the Mishna[7] quoted above state that that the obligation to obey the Halacha is founded on the basic norm: What was given by God at Mount Sinai (and not earlier or later). So what about a person who obeys the law, but not because of the basic norm? For example, assume a citizen of Israel crosses an intersection only at a green light and pays his taxes lawfully, but he does this not because he accepts the legislation of the Knesset (parliament), but because he considers the norms as morally correct. Is there a legal defect in his behaviour? Certainly not. Kelsen's basic norm does not appeal to the citizens but to the government; the basis of a prosecution of a citizen who does not obey the law is the basic law. This is the justification for punishing him. He must obey the law, and it does not matter what his motivation may be.

Maimonides in the book of Judges, Kings and Wars says something else. He states that if somebody obeys the obligations owing to reason and logic and not

---

[5] Free translation.

[6] where nothing else is stated the reference is to the Babylonian Talmud.
Talmud Bavli, The Schottenstein Edition, Mesorah Publications, Ltd, NY, 2008

[7] The Mishna or Mishna is the first major written redaction of the Jewish oral traditions called the "Oral Torah".

because of his obligation to the basic norm (The Torah at Mount Sinai), then his actions are not considered as Mitzvot (fulfillment of commandments). A person who puts on Tefillin (phylacteries) without believing in God, or without believing and feeling obliged to Mount Sinai, is not fulfilling a commandment. In principle he must put on the Tefillin a second time.

We see that the basic norm is central to Halacha and more important than in other legal systems. Here there is an appeal to the individual, and not just a theoretical justification for the government to act against the wrongdoer. In Halacha an action according to the basic norm is necessary for the action to be considered a Mitzva.

From Mount Sinai and on: The Development of the Oral Code.

The Jewish tradition states that at Mount Sinai Moses received two parts of the Torah: The Written Law (The five books of Moses — the Pentateuch) and additional principles and commentaries called the Oral Law.

From that point and on there is a chain of transmission from a teacher to his disciple, as described in the Mishna (Tractate Avot, chapter I, 1-2):[8]

> Moses received the Torah from Sinai, and transmitted it to Joshua, and Joshuah to the Elders, and the Elders to the Prophets, and the Prophets transmitted it to the Men of the Great Assembly...: Shimon HaTzaddik was [one] of the remnants of the Great Assembly... Antigenos, leader of Socho, received [the Mesorah] from Shimon HaTzaddik...: Yose ben Yoezer [the] leader of Tzredah and Yose ben Yochanan [the] leader of Jerusalem received [the Mesorah] from them... : Yehoshua be Perachyah and Nittai of Arbel received [the Mesorah] from them...: Yehudah be Tabbai and Shimon ben Shatch received [the Mesorah] from them...: Shemayah and Avtalion received [the Mesorah] from them...: Hillel and Shammai received [the Mesorah] from them...: Rabbi Yochanan ben Zakkai received [the tradition] from Hillel and Shammai...: Rabbi Yochanan be Zakkai had five disciples. They were: R'Eliezer ben Hyrkanos, R'Yehoshua be Chananiah, R'Yose the Kohen, R'Shimon ben Nesanel, and R'Elazar ben Arach.

This description is abridged, and in parallel sources one can find more detailed descriptions of the intermediate steps. At the end of the Tannaic[9] period it is decided to write down the principles of the Oral Law, and thus the Mishna is written by Rabbi Yehuda HaNassi (at the beginning of the third century CE).

After the Tannaic period outlined in the Mishna above, the tradition contin-

---

[8]The Mishna, Artscroll Mishna Series, Seder Nezikin, Vol. IV, Avos, Mesorah Publications, Ltd, NY, 2007.

[9]Tannaim (plural of Aramaic tanna,=one who studies or teaches), Jewish sages of the period from Hillel to the compilation of the Mishna .They functioned as both scholars and teachers, educating those in the synagogues as well as in the academies. Their opinions are found either in the Mishna or as collected in the Tosefta .

ues as described in the literature of the Rishonim[10], prefaces by Maimonides, and others: The Amoraim[11] created two works of Talmud: The Babylonian Talmud (often called the Gemara) and the Jerusalem (= Palestinian, = Israeli) Talmud. According to tradition the Jerusalem Talmud was completed by Rabbi Yochanan at the end of the fourth century CE, and the Babylonian Talmud was completed by Rav Ashi and Ravina at beginning of the sixth century CE. It is usually assumed that the finalising and editing of the two Talmuds was done over a period of several hundred years after the date given by tradition. After the Amoraim came the Savoraim[12], then the Gaonim[13] and then the Rishonim[8] (= sages of the Middle Ages). During the period of the Rishonim there was an large amount of Halachic activity, mainly interpretation of the Scriptures and the Babylonian Talmud. Exceptional during this period is Rabbi Moshe ben Maimon, Maimonides[1]. He created a monumental work, the Mishne Torah (the Code of Maimonides). In this book of fourteen parts Maimonides codifies all Halachic writings from the Talmudic and extra-Talmudic sources and the period of the Gaonim. This is a unique work in the long history of the Halacha. It is the only work that contains the entire Halachic corpus in a unified, methodical and organised structure. Other works do not cover all areas of the Halacha, and certainly do not classify the material and settle disputes in a systematic manner.

The beginning of Modern Times is the beginning of the Acharonim, leading rabbis and Poskim (Jewish legal decisors) living from roughly the 16th century to the present. During the period ending the Middle Ages and the beginning of Modern Times a major Halachic work, the Shulchan Aruch (Set Table), was created by Yosef Karo[14] in Safed and by Rabbi Moshe Isserles[15] in Krakow. This work which summarises the major commandments relating to everyday life at the time, does not include commandments that deal with the service in the (no more existing) Temple, with questions of cleanliness and purification (which are not observed today). Halachic developments continue of course also today.

The Work of the Sages: Types of Halacha.

The Halacha was given by God at Mount Sinai, but it expands and is elaborated all the time, to this very day. The Halacha is a legal system, and as such it is supposed to supply answers to the legal needs of Jewish society. It follows that each link in the chain of transmission described above is responsible for several

---

[10]Rishonim, leading rabbis who were deciders of Jewish law and lived between 1050 and 1500 CE

[11]Amoraim, renowned Jewish scholars who "said" or "told over" the teachings of the Oral law, from about 200 to 500 CE in Babylonia and the Land of Israel

[12]Savoraim (s. Savora, Aramaic "a reasoner") are the leading rabbis living from the end of period of the Amoraim (around 500 CE) to the beginning of the Geonim (around 700 CE).

[13]Gaonim (also transliterated Geonim) were the presidents of the two great Talmudic Academies of Sura and Pumbedita, in Babylonia, and were the generally accepted spiritual leaders of the Jewish community world wide in the early medieval era

[14]Joseph ben Ephraim Karo (also spelled Yosef Caro, or Qaro), Toledo, Spain 1488 – Safed, Israel 1575

[15]Moses Isserles (also spelled Moshe Isserlis, called the Remah), Kraków, Poland, 1520– May 11, 1572

tasks: Transmitting the knowledge accumulated so far, making new regulation and rabbinical decrees, responding to questions by ordinary people and passing judgments in rabbinical courts. However, it is true that the Halacha operated and developed at places and times when it has no full autonomy, under the rule of different legal systems.

It is customary to divide Halacha into two major categories: Halacha mainly revealed at Mount Sinai (Halacha DeOraita) and Rabbinical Halacha. It is a common mistake to believe that this distinction is entirely chronological. Halacha created by Biblical hermeneutics (to be dealt with below), or interpretation of oral traditions given to Moses at Mount Sinai is Halacha DeOraita. Halacha created by rabbinical legislation (and not by Biblical exegesis) is Rabbinical Halacha.

This means that Halachic items are created all through history, join the Halachic corpus and their status may be like oral traditions given to Moses at Mount Sinai., or their status is as rabbinical legislation.

Apart from the theoretical difference there is also a Halachic distinction between the two kinds of Halacha. Halacha DeOraita is more stringent than Rabbinical Halacha, and this difference has Halachic implications. Consider for example, the Halacha of Doubt. If Doubt concerning a Halacha DeOraita is strict, a person must exceed the bare requirements of the Halacha: If a person is about to eat meat, and he is not sure whether the meat is pork or veal, he must not eat it. In the case of Rabbinical Halacha one is more lenient.

The Anarchistic Character of Halacha

Based on our description above one would expect the Halacha to become well organised over time, and that fixed and constant Halachic procedures would develop. Surprisingly, Halacha has an anarchistic element that has not been eliminated through history. It has even been asserted that a modern legal system cannot be based on the Halacha because of this anarchistic trait[16].

Many consider this fundamental trait to be part of Jewish identity and nature, which is original, rebellious and argumentative, which is divisive into different lines of thought, and does not accept authority. Judaism in general and Halacha in particular are based on negotiation more than on a closed set of principles and obligatory specifics.

The anarchistic trait of the Halacha is expressed in several ways. It is found in the dispute among Halachic experts, but even more so it can be seen in the nature of the canonical works and their stature. We have already mentioned that throughout history we do not find any attempts to edit the various parts of Halacha and organise them in a classified manner. The attempt by Maimonides is exceptional, and his oeuvre was not acknowledged as binding. His work is considered one of the most important Halachic sources, but it is not a compulsory canonical codex.

---

[16] Hanina Ben-Menahem. Judicial Deviation in Talmudic Law: Governed by Men, Not by Rules. Jewish Law in Context, vol. 1. New York: Harwood Academic Publishers, 1991. xi, 220 pp.

If one wishes to speak about a binding canonical codex it must be the Talmud (especially the Babylonian Talmud). But many questions arise when the nature of this text is considered. It is not a codex in any sense. It is a collection of fragments (sugiot) that clarify various commandments. Among them are aggadatic (homiletic) fragments, stories, moral lessons, etc. Also the purely Halachic parts are formulated as discussion and debate among the Sages. They cite different sources, and only seldom do they state a definitive Halacha. In most cases the fragment ends by simply stating the different opinions and their Halachic conclusions. It is a description of discussions at various places, about different topics in different formulations. Sometimes there are contradictions between different Talmudic fragments, and also the textual versions are problematic. The Talmud is open textured, not what one may expect from a canonical text that aspires to be a codex.

So the central Halachic canon is only a collection of discussions and Halachic arguments, which also include elements that only relate to the discussions in an associative manner. It therefore looks very strange that such a text should be accepted as the central binding canon of a normative legal system. What is gained by this canonisation? What does it mean? As there is nothing final, as the questions remain open, what is canonical about this canon? In order to answer that question we must first consider the historical background leading to the acceptance of the Talmud as a binding canonical text.

The history of the Halacha as schematically described above can be considered as a chain of links; each link is a (not exactly defined) time period, with a name: Prophets, Men of the Great Assembly, the Couples, Tannaim, Amoraim, Savoraim, Gaonim, Rishonim and Acharonim. In some cases there is a Halachic significance in the passing from one period to the other: Amoraim do not disagree with Tannaim. A Tannaic source that contradicts an Amorai is usually considered a definitive proof against the Amorai. Similarly post-Talmudic sages do not disagree with the Talmud, most of the Rishonim do not usually disagree with the Gaonim (though the feature is less apparent), and similarly with Acharonim and Rishonim.

It would seem that this picture reduces the anarchistic nature we described above. However, we must remember that in each period there were several sages, each with his opinions, and they created different sources. Therefore, the general obligation towards a certain period does not mean much from a practical aspect. Nevertheless, the question remains what is the nature of the prohibition of sages from one period to disagree with sages from a previous period. This is particularly important in the (not too many) cases where the Talmudic fragment ends with a definite conclusion. This conclusion is binding on the following generations.

Maimonides (The Book of Judges, Rebels, chapter II, 1) states the following:

> If the Great Sanhedrin, by employing one of the hermeneutical principles, deduced a ruling which in its judgment was in consonance with the Law and rendered a decision to that effect, and a later Supreme Court finds a reason for setting aside the ruling, it may do so and act in accordance with its own opinion, as it is said: *and unto the judge that shall be in those days* (Deut. 17:9), that is, we are

bound to follow the directions of the court of our own generation.

It would seem that there is no restriction on the sages of one generation to formulate the Halacha as they wish. Their capability of disagreeing with their predecessors does not require that they are greater than the latter in learning, or any other requirement[17].

Rabbi Yosef Karo, the author of the Shulchan Aruch, in his commentary on Maimonides (Kesef Mishne[18]: On The Book of Judges, Rebels, chapter II, 1) considers the question why Amoraim do not disagree with the Tannaim, and why the Gaonim and Rishonim do not disagree with the sages of the Talmud: If there are no limitations on disagreement with previous generations, it is not clear why this does not happen in practice.

One might expect the explanation lies in praising the greatness of early generations. Thus we find several times in the Talmud, i.e. (Shabbat 112b):

> R' Zeira said in the name of Rava bar Zimona: If the early ones were sons of angels, we are sons of men; and if the early ones were sons of men, we are like donkeys.

but surprisingly, Kesef Mishne (loc. cit.) chooses another explanation. Its argument is that the authority of the Talmud is because we have decided not to challenge it. Thus, it is a technical acceptance only. In principle it could be possible to contradict any sage in any generation, but at the end of the Talmudic period the sages decided to accept the Talmud as a canonical corpus, not to be contradicted.

If there is no real Halachic constraint, why did the sages of that generation decide to stray from the Halachic anarchism and establish an obligatory text? The answer lies in processes that took place towards the end of the first Millennium CE (the beginning of the Middle Ages).Until then, Jews had been living in the Babylonian Diaspora for about a thousand years, they had legal autonomy, and an organised hierarchy headed by the Exilarch[19], who functioned in place of a king or president. At that time, this structure began to crumble. Jews began to spread all over the world, and form small communities at various distant places. There was therefore a danger that the Halacha would lose its coherence. Every little community, which may not have a person qualified in Jewish law, and no control over the ways of interpreting the law, could create some undisciplined legal interpretations. The Halacha would disintegrate, and Jewish social and legal cohesiveness would be destroyed. Therefore it was decided at that time to establish a framework for the further development of the Halacha. This framework is the Talmud.

It is important to understand that while the sages of those generations found it acceptable to deviate from the usual custom and establish a binding canon,

---

[17]In the next paragraph Maimonides introduces limitations on the capability of disagreeing with previous religious courts, but this relates only to Rabbinical legislation and regulations, and not to Halacha DeOraita, i.e. Biblical exegesis.

[18]Kesef Mishne, first printed Venice, 1574

[19]Exilarch (Hebrew: Rosh Galut, lit. "head of the exile") refers to the leaders of the Diaspora Jewish community following the deportation of the population of Judah into Babylonian exile after the destruction of the kingdom of Judah.

it seems that they also wished to preserve the open nature of the Halacha. The decision was therefore to select an open work like the Talmud as a binding canon. This step established a framework for discussion and development of the Halacha, enabled the discourse among communities and among sages all over the world, as indeed has been observed in all following generations. At the same time there is also room for considerable interpretational freedom. The result of this decision is the flowering of different communities and different interpretations of the sources of Halacha. During the thousand years since then the sages have acted autonomously, without a central Halachic authority, and without authority of enforcement. At the same time they have managed to keep up a debate among themselves. We believe this is a unique phenomenon, which has no analogue in the history of human civilisation.

Part of the debate is about the method of discussion itself. There are many conflicts about how to deal with controversy and different Halachic opinions. The debate is open, while at the same time its coherence is kept within the framework of the Talmud.

In order to illustrate the tension between the need for coherence and the wish to maintain freedom of opinions and dialectic, we shall describe a critical moment in the progress of Halachic disputation, which is found in several fragments of the Talmud and parallel writings.

The Way of Settling Controversy

Tractate Berachot 28a describes the forced abdication of R' Gamliel from the presidency[20] and the appointment of R' Elazar ben Azaryah in his stead, and states:

> And any place wherein 'on that day' is used, it is a reference to that day R' Elazar ben Azaryah was installed as Nasi

Let us attempt to clarify the importance of that day, which the Talmud has singled out in this manner.

In the second generation of sages in Yavneh a revolution took place, which has great importance for the further development of the Oral Law. The event is mentioned in several places in the Talmud, usually in a very dramatic way[21], but the historical correspondence between the descriptions is not clear at first sight. The words of Jewish Law are sparse in one place and rich in other places, so let us begin by examining a strange phenomenon in Tractate Avot.

As we saw above, the first chapter of Tractate Avot describes the transmission of the Torah from Moses to Yehoshua, to the Elders, etc. This process ends with the fifth couple: Hillel and Shammai (see quote on page 6). After that the Mishna brings sayings of sages from several generations, until chapter 2:9. There the description of the transmission is taken up again with the

---

[20]The Sanhedrin (Greek: synedrion, "sitting together," hence "assembly" or "council") was an assembly of twenty-three judges appointed in every city in the Biblical Land of Israel. The Great Sanhedrin was the supreme court of ancient Israel made of 71 members. The Nasi was the president of the Sanhedrin including when it sat as a criminal court.

[21]Tractate Baba Metziah 59, Tractate Berachot 28, Tractate Sanhedrin 68 and 101 and Tractate Chagiga 3.

words: "R' Yochanan ben Zakkai received [the transmission] from Hillel and Shammai".

Immediately after that the description of the transmissions ends. In the next Mishna it says: "Rabbi Yochanan be Zakkai had five disciples. They were: R'Eliezer ben Hyrkanos, R'Yehoshua be Chananiah, R'Yose the Kohen, R'Shimon ben Nesanel, and R'Elazar ben Arach", and this is the end of the narrative.

Until R' Yochanan ben Zakkai the process is described using the word 're-ceived': "Moses received from Yehoshua and transmitted..." R' Yochanan ben Zakkai is still described as 'receiving'. After that the words 'receive' and transmit' are not associated anymore in the Tractate Avot with respect to the process of transmission. The description of the process does not include these words. It should be noted that in the generation after R' Yochanan ben Zakkai there is no single prominent person or couple as before. The process becomes crowded, each sage has several disciples.

R' Yochanan ben Zakkai is considered the first generation of Tannaim. It is well-known that he asked the Romans for Yavneh[22] and its sages. The next generation was the generation of R' Gamliel from Yavneh, who was the president, R' Eliezer ben Hyrkanos (R' Eliezer the Great'), brother-in-law of R' Gamliel, R' Yehoshua ben Chananyah, his friend and opponent, R' Elazar ben Azaryah, who was younger, and R' Akiva ben Yosef, who was older but still a disciple, first of R' Eliezer the Great and at then of R' Yehoshua.

The change from the times of the terminology of 'receipt' of a disciple from his teacher to the era of multiple disciples learning from a teacher indicates a significant process that the Oral Tradition goes through in the first generation in Yavneh (second generation of Tannaim).

The Babylonian Talmud describes a dramatic incident, where R' Yehoshua and R' Eliezer the Great disagree about the law concerning an oven of Achnai[23] (Tractate Baba Metziah 59b):

> On that day R' Eliezer advanced all the arguments in the world, but [the Sages] did not accept his arguments. [R' Eliezer] said to them: If the Halacha accords with me, let this Carob tree prove it... Let the water canal prove it... Let the walls of the study hall prove it ... whereupon a Heavenly echo went forth and proclaimed: What argument do you have with R' Eliezer, whom the Halacha follows in all places. R' Yehoshua stood on his feet and declared: It [The Torah] is not in Heaven ... We pay no heed to a Heavenly echo in matters of Halacha, because You already wrote in the Torah at Mount Sinai: According to the majority [the matter] shall be decided.

Let us first remark that the expression 'bo bayom' ('on that day', see above, page 12) appears here. The meaning is probably not just the day of the discussion, but the day when R' Gamliel was forced from the presidency. Further

---

[22] After the destruction of the Second Temple in 70 CE, Rabban Yochanan Ben Zakkai moved the Sanhedrin[20] to Yavne. The Sanhedrin left Yavne for Usha in 80 CE and returned in 116 CE.

[23] The oven of Achnai is assembled rings of earthenware with sand in between them.

evidence for this can be brought from Tractate Berachot, which states that the entire Tractate of Eduyot was learned 'on that day'. Tractate Eduyot, chapter VII, 7 states:

> They testified about an [earthware] oven, that somebody cut into [horizontal] sections, and put sand between one section and the other, that it is susceptible to become unclean (tamei), because R'Eliezer rules such an oven clean (tahor).

In other words, the question of Achnai's oven was settled on the same day R' Gamliel was deposed from the presidency.

In order to understand the drama that took place that day, we must note that R' Eliezer the Great consistently represent the school that says that the Torah is all tradition, i.e., the law should be determined only by the information reaching us from the times of Moshe at Sinai. We shall show an example of this. In Tractate Sukkah 28a R' Eliezer states that he never said anything he had not heard from his teacher. R' Yochanan ben Zakkai praises R' Eliezer (Avot 2,8):

> Rabbi Eliezer the son of Hyrkanos is a cemented cistern that loses not a drop.

R' Eliezer himself said about himself: "Were all the seas ink, all the reed pens and all the men scribes they could not write all that I have studied" (Avot deRabbi Nathan, 80, 25). See also Tractate Sanhedrin 67-68 and 101, and many more examples. R' Eliezer was a great compiler of the knowledge of his teachers, and everything he said was in their name. His approach was one of tradition, he was a 'receiver'.

In the fragment in Tractate Baba Meziah 59b (Achnai's oven) R' Eliezer brings arguments that seem irrelevant: He makes miracles through the carob, the water canal, the heavenly voice. He attempts to prove that he is an expert, and therefore his viewpoint should be accepted. He does not prove the assertion itself. He does not bring reasons why his opinion is right, but reasons why he is a great man. This corresponds to his principled approach; with R' Eliezer the Halacha is decided because of his trustworthiness as conveyor of what he has learned from his teachers.

But R' Yehoshua, his friend and opponent, disagrees precisely on this point. He believes that the Halacha should be decided according to logic and wisdom: "[The Torah] is not in Heaven" (Deut 30:12). If there is no decision according to intellectual conviction there should be a vote, and the majority opinion should be the decision, as it is said; "yield to the majority" (Exodus 23:2). He does not accept the tradition that R' Eliezer presents without any reason and logic.

The end of the fragment (Tractate Baba Meziah 59a) describes how God himself says "My sons have vanquished me". Thus, according to the Talmudic tradition R' Yehoshua was victorious and overcame R' Eliezer. Even the Heavenly Voice did not help R' Eliezer, and the sages logically rejected his words. One may conclude that a 'Law of Debate' displaced a 'Law of Tradition', which had ruled until that day.

The President, R' Gamliel from Yavneh — friend and brother-in-law of R' Eliezer the Great — seems to have agreed to his concept of a 'Torah of Tradition'. This is why he, like R' Eliezer, was very careful to examine bearers of tradition. The Gemara tells us how he put guards at the entrance to the study hall (the academy), in order to allow entrance only to persons of like minds. According to R' Gamliel one has to ensure that the Torah is transmitted to persons who are trusted to transmit it on. When R' Gamliel was deposed, R' Elazar ben Azaryah was appointed in his place. He represented an opinion similar to that of R' Yehoshua: When the Torah is examined during a debate, it is not important to screen the participants according to their disposition and personality. Concepts are to be examined according to their nature, and not according to who expounds them. For that reason R' Elazar ben Azaryah decided to open up the study hall, and that day three hundred seats were added. The law of R' Elazar ben Azaryah is more democratic, as he does not examine the character of the disciples. According to him — and this was accepted from that moment and on — the Halacha is decided by debate and decisions are logical. No weight is given to the holiness and personality of the person expressing the opinion.

Apart from the discussion about the oven, the greater significance was the change from a 'Law of Tradition' to a 'Law of Debate'. This was a veritable revolution in the understanding of the Oral Code. A discussion about principles cannot be decided when the ruling system is 'Law of Tradition' — in a debate each side will be faithful to what he received from is teacher — and no conclusion can be reached.

In order to understand the timing and significance of this revolution one must consider the historical background. Maimonides in his preface to the Mishna describes how conflicts arose, when the disciples of Hillel and Shammai did not lend sufficient support to their teachers, tradition was lost and controversy arose (Tractate Sanhedrin 88b).

There had of course been disagreements before. The first one was in the Hellenistic period between Yose ben Yoezer and Yose ben Yochanan concerning the laying of hands on head of sacrifices on feast days. But in the times of Hillel and Shammai two schools of thought were created for the first time: Beit Hillel and Beit Shammai.

Such a situation cannot be resolved by the 'Law of Tradition' approach. One cannot decide between two schools based on different traditions. At that time the situation looked hopeless. It seemed like the Torah was about to crumble, and be lost to the world as a single and unique expression of Gods will. This is perhaps the way one should consider the account by the sages (Jerusalem Talmud, Tractate Shabbat, 81) saying that the disciples of Shammai actually murdered disciples of Hillel.

Hillel and Shammai belonged to the generation before R' Yochanan ben Zakkai. In Tractate Avot chapter I, 1-2 we saw that he received from both. In Tractate Sukkah he is described as the youngest of the disciples of the old Hillel. His disciple, R' Eliezer was already known as a Shammaite. So in the first generation in Yavneh a full scale controversy was already taking place. There was a danger of a general disintegration of the Torah.

The first generation of sages in Yavneh headed by R' Yehoshua ben Chananyah understood that such a situation warrants a real revolution in the approach to the Oral Tradition. It was necessary to develop a new approach in order to make decisions between the two schools that had arisen. In the case of open questions it was necessary to legitimise debate and decisions reached rationally or by plurality. This revolution, as described above in the case of Achnai's oven, was led by R' Yehoshua, and he was joined by his friend/disciple R' Elazar ben Azaryah, who as very young was appointed president instead of R' Gamliel.

The discussion in the case of Achnai's oven illustrates the type of issues in Tractate Eduyot, which were discussed 'on that day'. Right after his appointment R' Elazar be Azaryah brought all the open questions that could not be decided by the 'Law by Tradition' approach to a decision by debate and voting. Tractate Eduyot is somewhat exceptional in the Talmud as it does not have a definite subject which was learned 'on that day'. The tractate has, however, a very central theme, the new Oral Tradition and the decision of the issues that could not be decided before.

The Talmud describes how R' Eliezer the Great was ostracised by his friends/ disciples. Tractate Baba Metzia gives a heartbreaking description of his banishment, R' Akiva, his disciple, who volunteered to convey the bitter decision says to him: "My Teacher, it seems to me that your colleagues are removed from you" (Tractate Baba Metziah 59b), and they both wept. As we learn from Tractate Sanhedrin 88b, R' Eliezer stayed in isolation until his death. He stayed in Lud complaining that nobody pays him a visit, in order to learn from the vast amounts of Oral Tradition he knows.

It is not clear from the fragment itself what the banishment meant. It is not clear what sin R' Eliezer committed by daring to express a different Halachic viewpoint concerning the cleanliness of the oven. It is obvious that his demotion symbolises the end of the legitimacy of the Halachic approach that he represented: The "Law by Tradition". In view of the critical situation in the relationship among the sages (as described above), drastic measures were needed in order to introduce and settle the new face of the Oral Tradition in the study hall.

Also R' Gamliel, the brother-in-law of R' Eliezer, who held the same opinions, was deposed from the presidency in an unprecedented step. One may think the reason was the way R' Gamliel shamed R' Yehoshua (see e.g. Tractate Berachot 27b). However, that incident in reality shows the way R' Gamliel wished to impose the hierarchical approach as part of the 'Law by Tradition'. R' Yehoshua a rebel who went according to the logic and not the authority, gained the upper hand in the end. The Halachic anarchism was persecuted, but was victorious. The rebellion by R' Yehoshua in parallel to the acceptance by R' Gamliel of his authority (who was forced to desecrate what according to his view was the date of the Day of Atonement), may be denoted a 'Holy Rebellion'. R' Yehoshua was not interested in breaking totally with the past, but tried to convince his companions of the way of persuasion. In the words of the Mishna in Tractate Avot, chapter V, 17: "A debate for the sake of heaven will endure; but a debate not for the sake of heaven will not endure". The Mishna explains that disagreement and pluralistic views are good and important.

R' Gamliel accepted the rules of the game and was reinstalled. He rotated as president with R' Elazar ben Azaryah. R' Eliezer, on the other hand, staid in isolation until his death. He was not willing to change his approach of 'Law of Tradition'.

The development is illustrated by a fragment in Tractate Chagiga, 3a:

> There was once an incident involving R' Yochanan ben Broka and R' Eliezer (ben) Chisma, who went to visit R' Yehoshua in Pekiín. [R' Yehoshua] said to them: What novel teaching was expounded in the study hall today? They said to him: We are your disciples and we drink your waters. [R' Yehoshua] said to them: Even so, it is impossible for the scolars of the study hall without expounding a new teaching. Whose week was it to lecture in the study hall? It was the week of R' Elazar ben Azaryah. And on what subject was his discourse today?

R'Yehoshua says that 'Law of Debate" is a living and developing thing. It is not possible that there are no new developments in the study hall. So, while they wish to listen to his teachings, he wishes to learn from them.

The fragment in Tractate Chagiga, 3a continues with sayings by R' Elazar ben Azaryah., and R' Yehoshua continues (Tractate Chagiga, 3b):

> And he also started expounding "The words of the wise are like goads, and like nails well planted [are the sayings] of the masters of assemblies given from one shepherd"... Just as this plant is fruitful and multiplies, so the words of Torah cause one to be fruitful and multiply.

> The masters of assemblies – these are the wise scholars who sit in various groups and occupy themselves with Torah. There are those scholars who declare a thing ritually contaminated, and there are those who pronounce it clean. Those who prohibit and those who permit. Those who disqualify and those who declare fit. Perhaps a man will say: How can I ever learn Torah? Scripture states: All are given from one shepherd, one God gave them. One leader proclaimed them from the mouth of the Master, blessed is He. As is written: "And God spoke all these words". You make your ear like a mill-hopper, and acquire for yourself a discerning heart to hear intelligently the words of those that declare impure, and the words of those who declare pure, the words of those who prohibit, and the words of those who permit, and the words of those who disqualify and the words of those who declare fit.

Here we find the entire program of the Yavneh revolution, as carried out by R' Yehoshua and R' Elazar ben Azaryah. Next, R' Yehoshua stresses the importance for the Torah and the People of Israel (Tractate Chagiga, 3b):

> [R' Yehosua] then said in this language: It is not an orphaned generation that R' Elazar ben Azaryah dwells in.

The same fragment describes a meeting between R' Yose ben Durmaskis with his teacher R' Eliezer the Great (who sits excommunicated in Lud:

> There was once an incident involving R' Yose ben Durmaskis, who went to visit R' Eliezer in Lud. He said: What novel teaching was expounded in the study hall today? [R' Yose] told him: [The Sages] voted and decided Ammon and Moav must give the tithe of the poor in the seventh year. [R' Eliezer] replied to him: Yose stretch out your hands and darken your eyes. He stretched out his hands and darkened his eyes. R' Eliezer wept and declared: The secret of Hashem is to those who fear him and his covenant to inform them. [R' Eliezer] said to him: Go back and tell them: Do not fret about your voting. Thus I have received from R' Yochanan ben Zakkai, who heard it from his teacher, and his teacher from his teacher: A legal tradition to Moshe from Sinai that Ammon and Moav must give the tithe of the poor in the seventh year.

R' Eliezer speaks out against the sages of Yavneh, who 'innovate innovations', while he possesses the Halacha from the times of Moses at Sinai. This is a result of ignorance. If the sages were in need of the tradition that he knows, they did not need to have to debate at all.

Historically, and from parallel fragments, it is clear that the fragment from Tractate Chagiga deals with the revolution in Yavneh on 'that day'. The opposing beliefs of R' Eliezer and R' Yehoshua are here shown reflected in their assessment of what happened in Yavneh of R' Elazar ben Azaryah.

Let us now return to Tractate Avot, chapter I, 1-2 (cited above). Receipt and Transmission of the Torah is described only until the times of R' Yochanan ben Zakkai. R' Eliezer is characterised as a 'cemented cistern that loses not a drop', but eventually he is not the receiver from R' Yochanan ben Zakkai, but R' Yehoshua. He is not presented as a 'receiver' or part of a couple. The study hall is now wide open for everybody, because people are judged by the contents of what he says and not what he is.

In the generation of R' Yochanan ben Zakkai the split between the disciples of Hillel and Shammai took place, threatening the Torah and the people. The disciples of R' Yochanan ben Zakkai saved the situation by defining new ways of debating and decision making. This is the Yavneh revolution that happened on 'that day'.

The continuation is not linear anymore. The Torah transmitted from Yavneh in the following generations is a combination of the 'Law of Tradition' and the 'Law of Debate'. The process ended in a dialectic synthesis: The two extreme viewpoints were united in one comprehensive whole.

This is illustrated in the fragments in Tractate Sanhedrin 68 and 101. They contain parallel descriptions (with some important distinctions) of the visit of the disciples of R' Eliezer the Great on the day of his death.

In the Mishna (Tractate Sanhedrin 67a) R' Akiva learns the law of 'two [people] gathering cucumbers' from R' Eliezer. In the Gemara (Tractate Sanhedrin 68a) he receives the law as a tradition, but afterwards he asks R' Yehoshua for an explanation of the law, and only then does he accept it: R' Akiva considers both R' Eliezer and R' Yehoshua as his teachers. Also, in Tractate Sanhedrin, 101a, R' Eliezer remarks that R' Akiva is the only one who asks for his opinion, i.e. inquires about the tradition.

R' Akiva is the leader of the synthetic method. His style is a combination of tradition (which he learned from R' Eliezer) and debate (which he learned from R' Yehoshua). This approach continues in the following generations. Therefore R' Akiva is considered the father of the entire Oral Law as it has come down to us. The editor of the Jerusalem Talmud, R' Yochanan famously expressed this in the following way (Tractate Sanhedrin 86a):

> Stam Mishna [an anonymous passage in the Mishna is attributed to] Rabbi Meier, Stam Tosefta[24] R' Nechemiah, Stam Sifra[25] R' Yehudah, Stam Sifri[26] R' Shimon, and all of them according [to what they had learned from] Rabbi Akiva

The Understanding of Rules

So far we have examined the question of authority and adherence to binding precedents, but the Talmudic anarchy also expresses itself in other ways. One of the most salient expressions of this is the following example from Mishna in Tractate Eruvin, 26b (it is continued in our second book[41]):

> We may make an eruvei[27] [techumim] and a shitufei[28] [mevoot] with all [types of food] except for water and salt. And all [types of food] may be purchased with maaser[29] [sheni] funds except for water and salt.

This means that it is allowed to use money from maaser sheni or make an eruv with all foodstuffs, except water and salt. It seems this is a very precise definition, and one would not expect that other foodstuffs would also not be allowed to buy from maaser sheni. But the Gemara immediately brings the following saying (Tractate Eruvin, 27a):

R'Yochanan said: We cannot learn [i.e. extract categorical rulings] from general rules, and even where [the rule concludes] by saying 'except'

The Gemara brings an anarchistic rule (!), which states that we cannot learn anything from rules, even if they are specific, i.e., they itemise the exceptions. Indeed, the continuation of the fragment lists other foodstuffs that one cannot buy with maaser sheni money.

The Gemara later adds further rules to the anarchistic rule (Tractate Eruvin, 27a):

---

[24] The Tosefta (Aramaic: Additions, Supplements) is a compilation of the Jewish oral law from the period of the Mishnah. In many ways, it acts as a supplement to the Mishnah

[25] Sifra is the Halakic Midrash (classical Jewish legal Biblical exegesis), based on the biblical book of Leviticus.

[26] Sifri refers to either of two works of Halachic Midrash (classical Jewish legal Biblical exegesis), based on the biblical books of Bamidbar (Numbers) and Devarim (Deuteronomy).

[27] An Eruv is a ritual enclosure around most Orthodox Jewish and Conservative Jewish homes or communities

[28] A Shituf Mevo'ot is similar to an eruv

[29] The Maaser Sheni, meaning *Second Tithe* in Hebrew, is a tithing practice in Orthodox Judaism with roots in the Hebrew Bible

1. INTRODUCTION

> Since [R'Yochanan] said, Even where it says 'except', it is implied that the statement does not refer to here [our Mishna]. To where does it refer? It refers to there: "All positive mitzvoth that are time-bound, men are obligated [to perform them] and women are exempted, and those which are not time-bound, both men and women are obligated". And is this an [absolute] rule, that all positive mitzvoth that are time-bound women are exempted from performing? But there are [the positive mitzvoth of] matzah, happiness [during festivals], and assemblage, which are all positive mitzvoth that are time-bound – and [yet] women are obliged.
>
> And [is it true that] all positive mitzvoth which are not time-bound, women are obliged? But there are Torah study, being fruitful and multiplying, and redeeming a [firstborn] son, which are [all] positive mitzvoth that are not time-bound, and women are [nevertheless] absolved [from these obligations]. So R'Yochanan said: We cannot learn [categorical rulings] from general rules, and even where [the rule] states 'except'.

Thus, the exemption of women from time-bound obligations is a rule that should be examined carefully. It should not be taken too seriously. At the end of the fragment yet another non-obligatory rule is stated (Tractate Eruvin, 27a):

> Abayeh said, and some say R' Yirmiyah: We also learned this in a Mishna: also another rule was said about the laws of a zav:
>
> "All the things that are borne upon a zav are tamei, and all things which a zav is borne upon are tahor, except for [things which are] suitable for reclining or sitting [upon], and a person".
>
> And there are no more [exceptions]? But there is an object used for riding. This object for riding what is it like? If he sits on it, it is like sitting. We meant to say thus: There is the upper part of a saddle, [why was it not mentioned?] For it was taught in a Braita[30]: The saddle is subject to the tumah of moshav, and the pommel is subject to the tumah of merkav. So we learn from this, [that] we cannot learn [by making deductions] from general rules, and even in a place where it says 'except'.

The fragment ends by returning to the Mishna from above:

> Ravina said, and some say it was Rav Nachman: We also learned thus in our Mishna: With all [types of food] we may make an eruv [techumin] and a shituf [mevoot], except with water and salt. And there are no more exceptions? But there are truffles and mushrooms [also disqualified, but not mentioned]? So we learn from this, that we cannot learn [halachot by making deductions] from general rules, and even in a place where it says 'except'.

---

[30]Braita (pl: Braitot) refers to a statement or passage found in the Talmud that could have been included in the Mishna, but is nowhere to be found there.

As observed above, other foodstuffs not to be bought from maaser sheni money are here mentioned, despite the fact that the Mishna, supposedly, specified all excluded items.

The structure of the Talmud is casuistic. It seldom defines rules, and even when it does, it assigns them only limited warranty. The Talmud allows itself to change the interpretation of the Mishna and other Tannaic sources from the literal meaning, according to the judgement of the Amoraim. It distorts the words of the Mishna and the Braitot in such a way, that the declared obligation to these sources becomes almost ridiculous. There are cases where it is explained that a certain Mishna deals with a special case ('okimta'), or missing sentences are added ('chasurei mechasrei'). All this is done in order to make the Mishna fit to logic and what is reflected in parallel sources. The conclusion is that the relationship of the Halacha to obligatory texts and stringent rules is weak. The Halacha and the Talmud do not like rules, and when such rules do appear, they are of bounded status.

It is possible that the reason for formulating rules at all was the need to conserve knowledge passed orally. It is forbidden to write the Oral Torah down (see Tractate Gittin, 60a). This probably shows the wish to leave it open to interpretations and applications. At different times in history the sages decided to diverge from this prohibition, and write the information down in order not to forget it. This happened when the amount of knowledge became too big, and when the convulsions of the Diaspora threatened the capability of the collective memory to store all the oral knowledge. As a part of this aim the rules were created. The purpose was more to safeguard the knowledge, rather than a directive to Poskim (the practical deciders of the Halacha). Perhaps this is the reason for the contempt in which the rules are held.

Autonomy and Authority in Halachic Decision Making

The anarchism of the Halacha is also seen in the autonomy that the Halacha gives the Posek. We shall examine some post-Talmudic expressions of this, found in the lack of obligation to rules, and the lack of obligation to precedents and decisions by previous generations.

This subject was extensively discussed by Rabbi Asher[31]. He deals with the question whether the Gaonim[11], who came after the Talmud, have authority over the following generations (the Rishonim[8]). In Piskei haRosh[32] on Tractate Sanhedrin 84, section 6) he brings two major opinions: The Raavad[33] says that whoever disagrees with the Gaonim, errors in the Mishna, and to diverge from an obligatory canonical source has serious personal implications for the Dayan (judge). The Baal haMaor[34] says that whoever disagrees with the Gaonim,

---

[31] Asher ben Jehiel (or Asher ben Yechiel, sometimes Asheri) (1250 or 1259 – 1327) was an eminent rabbi and Talmudist best known for his abstract of Talmudic law. He is often referred to as Rabbenu Asher, "our Rabbi Asher" or by the Hebrew acronym for this title, the ROSH (literally "Head").

[32] Piskei haRosh is a summary of the Halacha derived from the Rosh's Talmudic commentary, compiled by his son.

[33] Rabbi Abraham Ben David, The Raavad (1125-1198), born in Posquieres, Provence, France. He was a a great commentator on the Talmud, Sefer Halachot of Rabbi Yitzhak Alfasi and Mishne Torah of Maimonides.

[34] Zerachiah ben Isaac Ha-Levi Gerondi (called the Baal Ha-Maor — author of the book

errors in his reasoning. They both agree that it is an error to disagree with the Gaonim. The question is the status of this error.

But the Rosh himself states that the judge has all the right to make Halachic decisions according to what he thinks, without building on precedents. Exceptional to this is the Talmud, which, as we have explained above, is an obligatory canon.

The Remah[13] establishes the law in Choshen Mishpat[35], section 25. He asserts that the Acharonim may disagree with the Rishonim, and even we are allowed not to accept their rulings, if there is a good reason for it.

One should keep in mind that this was written at a time, when autonomous decision making was on the wane. It appears in the Shulchan Aruch, despite the fact that the two authors are strong advocates of precedent based rulings. Much controversy arose at the beginning of modern times (the Acharonim) because of the change in direction (the codification controversy).

The Maharal[36] writes in Netivoth Olam ("Pathways of the World" — a work of ethics) that autonomous decision making has a most important value, even at the price of erroneous judgments. He states that God prefers the one who decides by his intelligence and not by precedent. Even if a judge makes a mistake, he is to be preferred to the one who judges according to a 'book' (precedent), who may be right.

On the other hand, Ri Megas[37] was asked whether it is allowed to let somebody decide Halacha according to the Gaonim, even if he does not know the Talmudic source and procedure. His answer (responsum 114) contradicts the opinion of Maharal: It is better that somebody decides according to the 'book', even if he does not fully understand (for he will usually reach the truth), than if he were to decide according to reason (which may be wrong).

It would seem that the disagreement is about whether there exists a single Halachic truth, or whether what the Dayan and Posek gives as a reasoned decision becomes the Halachic truth. However, if we examine the two sources carefully, we see that they actually agree in principle. The Maharal does not assert that there is no Halachic truth. He speaks about somebody who makes an error in his judgement (but he considers this preferable to the Posek who goes according to the 'book'). The Maharal believes that autonomous decision making has an intrinsic value, and this is sometimes better, even if in error. This is similar to what the Rosh had to say.

On the other hand, the Maharal does not conclude that just anybody can make such decisions. He ends the enquiry by saying that in his generation not many are capable of this. He also limits the recommendation of Halachic

---

Ha-Maor) was born about 1125 in the town of Girona, Spain and died after 1186 in Lunel. He was a famous rabbi, Torah and Talmud commentator and a poet.

[35] Choshen Mishpat (Hebrew for "Breastplate of Judgement"). The term is associated with one of the four sections of Shulchan Aruch. This section treats aspects of Jewish law pertinent to finance, torts, legal procedure and loans and interest in Judaism.

[36] Judah Loew ben Bezalel, (c. 1520 – 17 September 1609) known as the Maharal of Prague, or simply The MaHaRaL, the Hebrew acronym of "Moreinu Ha-Rav Loew," ("Our Teacher, Rabbi Loew"). He was an important Talmudic scholar, Jewish mystic, and philosopher who served as a leading rabbi in the city of Prague in Bohemia for most of his life.

[37] Joseph ben Meir ibn Megas or Megas (1077–1141) was a Rabbi, Posek, and Rosh Yeshiva in Lucena. He is also known as Ri Megas, the Hebrew acronym for "Rabbi Joseph Megas".

autonomy only to those who are really competent ('Bar Hachi' in the words of the Rosh)..

Examining the approach by Ri Megas we observe the same elements. The Ri speaks about the danger of a Halachic error, and is not prepared to let just any Posek make independent decisions. On the other hand it is clear from his words, that if somebody is indeed competent ('Bar Hachi'), he may decide according to his intelligence. But in the estimate of the Ri only few of his generation are qualified.

So the Maharal and Ri Megas actually say the same thing, and they only differ in their estimate of the factual situation: Are there or are there not competent ('Bar Hachi') people in their generation.

We see that there is indeed a place for Halachic competence and precedents, but only in a very limited manner. But apart from the discussion itself about this matter among the sages, even the most conservative among them do not believe in an absolute attachment to old sources.

The feeling of continuity that accompanies the Halachic study and debate is complemented by a sense of autonomy. The Posek feels obliged to express his private opinion and fight for it, even if it does not fully overlap the Godly truth. This is illustrated in the words of Rabbi Kook[38] on a contradiction between two Talmudic sources that both characterise R' Eliezer the Great. In one source (Tractate Sukkah, 28a) R' Eliezer states that he has never said anything he had not heard previously from his rabbi (see also Tractate Yomah, 66b and other places). The other source is in Avot d'Rabbi Natan[39] (86), where it is stated that R' Eliezer said things that 'had never been heard before'. Rabbi Kook explains that R' Eliezer in the second source did not say that 'these were things he had never heard' — which would indeed be a contradiction — but 'things that had never been heard before'. This means that his rabbi, R' Yochanan ben Zakkai actually said those things, but only R' Eliezer heard them, while other listeners did not.

Rabbi Kook here describes the feeling of innovation arising from continuity. On one hand the sage only discloses the tradition he has received, but this disclosure expands and generalises the tradition. It is full of novelties and new directions. This expresses the dichotomy in Halachic discourse. On one hand innovation is recognised and even encouraged, on the other hand continuity and convention are stressed. As we have seen, the attachment to custom is very flexible, and sometimes innovation is greater than tradition.

Should One Expect that there Exists a Logic of the Talmud?

So far we have seen a picture of a normative system, which varies over time, and goes through several improvements. It does not adopt strict rules or a rigid framework. So the question arises whether there is any purpose in examining

---

[38] Abraham Isaac Kook (1865–1935) was the first Ashkenazi chief rabbi of the British Mandate for Palestine, the founder of the Religious Zionist Yeshiva Merkaz HaRav, Jewish thinker, Halachist, Kabbalist and a renowned Torah scholar.

[39] Avot de-Rabbi Nathan, usually printed together with the minor tractates of the Talmud, is a Jewish aggadic work probably compiled in the geonic era (c.700–900 CE).

the logic of such a system? Or rather, whether a specific logic actually exists.

Let us first remark, that in a system where the debate is more important than the conclusions, one would expect a rich logic worthy of examination and analysis. Were the Halachic canon just a collection of laws, or even directions and values, perhaps there would not be any expectations of a clear logical basis. As we have shown in our fourth book[40] of the series, legal systems in general do not seek to apply a specific logic, and the logical research relating to such systems is minimal. One reason for that is that their development is not based on logical deduction and debating rules. They aim at specific purposes and the methodical formulation of agreements and social frameworks. The Halacha, on the other hand, is based on debate and the logical conclusions that arise from this. Hence, contrary to expectation, it would seem that there is a place for logical research.

A difficult problem of methodology arises here. The number of sources, periods and sages is large, and the question is whether there exists a Halachic or Talmudic logic as a unique category enabling separate research. In modern Talmudic research it is assumed that the development is unmethodical, the result of different cultural and intellectual directions and of varying social and environmental pressures. This is why the Talmudic research, in contrast to classical study of the Talmud, does not aim at harmonising among various Halachic sources. It considers each source as independent, and will at the most compare them.

On the other hand, as we have explained in our second book[41], we do not accept the situation described above. The relevant logic is indeed developing through the ages, but our historical and methodological assumption is that this logic is disciplined and consistent. Over time it becomes clearer that this is indeed one logic. Part of it is universal — and this is the part most interesting for us — and part of it is unique to the Talmud and to Halacha.

Our assumption is that examination of the later stages of development cast light upon the earlier stages. We believe that the way to understand the significance of the Talmudic-Halachic debate is through the prism of its later stages. This is also the assumption of the traditional scholar, but one should not be surprised to discover that only seldom has methodical research been based on this assumption.

In order to base our assertion we observe that despite the anarchistic picture described above, there is a continuous historic process, which seems entirely opposed to anarchy. It is a transition to causal and associative thinking, the use of rules and strengthening of methodology in the Talmudic and Halachic thinking. Talmudic research sees this as a later development. However, we suggest that one here sees a germination of seeds previously sown. Within the historical process each generation of sages decode the principles that form the basis of tradition received from previous generations. They begin to use such rules as more rigid rules of interpretation. The concepts crystallise, become

---

[40] Abraham M., Belfer I., Gabbay D., Schild U., *Temporal Logic in the Talmud* (in Hebrew), College Publications, King's College, London, UK, 2011

[41] Abraham M., Gabbay D., Hazut G., Maruvka Y.E., Schild U., *The Textual Inference Rules Klal uPrat* (in Hebrew), College Publications, King's College, London, UK, 2010

formalised and canonised. They are now rules of logic in some sense.

The significance of this has been described in detail in our second book[41] in the series, and will not be repeated here. The main assertion is that the Talmudic ways of thinking does not change, but become more general, methodical and logical. In later stages earlier types of thinking become systematic. In the second book we have shown that the rule of Klal uPrat, which was one single rule in the times of Hillel the Elder, became three or four rules in the list of R' Yishmael. This what has happened in general to Halachic thinking.

In this sense, our investigations form a continuation of this Halachic tradition. We too are attempting to discover the ways of reasoning of our predecessors, to conceptualise and give them a foundation, and analyse them using modern logical tools. The results so far are very encouraging, and show that this process has great opportunities to persist.

Two Important Distinctions

Before concluding we have to make two important distinctions between Talmudic Logic and Mathematical Logic. First of all, Talmudic Logic has more intuitive characteristics. Prima facie it does not seem to be formalistic, while Mathematical Logic and Natural Science in general are based on formal thinking.

This distinction may be understood at two different levels: Essence and Action. Talmudic thinking does not apply formal rules, at least not rules that have been explicitly formulated. That does not mean that such rules do not exist, as we have seen above — later stages of Talmudic thinking conceptualise rules that are based on earlier Tamudic thinking. But there is also an essential difference between standard logic and Talmudic thinking. Standard logic deals mainly with necessary and certain inferences, i.e., deduction. All that is not part of such inferences are not part of classical logic. Logic also considers other types of inference (induction, abduction and analogy), but does not provide a methodical and formal foundation for these types. The Talmud, on the other hand, is almost totally based on uncertain inferences.

Nachmanides[42], in his Milhamot Hashem (Wars of the Lord) defends the decisions of Alfasi[43] against the criticisms of Zerachiah ha-Levi of Girona. He explains that in the Talmud and in the Talmudic debate there are no absolute statements like in Mathematics, and not even empirical evidence like in Physics. There are disagreements about interpretation and what counts. There are not absolute logical proofs, but a criterion of what is or is not reasonable. This is Nachmanides' characterisation of the Talmudic debate.

All fields of knowledge and science, except Logic and Mathematics, belong to the category of domains with uncertain conclusions, like the Talmud and the Halacha. Hence, traditionally, inferences in those areas are considered outside standard logic. However, as we have shown in our books and papers, this is not

---

[42] Nahmanides, also known as Rabbi Moses ben Nahman Girondi, Bonastruc ça Porta and by his acronym Ramban, (Girona, 1194 -=- Land of Israel, 1270), was a leading medieval Jewish scholar, Catalan rabbi, philosopher, physician, kabbalist, and biblical commentator.

[43] Isaac ben Jacob Alfasi ha-Cohen (1013–1103) — also known as the Alfasi or by his Hebrew acronym Rif (Rabbi Isaac al-Fasi), was a Talmudist and Posek (decider in matters of Halacha)

true. Also uncertain inferences (like analogy and induction) may be formalised, and this is relevant to all science and human knowledge.

Rabbi David Cohen (the Nazirite Rabbi[44]), the great disciple of Rabbi Kook[32], devoted his book: *Kol Nevu'ah*, to this idea. He places two kinds of thought against each other. One is the Greek (scholastic) logic, which is material-visual, the other is the Jewish logic (Talmudic-Halachic), which is spiritual-acoustic. The Jewish philosophy is not single valued as the classical logic, but is based on sound and deep understanding. There is a preference of the reasonable over the less reasonable, and of what is heard over what is not heard well (even without sharp evidence, as also found in the words of Nachmanides).

The Nazirite Rabbi also asserts that the Halachic inferences are the foundation for this alternative logic, like the basic deductions in Aristotelian Logic. The Talmud prefers analogy and induction, i.e., softer inferences, in order to reach conclusions. The Talmud does not draw back from conclusions like 'perhaps it is also possible otherwise?', nor from the lack of certainty of the conclusions. It weighs the alternatives against each other, but is prepared to reach a decision where decision is not incontestable. Also obligations relating to doubts have a central place in Halachic thought, and there is an entire system of rules of decision and behaviour in the case of doubtful situations.

The Talmud and the Halacha live in an atmosphere where doubt is present at all times. They defer sharp conclusions, and prefer decisions based on preferences. The Talmud deals with life in all its complexities, and does not deal with abstract ideas. Its approach is usually casuistic, i.e., it will consider a concrete case and not the abstract idea itself. Generalisations arise from the consideration of the specific case, and do not precede it. Here too one sees the inductivity of Talmudic thought, which goes from the special case to the general one, and prefers this method to deductive thought, which goes from the general to the special case.

Our Series

So far four books have been published in our series. The two first books deal with rules of interpretation. As we have seen, these rules are the foundation of Halachic-interpretative deduction. The first book of the series deals with the logical rules of interpretation. It builds a methodical model, which explains reasoning with analogy and generalization in all ways of life. This supplies an explanation of some fundamental problems in the philosophy of scientific generalisation, in jurisprudence and legal interpretation. We believe that this is the first time that a general logical model has been developed for these types of reasoning and their combinations.

The second book of the series deals with the rules of textual interpretation. These ways of reasoning may seem specific to the biblical text and Halachic deduction. However, we show that they are actually universal modes of reasoning. We show that there exists a systematic manner of defining sets in an intuitive

---

[44]David Cohen (1887 – 1972) (also known as "Rav Ha-Nazir", The Nazirite Rabbi) was a rabbi, talmudist, philosopher, and kabbalist. A noted Jewish ascetic, he took a Nazirite vow after making aliyah to Israel.

manner. This is relevant also in the legal world and in other domains. In the book we present our alternative paradigm to Talmudic research, as explained above.

The third book of the series deals with Deontic Logic. We show that the Halacha has a unique approach to norms. We discuss the distinction between mandatory commands (mitzvot asey) and prohibitive commands (mitzvot lo ta'ase). We show that this distinction does not exist in other normative systems, whether legal or ethical. The formalism we propose solves many paradoxes and difficulties that exist in the usual deontic formalisation. In the fifth book we intend to deal with value-conflicts, that are problematic in the standard deontic logic, and show how they can be overcome with logical methods.

The fourth book of the series deals with temporal logic, especially in the context of actions conditional on future actions (Tenayim) and actions involving entities defined in future events (Breira). We deal with ideas of determinism, ideas of going back and inversion of time, also relative to modern Physics. In the last part of the book we examine one of the reasons why modern legal systems have problems dealing with these concepts. It relates to their practical nature which distances itself from the abstract definitions and.logical formalism.

The books of the series are written in Hebrew for the ease of the student of the Talmud. However, at the end of each book in the series appears a paper in English, which deals with the logical and mathematical aspects of the topic of the book. These papers deal less with the Talmudic content than with logical assertions. These papers have been published in various journals of Logic, and they form the basis for the present volume.

CHAPTER 2

ANALYSIS OF THE TALMUDIC ARGUMENTUM A FORTIORI INFERENCE RULE (KAL VACHOMER) USING MATRIX ABDUCTION

1 Introduction and Motivation

This section explains and motivates the intuitive use of the new method of Matrix Abduction to analyse the non-deductive rules of Analogy and Argumentum A Fortiori. This rule is a form of Induction rule when used in an Artificial Intelligence context and is a recognised Jurisprudence rule in Jewish, Islamic and Indian legal reasoning. In the Jewish Talmud it is known as the Binyan Abh and the Kal-Vachomer rules. In Islamic jurisprudence it is known as Qiyas (analogy) and in Sanskrit logic (Nyaya) it is known as Kaimatya Nyaya (or Kaimutika Nyaya, the *even more so*) rule.

1.1 Matrix Abduction in AI

Let us begin by trying to buy, over the Internet, two items:

1. An LCD computer screen

2. A digital camera

We start with the LCD screen. We want something good, within a price range we can afford and we would especially like it to have stereophonic speakers. So the usual thing to do in such cases is to go to a price comparison website. In our case.[1] We went to www.wallashops.co.il and got comparison tables for four candidates.

Screen 1. Xerox XM7 24A

Screen 2. Viewsonic FHD VX 2640w

Screen 3. Nec 2470 WVX

Screen 4. Nec 24 WMCX

The specifications of interest we got are shown in Figure 2.1 below.

It seems that for screen 3 there is no information about the stereophonic feature. It was not possible to get the information from other sites. Can we abduce the information from the table itself? How do we do that?

Let us check another example, where a similar problem arises. We look for cameras at the same site.

---

[1] This is a real example we are describing, of what we did on 1.2.09.

	P price over £450	C self collection	I screen bigger than 24inch	R reaction time below 4ms	D dot size less than 0.275	S stereo- phonic
Screen 1	0	1	0	1	0	1
Screen 2	0	0	1	1	0	1
Screen 3	0	0	0	0	1	?
Screen 4	1	1	0	0	1	1

$1 = $ yes; $0 = $ no; $? = $ no data given

Figure 2.1.

Camera 1.   Canon A590 8MP + 4GB

Camera 2.   Olympus FE20 (thin) 8MP + 4GB

Camera 3.   Olympus FE60 + 2GB

Camera 4.   Olympus 8MP in Hebrew + 1GB.

Figure 2.2 gives the specifications for comparison

	P price over £100	M over 12 monthly payments	D quick delivery	B more than one battery	W weighs more than 150g	F flash has more than 3 states	E can edit image afterwards
Camera 1	1	1	0	1	1	0	?
Camera 2	0	0	0	0	0	1	1
Camera 3	0	0	1	0	0	1	1
Camera 4	1	0	1	0	0	0	1

Figure 2.2.

Again, there is no information whether Camera 1 can edit an image taken into the camera memory. Our question is, can we assume that this type of camera, as compared with the others, will have this feature? Can we use the matrix to get the answer? See Example 2.29 for a solution.

We can now formulate the general problem:

DEFINITION 2.1 (Matrix abduction problem). Let $\mathbb{A} = [a_{i,j}]$ be a 0–1 matrix, where $a_{i,j} \in \{0, 1, ?\}$ $i = 1, \ldots, m$ (m rows) $j = 1, \ldots, n$ (n columns) such that the following holds:

a. $m \leq n$ (there are more columns than rows[2]

b. exactly one a_{i_0, j_0} is undecided all the others are in $\{0, 1\}$.

---

[2]This condition does not matter in the formal abstract case, since we can rotate the matrix. However, in some applications the rows and columns may have special meaning. The formal machinery works even if $n < m$.

2. ANALYSIS OF THE TALMUDIC KAL VACHOMER RULE

The abduction problem is to devise some algorithm which can decide whether $a_{i_0,j_0} =?$ should be 1 or $a_{i_0,j_0} =?$ should be 0 or $a_{i_0,j_0} =?$ must remain undecided

We cannot solve this problem without further assumptions on the meaning of the entries. Put in different words, if we give an algorithm $\mathcal{A}$ to be applied to $\mathbb{A}$, we need to specify its range of applicability. To specify whether $\mathcal{A}$ can be meaningfully applied to $\mathbb{A}$, we need to know how $\mathbb{A}$ was constructed. In other words, we need some assumptions about the meaning of the rows and columns of $\mathbb{A}$.

The examples above suggest that we can look at the roles of $\mathbb{A}$ as representative agents or causes, which can generate various features. The columns of the matrix represent the features. So objects like cameras or LCD screens can "generate" the properties listed in the columns. There are other examples, for instance, hurricanes can generate a lot of damage through various features. If we go to the web, we can find a list of names for hurricanes and a list of the main kinds of features they generated. We can construct, for example, Figure 2.3.

	rip tide	winds	storm surge	flooding	tornado
Katrina					
Andrew					
Ivan					
Hugo					
Camille					
⋮					

Figure 2.3.

The $a_{i,j}$ slots usually contain numerical data or even qualitative data. For example, the wind column may contain the maximum speed in miles per hour of each hurricane.

To turn the data into $0-1$ data we need to decide on a cut-off point. Say for winds we choose 150 miles per hour. We have two choices for the wind column. Do we take 1 to mean over 150 miles per hour or do we take it to be $1 =$ under 150 miles per hour? The reader might think it is a matter of notation but it is not! We need to assume that all the column features pull in the same direction. In the hurricane case the direction we can take is the capacity for damage. In the LCD screen and camera case it is performance. So to put 1 as opposed to 0 in a box indicates more strength to the feature in the general agreed shared direction. So the representation of the columns must be compatible with the chosen direction. So if 1 in the winds means over 150 miles (in direction of increased damage), then 1 in the tornadoes column must go in the same direction. To give an example of a matrix where there is no direction to the columns, take a simple graph, see Figure 2.4.

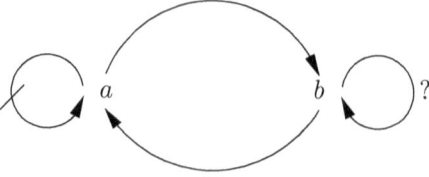

Figure 2.4.

This is a binary relation R

$$(a, b) \in R, (b, a) \in R, (a, a) \notin R.$$

We ask is $(b, b) \in R$? Form the characteristic matrix in Figure 2.5

	a	b
a	0	1
b	1	?

Figure 2.5.

There is no direction or meaning here. We might apply our algorithm formally and get an answer but it means nothing.

Let us give another example. Imagine a society of agents and various context in which the agents might wish to apply actions. Say action **a** might be to shoot to kill and the context B might be a burglar in the middle of the night. The matrix $\mathbb{A}$ might give $0 - 1$ values to indicate the accepted norms.

So we may get Figure 2.6

	A	B	C	D
a	0	1	1	0
b	1	?	0	0
c	1	1	0	1

Figure 2.6.

a, b, c are actions and A, B, C, D are situations.

We know that action **b** for example is allowed in situation A but we don't know about situation B.

The reader may ask how can such a problem arise? If actions are described by pre conditions and post conditions and situations (states) are also described properly then we can check whether the preconditions hold and whether there are any restrictions on the execution of the action. The problem is that the above presentation is already a formal model.

If we construct a table and use common sense, there may be clear answers in some places and question marks in others. Figure 2.7 is such a case:

This example also has a "direction". We allow severe actions for severe situations. So we may decide on the basis of the matrix that if the burglar may

2. ANALYSIS OF THE TALMUDIC KAL VACHOMER RULE

	burglar unarmed	burglar armed	burglar could be armed	burglar could be armed but several murders same week
shoot the burglar	0	1	?	1
beat up the burglar	?	1	1	1

Figure 2.7.

be armed then better shoot him and maybe then decide that if he is definitely not armed then beat him up, sensing the general "severe" spirit of the case.

Another example could be from monadic predicate logic over a finite domain. The domain can be $\{d_1, \ldots, d_n\}$ and the monadic predicates $A_1(x), \ldots, A_m(x)$. Assume we know all values of $A_i(d_j) = e_{i,j}$ except one, say $A_k(d_r) = ?$. We get the matrix of Figure 2.8

	d_1	d_2	...	d_r	...	d_n
A_1	$e_{1,1}$	$e_{1,2}$				
A_1	$e_{2,1}$	$e_{2,2}$				
$\vdots$						
A_k	$e_{k,1}$	$e_{k,2}$		?		
$\vdots$						
A_m	$e_{m,1}$	$e_{m,2}$				

Figure 2.8.

Our method allows us, under certain assumptions, to get a value for $A_k(d_r) = e_{k,r}$. More on this example in Appendix D.

The above discussion gives us an idea of when a matrix $\mathbb{A}$ is within the range of applicability of our matrix abduction algorithm. However the explanation is not formal but in terms of examples showing how the matrix is constructed we have not given a formal definition which says when an arbitrary $0-1$ matrix is within the range of applicability.

We shall do this in Section 3 where we develop some matrix machinery. Definition 2.11 describes when a matrix has a 'direction'. Meanwhile consider the two matrices in Figure 2.9. The first is not within range, it has no direction, the second is within range, as we shall see later.

1.2 The Talmudic Kal-Vachomer[3]

Here we give a small example. An extensive model will be given later in the chapter.

---
[3] Also written as Qal-Vahomer, or Qal-Vachomer.

(1)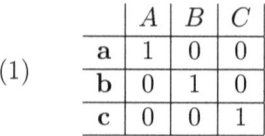

(2)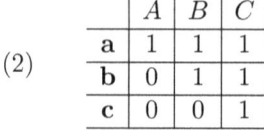

Figure 2.9.

A bull can do damage in two ways.[4] It can trample something with its feet or it can use its horns. Also the location of the arena of the damage can either be in a public place or a private place (e.g. a public road or a private garden). The amount of compensation paid by the owner of the bull depends on these features.

Figure 2.10 describes the situation.[5] The entries indicate proportion of the damage to be paid, as indicated in the Bible.

	public place	private place
Foot action	0	1
Horn action	$\frac{1}{2}$	$x = ?$

Figure 2.10.

The Talmudic law specifies that foot damage by a bull at a public place needs to pay 0 compensation. Horn damage at a public place pays $\frac{1}{2}$ the cost of damage as compensation.

In a private area foot damage must be paid in full. What can we say now about payment for horn action in a private place? This is not specified explicitly in the Biblical written law and the Talmud is trying to abduce it from the above matrix using Kal-Vachomer.

The next section shows how the Talmud does it.

1.3 Preview of the model

We use the bull example of Section 1.2 to show how the model works.

First the intuitive argument:

We see from the public arena, that horn damage is considered more serious

---

[4]Actually a bull can damage in three ways. He can eat (Tooth), trample (Foot) and gore (Horn). The Horn is intentional damage. The Tooth and Foot are not intentional, but the Tooth gives benefit to the perpertrator and the Foot gives no benefit.

[5]If we insist on $\{0, 1\}$ values in the matrix we can read the entries as taking either the value 0 or taking the value of $\frac{1}{2}$ or 1 in which case the (Horn, public place) square will be 1. Subsequent considerations for $x = ?$ in Section 1.3 always use $x \geq \frac{1}{2}$ or $x = 0$ as options anyway.

2. ANALYSIS OF THE TALMUDIC KAL VACHOMER RULE

than foot damage. You need to walk but certainly you don't need to use your horn in a public road! If this is the case, then if in a private place foot damage has to pay in full, then certainly horn damage has to pay in full.

We can also look at Figure 2.10 from the row point of view. We see from row 1 that damage in private area is considered more seriously than damage in public area. You are allowed routinely to walk and move in public areas but not in a private area. So if horn action in public area pays $\frac{1}{2}$ then certainly it has to pay at least half if done in a private area!

We now give you a glimpse of the maths of the model. Consider the matrix of Figure 2.10 and consider columns as vectors and consider two cases:

Case 1 we put for ? the value $x \geq \frac{1}{2}$.
Case 2 we put for ? the value $x = 0$.

For $x \geq \frac{1}{2}$ we have

$$\begin{array}{cc} \text{Public} & \text{Private} \\ \begin{pmatrix} 0 \\ \frac{1}{2} \end{pmatrix} \leq & \begin{pmatrix} 1 \\ x \end{pmatrix} \end{array}$$

but for $x = 0$ we get that the two columns are not comparable.

We get two types of orderings, described in Figures 2.11 and 2.12. a, b are two abstract points of ordering which in our case can represent the public column and the private column. The two abstract orderings we get are

$$a \quad \rightarrow \quad b$$

Figure 2.11.

• b • a

Figure 2.12.

So one is a linear ordering $a \leq b$ and the other is no ordering of a, b. We ask which one is "nicer". The intuitive answer is that Figure 2.11 is nicer. So $x \geq \frac{1}{2}$ is our answer to the question in this case.

Comparing rows we get for $x = 1$:

$$\text{Horn}\,(\tfrac{1}{2}, 1) \geq \text{Foot}(0, 1),$$

i.e. the abstract ordering of Figure 2.11 again, where now a, b represent foot and horn rows.

For $x \leq \frac{1}{2}$ we get two incomparable rows, i.e. Figure 2.12 again. So again, if Figure 2.11 is considered "nicer", we must take $x = 1$ as our answer.

The actual case is decided in Jewish law as $x = \frac{1}{2}$.

1.4 Qiyas and Kaimutika Nyaya

We saw that the Talmudic rule of Kal-Vachomer is used in Jewish Jurispurdence to derive further conclusions and laws from the explicit existing laws in the Bible. A similar rule in Islamic Jurisprudence is in the Qiyas, see [77] and [70].

Literally Qiyas means measuring or ascertaining the length, weight or quality of something. It is used to extend a Shariah ruling from an original case to a new case. This is done by identifying a common cause between the original case and the new case. See Examples 2.2 and 2.3.

EXAMPLE 2.2 (Example of Qiyas (from Wikipedia)).
For example, Qiyas is applied to the injunction against drinking wine /wiki/Wine to create an injunction against cocaine /wiki/Cocaine use.

1. Identification of a clear, known thing or action that might bear a resemblance to the modern situation, such as the wine drinking.

2. Identification of the ruling on the known thing. Wine drinking is prohibited.

3. Identification of the reason behind the known ruling. For example, wine drinking is prohibited because it intoxicates. Intoxication is bad because it removes Muslims /wiki/Muslim from mindfulness of God.

4. The reason behind the known ruling is applied to the unknown thing. For instance cocaine use intoxicates the user, removing the user from mindfulness of God. It is therefore prohibited.

EXAMPLE 2.3. This example is from www.islamtoday.com.

What is the ruling on giving one's parents a good smack?

We will not find any text in our scriptures that directly addresses this question. However, we are in no doubt that it is absolutely prohibited and sinful to do so.

We find in the Qur'ân that it is sinful to even mutter "ugh" or "uff" to our parents in exasperation when they ask us to do something for them.

Allah says: "And your Lord has commanded that you shall not worship any but Him, and that you show kindness to your parents. If either or both of them reach old age with you, say not to them so much as "ugh" nor chide them, but speak to them a generous word." [Sûrah al-Isrâ: 23]

We are prohibited to say "ugh" to our parents, because it is abusive behaviour. At the very least, it hurts their feelings. We can have no doubt that shoving them or smacking them is even more abusive and hurtful. Since the reason for prohibition is even more evident here, we can be certain that smacking our parents is unlawful and very sinful.

A similar rule exists in Indian Logic. We quote an example:

EXAMPLE 2.4. (**Kaimutika Nyaya (from sadagopan.org)**
http://www.biblio.org/sadagopan/ahobilavalli/sus_v2p2.pdf)

It has been said also in SANdilya-smriti: "There may be doubts concerning the redemption of those who serve AchArya, but there is absolutely no doubt about the redemption of those who delight in the service of His devotees" (1-95). So, in the case of those who depend solely on the AchArya, there is no doubt at all concerning the fruition of prapatti, by the principle of "kaimutika nyAya".

> (Will not the Lord, who saves those who take refuge in His devotees, save those who take refuge in their AchAryas? Will not a benefit, which is got by one who is not qualified, be obtained by one who is qualified?).
>
> It is thus established that sarveSvara, the Lord of all, will not grant us the supreme goal of existence, unless prapatti is performed in any of these two forms, and by some one or other. Thus the Lord has done another favour by revealing these important messages inbuilt in these mantras, said SwAmi Desikan, in this sub-section

It is now time to define the mathematical model.

2 Motivating the matrix model

Before we give the algorithm, let us say how it is to be used.

The algorithm works as follows. We are given a matrix $\mathbb{A}$ with one place with $x = ?$ and all the rest are entries from $\{0, 1\}$. We need to decide which is better $x = 0$ or $x = 1$ or declare the case as formally undecided.

Let $\mathbb{A}^1$ be the matrix with $x = 1$ and $\mathbb{A}^0$ be the matrix with $x = 0$.

Step 1
Let Π_1 be the partial order of the columns of $\mathbb{A}^1$, taken as vectors and compared coordinate wise. Let Π_0 be the same for $\mathbb{A}^0$.

Step 2
Decide, if you can, which is "nicer". (Formal definitions will be given later.)

Step 3
If Π_1 is definitely nicer than Π_0 then say $x = 1$ is the output. If Π_0 is definitely nicer than Π_1 then let output be $x = 0$.

If neither can be shown to be nicer then say that x is undecided.

Thus we need an algorithm on two partial orders X and Y to say either "X is better than Y" or "Y is better than X" or "X, Y are not comparable".

This algorithm must be compatible with the meaning of the rows and columns of the matrix as discussed in Section 1.1 and may use the matrix for help.

The next section will give precise mathematical definitions but before than we need to give some methodological remarks.

The Kal-Vachomer rule (and the algorithms supporting it) are nonmonotonic rules of induction. This means they are not absolute deductive rules but defeasible common sense rules. So we may use these rules to obtain a conclusion A, but further information and further arguments may force us to doubt A or even come to accept $\sim A$.

Let us compare this rule with ordinary Abduction.

Imagine we have hard facts, accepted statements of the form $\Delta = \{A_1, \ldots, A_m\}$, we are looking for further information. We consider Δ and using common sense, experience, our knowledge of the way the world works, our creative imagination, our religion and whatever else we bring to bear on the case, we put forward that H should be added to Δ. The decision to add H is defeasible. We may find out later, through more facts, etc., that H was the wrong addition.

On the other hand, compare this with a proof in school geometry. If $A_1, \ldots, A_m$ are assumptions about geometric figure and we *prove* H, then H follows absolutely! It is not defeasible no matter how much more information we get.

Matrix abduction is a defeasible rule. We looked for the missing information about the camera and could not get it. We may use matrix abduction to conjecture that the camera did have a stereophonic feature and decided to order it from the dealer. It is quite possible that when we get the camera we find out that it does not have this feature. This does not mean our matrix abduction rule was wrongly applied. The rule was correctly applied but was defeated by further data.

Another typical case of abduction can be described as follows. Given a theory Δ, say $\Delta = \{A, A \wedge B \to C, X\}$ and a result G, say that $G = C$ such that we know that $\Delta \vdash G$ must hold. However without knowing what X is, G does not follow from Δ. We therefore want to *abduce* a hypothesis H such that

1. $H \nvdash G$

2. $\Delta + H \vdash G$.

There may be several such candidates but we decide that a certain algorithm is the one we use. Once we decide on that, we can calculate H and let $X = H$. In the above case we can use a goal directed algorithm for $G = C$ which goes as follows:

1. What can give us C? We can get C from the data $A \wedge B \to C$ if we have two items A and B.

2. We do have A, but B is not available, however we have X which we don't know what it is.

3. So abduce $X = B$.

Thus $H = B$

Note that the weaker assumption $X = (A \to B)$ would also do the job but this is not what our algorithm does.

So for the case of the matrix $\mathbb{A}$ the inductive/abductive step is to use our specific algorithm. Once we decide on that, the answer becomes mathematically determined. However the whole process gives us defeasible conclusions, not absolute conclusions.

3 Superiority relation on partial orders

This section develops the mathematical machinery for our Matrix Abduction algorithm.

DEFINITION 2.5 (Graphs).

1. A partial order is a set S with a binary relation $<$ which is transitive and irreflexive. We write $\tau = (S, <)$ for a partial order. We write $\leq$ for the reflexive closure of $<$.

2. Let $x \prec y$ be the relation

$$x \prec y \text{ iff } x < y \wedge \sim \exists z(x < z < y)$$

We represent graphically "$x \prec y$" by "$x \leftarrow y$". So for example in Figure 2.13, we have $x_1 \prec x_2, x_2 \prec x_3, y_1 \prec x_3$, etc., etc.

$x \prec y$ means that x is an immediate predecessor of y (or equivalently y is an immediate successor of x).

We have that $<$ is the transitive closure of $\prec$. From now on we look at $(S, \prec)$.

3. A path in $(S, \prec)$ of length n, is a chain of the form $x_1 \prec x_2 \prec \ldots \prec x_n$.

A path is maximal if there is no longer path containing it.

4. Let $T \subseteq S$. Let T^*, the projection of T, be the set

$$T^* = \{y \mid y \leq t, t \in T\}.$$

5. Let T be a maximal path in $(S, \prec)$. T is said to be maximal thin path if there is no other maximal path T_1 such that T_1^* has less elements than T^*.

6. Figure 2.13 is a good graph to serve as an example for our concepts. There are two maximal paths.

$$T_1 : x_1 \prec x_2 \prec x_3 \prec z \prec x_4 \prec v$$

and

$$T_2 : x_1 \prec x_2 \prec x_3 \prec z \prec x_4 \prec x_5.$$

The path ending up in v is thinner, because $y_3 \in T_2^*$ but $y_3 \notin T_1^*$.

7. We now divide $(S, \prec)$ into levels.
Level 1
All minimal points, i.e. all points x such that $\sim \exists y(y < x)$.
Level $n+1$
Let $P_r(y)$ be the set of all predecessors of y. Then y is of level $n+1$ if all predecessors of y are of level $\leq n$, with at least one such preceessor being of level n.

For example, in Figure 2.13, the following are the levels of the nodes:
Level 1 x_1, y_1, y_2, y_3

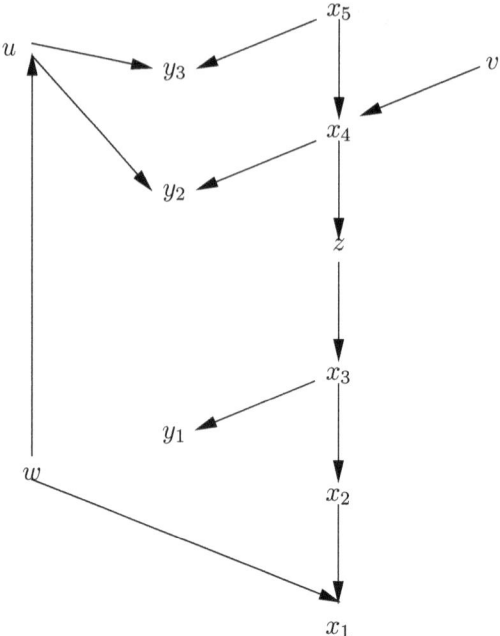

Figure 2.13.

Level 2 x_2, u
Level 3 x_3, w
Level 4 z
Level 5 x_4
Level 6 x_5, v.

8. A point $z \in S$ is a critical point if the following holds:

   (a) z has at least two predecessors
   (b) there exists y such that $\sim (z < y)$ and all predecessors of z are less than y.

DEFINITION 2.6 (Abduction matrices). An abduction matrix $\mathbb{A}$ has the form

$$\mathbb{A} = [a_{i,j}], 1 \leq i \leq m, 1 \leq j \leq n$$

where i runs over rows and j over columns we require

1. $m \leq n$
2. $a_{i,j} \in \{0, 1, ?\}$
3. exactly one $a_{i,j}$ has value ?

DEFINITION 2.7.

2. ANALYSIS OF THE TALMUDIC KAL VACHOMER RULE

1. A matrix $\mathbb{A}$ is definite if $a_{i,j} \neq ?$ for all i, j, that is we always have values in $\{0, 1\}$ for the entries.

2. Given a definite matrix $\mathbb{A}$, its columns are $0 - 1$ vectors of length m, i.e.
$$V_j = (a_{1,j}, a_{2,j}, \ldots, a_{m,j}).$$

Define an ordering on two vectors V, V', by comparing coordinates.
$$V \leq V' \text{ iff for all } i, v_i \leq v'_i,$$
where
$$V = (v_1, \ldots, v_m), V' = (v'_1, \ldots, v'_m).$$
We also indicate the ordering by writing
$$V \to V'.$$

LEMMA 2.8 (Graph representation theorem). *Let $(S, <)$ be an abstract partial ordering based on a finite set $S = \{a_1, \ldots, a_n\}$. Then there exists a definite matrix with m column and m rows such that the column ordering is the same as $(S, \leq)$.*

Proof. Let $\mathbb{A} = [a_{i,j}], 1 \leq i, j \leq 1$ be the matrix defined by $a_{i,j} = 1$ iff $a_i \leq a_j$.

This is the characteristic matrix of the ordering. We shall see that we can identify that column V_i with the element a_i
we have
$$V_k \leq V_j$$
iff (by definition)
$$\text{for } i = 1, \ldots, n \text{ we have } a_{i,k} \leq a_{i,j}$$
iff for $i = 1, \ldots, m$
$$a_i \leq a_k \Rightarrow a_i \leq a_j$$
$$\text{iff } \forall x \in S(x \leq a_k \to x \leq a_j)$$
iff (since $\leq$ is reflexive and transitive
$$a_k \leq a_j.$$

■

REMARK 2.9. The lemma is important because we can assume that the definition for "nicer" or superiority among ordering can use conditions and properties of the matrix generating them.

So from now on we can assume that every ordering $\tau = (S, \leq)$ comes from a matrix $\mathbb{M} = \mathbb{M}_\tau$, or $\tau = \tau(\mathbb{M})$.

We now want to get some intuition about when one ordering is superior to another. Our strategy is as follows

1. Look at some orderings and give some plausible mathematical definition of when one is superior to another. Such a definition must use topological and mathematical properties of the ordering and in no way have any connection with problems of abduction and reasoning.

2. It is inevitable that such a definition will be partial and incomplete and in many cases will have nothing to say.

We now run our definition on orderings derived from matrices arising from actual reasoning cases where we know what answers we should be getting. We use these cases to make our partial definitions more precise.

If the extra precision required turns out to be topologically meaningful, then we can say we got a good model, because of the intuitions of the reasoning do correspond to topological conditions on the ordering.

EXAMPLE 2.10 (Examples of ordering). The following (Figure 2.14) are some examples of orderings. Note that for $b \prec a$ we also write

$$a \to b$$

or

$$a \\ \downarrow \\ b$$

when we present the ordering as a graph.

We now give a partial definition of superiority. To expand the partial definition into a full definition we need to know the application area, and take it into consideration.

DEFINITION 2.11 (Multisets).

1. Let $\mathbb{L}$ be a set of labels $\mathbb{L} = \{\alpha_1, \alpha_2, \ldots\}$. Let $\mathbb{M}(\mathbb{L})$ be the family of all multisets based on $\mathbb{L}$. So these are subsets with copies from $\mathbb{L}$. For example $\{2\alpha, 3\beta\}$, this is a multiset with 2 copies of α and 3 copies of β.

2. Let $\mathbb{M}_1(\mathbb{L})$ be all multisets of the form $\{m\alpha, \beta_1, \ldots, \beta_{k-1}\}$, i.e. at most one element appears with more than one copy. So for example $\{2\alpha, 3\beta, \gamma\}$ is not in $\mathbb{M}_1(\mathbb{L})$.

   We call the number k in $\{m\alpha, \beta_1, \ldots, \beta_{k-1}\}$ the dimension of the element and the number m in its (multi-valued) index.

3. Let E be a finite subset of $\mathbb{M}_1(\mathbb{L})$. Define the dimension and index of E as the maximum of the respective dimensions and indices of its elements.

DEFINITION 2.12 (Multiset representation of ordering). Let $(S, <)$ be a partially ordered set and let $\mathbb{L}$ be a set of labels. A function $\mathbf{f}$ giving for each $x \in S$ a multiset $\mathbf{f}(x)$ be in $\mathbb{M}_1(\mathbb{L})$ is called an $(\mathbb{L}, \mathbf{f})$ realisation of $(S, <)$ iff the following holds:

(∗) $x \leq y$ iff $\mathbf{f}(x) \subseteq \mathbf{f}(y)$ where $\subseteq$ is a multiset inclusion

2. ANALYSIS OF THE TALMUDIC KAL VACHOMER RULE

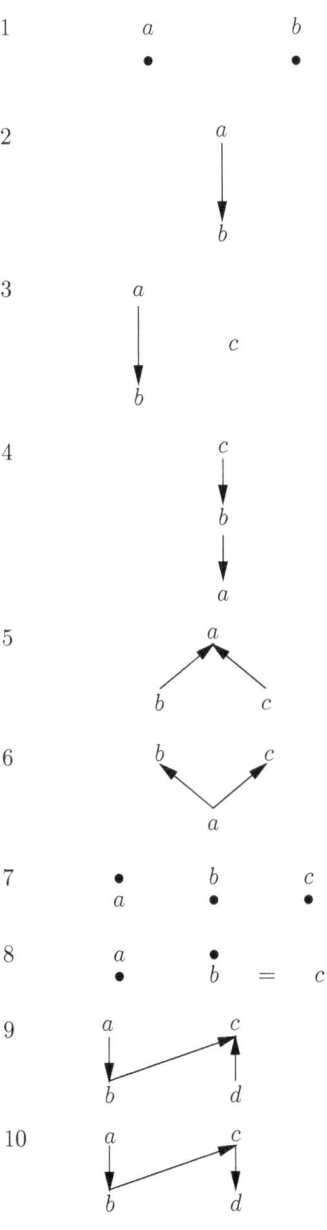

Figure 2.14.

The dimension and index the realisation are defined as those of $E = \{\mathbf{f}(x)|x \in S\}$.

LEMMA 2.13. *For every $(S,<)$ there exists an $\mathbb{L}$ and $\mathbf{f}$ such that $(\mathbb{L},\mathbf{f})$ is a realisation of $(S,<)$.*

Proof. Let $\mathbb{L} = S$ and let $\mathbf{f}(x) = \{y|y \leq x\}$. ■

DEFINITION 2.14 (Multiset representation of matrices). Let $\mathbb{A} = [a_{i,j}]$ be a definite abduction matrix. Let $V_1, \ldots, V_n$ be its columns and $U_1, \ldots, U_m$ be its rows. Let $\mathbb{L}$ be a set of labels.

1. A function $\mathbf{f}$ giving each column and each row X a multiset $\mathbf{f}(X) \in M_1(\mathbb{L})$ is considered a realisation of $\mathbb{A}$ iff the following holds

   (*) $\qquad\qquad\qquad a_{i,j} = 1 \text{ iff } \mathbf{f}(U_i) \supset \mathbf{f}(V_j)$

2. We say that the matrix $\mathbb{A}$ *has a direction* if it has a representation where the number of labels in $\mathbb{L}$ is strictly less than the number of columns in $\mathbb{A}$.

LEMMA 2.15. *Let $\mathbb{A}$ be a definite matrix. Let U_i, V_j be the rows and columns respectively. Let $\mathbb{L} = \{V_j\}$. Let $\mathbf{f}$ be defined as follows:*

$$\mathbf{f}(V_j) = \{V_j\}$$
$$\mathbf{f}(U_i) = \{V_j | a_{i,j} = 1\}.$$

Then $\mathbf{f}$ is a representation for $\mathbb{A}$.

Proof. We have indeed

$$\mathbf{f}(U_i) \supseteq \{V_j\} \text{ iff } a_{i,j} = 1.$$

■

We now define the concepts we shall use to give a definition of when one ordering τ_1 is superior to another ordering τ_2.

DEFINITION 2.16 (Minimal realisation). Let $(S,<)$ be an ordering and let $(\mathbb{L},\mathbf{f})$ be a realisation of it. The realisation is said to be *label-minimal* iff there is no other realisation $(\mathbb{L}',\mathbf{f}')$ with less labels, i.e. the dimension of $(\mathbb{L},\mathbf{f})$ is minimal among all the realisations of $(S,<)$.

The proof of Lemma 2.13 presented a multiset realisation for $(S,<)$, using the same number of labels as the number of points in S. It is important for us to minimise the number of labels needed for the realisation, as we use this number as a simplicity indicator for the ordering. We shall therefore give a construction for obtaining realisations a with minimal number of points.

To explain to the reader the ideas and difficulties with this algorithm,[6] we begin by executing it for the graph in Figure 2.13 and pointing step-by-step all key points. Examples 2.17, 2.18 and 2.19 do the job.

2. ANALYSIS OF THE TALMUDIC KAL VACHOMER RULE

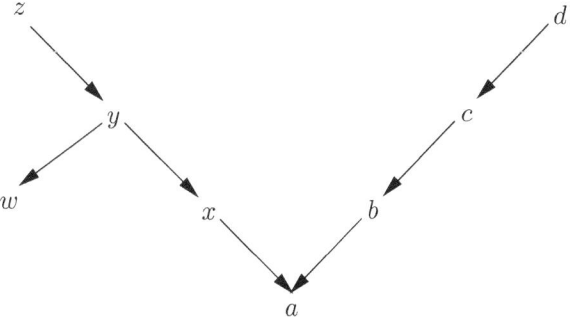

Figure 2.15.

EXAMPLE 2.17 (Maximal chains).
First note some important strategic points. Consider the graph in Figure 2.15.

We want to give it a realisation with a minimal use of labels. We are allowed to duplicate only one label, say α. So we can use $2\alpha, 3\alpha, \ldots$.

For this purpose it is good to identify a long chain and increase the number of copies of the α label along the chain. In Figure 2.15 we have two chains

$$a < b < c < d$$

and

$$a < x < y < z.$$

The second chain has $w < y$, this contributes a new label to y and so saves us from the need of duplicating α. It is therefore better to increase the α along the other chain.

Figures 2.16 and 2.17 show the two options

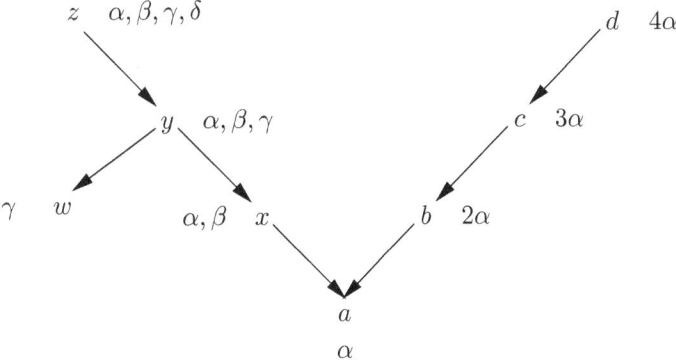

Figure 2.16.

---

[6]This algorithm does not always give the minimal realisation. There are examples by Karl Schlechta showing that there cannot be a recursive algorithm. We need brute force.

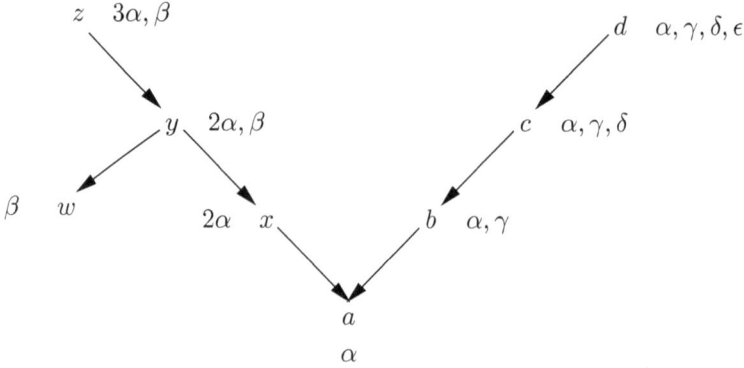

Figure 2.17.

Obviously Figure 2.17 requires more labels.

We can be clever and duplicate α along both chains. So in Figure 2.17 we can make $\delta = \alpha$ (i.e. increase α and have for c $2\alpha, \gamma$). This will not work because it makes $x < c$. Similalry we cannot make $\delta = \alpha$ in Figure 2.16 because this will make $b < z$. So our strategy is to choose a maximal chain with as little as possible points smaller than members of it.

This is what we called thin chain in Definition 2.5.

There is a trick we can use when the number of points in S is finite, say less than a fixed k. In our Figure 2.15 the number of points is less than 8.

So we progress with α along the main axis along the progression $\alpha, (m+1)\alpha, (m+2)\alpha$, etc., where m is the number of points remaining in the chain and $m \leq k$.

Using this trick Figure 2.16 becomes Figure 2.18.

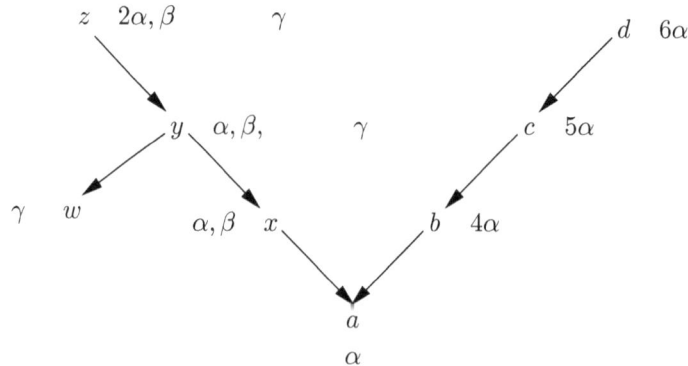

Figure 2.18.

Similarly Figure 2.19 can improve on Figure 2.17.

So the strategy is to choose a good maximal chain and increase α by at most by multiples of $k\alpha$ as necessary along the chain and increase α by 1 in all other

2. ANALYSIS OF THE TALMUDIC KAL VACHOMER RULE

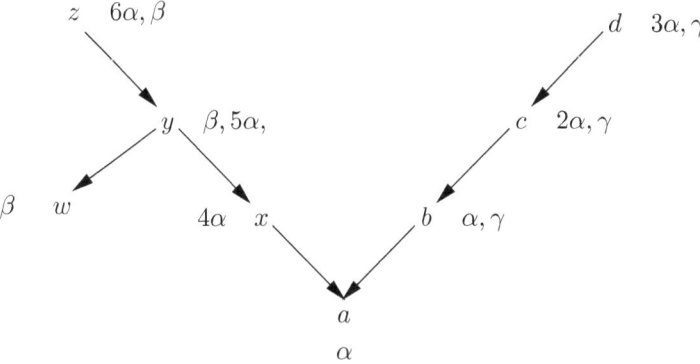

Figure 2.19.

directions.

The reason we advance possibly in multiples of $k\alpha$ along the main chain is because of the following possible situation in Figure 2.20

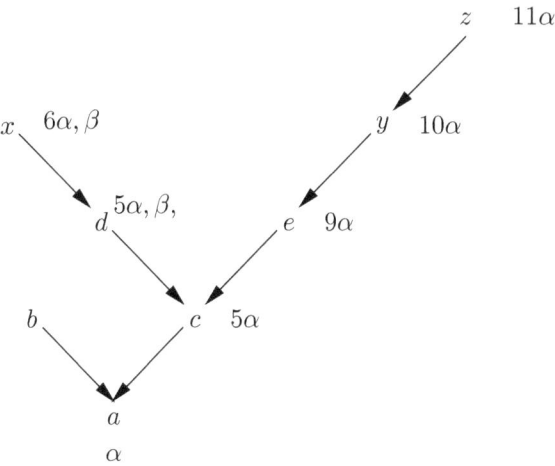

Figure 2.20.

We would have had $e < x$ if we had not advanced in more than just one α along the main chain $a < c < e < y < z$.

Note that we don't really need to increase the numbers of α by a jump of up to $k\alpha$ at every point of the main chain. We need to do that only after split points such as c in Figure 2.20. Since at e there is no split y can get 10α and similarly z can get 11α.

In fact, we need to increase after a split at point s by at most the number $d(s) + 1$, where $d(s)$ is equal to the remaining points in the chain. In the case of the point c, there were 3 points remaining in the chain so we jumped by 4α.

The reason this is OK is that we are on a maximal chain and so other points in other directions, e.g. x cannot accumulate more αs than the jump.

In fact in many cases we need less than $d(s)+1$. One strategy is to jump in each case by some variable letter $\mathbf{k}(s)$ and adjust it at the end so that all is OK.

EXAMPLE 2.18 (Critical nodes). This example explains another problem we have to watch for. Consider the situation in Figure 2.21.

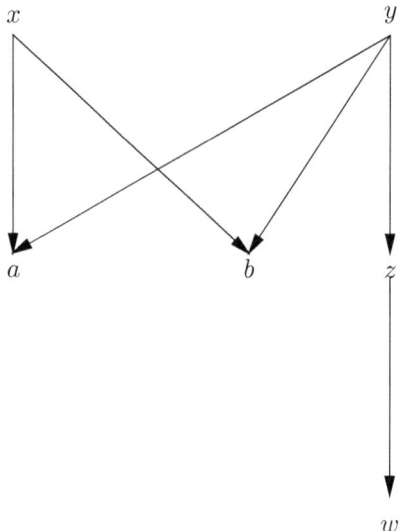

Figure 2.21.

The longest chain in this figure is

$$w < z < y.$$

So we allocate

$$w : \alpha < z : 2\alpha.$$

We allocate $a : \beta$, and $b : \gamma$ and now since x comes immediately above a and b it gets $x : \alpha, \beta$ and similarly y gets $\gamma, \beta, 2\alpha$. This algorithm however makes $x < y$.

We need to recognise the critical points x such that there is a y such that $\sim (x < y)$ and y is such that it is above all the immediate predecessors of x. In such a case to avoid the result $x < y$, we add a label to x. We do not need to worry if x has only one predecessor. In such a case we add additional label to x anyway. It is only when x has more than one predecessor that we need to worry. Hence the definition of critical points in Definition 2.5.

So the labelling becomes as in Figure 2.22, where we added an additional label to the critical node x.

Critical points can be identified from the ordering.

In Figure 2.23, both x and y are critical, and so is z.

2. ANALYSIS OF THE TALMUDIC KAL VACHOMER RULE

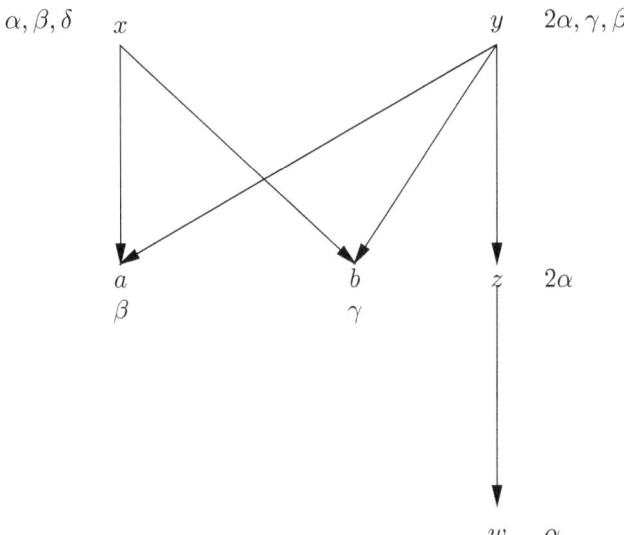

Figure 2.22.

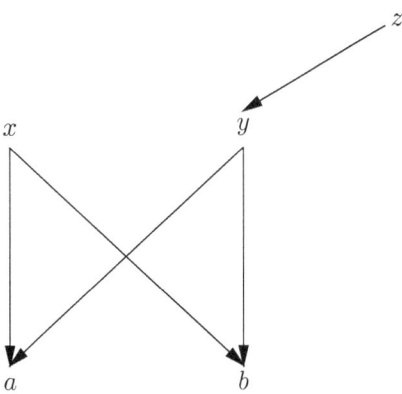

Figure 2.23.

However, if we deal with x, y, we do not need to deal with z. Our algorithm will pay attention to do that.

Also if $a = b$, then x, y are not critical because we increase the allocation of both x and y.

EXAMPLE 2.19. We now apply our algorithm to be given in Construction 2.20 Figure 2.13.

Step 0 (Preparatory step)
Identify the set of critical points C and a maximal thin chain T.
In our case
$$C = \{u\}$$
$$T = \{x_1 < x_2 < x_3 < z < x_4 < v\}$$
Identify the number of points fo the graph. In Figure 2.13, $k = 12$.

Step 1
Consider all points of level 1. Give a different atomic label to each point. Give α to the point which is on the chain T. Let the function be λ. In our case
$$\lambda(y_1) = \beta_1$$
$$\lambda(y_2) = \beta_2$$
$$\lambda(y_3) = \beta_3$$
$$\lambda(x_1) = \alpha$$

Step 2
Identify the points of level 2.

In this case, we have point x_2 and u. x_2 is on the main chain T_1 and u is a critical point. We allocate
$$\lambda(x_2) = 5\alpha$$
$$\lambda(u) = \{\beta_3, \beta_2, \gamma\}.$$

Step 3
Identify points of level 3. These are x_3 and w.

x_3 is immediately above x_2 and y_1, so we allocate
$$\lambda(x_3) = \{\beta_1, 5\alpha\}$$
w is above u and x_1 so
$$\lambda(w) = \{\alpha, \beta_3, \beta_2, \gamma\}.$$

Step 4
Identify level 4 points. This is z. It is on T, so we advance α (add α to the allocation of its predecesor)
$$\lambda(z) = \{\beta_1, 6\alpha\}$$

Step 5
Consider nodes of level 5. This is x_4. x_4 has two immediate predecessors, z and y_2. It is on T but we do not need to advance α because its allocation will increase anyway from y_2 and z. It is not critical so we do not need to add extra. So
$$\lambda(x_4) = \{\beta_1, \beta_2, 6\alpha\}$$

Step 6
Level 6 points are x_5 and v. We allocate

$$\lambda(x_5) = \{\beta_1, \beta_2, \beta_3, 6\alpha\}$$
$$\lambda(v) = \{\beta_1, \beta_2, 7\alpha\}$$

We advanced α to v because $v \in T$.

To summarise, we get Figure 2.24. The algorithm can be improved to decide more carefully how much to advance α but we don't do that in order to keep the algorithm simple. See Remark 2.21.

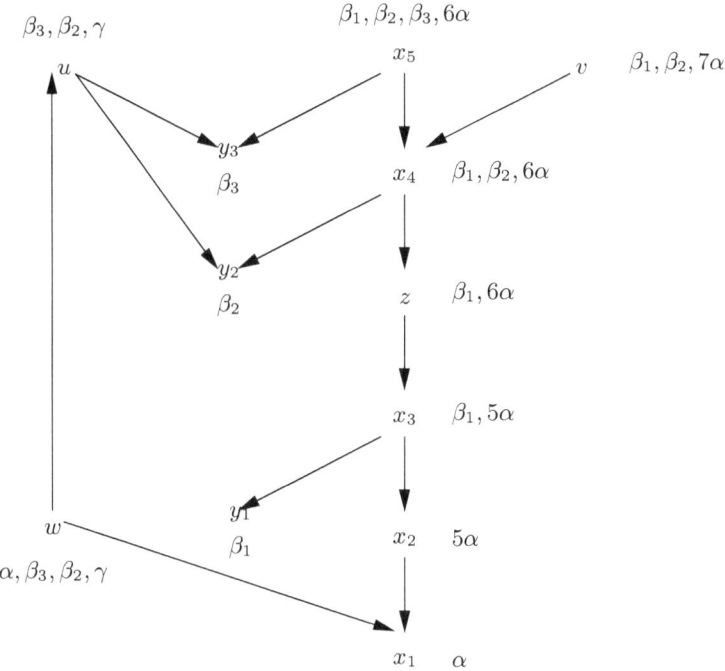

Figure 2.24.

We are now ready to give the algorithm for allocating multiset labels to any finite graph.

Construction 2.20 (Multiset realisations for finite graph).
Let $(S, <, \prec)$ be a graph, as defined in Definition 2.5. We shall construct a realisation λ on $(S, \prec)$ using the partition into levels of S as presented in Definition 2.5. The construction proceeds by induction on the levels. We assume we have an infinite sequence of labels $\{\alpha, \beta_i\}$ to use as we need. α is the only label that we allow to make copies, $2\alpha, 3\alpha$, etc.

We define a function λ in steps 1, 2, 3,... defining λ in step n on all points of level n. Step 0 just prepares the gound for the induction by doing some preliminary processing.

Step 0

Identify and choose one maximal thin path in $(S, \prec)$, call it T. For example in Figure 2.13 this is T_1. Also identify all critical points.

Step 1

Consider all level 1 points (i.e. minimal points). One of them, say x_1 is in T. Let $\lambda(x) = \{\alpha\}$. If the other minimal points are $y_1, \ldots, y_n$ let $\lambda(y_i) = \beta_i$, β_i are all differnet labels. In Figure 2.13, $n = 3$.

Step $n+1$

Consider all level $n+1$ points. One of them, say w is in T. Let the others be $a_1, \ldots, a_k$. In Figure 2.13, for $n = 2$, we have $w = x_2$ is in T_1 and $a_1 = u$.

There are the following possibilities for a level $n+1$ point e.

a. e has only one predecessor and e is in T.

b. e has only one predecessor and e is not in T

c. e has several predecessors and e is the only one with these predecessors. We have two subcases:

   c1. e is not a critical point

   c2. e is critical

d. e and $e_1, \ldots, e_k$ have the same set of predecessors and $e \notin T$

e. e and $e_1, \ldots, e_k$ have the same set of predecessors and $e \in T$.

In Figure 2.13 for level 2, point u is of Case (c1) and point x_2 is of case (a).

We now extend λ to the new level $n+1$ points of the graph. Let e be of level $n+1$. We use case analysis and define $\lambda(e)$ as follows:

Case (a)

Let y be the single predecessor of e. Then since $e \in T$, we also have $y \in T$.

We distinguish two subcases:

(a1) e is the only immediate successor of y.

   Let $\lambda(e) = \lambda(y) \cup \{\alpha\}$.

(a2) y has other immediate successors besides e. Let $m(y)$ be the remaining number of nodes above y in the chain T. Then let $\lambda(e) = \lambda(y) \cup \{(m+1)\alpha\}$.

Note that the choice to advance by $(m+1)\alpha$ is safe but in many cases not minimal. Let $\mathbf{k}(y)$ be a variable letter which can take values $1 \leq \mathbf{k}(y) \leq m+1$. We can advance α by $\mathbf{k}(y)$, i.e. $\lambda(e) = \lambda(y) \cup \{\mathbf{k}(y)\alpha\}$. We can carry on the construction until we finish. We get allocations of multisets with some numerically bound variables $\mathbf{k}(y), y \in T$ in it. We can now check by a computer program what values of $\mathbf{k}(y)$ will maintain the graph ordering. These are the values we take. The program terminates because $\mathbf{k}(y) \leq m(y)+1$. See Remark 2.21.

Case (b)

Here $y \notin T$. We distinguish two subcases:

(b1) $\alpha \in \lambda(y)$. Let $\lambda(e) = \lambda(y) \cup \{\alpha\}$.

(b2) $\alpha \notin \lambda(y)$. Let δ be a new atomic label and let $\lambda(e) = \lambda(y) \cup \{\delta\}$,

(b3) $\alpha \in \lambda(y)$ and there exists a point z is above y and also above some point in T. In this case let δ be new label and let $\lambda(e) = \lambda(y) \cup \{\delta\}$. See for example Figure 2.63, node G. Here $T = A < H < G, e = G, y = K$. Point Y is above K and if we advance α and let G have $2\alpha, \beta$ it will become below Y. The reason is that Y is above $H \in T$ and so gets more α from H.

Case (c)
Let the predecessors of e be $y_1, \ldots, y_k$.

(c1) e is not critical. Let D be the smallest multiset containing $\lambda(y_i)$ for all $i = 1, \ldots, k$. Let $\lambda(e) = D$.

(c2) e is critical. In this case let δ be a new atomic label. Let $\lambda(e) = D \cup \{\delta\}$.

Case (d)
Let $y_1, \ldots, y_k$ be the predecessors. Let $\delta, \delta_1, \ldots, \delta_k$ be completely new set of labels.

Let $\lambda(e_i) = E \cup \{\delta_i\}$ where E is the smallest multiset containing all of $\lambda(y_i)$. Similarly $\lambda(e) = E \cup \{\delta\}$.

Case (e)
This case is like Case (d) except that $e \in T$. In this case we proceed just like Case (d), we take $\delta_i, i = 1, \ldots, k$ new atoms, let $\lambda(e_i) = E \cup \{\delta_i\}$. However, for e we take $\lambda(e) = E \cup \{(m+1)\alpha\}$.

REMARK 2.21. We are pretty sure that the previous construction gives a minimal realisation as far as the number of different letters is concerned. It does not minimise the number of copies of α. For a practical strategy, we find the number of letters and copies of α we need using the algorithm possibly with some variables $\mathbf{k}(y)$ and then use another complete adjustment program to optimise the allocations and assign values to the variables $\mathbf{k}(y)$.

It is like the Newton method for finding roots of a polynomial. We get an approximate root first and then use a computer to get a better solution. In our cse, get a realisation from the algoirthm possibly with some variables and then simplify and optimise it.

Construction 2.22 (Multiset realisation for matrices). Let $\mathbb{A}$ be a matrix with $0, 1$ values construct the graph of the columns of $\mathbb{A}$. If V_1 and V_2 are two columns, define $V_1 \leq V_2$ iff for every row in the matrix, the value of V_1 is bigger than that of V_2 (thus larger values are lower in the order. Remember the more 0 in the column, the harder it is to achieve whatever that column represents, hence the column is higher in the ordering).

We also write graphcially
$$V_1 \leftarrow V_2$$

So we get a graph $(S, \prec)$. Now apply the construction to get a realisation $\mathbf{f}$ for the graph. Since the elements of the graph are all the columns of the matrix, we get a multiset value assigned for each column. Suppose $\mathbb{A} = [a_{i,j}], i =$

$1, \ldots, m, j = 1, \ldots, n$. Then $V_j = (a_{1,j}, \ldots, a_{m,j})$. $\mathbf{f}(V_j), j = 1, \ldots, n$ is now available.

We can now compute a multiset value for each row. Let $U_i = (a_{i,1}, \ldots, a_{i,n})$ be the ith row. We define $\mathbf{f}(U_i)$ to be the smallest multiset containing all the column multisets $\mathbf{f}(V_j)$ for which $a_{i,j} = 1$. With this definition we get a multiset representation for the matrix $\mathbb{A} = [a_{i,j}]$. We have

$$a_{i,j} = 1 \text{ iff } \mathbf{f}(U_i) \supseteq \mathbf{f}(V_j).$$

This is a more minimal realisation than the one proposed in Lemma 2.15.

DEFINITION 2.23. Let $(S, <)$ be given. Define xRy as $x < y \vee y < x$. Let R^* be the transitive closure of R.

1. For $s \in S$, let $[s]$ be the set of all elements such that sR^*y. We get $S = S_1 \cup \ldots \cup S_k$ where each S_i is R^* connected, and for $i \neq j$, $S_i \cap S_j = \emptyset$.
   Let ξ be the number k of connected components.

2. Take two points x and y such that xR^*y. Then there exist $z_1, \ldots, z_k$ such that
   $$xR_1z_1R_0z_2R_1z_3, \ldots, R_iz_kR_{1-i}y$$
   where
   $$R_1, R_0 \text{ are in } \{<, >\} \text{ and } R_1 \neq R_0$$
   Let $\rho(x, y)$ be the minimal number k such that a sequence $z_1, \ldots, z_k$ exists.

   Let $\rho = \max_{x,y} \rho(x, y)$.

   ρ measures the maximal number of changes in direction required to move from one point to another. This is a measure of the complexity of the ordering.

We call ρ the index of directional change is $(S, <, >)$ and ξ the index of connectivity.

EXAMPLE 2.24. Consider Figure 2.25

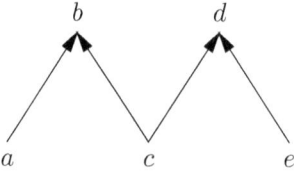

Figure 2.25.

To get from a to e we change direction three times. From c we can get to any point by changing direction once only. Here $\rho = 3$.

To get a better feel for this example, consider this ordering as a temporal ordering of temporal points. $a < b$ means b is in the future of a and a is in the past of b.

The temporal logic K_t has two temporal connectives FA and PA. We have

- $X \vDash FA$ iff $\exists x(x < y \wedge y \vDash A)$
- $X \vDash PA$ iff $\exists y(y < x \wedge y \vDash A)$

If A were true at point c, then we have

$$a \vDash FPFPA$$

We see that we require three changes of connectives.

$FPFP$ is known as a "modality", and in modal logic there are many theorems for many logics about how their modalities relate to one another.

REMARK 2.25 (Summary of topological indices and their meanings).

1. **Number of points**
   This parameter is obvious. We have that less number of points makes a simpler ordering.

2. **Connectivity**
   This is a known topological notion. More connectivity make a simpler graph.

3. **Changes of direction**
   Less changes makes a better graph. As we have seen in Example 2.24, it makes for a simpler logic.

4. **Dimension**
   A realisation with lower dimension and lower index is better. I shows more connections in the graphs.

5. **Other indices**
   Note that the indices we use must have a direction. So if a small number of points is a good index, then the smaller the better. Consider for example, the graph theory criterion of how many arrows go into a point. In Figure 2.29 for example, node A has index 2 while node N has index 1.

   We now argue that this topological feature is not a good index.

   Consider Figure 2.14, the graphs of items 4, 5, and 7. In order of simplicity, 4 is best, 5 is middle and 7 is worst. The proposed graph index is one for 4, two for 5 and 0 for 7. So it has no direction, it just goes up and down.

We now discuss the meaning of a realisation and the meaning of dimension. First observe that giving realisations (or representations) is common in mathematics.

Representing algebraic structures by matrices is very common and also representing orderings by set inclusion. So the idea of representing a partial order by inclusion of multisets is a move every mathematicians will understand. The question is what more does it give us? We mentioned in Section 1.1 that the matrices should have the meaning that the rows are actions and the columns are features generated by the actions. We also argued that all features should be pulling in the same direction. We gave some examples. We give one more which will help us with our notation. Consider a matrix where the rows are types of foods and the columns are health features. Here is a partial matrix (Figure 2.26):

	heart	blood flow	eyes	bones
carrots			1	
eggs		0		
coffee	0	1		
milk				1

Figure 2.26.

Eggs are bad for the veins, caffeine for the heart, carrots good for the eyes, etc.

The reason behind this table are the specific ingredients the foods contain. It is the ingredients that do the job. If the columns are represented correctly, i.e. all pulling in the same general direction of better health, then 1 in the caffeine or egg column means quantity while 1 in the carrot column means larger quantity. So in this case, if the egg heart slot gets represented by say $\{3\alpha, \beta, \gamma\}$ this means there are some ingredients in eggs (say β, γ) that give the effects on the heart. α is the only label that can have a strength index, so here 3α means average strength in the direction of health.

Mathematically it is sufficient to allow for only one parameter to indicate strength.

Consider Figure 2.27

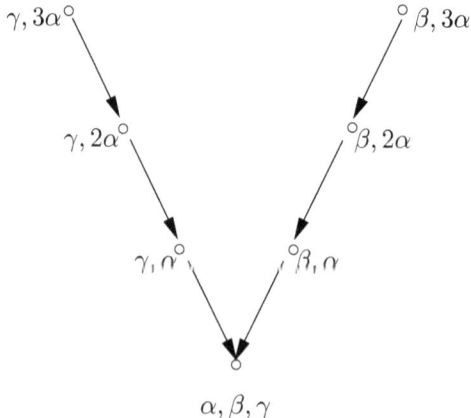

Figure 2.27.

β, γ give the qualitative directions and α gives the strength. This representation has dimension 3 (3 ingredients) and index 3 (strength of α).[7] So if we have an ordering which can be realised with less ingredients (dimension) and lower index, then it is a better ordering, giving a more detailed picture of what is going on.

EXAMPLE 2.26 (Restriction on the representation). We saw that a lower dimension on the representation is an indication of a superior ordering. Therefore any restriction imposed on the representation might increase the dimension for the same ordering and we expect it must make sense. We best explain through an example. Consider the matrix of Figure 2.28

	N	A	P	Y
m	0	1	1	0
h	1	x =?	0	0
b	1	1	0	1

Figure 2.28.

We use the notation of capital letters for columns and small bold letters for rows.

To decide whether we should recommend $x = 0$ or $x = 1$, let us do the graphs for each case, and calculate the realisation using our algorithm

For the choice $x = 1$, we get Figure 2.29

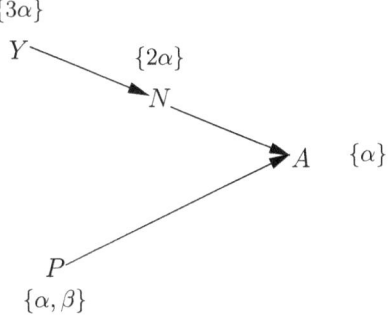

Figure 2.29.

For the choice $x = 0$ we get Figure 2.30
We now have to check the various criteria for the two orderings.
The table in Figure 2.31 gives the answers:
The dimension and index needs to be checked against all possible realisations of the graphs. The following Figure 2.32 is a table of realisations with dimension

---
[7] Technically in the finite case we can manage with just α, β. So in our graph of Figure 2.27, let $\gamma = 3\alpha$ and the left branch becomes $4\alpha, 5\alpha, 6\alpha$. This representation is only technical. We want γ to indicate quality not quantity.

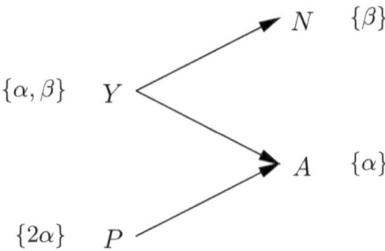

Figure 2.30.

	Dimension	connectivity	change direction	number points
Case $x = 1$	2	1	1	4
Case $x = 0$	2	1	2	4

Figure 2.31.

2 (labels $\{\alpha, \beta\}$). We need to prove that neither graph can manage to have a realisation with only one label $\{\alpha\}$. This is easy to see.

	N	A	P	Y
Case $x = 1$	2α	α	α, β	3α
Case $x = 0$	β	α	2α	α, β

Figure 2.32.

According to this $x = 1$ has a better ordering because it has less change of direction. So the answer to the abduction problem of Figure 2.28 is to take $x = 1$.

We can now compute the realisation **g** for the rows matrix of Figure 2.28, using the algorithm of Construction 2.22. We get two fuctions, $\mathbf{g}_1$ for the case $x = 1$ and $\mathbf{g}_0$ for the cae $x = 0$. The values of $\mathbf{g}_1$ and $\mathbf{g}_0$ for the columns can be read from Figures 2.29 and 2.30 respectively.

To find what ingredient row i has in a representation, we must find a minimal multiset $\mathbf{g}(U_i)$ such that

$$\mathbf{g}(U_i) \supseteq \mathbf{f}(V_j), j = 1, \ldots, n, \quad a_{i,j} = 1.$$

So in the matrix for $x = 1$ we get

$$\mathbf{g}_1(\mathbf{m}) = \{2\alpha, \beta\}$$
$$\mathbf{g}_1(\mathbf{h}) = \{2\alpha\}$$
$$\mathbf{g}_1(\mathbf{b}) = \{3\alpha\}$$

For the matrix $x = 0$ we get

$$\mathbf{g}_0(\mathbf{m}) = \{2\alpha\}$$
$$\mathbf{g}_0(\mathbf{h}) = \{\beta\}$$
$$\mathbf{g}_0(\mathbf{b}) = \{\alpha, \beta\}$$

Let us now add the restriction that rows **m** and **b** (i.e. the actions **m** and **b**) must contain an ingredient which is not in **h**. For example, if the rows are foods or medicines, we may know that there is something (e.g. vitamin present in **m** and **b** and not in **h**).

Both realisations g_0 and g_1 fail to satisfy the restriction.

The following Figures 2.33 for the case $x = 1$ and 2.34 for the case $x = 0$ give realisations which do satisfy the condition. However, the dimension goes up. We need to prove mathematically that it is not possible to give any realisation of dimension 2 which satisfies the restriction.

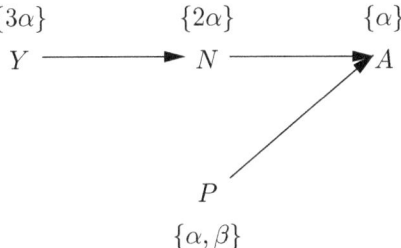

Figure 2.33.

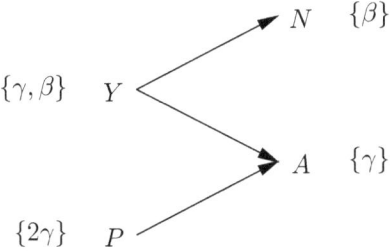

Figure 2.34.

	$x = 1$	$x = 0$
g(m)	$\{\alpha, \beta, \gamma\}$	$\{2\gamma\}$
g(h)	$\{2\alpha\}$	$\{\beta\}$
g(b)	$\{2\alpha, \gamma\}$	$\{\gamma, \beta\}$

Figure 2.35.

Again the case $x = 1$ wins because of changes of direction. We get in this case, Figure 2.35

Clearly γ is an ingredient in **m** and **b** but not in **h**.

DEFINITION 2.27 (Superiority). Given two graphs τ_1 and τ_2 we calculate the value of the parameters for each graph.

1. If graphs τ_1 (resp. τ_2) has better or equal values to all parameters than τ_2, (resp. τ_1), with one parameter strictly better, then τ_1 is superior.

2. If all parameters are equal or if one graph is better in one parameter and the other graph is better in another then the answer is undecided.

We now describe how we reason and argue with these matrices. We imagine a proponent and an opponent.

The proponent puts forward a matrix $\mathbb{A}$ with $a_{i,j} =?$. All the entries except $a_{i,j}$ are considered known and agreed values. He applies the matrix abduction rule to $\mathbb{A}$ and proves (i.e. the algorithm of Section 3 shows) that $x = 1$ is a winning value. Thus the proponent showed non-monotonically using the matrix $\mathbb{A}$ and our rule that $x = 1$.

Remember that these entries have meaning: so for example if the entries are from monadic predicate logic with predicates $A_i(x), i = 1, \ldots, m$ and the elements of the domain are $d_1, \ldots, d_n$ then the proponent proved that $A_i(d_j) = 1$.

How can the opponent attack? He adds more facts to the argument by adding more columns and rows to the matrix. So assume $\mathbb{A} = [a_{i,j}], 1 \leq i \leq m, 1 \leq j \leq n$. The opponent expands the matrix to $\mathbb{A}^* = [a_{i,j}] 1 \leq i \leq m^*, 1 \leq j \leq n^*$, where $m \leq n^*$ and $n \leq n^*$ and at least one of $m \not\geq m^*$ and $n \not\leq n^*$ holds.

All the new entries in $\mathbb{A}^*$ are in $\{0, 1\}$ (i.e. $a_{i,j} =?$ is still the only unknown, ? entry). Furthermore, when we apply our matrix abduction algorithm to $\mathbb{A}^*$ we get 'undecided' as values.

The proponent can defend by expanding $\mathbb{A}^*$ to $\mathbb{A}^{**}$ where in $\mathbb{A}^{**}$ we do get that $a_{i,j} = 1$ is a winning value. This attack and defence can go on and on until it stops. The last value is the conclusion value.

EXAMPLE 2.28. Here is a sequence of attacks and counterattacks

	N	A	Y
h	1	x =?	0
b	1	1	1

Figure 2.36.

In the matrix $\mathbb{A}$ of Figure 2.36 without column $Y, x = 1$ wins. When we add Y to it to get $\mathbb{A}^*$ we get 'undecided'.

Let us check this, see Figures 2.37 and 2.38.

EXAMPLE 2.29 (Screens and cameras). We can now settle the question of whethr the NEC2470/WVX LCD screen has stereophonic spakers.[8]

Let us do the graph for the columns of the matrix of Figure 2.1. This is displayed at Figure 2.39.

Clearly the case $x = 1$ is superior because it is connected.

We now consider the camera example of Figure 2.2.

The two graphs for case $x = 1$ and case $x = 0$ are displayed in Figure 2.40

---
[8]Searched the web again today, 1 March 2009. Could not find a definite answer.

Graph of $\mathbb{A}$ for $x = 1$

•
$N \; = \; A$

Graph of $\mathbb{A}$ for $x = 0$

$A \longrightarrow N$

Here $x = 1$ wins because it has less points ($N = A$)

Figure 2.37.

Graph of $\mathbb{A}^*$ for $x = 1$

$Y \longrightarrow N, A$

Graph of $\mathbb{A}^*$ for $x = 0$

$A, Y \longrightarrow N$

Neither graph wins.

Figure 2.38.

Case $x = 1$

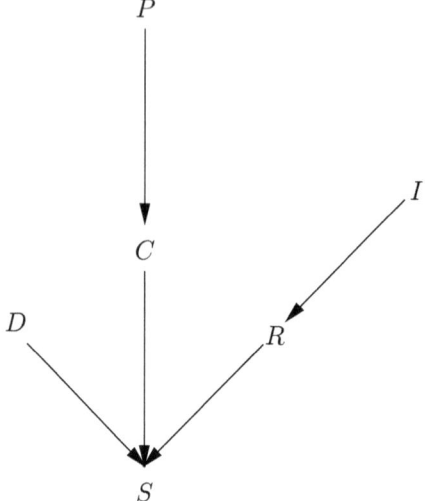

Case $x = 0$

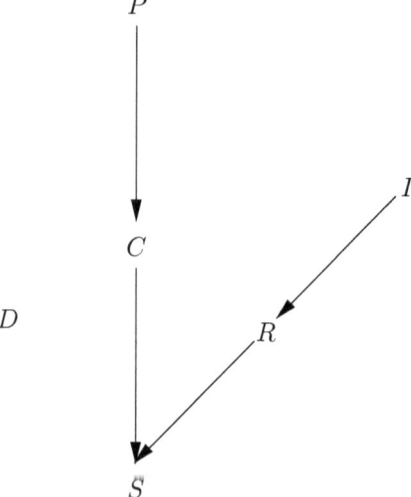

Figure 2.39.

2. ANALYSIS OF THE TALMUDIC KAL VACHOMER RULE

Case $x = 1$

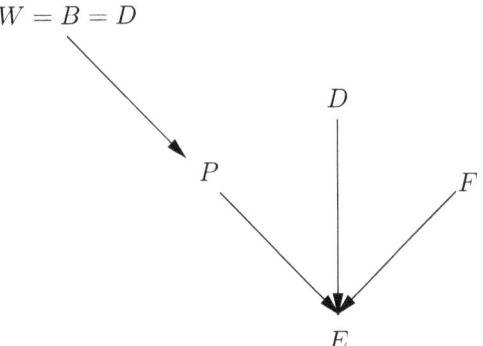

Case $x = 0$

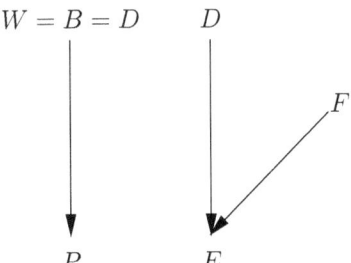

Figure 2.40.

Again the case $x = 1$ wins, because for $x = 0$ we get a disconnected graph.

REMARK 2.30 (Two question marks). How do we deal with abduction matrices which have more than one slot with a question mark? Say, for example $a_{i_0,j_0} = ?$ and $a_{i_1,j_1} = ?$. The simplest course of action is to substitute all possible $0, 1$ values and see which combination wins.

In our Hebrew paper [2] there are examples of this sort. It is possible to find, for example, that no matter what the value of a_{i_0,j_0} is we have that $a_{i_1,j_1} = 1$ is a winning substitution (over the option $a_{i_1,j_1} = 0$) while when we substitute $a_{i_1,j_1} = 1$ in the matrix, we find no winning value for $a_{i_0,j_0} = ?$.

EXAMPLE 2.31 (Dependency of columns). Assume we are given a definite $\{0,1\}$ matrix $\mathbb{A}$. Our procedures so far for handling it run through the following steps:

1. Describe the column graph of the matrix
2. Apply an algorithm to find a minimal multiset realisation of the graph
3. Use the above to find a minimal multiset realisation $\mathbf{f}$ of the matrix.

Let us concentrate our attention on (3) above.

First note that if we have a multiset realisation of the matrix we can get (1) and (2) anyway. Namely, we have

(*) $\quad a_{i,j} = 1$ iff $\mathbf{f}(U_i) \supseteq \mathbf{f}(C_j)$ where U_i is row i and C_j is column j of the matrix.

(**) We have $C_j \leq C_k$ iff $\mathbf{f}(C_j) \subseteq \mathbf{f}(C_k)$

Thus $\mathbf{f}$ actually determines everything using (*) and (**).

We now consider a new type of restriction on the realisation $\mathbf{f}$. We call it column dependencies. It arises from applications and it is a new interpretation of the matrix entries.

Consider the matrix of Figure 2.1. Consier the two columns R-reaction time and D-dot size. We can easily imagine that for technical reasons, the reaction time of Screen 3 is enhanced because Screen 3 has also small dot size. In other words the technical modifications required to make small dot size also help with reaction time. The entry therefore for Screen 3 column R depends (or is helped by) the entry for Screen 3 Column D. How do we express this formally? The answer is that it manifests itself in the restrictions on the realisation $\mathbf{f}$ of the matrix of Figure 2.1.

Instead of the equation(*)

- $a_{3,R} = 1$ iff $\mathbf{f}(\text{Screen 3}) \supseteq \mathbf{f}(R)$

we have

- $a_{3,R} = 1$ iff $\mathbf{f}(\text{Screen 3}) \cup \mathbf{f}(D) \supseteq \mathbf{f}(R)$.

It is clear that $\mathbf{f}(\text{Screen 3})$ is helped by the multiset $\mathbf{f}(D)$.

This example prompts us to change (*) to (*1) as follows: Given a definite matrix $\mathbb{A}$ with dependencies $\mathbb{D}$ of the form

2. ANALYSIS OF THE TALMUDIC KAL VACHOMER RULE

- $a_{i,j} = 1$ provided column j depends on columns $k_1^{i,j}, \ldots, k_r^{i,j}$.

Then a function $\mathbf{f}$ assigning multisets to rows and columns is a realisation of $(\mathbb{A}, \mathbb{D})$ provided (*1) holds

(*1) $\quad a_{i,j} = 1$ iff $\mathbf{f}(U_i) \cup \bigcup_{m=1}^{r_{i,j}} \mathbf{f}(C_{k_m^{i,j}}) \supseteq \mathbf{f}(C_j)$.

To see the difference in a real Talmudic example, consider the argument of Figure 2.46 below for the cases $x = 1$ and $x = 0$.

The graphs for it are in Figure 2.47. The realisation we get from the graphs are $\mathbf{f}_1$ and $\mathbf{f}_0$ as follows. See Figure 2.41 below.

Case $x = 1$	
$\mathbf{f}_1(A)$	α
$\mathbf{f}_1(N)$	2α
$\mathbf{f}_1(\mathbf{m})$	α
$\mathbf{f}_1(\mathbf{h})$	2α

Case $x = 0$	
$\mathbf{f}_0(A)$	α
$\mathbf{f}_0(N)$	β
$\mathbf{f}_0(\mathbf{m})$	α
$\mathbf{f}_0(\mathbf{h})$	β

Figure 2.41.

The Talmudic argument is for $x = 1$ to win, as indeed it does.

This argument is attacked by claiming that there is a dependency, and that actually the value $a_{\mathbf{h},N}$ at the square $(\mathbf{h}, N)$ depends on the column A. Thus we need a new matrix realisation $\mathbf{f}^*$ which satisfies

$$a_{\mathbf{h},N} = 1 \text{ iff } \mathbf{f}^*(\mathbf{h}) \cup \mathbf{f}^*(A) \supseteq \mathbf{f}^*(N).$$

If this is the case we get the following realisations $\mathbf{f}^*$ for the matrices, for cases $x = 0$ and $x = 1$. See Figure 2.42

Case $x = 1$	
$\mathbf{f}_1^*(A)$	α
$\mathbf{f}_1^*(N)$	2α
$\mathbf{f}_1^*(\mathbf{m})$	α
$\mathbf{f}_1^*(\mathbf{h})$	α

Case $x = 0$	
$\mathbf{f}_0^*(A)$	α
$\mathbf{f}_0^*(N)$	1.5α
$\mathbf{f}_0^*(\mathbf{m})$	α
$\mathbf{f}_0^*(\mathbf{h})$	0.5α

Figure 2.42.

We need to formulate algorithms to find minimal realisations for matrices $(\mathbb{A}, \mathbb{D})$ with dependencies as well as criteria to compare realisations, but clearly the attack succeeds as Case $x = 1$ of Figure 2.42 is not superior to Case $x = 0$.

4 Case study: Sentences for traffic offences

As an additional example of our general method we shall consider an application in the domain of Traffic Offences. We stress that it is not our intention to suggest that traffic judges should actually use a computer system implementing this approach. It is though conceivable that some day in the future decision support systems for judges could incorporate this method.

Let us first briefly survey the area of sentencing within the framework of law and order in society. This is usually the point of view taken by judges about to pass sentence on an offender. One distinguishes four classical approaches to punishment: Retribution, Deterrence, Prevention and Rehabilitation [Lawton L.J., in: Sargeant (1974) 60 Cr. App. Rep. 74 C.A. at pp.77-84].

This classification does not mean that a judge about to pass sentence on an offender asks himself an explicit question: "Which approach shall I use here?" It is generally assumed that he forms an opinion about which approach (or approaches) to apply in an intuitive manner. The next step is then to decide on a sentence appropriate for the specific offender and offence within the sentencing approach (or approaches). This is also an intuitive process: "It comes from within", as several judges have expressed it. Our formulation would be that the sentence chosen by the judge is the one that he intuitively believes includes the appropriate mixture of 'microscopic elements', thus leading to one or more of the four sentencing aims.

The possible punishments for traffic offences are (in Israel): Imprisonment, driving disqualification, fine, community service. These punishments may also be suspended, i.e. applied only if the offender commits a new offence. Sentences are often a combination of the above, e.g., suspended driving disqualification plus fine. In the following we shall not consider community service.

Consider now the following example. A judge has passed sentence on six traffic offenders. He has already decided on part of a sentence for a seventh offender, but has not made up his mind whether to sentence him to imprisonment or not. Our algorithm will indicate what would be a logical decision, based on the previous six sentences.

Offender 1: Killed a pedestrian. The sentence: Suspended imprisonment and actual disqualification.
Offender 2: Killed pedestrian while driving under licence disqualification. The sentence: Imprisonment, disqualification, and also suspended imprisonment and suspended disqualification.
Offender 3: Drunk driving. The sentence: Disqualification, fine, and also suspended disqualification and suspended fine.
Offender 4: Driving through a red light. The sentence: Fine and suspended disqualification.
Offender 5: Driving while under disqualification. The sentence: Disqualification, fine and suspended fine.
Offender 6: Driving without valid driver's licence. The sentence: Fine and suspended fine.
Offender 7: Driving while under the influence of drugs. The sentence: Disqualification, fine and suspended disqualification and suspended fine. In addition the judge has decided on suspended imprisonment and is thinking about an actual prison sentence.

What advice should we give him, in order to preserve a logical uniformity of sentencing?

It is important to assume that the above sentences were passed by the same judge. Only by this assumption can we be sure that the "microscopic ingredients' are the same. For different judges may use different ingredients in different amounts.

2. ANALYSIS OF THE TALMUDIC KAL VACHOMER RULE

This of course is strongly related to the problem of uniformity of punishment, or rather the lack of uniformity. Were different judges to use the same ingredients in the same amounts the problem of sentencing disparity would diminish. It is interesting to speculate that iterative use of our approach on sentences by different judges could lead to some kind of convergence bringing increased uniformity.

The following table 2.43 represents the cases described above. The undecided sentence for offender 7 is indicated by a ? sign.

	O1	O2	O3	O4	O5	O6	O7
imprisonment	0	1	0	0	0	0	?
suspended imprisonment	1	1	0	0	0	0	1
disqualification	1	1	1	0	0	0	1
suspended disqualification	0	1	1	1	1	0	1
fine	0	0	1	1	1	1	1
suspended fine	0	0	1	0	1	1	1

Figure 2.43.

The following diagram 2.44 represents the choice: actual imprisonment, i.e. the value 1 is substituted for the question mark.

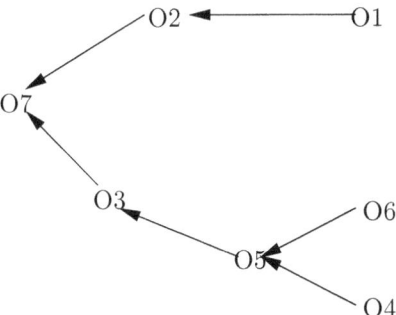

Figure 2.44.

The following diagram 2.45 represents the choice: No actual imprisonment, i.e., the value 0 is substituted for the question mark.

We immediately realize that the first diagram is superior to the second one. This means that our approach will recommend that the judge imposes an actual prison sentence on offender seven.

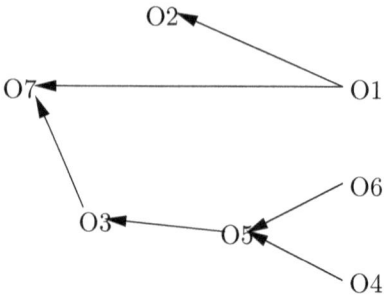

Figure 2.45.

5 Analysis of the Talmudic Kal-Vachomer from Kidushin 5a–5b

The Talmud was finalised in the fifth century AC. It contains many legal arguments about a variety of issues and one of the rules used was the Kal-Vachomer. The following text is one of the most complicated uses of this rule. The rule has never been properly formulated, though there have been many attempts.

Louis Jacobs [74], distinguishes two types of Kal-Vachomer. The simple one and the more complex one. The simple one has the structure:

- If A has x then B certainly has x.

The complex one has the structure

- If A, which lacks y, has x, then B which has y certainly has x.

The following are examples of the simple case from the Old and New Testaments. We already saw examples of the complex case in Sections 1.2 and 1.3.

The Bible does not contain instances of the complex case. This has emerged later, after the Bible.

EXAMPLE 2.32 (Kal Vachomer in the Old and New Testaments).
Exodus 6
10 And Jehovah spake unto Moses, saying,
11 Go in, speak unto Pharaoh king of Egypt, that he let the children of Israel go out of his land.
12 And Moses spake before Jehovah, saying, Behold, the children of Israel have not hearkened unto me; how then shall Pharaoh hear me, who am of uncircumcised lips?

Deuteronomy 31
27 For I know thy rebellion, and thy stiff neck: behold, while I am yet alive with you this day, ye have been rebellious against Jehovah; and how much more after my death?

Matthew 12
9 And he departed thence, and went into their synagogue:

10 and behold, a man having a withered hand. And they asked him, saying, Is it lawful to heal on the sabbath day? that they might accuse him.

11 And he said unto them, What man shall there be of you, that shall have one sheep, and if this fall into a pit on the sabbath day, will he not lay hold on it, and lift it out?

12 How much then is a man of more value than a sheep! Wherefore it is lawful to do good on the sabbath day.

Luke 13

14 And the ruler of the synagogue, being moved with indignation because Jesus had healed on the sabbath, answered and said to the multitude, There are six days in which men ought to work: in them therefore come and be healed, and not on the day of the sabbath.

15 But the Lord answered him, and said, Ye hypocrites, doth not each one of you on the sabbath loose his ox or his ass from the stall, and lead him away to watering?

16 And ought not this woman, being a daughter of Abraham, whom Satan had bound, lo, /these/ eighteen years, to have been loosed from this bond on the day of the sabbath?

17 And as he said these things, all his adversaries were put to shame: and all the multitude rejoiced for all the glorious things that were done by him.

Romans 5

8 But God commendeth his own love toward us, in that, while we were yet sinners, Christ died for us.

9 Much more then, being now justified by his blood, shall we be saved from the wrath /of God/ through him.

10 For if, while we were enemies, we were reconciled to God through the death of his Son, much more, being reconciled, shall we be saved by his life;

11 and not only so, but we also rejoice in God through our Lord Jesus Christ, through whom we have now received the reconciliation.

The simple Kal-Vachomer was analysed as an Aristotelian syllogism by A. Schwarz [93]. Compare Barbara with what moses says:

Barbara:

1. All men are mortal.

2. Socrates is a man,
   therefore

3. Socrates is mortal

1. $\forall x (\text{Men}(x) \rightarrow \text{Mortal}(x))$

2. Men(Socrates)
   therefore

3. Mortal(Socrates)

Deuteronomy 31:

Let s be something Moses says or demands. We have

1. $\forall x\neg\, \text{ListenIsrael}(x) \to \neg\text{ListenPharaoh}(x)$

2. $\neg\text{ListenIsrael}(s)$
   therefore

3. $\neg\text{ListenPharaoh}(x)$.

Louis Jacobs refutes the similarity, see [74, chapter 1], see also [80].
Certainly the more complex cases of Kal-Vachomer are not syllogisms at all.
We now analyse one of the most involved arguments in the Talmud. We first quote the text. A detailed analysis of the Kal-Vachomer in general and of this text in particular can be found in our companion paper in Hebrew [2].

Consider the following text from the Talmud, Kidushin 5a–5b.[9]

> (1a) Rav Huna said: *Huppa* acquires a fortiori, since money, which does not allow one to eat *teruma* does acquire, *Huppa* which allows one to eat *teruma*, how much more should it acquire.
>
> (1b) And does money not allow one to eat. But 'Ulla said: According to the Torah, a betrothed Israelite daughter eats of *teruma*, for it is said *"But if a priest acquire any soul, the acquisition of his money"*, and this is the acquisition of his money. For what reason did they say that she does not eat? It was feared that a cup may be poured for her in her father's house, and she will let her brothers and sisters drink it.
>
> (2) Rather argue thus: If money, which does not finalise, does acquire *Huppa*, which does finalise how much more should it acquire.
>
> (3) As to money, it is because one can redeem it with *heqdeshoth* and the Second Tithe.
>
> (4) Intercourse shall prove it.
>
> (5) As to intercourse, it is because it acquires in the case of a *Yevama*.
>
> (6) Money shall prove it.
>
> (7) And the inference revolves; the character of this is not like the character of that is not like the character of this:
>
> (8) the feature common to them is that they acquire elsewhere and they acquire here. I can also bring *Huppa*, which acquires elsewhere and acquires here.
>
> (9) As to the feature common to them, that is that their enjoyment is great!
>
> (10) 'Writ' shall prove.
>
> (11) As to writ, that it sets free an Israelite daughter,
>
> (12) money and intercourse shall prove.
>
> (13) Again the inference revolves. The character of this is not like the character of that and the character of that is not like the character of this.

---

[9]The insert numbers refer to the steps in arguments. The translation is from the El-Am edition.

2. ANALYSIS OF THE TALMUDIC KAL VACHOMER RULE

(14) The feature common to them is that they acquire elsewhere and they acquire here. I can also bring *Huppa* which acquires elsewhere and acquires here.

(15) As to the feature common to them, it is that they are possible by compulsion.

(16) And Rav Huna? Money, however, we do not find in matrimony by compulsion.[10]

We now give the argument sequence of the text above. First, some background material. When a boy wants to wed a girl as his wife, he can do it in stages. First he can give her a ring and if she accepts they are engaged. The text refers to this state as *Kidushin*. It has to be done by giving the girl a ring or something of value. The important point is the value. So the text refers to the act as "money" (i.e. something of value). The next step is the marriage ceremony which the text calls '*Huppa*'. It is known that the ceremony is essential for marriage and cannot be replaced by another ring. So if the boy gives the girl another ring this does not make her his wife. She just gets a second ring for noting. He has to go through the ceremony. There are other options for marriage. For example they can be together in a 'familiar way', which can be anything you are not supposed to do otherwise, e.g. a kiss or a short period alone in a room (long enough to be naughty), etc. This is why for example, in a marriage ceremony the boy is allowed to kiss the bride. The text calls this 'intercourse'. The question we ask here is whether the marriage ceremony can do the job of the ring. So imagine that you are ready to get married and your silly best man forgot the ring. Can we go on or do we actually have to wait for the ring? The first argument by the proponent named Rav Huna is to prove that the ceremony itself can do the job of the ring, i.e. it can do the engagement as well as the marriage itself. Figure 2.46 is this argument (item 2 in the text).

	N = married	A = engaged
m (ring)	0	1
h (*Huppa*)	1	$x = ?$

Figure 2.46.

We do the graphs for $x = 1$ and $x = 0$, and get Figure 2.47

Clearly the case $x = 1$ is a better graph. It is more connected. We also wrote the multiset assignment in the figure.

The opponent (the audience to Rav Huna) attacks this in item 3 in the text and adds column 3 to the matrix. See Figure 2.48.

The two graphs are now in Figure 2.49

---

[10] Glossary
Money = ring
Kidushin = engaged
Huppa = religious marriage ceremony
Writ = official document/contract.

1. Graphs for $x = 1$

$$N \longrightarrow A$$
$$2\alpha \qquad \alpha$$

2. Graph for $x = 0$

$$\bullet \quad \bullet$$
$$N \quad A$$
$$\beta \quad \alpha$$

Figure 2.47.

	N	A	P
m	0	1	1
h	1	x=?	0

Figure 2.48.

1. Graph for $x = 1$

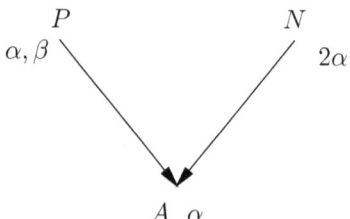

2. Graph for $x = 0$

$$N\bullet \quad \bullet A = P$$
$$\beta \qquad \alpha$$

Figure 2.49.

2. ANALYSIS OF THE TALMUDIC KAL VACHOMER RULE

In Figure 2.49 the result is undecided. The graph of $x = 1$ is better in the aspect of being connected, and the graph for $x = 0$ is better in the aspect of having less points. So it is a draw and the verdict is 'undecided'.

This means the proof of the proponent fails to be conclusive.

Now the proponent tries again (item 4 in the text) and presents a different table, using **b**= Intercourse, see Figure 2.50

	N	A
b	1	1
h	1	$x =?$

Figure 2.50.

The two graphs are in Figure 2.51, and clearly $x = 1$ wins.

1. Graph for $x = 1$

$$\bullet$$
$$A = N$$
$$\alpha$$

2. Graph for $x = 0$

$$A \quad\quad N$$
$$\longrightarrow$$
$$2\alpha \quad\quad \alpha$$

Figure 2.51.

The opponent now attacks by adding column Y for the case of yevama (item 5 of the text). We explain this case: an unmarried man must marry the widow of his brother if she is without children by biblical law. This cannot be done by ceremony (*Huppa*) but must be done by familiarity, **b**. In practice of course, if they don't want to marry then a 'divorce'-like procedure must be done.

We get Figure 2.52

	N	A	Y
b	1	1	1
h	1	$x =?$	0

Figure 2.52.

The graphs we get are in Figure 2.53

1. Graph for $x = 1$

$$Y \longrightarrow N = A$$
$$2\alpha \qquad\qquad \alpha$$

2. Graph for $x = 0$

$$A = Y \longrightarrow N$$
$$2\alpha \qquad\qquad \alpha$$

Figure 2.53.

Clearly they are of equal strength and the answer is undecided.

The proponent now combines both tables to get $x = 1$ to win(items 6–8 of the text). We get Figure 2.54

	N	A	P	Y
m	0	1	1	0
h	1	$x =?$	0	0
b	1	1	0	1

Figure 2.54.

The two graphs are in Figure 2.55

The case $x = 1$ wins because it has only value 1 for change of direction. In the graph for $x = 0$, to get from N to P we have to change direction twice.

The opponent now attacks by adding a column of H (pleasurable activity, item 9 in the text). He argues that money (**m**) and intercourse (**b**) give pleasure, while the marriage ceremony **h** does not.

We get Figure 2.56

The graphs are in Figure 2.57 and the result is undecided

Clearly case $x = 1$ has the advantage in change of direction index (1 change of direction while the graph for $x = 0$ has 2 changes), but the case $x = 0$ identifies $A = H$ and this gives it advantage over the case $x = 1$. The result is a draw.

The proponent tries again by adding a column G for divorce which can be done by a writ, **w**. This discussion is in items 9–14 of the text. Figure 2.58 gives the table.

The graphs for this are given in Figure 2.59

The case $x = 1$ wins because its graph has only one change of direction and the graph of $x = 0$ has two changes.

The opponent now attacks by adding a column with K — meaning without consent, like a girl being married by her parents without her consent. A practice still followed by some parts of the world. This is item 15 of the text.

1. Graph for $x = 1$

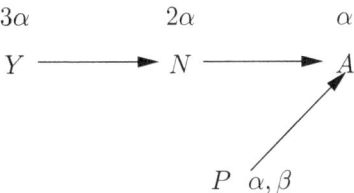

2. Graph for $x = 0$

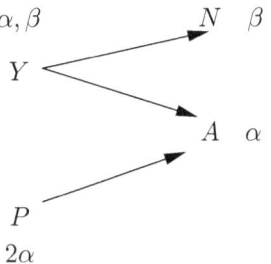

Figure 2.55.

	N	A	P	Y	H
m	0	1	1	0	1
h	1	$x = 1$	0	0	0
b	1	1	0	1	1

Figure 2.56.

1. Graph for $x = 1$

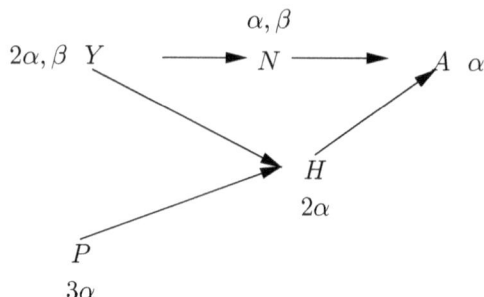

2. Graph for $x = 0$

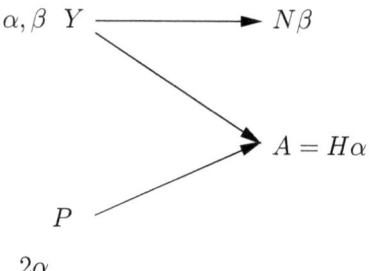

Figure 2.57.

	N	A	P	Y	H	G
m	0	1	1	0	1	0
ñ	1	$x=?$	U	U	U	U
b	1	1	0	1	1	0
w	0	1	0	0	0	1

Figure 2.58.

2. ANALYSIS OF THE TALMUDIC KAL VACHOMER RULE

1. Graph $x = 1$

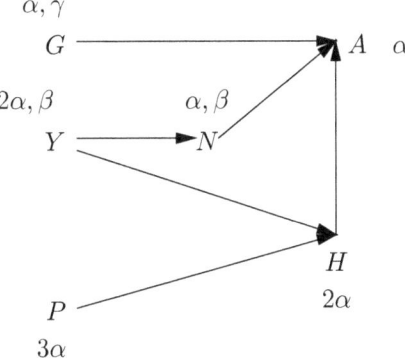

2. Graph $x = 0$

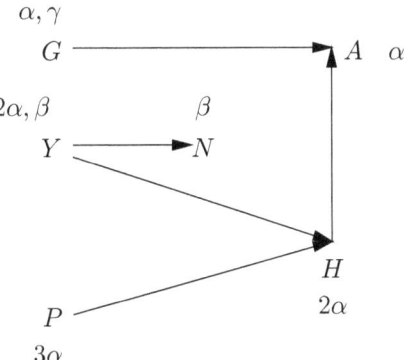

Figure 2.59.

We get the following matrix of Figure 2.60

	N	A	P	Y	H	G	K
m	0	1	1	0	1	0	1
h	1	x =?	0	0	0	0	0
b	1	1	0	1	1	0	1
w	0	1	0	0	0	1	1

Figure 2.60.

The two graphs are given in Figure 2.61

The comparison of the two graphs is undecided. The graph for $x = 1$ has the advantage of one change of direction, as compared with that of $x = 0$ which has 2. On the other hand, the graph for $x = 0$ has the advantage of making $A = K$ i.e. has less points.

So it is an undecided draw and so the proponent has not successfully proved that $x = 1$ wins.

The proponent counters that he disagrees with the matrix of Figure 2.60, in which the opponent put value 1 in the slot $(\mathbf{m}, K)$. The proponent's opinion is that a value 0 should be there. This gives us the matrix of Figure 2.62. This corresponds to item 16 in the text.

The two graphs are in Figure 2.63

Clearly Case $x = 0$ is inferior because it has 2 changes in direction to get from G to N.

This completes the analysis of the text.

Remark: Achievement

Let us discuss what we have done here. We built a matrix abduction model whose components and concepts use only topologically meaningful notions (and hence the model is culturally independent) and we used it to analyse an involved Talmudic argument and we got a perfect and meaningful fit.

2. ANALYSIS OF THE TALMUDIC KAL VACHOMER RULE

1. Graph for $x = 1$

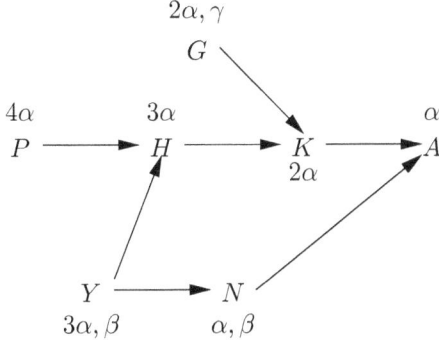

2. Graph for $x = 0$

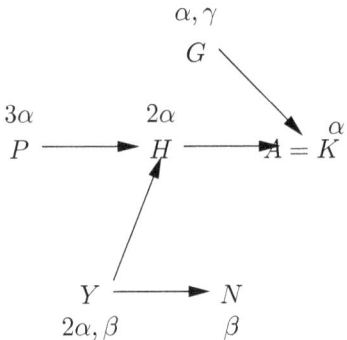

Figure 2.61.

	N	A	P	Y	H	G	K
m	0	1	1	0	1	0	0
h	1	?	0	0	0	0	0
b	1	1	0	1	1	0	1
w	0	1	0	0	0	1	1

Figure 2.62.

1. Graph for $x = 1$

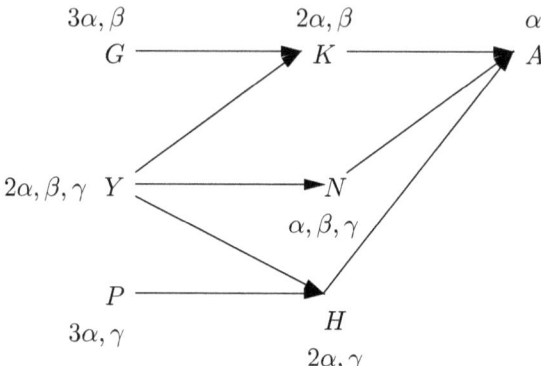

2. Graph for $x = 0$

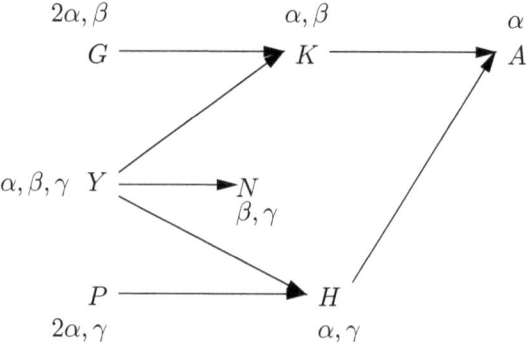

Figure 2.63.

6 Conclusion and discussion

This chapter introduced a new method of abduction, which we called matrix abduction and showed that it can be applied in a variety of areas. The method arose directly from the study of the Talmudic non-deductive inference rules of Kal-Vachomer, the Argumentum A Fortiori. See our Hebrew paper [2] for a very detailed analysis.

We would like in this concluding section to make some epistemological comments.

Jacob Neusner [81] has argued (1987) that Talmudic thinking is very differnet from western thinking that produced science. This explains why the Jewish people through the ages did not make scientific achievements to the level of other nations. This view has been strongly criticised by other writers such as M. Fisch [43], who argues to the contrary, that rabbinic thinking is very similar to that of western science.[11]

We put forward to the reader that the results of this chapter exemplifies and supports the claim by M. Fisch. Matrix abduction is a new form of induction, arising from the Talmud, which can solve problems currently in the scientific community. (See [47] for a comprehensive treatise on abduction.)

We will venture to say that the logic of the Talmud is far richer and complex than currently available western logic. We hope to make this point in this current monograph.

Appendices: General applications of matrix abduction

Appendix A: Application to argumentation networks

Argumentation networks were introduced by P. M. Dung in a seminal paper in 1995. Since then a strong community arose working in the area. Our matrix abduction ideas can make a contribution to this area, as we shall now discuss.

An abstract argumentation network has the form (S, R), where S is a nonempty set of arguments and $R \subseteq S \times S$ is an attack relation. When $(x, y) \in R$, we say x attacks y.

The elements of S are atomic arguments and the model does not give any information on what structure they have and how they manage to attack each other.

The abstract theory is concerned with extracting information from the network in the form of a set of arguments which are winning (or 'in'), a set of arguments which are defeated (or are 'out') and the rest are undecided. There are several possibilities for such sets and they are systematically studied and classified. See Figure 2.64 for a typical situation. $x \to y$ in the figure represents $(x, y) \in R$.

A good way to see what is going on is to consider a Caminada labelling. This is a function λ on S distributing values $\lambda(x), x \in S$ in the set {in, out, ?} satisfying the following conditions.

1. If x is not attacked by any y then $\lambda(x) = 1$

---

[11] Jews have had hard life throughout history. We don't think they had the same opportunities as western scientists.

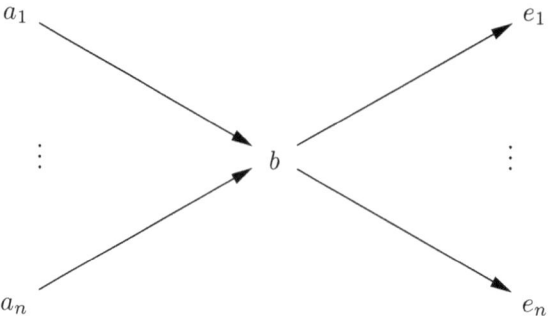

Figure 2.64.

2. If $(y,x) \in R$ and $\lambda(y) = 1$ then $\lambda(x) = 0$

3. If all y which attack x have $\lambda(y) = 0$ then $\lambda(x) = 1$.

4. If one y which attack x has $\lambda(y) =?$ and all other y have $\lambda(y) \in \{0, ?\}$ then $\lambda(x) =?$.

Such λ exist whenever S is finite and for any such λ, the set $S_\lambda^+ = \{x \mid \lambda(x) = 1\}$ is the set of winning arguments, $S_\lambda^- = \{x \mid \lambda(x) = 0\}$ is the set of defeated arguments and $S_\lambda^? = \{x \mid \lambda(x) =?\}$ is the set of undecided arguments.

The features of this abstract model are as follows:

1. Arguments are atomic, have no structure.

2. Attacks are stipulated by the relation R; we have no information on how and why they occur.

3. Arguments are either 'in' in which case all their attacks are active or are 'out' in which case all their attacks are inactive. There is no in between state (partially active, can do some attacks, etc.). Arguments can be undecided.

4. Attacks have a single strength, no degrees of strength or degree of transmission of attack along the arrow, etc.

5. There are no counter attacks, no defensive actions allowed or any other responses or counter measures.

6. The attacks from x are uniform on all y such that $(x,y) \in R$. There are no directional attacks or coordinated attacks. In Figure 2.64, $a_1, \ldots, a_n$ attack b individually and not in coordination. For example, a_1 does not attack b with a view of stopping b from attaching e_1 but without regard to $e_2, \ldots, e_n$.

7. The view of the network is static. We have a graph here and a relation R on it. So Figure 2.64 is static. We seek a λ labelling on it and we

may find several. In the case of Figure 2.64 there is only one such λ. $\lambda(a_i) = 1, \lambda(b) = 0, \lambda(e_j) = 1, i = 1, \ldots, j = 1, \ldots, n$.

We do not have a dynamic view, like first a_i attack b and b then (if it is not out dead) tries to attack e_i. Or better still, at the same time each node launches an attack on whoever it can. So a_i attack b and b attacks e_i and the result is that a_i are alive (not being attacked) while b and e_j are all dead.

We use the words 'there is no progression in the network' to indicate this. The network is static.

We have addressed point 4 above in our paper [21], but points 1–3, 5–7 were addressed in [38].

There are several authors who have already addressed some of these questions. See [24; 32].

Obviously, to answer the above questions we must give contents to the nodes. We can do this in two ways. We can do this in the metalevel, by putting predicates and labels on the nodes and by writing axioms about them or we can do it in the object level, giving internal structure to the atomic arguments and/or saying what they are and defining the other concepts, e.g. the notion of attack in terms of the contents.

EXAMPLE 2.33 (Metalevel connects to nodes). Figure 2.65 is an example of a metalevel extension.

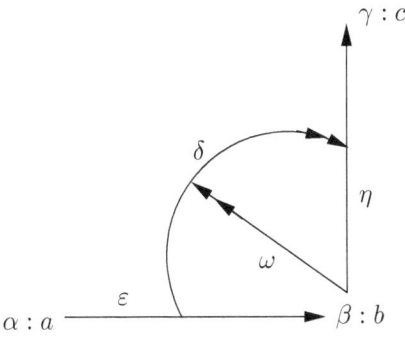

Figure 2.65.

The node a is labelled by α. It attacks the node b with transmission factor ε. Node b is labelled by β. The attack arrow itself constitutes an attack on the attack arrow from b to c. This attack is itself attacked by node b. Each attack has its own transmission factor. We denoted attacks on arrows by double arrows.

Formally we have a set S of nodes, here

$$S = \{a, b, c\}.$$

the relation R is more complex. It has the usual arrows $\{(a, b), (b, c)\} \subseteq R$ and also the double arrows, namely, $\{((a, b), (b, c)), (b, ((a, b), (b, c)))\} \subseteq R$. We have a labelling function **l**, giving values

$$l(a) = \alpha, l(b) = \beta, l(c) = \gamma,$$
$$l((a,b)) = \varepsilon, l((b,c)) = \eta,$$
$$l(((a,b),(b,c))) = \delta$$
$$l((a,((a,b),(b,c)))) = \omega.$$

We can generalise the Caminada labelling as a function from $S \cup R$ to some values which satisfy some conditions involving the labels. We can write axioms about the labels in some logical language and these axioms will give more meaning to the argumentation network. See [21] for some details along these lines. The appropriate language and logic to do this is Labelled Deductive Systems (LDS) [46].

We shall not pursue the metalevel extensions approach in this chapter except for one well known construction which will prove useful to us later.

Our matrix methods allow us to give new kind of content to the nodes and define a new mode of attack. This we now discuss.

Consider Figure 2.66

$$a \longrightarrow b \longrightarrow c \longrightarrow d$$

Figure 2.66.

As an argumentation network, any finite acyclic graph is very simple. We start with the nodes x that are not attacked, they get $\lambda(x) = 1$ and then we propagate λ along the arrow.s In Figure 2.66 we get

$$\lambda(a) = 1, \lambda(b) = 0, \lambda(c) = 1, \lambda(d) = 0.$$

The story becomes more interesting when we try and give contents to the nodes. The main way of doing this in the literature is proof theoretical. The nodes are theories or proofs and one node x attacks another node y if it obstructs its proof by proving the opposite.

Figure 2.67 is such an example

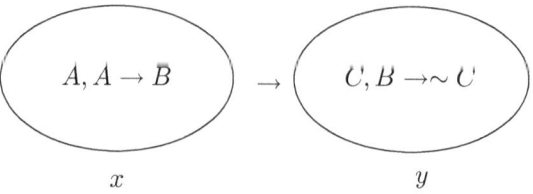

Figure 2.67.

x attacks y because x proves B but y proves $\sim B$.

Besnard and Hunter in [24] take the classical logic approach. The paper of Amgoud and Caminada [32] surveys other approaches where the logic may be nonmonotonic, i.e. we may have several defeasible arrows.

Anyway, all existing approaches are proof theoretical or classical semantical involving consistency.

Our matrix system can give a completely different content to an abstract argumentation network. Section 5 is an example of a series of attacks. Figure 2.68 is an example.

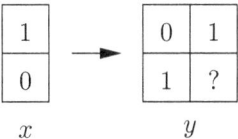

Figure 2.68.

x attacks y by joining it from the right to form Figure 2.69

0	1	1
1	?	0

Figure 2.69.

Our matrix abduction will tell y it must put 1 in the blank "?" place. In Figure 2.69, the result of the attack by x, we get that "?" remains undecided.

We can have new kind of attacks, as in Figure 2.70. z attacks y by wrapping around it.

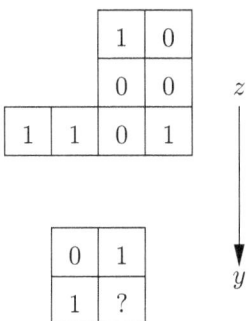

Figure 2.70. z wraps around y

The result is Figure 2.71

Figure 2.72 is a schematic joint attack.

We get Figure 2.73

Our matrix abduction can deal only with rectangular matrices. So we need to be careful with joint attacks, unless we extend our algorithms to deal with

0	1	1	0
1	?	0	0
1	1	0	1

Figure 2.71.

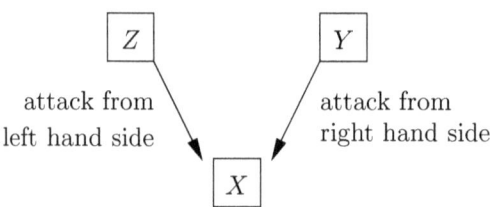

Figure 2.72.

general shapes, as for example in Figure 2.74.

We shall stop here. The full machinery can be developed in another paper.[12]

REMARK 2.34 (Summary). Let us summarise what our matrix example does for argumentation theory.

Consider again the chain in Figure 2.66. a attacks b by joining it and forming a new matrix ab, which joins c to form $(ab)c$ and then we get $((ab)c)d$. The new matrix may still have 1 as a solution in which case the attack did not kill d. It may have undecided or 0 as a solution in which case the attack succeeded. In any case, we present a new form of attack in argumentation networks.

---

[12]One way to deal with general shapes is to expand the shape into a rectangle and regard all missing squares as having N/A (not applicable) value. This turns the matrix $\mathbb{A} = [a_{i,j}]$ into a partial function on the index (i,j). It can give $a_{i,j} = 0$ or $a_{i,j} = 1$ or $a_{i,j} = $ N/A = undefined, and exactly once it can give $a_{i,j} = ?$. The columns become partial functions into $\{0,1\}$ and the ordering graph can be defined between columns as $\leq$ on all coordinates in which they are both defined. See our paper in Hebrew [2] for examples of such matrices arising from Talmudic reasoning.

2. ANALYSIS OF THE TALMUDIC KAL VACHOMER RULE

Z	X	Y

Figure 2.73.

	0	1
1	x=?	0
1	1	0

Figure 2.74.

Appendix B: Application to Voting paradoxes

We now give a voting case study, (see [26]).

A group of 13 farmers from southern Germany rent a bus and go to London for a week's holiday. They are offered 3 extra events in London, for which they have to pay individually, in addition tot he agreed holiday package cost. These are:

T Evening at the theatre (the Globe)

D Fancy dinner at a posh London restaurant

B A tour in a boat along the Thames.

The farmers are asked to vote. We get the following result, where 1 means 'I want it', see Figure 2.75

	A	B	C	D	E	F	G
T	0	1	1	0	1	1	0
D	1	1	0	0	0	1	1
B	1	1	0	1	1	0	0
No. of farmers voting for this column	1	1	3	3	1	1	3

Figure 2.75.

The question is what to do? Where to go?

If we consider the options as packages, then packages

$$C = T \wedge \sim D \wedge \sim B$$
$$D = \sim T \wedge \sim D \wedge B$$
$$G = \sim T \wedge D \wedge \sim B$$

each received three votes and so they draw the winning package. We cannot, however, decide between them.

	No. of farmers voting yes	No. of farmers voting no
T	6	7
D	6	7
B	6	7

Figure 2.76.

If we regard the voting procedure as collecting individual votes for each of the options $\{\mathbf{T}, \mathbf{D}, \mathbf{B}\}$, then we get Figure 2.76

The winning combination is $\sim \mathbf{T} \wedge \sim \mathbf{D} \wedge \sim \mathbf{B}$, namely, go to no event.

This is known as the multiple voting paradox, for three issues ($\mathbf{T}, \mathbf{D}$ and $\mathbf{B}$) and 13 voters. We can generate a paradox for four issues for example, in this case we need 31 voters, see [26].

The paradox is that by majority vote we get a result that nobody wants, in our case this result is not to go anywhere! Nobody voted for $(0,0,0)$ as a column.

Let us see whether our matrix abduction point of view can help. Our first question is whether the method of matrix abduction is applicable to the voting problem. Do the criteria discussed in Section 1.1 apply here? The answer is yes. Each farmer wants something. Each option has ingredients to offer. If the option can satisfy what the farmer wants he will vote for it. This example is also slightly different. There are connections between the rows, maybe giving rise to constraints (see Example 2.24. There is also the question of cost, some farmers must have chosen 2 out of the three options simply because they didn't have enough money.

Let us construct the graph for this matrix. We get Figure 2.77.[13] The table in Figure 2.78 tells us what are the ingredients of the options. The way we get the ingredients, is to look at Figure 2.75. $\mathbf{T}$ has 1 for columns B, C, E, F. So $\mathbf{T}$ must have enough ingredients to satisfy the needs of each of B, C, E, F. These needs we get from the allocation of Figure 2.77. So $\mathbf{T}$ needs $\{2\alpha, \beta\}$. If we take into account how many voters voted for each column, then $\mathbf{T}$ needs $\{6\alpha, 3\beta\}$, since 3 voters voted for C. Thus we put in Figure 2.78 $\{6\alpha, 3\beta\}$ for $\mathbf{T}$. Similarly we calculate $\{6\alpha, 3\gamma\}$ for $\mathbf{D}$ and $\{3\alpha, 3\beta, 3\gamma\}$ for $\mathbf{B}$. Remember, we give $\mathbf{T}$ not the union of allocations of the relevant columns, but the minimum

---

[13]Note that the voting matrix has columns corresponding to all Boolean combinations of $\{\mathbf{T}, \mathbf{D}, \mathbf{B}\}$.

Thus in Figure 2.77 if we were to annoate with sets (not multisets) and annotated B with $\varnothing$, we would have annotated as follows:

$$A : \{\alpha\}, E : \{\beta\}, F : \{\gamma\}$$
$$D : \{\alpha, \beta\}, G : \{\alpha, \gamma\}, C : \{\beta, \gamma\}.$$

These are Boolean allocations representing the Boolean algebra with $\mathbf{T},\mathbf{D},\mathbf{B}$ as a Boolean algebra of subsets of $\{\alpha, \beta, \gamma\}$ with Truth $=\varnothing$, Falsity $=\{\alpha, \beta, \gamma\}$ and $\wedge$ becomes $\vee$ and $\vee$ becomes $\wedge$.

We get nothing new. So the two new mathematical steps we are making are assigning α to B and using multiples of α.

that we need!

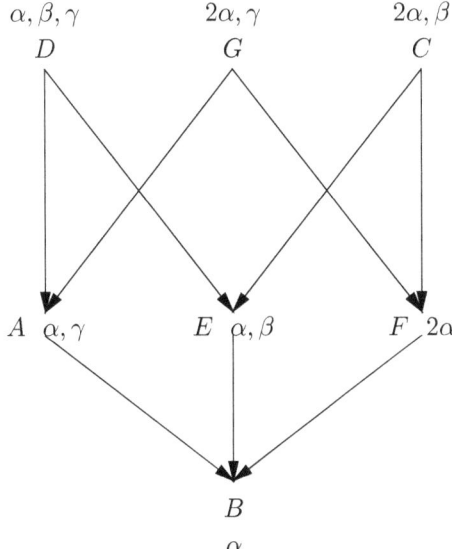

Figure 2.77.

	Ingredients
T	$6\alpha, 3\beta$
D	$6\alpha, 3\gamma$
B	$3\alpha, 3\beta, 3\gamma$

Figure 2.78.

Let us now try and guess what α, β, γ can be. **D** and **B** have γ in common. Our guess is that we can take γ to be 'non-intellectual activity'.

B and **T** have β in common. Our guess would be that β is a sightseeing factor. Food you get in Germany. Theatre and the Thames are characteristic of London.

α is common to all. Our guess is that it can be cost. A boat ticket costs less (per person) than a theatre ticket or a dinner check.

So how can this help our decision about what to do?

We would go for **B** and only one of **T** and **D**. Let us check the vote for the $(\mathbf{T}, \mathbf{D})$ component only. We have four possibilities. See Figure 2.79

We get a tie between $\mathbf{T} \wedge \sim \mathbf{D}$ and $\sim \mathbf{T} \wedge \mathbf{D}$. Which one to choose? Looking at the ingredients, they are symmetrical, $\{6\alpha, 3\beta\}$ compared to $\{6\alpha, 3\gamma\}$. It is really a vote between β and γ. We must ask the farmers.

Note that the graph is symmetrical. So we could have assigned the α, β, γ differently.

	No of votes
T ∧ **D**	2
T ∧ ∼ **D**	4
∼ **T** ∧ **D**	4
∼ **T** ∧ ∼ **D**	3

Figure 2.79.

There are two more possibilities, assign in Figure 2.77 the value 2α to E or assign the value 2α to A.

We get Figures 2.80 and 2.81 respectively.

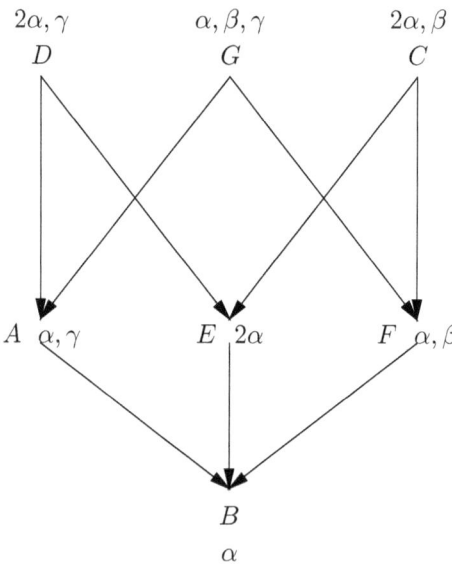

Figure 2.80.

The following table, Figure 2.82, summarises the possible ingredients for **T**, **D**, **B** according to which figure we use. It extends Figure 2.78.

We see that the graphs and the tables, including Figure 2.75 are completely symmetrical. So the conclusion is that the farmers should do any two events. Only a combination of two events can have enough ingredients for all columns. Namley the vote concludes with

$$\mathbf{V} = (\mathbf{T} \wedge \mathbf{D} \wedge \sim \mathbf{B} \bigvee \mathbf{T} \wedge \sim \mathbf{D} \wedge \mathbf{B} \bigvee \sim \mathbf{T} \wedge \mathbf{D} \wedge \mathbf{B}).$$

Note that this matrix abduction approach is pretty revolutionary. We follow neither the drawing contenders for the maximal vote (of 3, namely, C, D and G), i.e. we do not take exactly one of $\{\mathbf{T}, \mathbf{D}, \mathbf{G}\}$, i.e. **T**∧ ∼ **D**∧ ∼ **B** or ∼ **T**∧**D**∧ ∼ **B** or ∼ **T**∧ ∼ **D**∧**G**, nor do we follow the result of the component vote of Figure 2.76, namely ∼ **T**∧ ∼ **D**∧ ∼ **B**.

2. ANALYSIS OF THE TALMUDIC KAL VACHOMER RULE   87

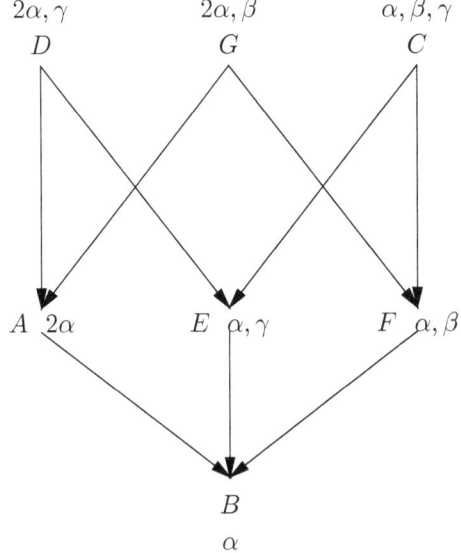

Figure 2.81.

	Ingredients Figure 2.78	Ingredients Figure 2.80	Ingredients Figure 2.81
T	$6\alpha, 3\beta$	$6\alpha, 3\beta$	$3\alpha, 3\beta, 3\gamma$
D	$6\alpha, 3\gamma$	$3\alpha, 3\beta, 3\gamma$	$6\alpha, 3\beta$
B	$3\alpha, 3\beta, 3\gamma$	$6\alpha, 3\gamma$	$6\alpha, 3\gamma$

Figure 2.82.

We follow a compromise, as suggested by the matrix abduction.

This is already more than the voting procedures can give us. Also we know what to ask the farmers in order to decide the matter!

Let us now check what happens in the case of the four issues, 31 voters paradox, see [26]. This paradox has issues **a, b, c, d**. **a** ∧ **b** ∧ **c** ∧ **d** is a winning combination, and yet, calculated coordinatewise we get complete reversal, ∼ **a**∧ ∼ **b**∧ ∼ **c**∧ ∼ **d**, which is an option for which nobody voted!

Figure 2.83 gives the voting table.

	X_1	X_2	X_3	X_4	X_5	X_6	X_7	X_8	X_9	X_{10}	X_{11}	X_{10}	X_{13}	X_{14}	X_{15}
a	1	1	1	1	1	1	1	1	0	0	0	0	0	0	0
b	1	1	1	1	0	0	0	0	1	1	1	1	0	0	0
c	1	1	0	0	1	1	0	0	1	1	0	0	1	1	0
d	1	0	1	0	1	0	1	0	1	0	1	0	1	0	1
No of Voters for this column	5	1	1	1	1	1	1	4	1	1	1	4	1	4	4

Figure 2.83.

If we count the numbers of voters who voted for a column containing 1 for **a** (i.e. who wanted **a**) we get 15, as opposed to 16 voters who wanted ∼ **a**. Similarly we have for **b,c** and **d**. This is why we have a paradox.

If we follow the majority package vote we have to go for **a**∧**b**∧**c**∧**d** because 5 voters went for it, the biggest number of voters. This makes 26 other voters unhappy. If we go for the issue by issue result, then ∼ **a**∧ ∼ **b**∧ ∼ **c**∧ ∼ **d** wins, since each issue got voted 0 by 17 against 16 who voted 1. But then this is not good either since everyone voted for something. Nobody wanted the 'nothing' option.

So we propose the matrix method. Figure 2.84 draws the graph of the columns of Figure 2.83, with an indicated allocation of ingredients.

If we collect the ingredients from Figure 2.84 using the table of Figure 2.83 we get Figure 2.85. Note that we make allowance for the number of voters.

To satisfy the needs of all voters we need at least two of {**a, b, c, d**}. We do not take more because each individual **a, b, c**, or **d** was voted 0 by the majority. The winning single package **a** does not have enough α to satisfy the X_8, X_{10}, X_{14} and X_{15} voters.

Thus we need two from {**a, b, c, d**}. Note that we relied here on the allocation of $\alpha, \beta, \gamma, \delta$ on the graph. There are three other ways of doing this allocation, giving α to X_1 but $\beta\alpha$ either to X_1, X_3 or X_0.

Since both the graph of Figure 2.84 and the table of Figure 2.83 are completely symmetrical in the swapping of X_2, X_3, X_5 and X_9, our conclusion that we need two of {**a, b, c, d**} to make everyone happy does stand!

Thus our recommendation for the vote of Figure 2.83 is

$$\mathbf{F} = (\mathbf{a} \wedge \mathbf{b} \wedge \sim \mathbf{c} \wedge \sim \mathbf{d} \bigvee \mathbf{a} \wedge \sim \mathbf{b} \wedge \mathbf{c} \wedge \sim \mathbf{d}$$
$$\bigvee \mathbf{a} \wedge \sim \mathbf{b} \wedge \sim \mathbf{c} \wedge \mathbf{d} \bigvee \sim \mathbf{a} \wedge \mathbf{b} \wedge \mathbf{c} \wedge \sim \mathbf{d}$$
$$\bigvee \sim \mathbf{a} \wedge \mathbf{b} \wedge \sim \mathbf{c} \wedge \mathbf{d} \bigvee \sim \mathbf{a} \wedge \sim \mathbf{b} \wedge \mathbf{c} \wedge \mathbf{d})$$

2. ANALYSIS OF THE TALMUDIC KAL VACHOMER RULE

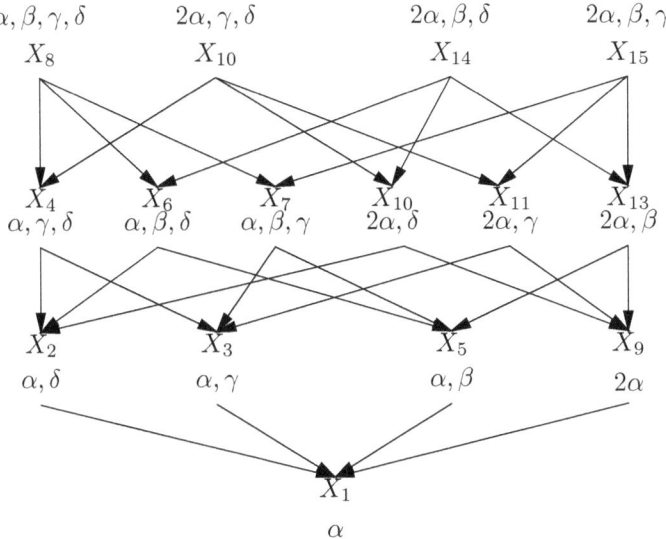

Figure 2.84.

	ingredients
a	$5\alpha, 4\beta, 4\gamma, 4\delta$
b	$8\alpha, 4\gamma, 4\delta$
c	$8\alpha, 4\beta, 4\delta$
d	$8\alpha, 4\beta, 4\gamma$

Figure 2.85.

Again note that this is contrary to both the winning package vote (a∧b∧c∧d which is winning by 5 voters) and the winning issue by issue vote (∼ a∧ ∼ b∧ ∼ c∧ ∼ d where each ∼ a, ∼ b, ∼ c, ∼ d wins by 17 against 16 votes).

Again a revolutionary compromise (suggseted by the matrix method) between the two extreme components of the paradox.

REMARK 2.35. We stress that we are not necessarily offering here the matrix method as new voting procedure. The matrix method relies on ingredients, not on numerical aggregation of votes. It can help when the voting aggregation is parasdoxical.

We shall examine the matrix method as a voting procedure in a future paper.

To show the coherence and solidity of our matrix approach, let us increase the number of voters by 2, from 31 to 33, and let them vote for X_1. Figure 2.83 will change in the bottom of column X_1 from 5 to 7.

X_1 will continue to be the winning package but now the paradox will disappear. Each of **a, b, c** and **d** will get coordinatewise 17 votes as opposed respectively 16 to ∼ **a**, ∼ **b**, ∼ **c** and ∼ **d**.

The graph in Figure 2.84 remains the same, with its allocations of $\alpha, \beta, \gamma, \delta$. What will change is Table 2.85, which describes the amount of ingredients $\alpha, \beta, \gamma, \delta$ to each row. Each of **a, b, c, d** will get 2 more α. So **a** now has 7α. Still not enough to satisfy the needs of the voters of X_{10}, X_{14} and X_{15} which require 8α.

So although there is no paradox, the majority of X_1 is still not strong enough to go alone. If we add one more voter who votes for X_1, (bringing the number of voters to 34) then **a** will get 8α, now enough to satisfy on its own all voters.

We see here that our method is different but still resonable and paradox free.

As we said, a detailed study of this approach will be pursued in another paper. Further connections with argumentation networks will be discussed in our chapter on loops, Chapter 7.

Appendix C: Application to Paradoxes of judgement aggregation

We begin with the *doctrinal paradox*, indentified by Kornhauser and Sager [78; 79]. The paradox arises when majority voting can lead a group of rational agents to endorse an irrational collective judgement. Consider the question of liability following a breach of contract. Three judges have to decide whether

> **a**= there was a binding contract

and

> **b**= there was a breach of that contract.

We get liability only when both **a** and **b** are upheld.

The table in Figure 2.86 describes the situation.

Judges A and C think the evidence for **a** is convincing but not so for **b**. Judges B and C think the evidence for **b** is convincing but not so for **a**. Thus each judge individually would express judgement as in row **a** ∧ **b**. Therefore

2. ANALYSIS OF THE TALMUDIC KAL VACHOMER RULE

	Judge A	Judge B	Judge C	majority vote
a	1	0	1	1
b	0	1	1	1
liability **a ∧ b**	0	0	1	$x = 0$

Figure 2.86.

two judges will give verdicts of no liability and only one, Judge C, will give a verdict of liability. Going by majority of verdicts — the final verdict is $x = 0$.

On the other hand, if we were to take majoirty judgement first on **a** and **b** individually, then we get that both **a** and **b** get 1 having a majority of two judges, and so x must be 1 and not 0.

This is the paradox.

We see this paradox as a special matrix abduction problem.

We can now formulate the *general matrix aggregation problem*.

DEFINITION 2.36 (Matrix aggregation problem).

1. Let $V = (x_1, \ldots, x_n)$ be a vector of numbers in $\{0, 1\}$. An *aggregation function* **g** is a function giving a value $\mathbf{g}(V) \in \{0, 1\}$, for any such vector.

   For example
   $$\mathbf{g}_{\text{majority}}(V) = 1 \text{ iff } \sum_{i=1}^{n} x_i > \tfrac{1}{2}$$
   $$\mathbf{g}_\wedge(V) = 1 \text{ iff } x_i = 1 \text{ for all } i$$
   $$\mathbf{g}_\vee(V) = 1 \text{ iff } x_i = 1 \text{ for some } i$$

2. Let $\mathbf{g}_{\text{row}}$ and $\mathbf{g}_{\text{column}}$ be two aggregation functions.

A matrix $\mathbb{A}$ with $m + 1$ rows and $n + 1$ columns is a *matrix aggregation problem* if it has the form described in Figure 2.87.

	A_1	...	A_n	Row aggregation
$\mathbf{a}_1$				$\mathbf{g}_{\text{row}}(\mathbf{a}_1)$
$\vdots$				
$\mathbf{a}_m$				$\mathbf{g}_{\text{row}}(\mathbf{a}_m)$
Column aggregation	$\mathbf{g}_{\text{column}}(A_1)$		$\mathbf{g}_{\text{column}}(A_n)$	$x = ?$

Figure 2.87.

The row aggregation column gives the aggregated value for each row. The column aggregation row gives the aggregated value for each column. We get a matrix abduction problem if we ask what should $x = ?$ be. Do we aggregate the column above the $x = ?$ square, i.e. let $x = \mathbf{g}_{\text{column}}(\mathbf{g}_{\text{row}}(\mathbf{a}_1), \ldots, \mathbf{g}_{\text{row}}(\mathbf{a}_m))$ or do we aggregate the row to the left of the $x = ?$ square, i.e. let $x = \mathbf{g}_{\text{row}}(\mathbf{g}_{\text{column}}(A_1), \ldots, \mathbf{g}_{\text{column}}(A_n))$ or do we do some matrix abduction algorithm $\mathcal{A}$ on the matrix and get a value for x?

Figure 2.88 describes the situation of Figure 2.86 seen as a matrix aggregation problem.

	A	B	C	D=$\mathbf{g}_{\text{majority}}$
a	1	0	1	1
b	0	1	1	1
c = $\mathbf{g}_\wedge$	0	0	1	$x = ?$

Figure 2.88.

If we apply our graph technique to this figure, we get the graphs in Figure 2.89.

Case $x = 1$

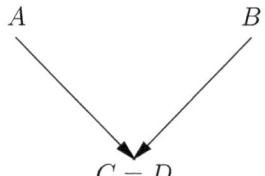

Case $x = 0$

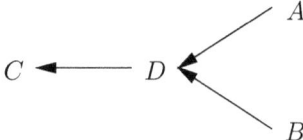

Figure 2.89.

Clearly by our criteria of Section 3, $x = 1$ wins. Of course we need to formulate new criteria suitable for the voting and the aggregation application area. We have here different kinds of matrices. So we need to look at some examples and match the intuitive ideas embedded in the examples with criteria on graphs.

There is also symmetry between rows and columns in this problem. In general we have two aggregation functions without any special conditions on them. So we must also consider the graphs arising from the rows. This we show in Figure 2.90 for our specific example.

Again, according to our criteria of Section 3, case $x = 1$ wins.

2. ANALYSIS OF THE TALMUDIC KAL VACHOMER RULE

Case $x = 1$

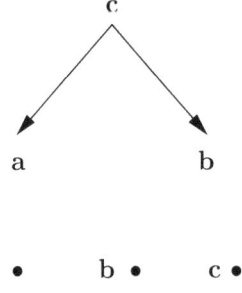

Case $x = 0$

a •   b •   c •

Figure 2.90.

The interested reader can look up a recent penetrating analysis of the paradox in [69]. The paper uses probabilistic methods, looking at the reliability of the judges involved and aggregating accordingly. If we adopt the reliability idea into our matrix we get the matrix in Figure 2.91.

	Judge A	Reliability of A	Judge B	Reliability of B	Judge C	Reliability of C	Majority vote
a	1	$r(A,\mathbf{a})$	0	$r(B,\mathbf{a})$	1	$r(C,\mathbf{a})$	
b	0	$r(A,\mathbf{b})$	1	$r(B,\mathbf{b})$	1	$r(C,\mathbf{b})$	
a ∧ b	0		0		1		

Figure 2.91.

The reliabilities $r(A,\mathbf{a}), r(A,\mathbf{b})$ are the numbers in $\{0,1\}$ telling us whether Judge A is reliable on issues **a** and **b**. Similarly, $r(B,\mathbf{a}), r(B,\mathbf{b}), r(C,\mathbf{a})$ and $r(C,\mathbf{b})$.

It was suggested to us by S. Hartmann that we process the columns first in the matrix and then aggregate. We use the following processing formula.

- x with reliability 1 is processes as $x' = x$
- x with reliabiltiy 0 is processed as $x' = 1 - x$.

So the formula is

$$x' = x \cdot r(x) + (1-x)(1(r(x))$$

So in the matrix of Figure 2.91 we first process the pairs of columns and get the matrix of Figure 2.92.

Note that such preprocessing is done in the Talmud. We discuss this in our Hebrew paper [2, Part 2, Section A].

Summary

The general theory of the matrix aggregation problem needs to be developed. We see however already at this stage that we have a clear mathematical formulation of the problem and we have a machinery to offer a solution. This is good news for the judgment aggregation community.

	new Judge A	new Judge B	new Judge C	vote
a	$r(A,\mathbf{a})$	$1-r(B,\mathbf{a})$	$r(C,\mathbf{a})$	
b	$1-r(A,\mathbf{b})$	$r(B,\mathbf{a})$	$r(C,\mathbf{b})$	
a ∧ b				

Figure 2.92.

We hope to address this problem in a subsequent paper.

We note that we have not explained away the aggregation paradox but offered a possible third computation to bail us out of the aggregation problem.

Appendix D: Learning, Labelling and Finite Models

We continue to examine the example of monadic predicate logic introduced in Figure 2.8. We have a finite model with predicates $A_1, \ldots, A_m$ and elements $d_1, \ldots, d_n$. Let us assume that the definite matrix $\mathbb{A} = [a_{i,j}], i = 1, \ldots, m$ and $j = 1, \ldots, n$ describes the model. That is we have for all i, j

$$a_{i,j} = 1 \text{ iff } A_i(d_j) \text{ is true.}$$

Our question is what can we learn from this data?

To explain how we can make use of our matrix realisation method, let us take an example we have already analysed. Consider the matrix of Figure 2.60 for the case $x = 1$.

We consider this matrix as a matrix of a model with elements

$$d_1 = N$$
$$d_2 = A$$
$$d_3 = P$$
$$d_4 = Y$$
$$d_5 = H$$
$$d_6 = G$$
$$d_7 = K$$

and predicates

$$A_1 = \mathbf{m}$$
$$A_2 = \mathbf{n}$$
$$A_3 = \mathbf{b}$$
$$A_4 = \mathbf{w}$$

The graph for this matrix is in Figure 2.63, case 1.

Let us insist on a realisation for this graph using sets, not multisets. This means we do not allow multiples of α.

Therefore we would get the following realisation **f** in Figure 2.93.

Figure 2.94 gives the coresponding matrix realisation.[14]

---

[14]This is hardly surprising. Let $\mathbb{A} = [a_{i,j}]$ be a definite matrix with m rows and n columns, $m \leq n$. Let $\mathbf{a}_1, \ldots, \mathbf{a}_m$ be the rows and $C_1, \ldots, C_n$ be the columns. Then each column C is a subset $\mathbf{C}$ of the set $M = \{\mathbf{a}_1, \ldots, \mathbf{a}_m\}$ of all rows. We have $\mathbf{a}_i \in \mathbf{C}_j$ iff $a_{i,j} = 1$. Thus the

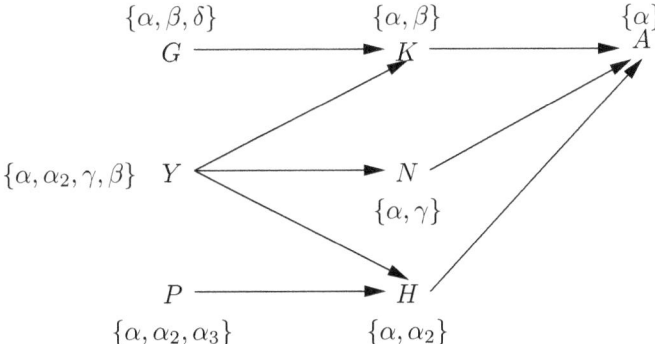

Figure 2.93.

$$\mathbf{m} : \{\alpha, \alpha_2, \alpha_3\}$$
$$\mathbf{h} : \{\alpha, \gamma\}$$
$$\mathbf{b} : \{\alpha, \alpha_2, \beta, \gamma\}$$
$$\mathbf{w} : \{\alpha, \beta, \gamma\}$$
$$N : \{\alpha, \gamma\}$$
$$A : \{\alpha\}$$
$$P : \{\alpha, \alpha_2, \alpha_3\}$$
$$Y : \{\alpha, \alpha_2, \beta, \gamma\}$$
$$H : \{\alpha, \alpha_2\}$$
$$G : \{\alpha, \beta, \delta\}$$
$$K : \{\alpha, \beta\}$$

Figure 2.94.

$$A_i(d_j) = \text{True iff } \mathbf{f}(A_i) \supseteq \mathbf{f}(d_j).$$

Note that instead of a model with 7 elements, we found a model of 6 elements (a saving in the number of elements) which contains all the information. In this new smaller model we have that A_i, d_j are all predicates and the meaning of $A_i(d_j)$ is $\forall x(d_j(x) \to A_i(x))$.

Independently of whether we save on the number of points, this method suggests a translation of the monadic first order theory into itself.

We prepare the ground for the translation by observing that all monadic models for m monadic predicaes $\{A_1, \ldots, A_n\}$ can be reduced equivalently to models with at most 2^m elements. This holds since each element d in the domain has a type $\bigwedge_i \pm A_i(d)$, and there are at most 2^m such types. So any formula with quatifiers can be rewritten to a formula without quantifiers. If we have 2^m constants in the language $\mathbf{d}_1, \ldots, \mathbf{d}_{2^m}$. We write $\forall x \varphi(x) \equiv \bigwedge_{i=1}^{2^m} \varphi(\mathbf{d}_i)$ and $\exists x \varphi(x) \equiv \bigvee_{i=1}^{2^m} \varphi(\mathbf{d}_i)$.

So any ϕ becomes ϕ^* by eliminating the quantifiers in this manner. So, for example
$$\phi = \forall x \exists y (A(x) \to B(y))$$
becomes
$$\phi^* = \bigwedge_i \bigvee_j (A(\mathbf{d}_i) \to B(\mathbf{d}_j))$$

We can translate now any ϕ into ϕ^{**} as follows:

Let $D_1, \ldots, D_{2^m}$ be additional predicates. Translate any $A_i(\mathbf{d}_j)$ into $\forall x(D_j(x) \to A_i(x))$. Now given any closed formula ϕ translate first into ϕ^* by using $\mathbf{d}_j$. ϕ^* will have no quantifiers. Now replace in ϕ^* any $A_i(\mathbf{d}_j)$ as above and get ϕ^{**}.

We have

LEMMA 2.37. ϕ has a monadic model iff ϕ^{**} has a monadic model.

Proof. ϕ has a monadic model iff ϕ has a monadic model $\mathbf{M}$ with 2^m elements iff ϕ^* has this same monadic model. We now construct the matrix $\mathbb{A}$ for the model $\mathbf{M}$, and construct a set realisation of it using a set of labels $\mathbb{L}$. Then ϕ^* holds in $\mathbf{M}$ iff ϕ^{**} holds in $\mathbb{L}$. ∎

REMARK 2.38. We are aware that we can have a similar translation by regarding any element d_j of the doamin as a predicate D_j with an extension of exactly the element d_j. Thus $A_i(d_j)$ becomes
$$\forall x(D_j(x) \to A_i(x)).$$

We need to add the axioms

---

columns are elements of the Boolean algebra of the powerset 2^M. The graph of the columns is a subgraph of the lattice of the algebra 2^M with M as the smallest element and $\varnothing$ as the top element. Since we give α to the bottom element of the graph, this observation implies that we can get a set realisation to the graph with $m+1$ elements. In practice many graphs can manage with less, but some might need more, since we need to realise the cancellation of edges and some possible restrictions as well.

1. $\exists x D_j(x), j = 1, \ldots, n$

2. $\sim \exists x [D_j(x) \wedge D_i(x)], i \neq j$

We hae ϕ has a model of n elements iff $(1) \wedge (2) \wedge \phi^{**}$ has (the same) model.

This translation does not decrease the number of elements because (1) and (2) ensure the same number of elements is used.

Furthermore, we can use the Lemma for the previous translation and a theorem Prover to find a minimal model for ϕ^{**}. This will give us the minimal number of labels for the columns withot using the graphs. We summarise

LEMMA 2.39. *Let $\mathbb{A}$ be a definite $m \times n$ matrix. Consider it as a model with rows as predicates and columns as elements as in Figure 2.8.*
Let φ be the following formula

$$\varphi_{\mathbb{A}} = \bigwedge_{a_{i,j}=1} \forall x (D_j(x) \to A_i(x)).$$

Let a theorem prover find a minimal model $\mathbf{M}$ for $\varphi_{\mathbb{A}}$.
Then the sets

$$D_j = \{a \in \mathbf{M} \mid D_j(a) \text{ is true}\}$$

form a set realisation for $\mathbb{A}$.

Proof. Follows from our previous constructions and lemmas. ∎

REMARK 2.40. How do we use a theorem prover to find a multiset realisation?

Let $\mathbb{A}$ be given. Write $\varphi_{\mathbb{A}}$. Add constants to the language $\alpha_1, \alpha_2, \ldots, \alpha_n$. We do not need more than n since we know we can find a realisation with n elements. We think of α_k as $k\alpha$. This means that we add the axiom

$$\alpha = \bigwedge_{i=1}^{n} \bigwedge_{j=1}^{n-1} D_i(\alpha_{j+1}) \to D_i(\alpha_j))$$

This means that if $(j+1)\alpha$ labels a node then so does $j\alpha$.

We use a theorem prover to find a model for $\alpha \wedge \varphi$ and minimise the number of elemnets in the model which are not α_j.

Appendix E: Applications to Access Control Reasoning

Matrix abduction can be also employed in reasoning with incomplete information about access control policies.

Access control consist of determining whether a principal (machine, user, program ...) which issues a request to access a resource should be trusted on its request, i.e. if it is authorized.

A classical way of representing access control policies is the employment of an "Access Control Matrix" which characterizes the rights of each principal with respect to every object in the systems.

For instance, suppose we have an access control policy expressed in Figure 2.95, where in cell (i, j) we place 1 if principal i can read $file_j$. Where the

	$file_1$	$file_2$	$file_3$
A	1	1	1
B	0	1	0
C	1	?	0

Figure 2.95. Access Control Matrix

'?' means that the specification of the access control policy is unknown or incomplete. The question is: what to do? Should a reference monitor deny the access to read $file_2$ to C or not?

There are many ways to reply to the raised questions, here we report two simple examples

- The reference monitor can query his knowledge about the principals A, B and C. For instance, if C has more power than A (maybe C is *root* and A a *user*), the reference monitor can than derive that C has the right to read $file_2$.

- The reference monitor can rely on some knowledge about how the files are organized, so if $file_1$ has a higher protection level the reference monitor may assume that $file_2$ can be read by C.

Another possibility is to employ the methods of Matrix Abduction proposed in this article. We leave for future research the formalization of an ordering between components of access control matrices in order to be able to craft access control policies that can be employed in reasoning without complete knowledge of the domain. Recently, in [22] abduction in access control policies has been also applied to compute a specification of missing credentials in decentralized authorization languages. We believe that matrix abduction can provide a practical tool to craft new access control models, as future work we plan to extend the logical framework presented in [18] with abductive reasoning methods.

CHAPTER 3

LOGICAL ANALYSIS OF THE TALMUDIC RULES OF GENERAL AND SPECIFIC (KLALIM-U-PRATIM)

1 Introduction

Chapter 1 addressed the Talmudic Rule of *Kal-Vachomer*, known also as *Argumentum a Fortiori* , as well as analogy (Binyan-Ab) and their interactions. This chapter deals with the Talmudic rules of General and Specific, known as Klal and Prat (KP), Prat and Klal (PK), Klal and Prat and Klal (KPK) and Prat and Klal and Prat (PKP). Related are the rules of Ribbuy and Miyut (RM) and Miyut and Ribbuy (MR).[1]

We begin in this section with the philosophy of our approach and then general specific details of the KP rules. We denote the family of the KP rules by **KPR**.

1.1 General discussion

The reader may ask: what is it we are trying to do? Why logically analyse the Talmudic rules? There are three reasons.

1. To show the present day logic community the kind of rules the Talmud uses and the wealth of cultural logical material in it. This is interesting in itself as a cultural historical enterprise. Such work is done not only in history and philosophy departments, but in the logic community itself. There is strong interest in the history of logic, see the 12 volume *Handbook of the History of Logic*, edited by D. M. Gabbay and J. Woods.

   There is a book published in the 1950s: J. Lukasiewicz, *Aristotle's Syllogism from the point of view of modern logic*, OUP, 1951, second edition, 1957. This is a typical example of this general interest. Aristotle invented logic and yet, present day logic communities want to know what he did and what it looks like cast in today's language and concepts.

   Another example is Maimonedes (1135–1204). The first thing Maimonedes did, when he was 16 years of age, was to write his own book on Aristotelian logic. He wanted to embark on his career and he needed to start by re-writing the logical foundations in his own terms.

   In fact, Aristotle himself said that to start his series of books he needed to establish logic first (the Organon — the tool). This is the same kind of

---

[1] In Hebrew
Klal — a general rule or predicate
Prat — an item, as specific detail
Miyut — making less
Ribbuy — making more.

reasoning as the authors use — we are asking what are our logical tools in the Talmud.

2. The second reason is more intrinsic. The Talmud is so full of logic, we can learn much from it. Some of its principles, which were developed 1600–2000 years ago, are still new for modern logic and can be useful in today's AI and common sense reasoning. We have shown this in the chapter on the Kal-Vachomer and we will see this again in this chapter.

3. Going back to the tool idea, the organon, analysing and modelling the logic of the Talmud can help with Talmudic studies either pedagogically or even clarify various difficulties and puzzles. This will depend whether our analysis goes beyond the descriptive (from Aramaic into logical language) which is sufficient for (1) and (2) above and offers a really innovative deep analysis of the concepts we study. We believe we have such analysis in our previous chapter analysing the Kal Vachomer, using **KPR** we will show (see [4]) that some Talmudic passages such as Hulin page 66 onwards can be seriously clarified using our model.

Our approach

Our approach to KPK and other related rules is that the Talmud has its own commonsense way of defining sets. Modern logic has not yet addressed this problem. Modern logic has a large area of nonmonotonic commonsense deduction but has not yet investigated commonsense Theory of Definition. We are showing that the Talmud has a method of commonsense Theory of Definition.

Our reading of how the Talmud uses these rules is different from other well establiehed opinions. Menachem Elon in his famous 4-volume work on Jewish Law takes the view that what the Talmud does in **KPR** and the like is a way of resolving apparent contradictions in the biblical text (see his [39] Vol 1, pp. 277). He says:

> The Halachic sages found the answer to this internal contradiction.

Our view is that the Bible and the Talmud uses these rules as ways of defining sets.

2 How to define a set of elements

This section offers the set theoretical background we need.

We all know about sets and operations with sets. In this section we want to set up the scene of specific ways in which sets can be defined. We then present the rules of General and Specific as Talmudic ways to present a set.

There are three basic methods of defining a set.

B1. *Defining sets by using properties of the elements, as done in traditional set theory*
We need a logical language in which we can express complex predicates. We can also use natural language for that purpose if we want to be semi-formal and intuitive. Natural language will be less precise but more

accessible. Assume we have a language $\mathbb{L}$ in which we can express properties of individuals. We make the following observations from our general experience.

1. Some sets will not have an adequate description.
2. Some of the sets which do have a description, will not have an easy to understand, intuitive description.
3. Some formal descriptions of a set, although simple formally, may not be compatible with the intuitive way in which we the people perceive the set (compare, for example, 'water' with 'H_2O').
4. Even if we succeed in giving a formal description of a set it may not change in time the way we want it. In legal contexts we may want definitions that can be reinterpreted in the future and so the use of common sense is essential. See also Section 4 about this point.

The above shows that the question of how we present a set in practice is very important to the layman public and is not so simple.

We shall see later that the (**KPR**) rules of the Talmud are really very simple intuitive ways of presenting sets to ordinary commonsense people.

To summarise formally, method (B1) goes as follows:

Let $\mathbb{L}$ be a language. Let $\varphi(x)$ be a property expressed in the language about any element x. Then we define a set $\hat{x}\varphi(x) = \{$all x satisfying $\varphi\}$.

Such a φ can be referred to as a General Rule or *Klal*.

B2. *Defining sets by using operations exhibiting the set*
The simplest operation or algorithm for exhibiting a set is to list the elements of the set. For example, define the set containing {John, Mary and the number 77}. This is called *Prat*.

Example: From Numbers (Sefer Bamidbar). Here is an example from the Bible: Numbers, Chapter 1, containing both methods (we include the verse numbers in the text).
Method B1
1 And the LORD spoke unto Moses in the wilderness of Sinai, in the tent of meeting, on the first day of the second month, in the second year after they were come out of the land of Egypt, saying: 2 'Take ye the sum of all the congregation of the children of Israel, by their families, by their fathers; houses, according to the number of names every male, by their polls; 3 from twenty years old and upward, all that are able to go forth to war in Israel: ye shall number them by their hosts, even thou and Aaron. 4 And with you there shall be a man of every tribe, every one head of his fathers' house.
Method B2
5 And these are the names of the men that shall stand with you: of Reuben, Elizur the son of Shedeur. 6 Of Simeon, Shelumiel the son of Zurishaddai. 7 Of Judah, Nahshonthe son of Amminadab. 8 Of Issachar, Nethanel the son of Zuar. 9 Of Zebulun, Eliab the son of Helon. 10

Of the children of Joseph: of Ephraim, Elishama the son of Ammihud; of Manasseh, Gamaliel the son of Pedahzur. 11 Of Benjamin, Abidan the son of Gideoni. 12 Of Dan, Ahiezer the son of Amishaddai. 13 Of Asher, Pagiel the son of Ochran 14 Of Gad, Eliasaph the son of Deuel. 15 Of Naphtali, Ahira the son of Enan.' 16 These were the elect of the congregation, the princes of the tribes of their fathers,

B3. *Defining sets by iterations of B1 and B2*
Sets can also be defined by successive iterations of method B1 an B2. We can start for example by defining a set A_1 by a rule φ_1, i.e. all elements x satisfying φ_1 and then make a list of names to be taken out of A_1.

So the set A_2, which is the set we are really after, is $A_2 = A_1$-list.

We can have a sequence of such iterations

A_1 defined by φ_1

A_2 $= A_1$-list

A_3 defined as all elements *not* in A_2 satisfying φ_3, (i.e. we are using the complement of A_2).

A_4 $= A_3+$ another list, etc, etc.

A mathematician logician will not think much of these methods. He will write a four line definition of how to generate sets and leave it at that. No big deal. However for a practical person trying to identify a collection of individuals to a crowd, the problem of how to present the set is a difficult one. We do not want a mathematical definition, we want something simple, intuitive, quick, which the crowd can easily grasp.

You may think that trying to define sets in this manner puts us at a disadvantage, however this is not necessarily the case. The crowd is a collection of commonsense reasoners with intuitive knowledge of the world around them. We can use that in our definition of our set. Mathematics and logic cannot do that. Formal logic will have to formalise the knowledge of the crowd and put it into its formula φ. We in comparison can allude to it and use it.

Formally what we are doing here is the nonmonotonic theory of definitions of sets, i.e. using commonsense reasoning for defining sets. Of course, such definitions are not crisp. There will be some elements where it is not clear whether they are included in the set or not. But on the whole the set is more or less clearly defined.

The following table, see Table 3.1 explains our position, by drawing a parallel between definitions and reasoning.
So we are in fact launching the new area of

commonsense nonmonotonic definitions of sets

and showing how the Talmud has been doing it, over 1500 years ago.

Let us be more specific.

Given a set K defined by some rule $K = \hat{x}\mathbf{K}(x)$, see Figure 3.1

We want to identify part of it, the set A. What are our options for doing so? Well, we can give another predicate $\mathbf{K}_A$ and define A

Table 3.1.

	Formal	Informal
Reasoning	deductive formal reasoning	commonsense nonmonotonic reasoning
Defining sets	formal set-theoretic definition of sets	commonsense nonmonotonic definition of sets

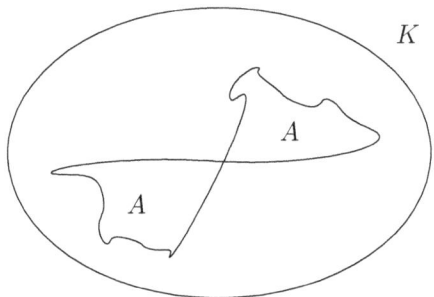

Figure 3.1.

$A = \{$all x such that $\mathbf{K}_A(x)$ holds$\}$

This is OK except for two possible problems.

1. We may find it difficult to find or write down a $\mathbf{K}_A$.

2. A may be such that it is not easy to list

So neither method B1 or B2 or B3 are easy for this set.

The difficulty may be mathematical or practical. Mathematically the language of the properties may not have any φ such that we can write

$$A = \{x|\varphi(x)\}$$

This is a problem of definability. There are many examples in logic of undefinble sets relative to a given logical system.

Practically the difficulty may be that the set may be definable in a mathematical way but the definition is formal and not transparent or the use of language (natural language) is vague, etc.

Furthermore, going back to our example, even if we find a $\mathbf{K}_A$ or take the trouble to list the members of A, we may feel that we are not making good use of the fact that A is a part of K, especially if K is a very clear and helpful context. In other words, there may be simpler commonsense ways of identifying A with the help of K. So how do we do it?

EXAMPLE 3.1. Start with a set of young girls ages 16–30. This is a clear definition. Now we want to explain/highlight the subset of those which are 'real beauties'.

How are we going to identify this set? The language is vague and cannot be formalised. We can give 'measurements' of weight, bust, proportions, etc., or some algorithms of community voting, etc., etc., etc., but that will not easily capture the concept. There are too many beauties to list by name and any other procedure may be complex and costly. So how do we do it?

One way is to list the names of well known beauty queens (Miss World) 2000–2008 and let the reader get the idea using his commonsense and imagination. All girls that look more or less like the ones in the list are our set of "beauties".

This is much more effective but may be open to discussion.

So we must indicate by some 'code of words' how to generalise from this list of girls and get the rest of the beauties in the set. So we may say:

> All girls in town between 16–30 such as the well admired Mary, Tracy and Abigail, or any other pleasant and delightful girl.

So the last phrase tells us to generalise and gives us a hint how to generalise. The hint may be more detailed, for example, we may say "or any other pleasant and delightful hard working girl". This will exclude "useless" celebrities. The Talmudic way of describing a set is something like that.

It is simple, intuitive, descriptive and takes advantage of our commonsense and knowledge of the world.

Here are the general possible options for (KPK) rule.

Step 1: First describe a set K_1 by some rule.

Then:

Step 2 Option M1: List some individuals in K_1.

Then give a clue allowing us to take any other members of K_1 which have common properties with these individuals.

Say we choose four names

$$e_1, \ldots, e_4$$

we know $\mathbf{K}_1(e_1), \ldots, \mathbf{K}_1(e_4)$ hold.

1. We can look at typical properties which at least one of them has e.g. $\pi_1^1, \pi_2^1 \ldots$.

2. We can look at typical properties which any two of them have, e.g. $\pi_1^2, \pi_2^2, \pi_3^2, \ldots$.

3. We can look at properties which any three of them have, e.g. $\pi_1^3, \pi_2^3, \ldots$.

4. We can look for poperties which all four of them have, e.g. '$\pi_1^4, \pi_2^4, \ldots$.

Commonsense and context allows you to identify such properties. In fact in many examples the text itself might hint at the intended properties.

We then decide on a sublist of properties which are the ones we actually use to define the set.

Of course there may be a debate on which ones to take.

Then define a subset of K_1 to be all elements satisfying such properties. We can even say explicitly which π_j^i we want to use, i.e. first identify some $\alpha, \beta, \gamma \in \{$set of all $\pi_j^i\}$ then generalise using them and get the set.

Exactly what you do is the option you may wish to use.

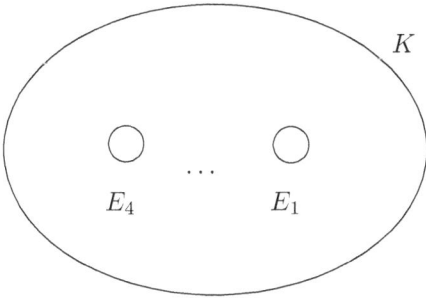

Figure 3.2.

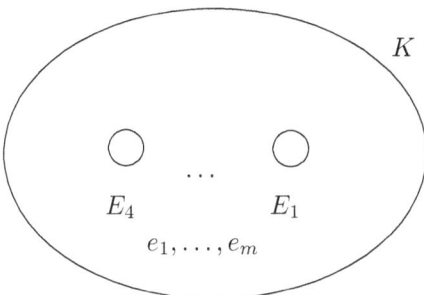

Figure 3.3.

Step 2 Option M2: We can define some subsets of K_1 using easy simple predicates $E_1, \ldots, E_k$. See Figure 3.2

Here we use small sets instead of individuals and again seek common properties. The game is slightly different when we deal with sets and so we may get different kinds of π_j^i.

Step 2 Option M3: Use a mixed approach, see Figures 3.3 and 3.4 containing both sets and individuals. The simplest case is Figure 3.4.

E_1 is a stronger context than K and e_1 is the indivudal whose properties we generalise.

Note that the process can be iterated. So the sets E_τ can themselves be defined using our method and then be used in Figure 3.3 to define more sets.

The above discussion presented (KPK). We similarly have the (PKP) or just (PK) or (KP). Each case has its agreed ways of use.

We conclude this section with a complex example just to show how complicated these concepts can be.

EXAMPLE 3.2 (Recursively enumerable sets). The traditional definition of recursive functions is to generate them

1. Addition $+$ and multiplication $\times$, as well as the constant functions are recursive.

2. If $f(x_1, \ldots, x_n, y_1, \ldots, y_k)$ and $g_i(z_k, y_j), i = 1, \ldots, n$ are recursive then

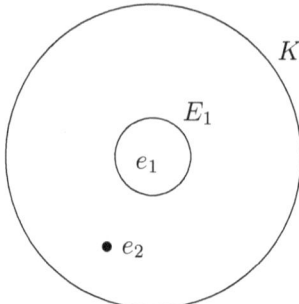

Figure 3.4.

so is $f(x_1/g_1, \ldots, x_n/g_n, y_j)$

3. If $f(x, y_j)$ is recursive so is $\mu x f(x, y_j)$ where $\mu x f(x)$ gives the least x such that $f(x, y_j) = 0$, if it exists.

4. Iteration. If $h(y, z, x_i)$ and $g(x_i)$ are recursive so is the function f satisfying
$$\begin{aligned} f(0, x_j) &= g(x_j) \\ f(n+1, x_j) &= h(n, f(n, x_i), x_j). \end{aligned}$$

We can now use recursive function to define recursively enumerable sets. These are generated by letting recursive fuctions compute and generate a range of numbers. Such ranges are recursively enmerable sets.

The predicate definition of such sets comes from a theorem of Matiyaseich. A set K is recursively enumerable iff there exists a polynomial with integer coefficients $f(x, n_1, \ldots, n_k)$ such that $K = \{n | f(n, n_1, \ldots, n_k) = 0\}$.

Both of these options are highly complex and mathematical.

The intuitive commonsense definition of a recursively enumerable set is as follows.

These are sets of numbers obtained by allowing some computer program to keep on running, churning out numbers. If we let it run forever and collect the numbers and ignore repetitions we get a recursively enumerable set generated by the program. Try all possible programs and you will get all possible sets.

This is a simple intuitive definition and it is actually 100% correct. It relies on our familiarity with computers, not in the technical sense but in the commonsense daily life sense

Now think of the Bible and its desire to define some sets for a crowd of former slaves just out of Egypt. How is it going to make things clear to them? What device to use? Well it used the method of (KPK), (PKP), etc., etc.

In fact the Bible uses another device. If we presented a set using (KP), we know we cannot change it any more and we are not allowed to apply further operations to it. If we use other rules, then maybe we can. This is a Talmudic convention. In modern terms this is a principle of reactivity. Each use of a rule tells us which other rules can be used. The **KPR** rules cannot string together but one is allowed to use the rule of analogy (Binyam-Ab) after a **KPR** rule and this possibility can be switched off.

Here is an example (not Biblical).

EXAMPLE 3.3 (The wedding). Mary is planning a wedding for her daughter. She has a big family and not all of them get along with each other. For example we have

$$a \longrightarrow b$$

a does not speak with b. If b is invited, a will not come.

We also have

$$c \longrightarrow d$$

d is a relative, c is a friend, not a relative. Now rich Uncle Morris from the US says: "I will pay for the wedding. Invite all the relatives (this is K-rule), for example b (this is P-rule) and any friend you like (this is another K)". Now which set has Uncle Morris defined? The set K_1 of all the relatives he mentioned first. This set is problematic. If b is invited, a will not come. But Uncle Morris mentioned b, so b has to be invited and not a.

Now that we clarified that we get K_2 — all the friends. Can we invite them all? No, because if $d \in K_1$ is invited then friend $c \in K_2$ will not come. Who has priority? K_2 or K_1? Do we invite c or do we invite d? This is a matter of how we perceive the rule of $(K_1 P K_2)$. In fact there are two opinions in the Talmud about this. One says K_2 has priority and the other says K_1 has!!

3 The Talmudic options

To use a **KPR** rule (for example KPK) in the Talmud we go through five stages.

1. Identify the Biblical text which seems to be a **KPR** definition of a set. This may suggest the form illustrated for example, in Figure 3.3. This text may involve one or two general rules K_1 and K_2 and several specific items $e_1, \ldots, e_m$ and more items $E_1, \ldots, E_4$ which can be specific small descriptions of subsets. These serve as P_1 and or P_2. We need to decide which rule of **KPR** is to be used. E.g/ $K_1 P K_2$ or $K_1 P$ or $P_1 K P_2$, etc.

2. We need to decicde from the text whether we have here one single application of the rule, with all the items $\{E_1, \ldots, E_4, e_1, \ldots, e_m\}$ or perhaps the intention is to use several applications of the rule in parallel, for example one with $K, \{E_1, \ldots, E_4\}$ which we call the E-application and one with $K, \{e_1, \ldots, e_m\}$, which we call the e-application, thus obtaining two sets Y_E and Y_e and then continuing with these sets.

   We can usually expect some textual hint as to the itention.

   Another possibility is to use **KPR** on each of $e_1, \ldots, e_m$ individually obtaining $Y_{e_1}, \ldots, Y_{e_m}$ and then use $E_1, \ldots, E_m$, not as the objects of **KPR** but on the results $Y_{e_1}, \ldots, Y_{e_m}$ of **KPR** on each e_i as a means to decide which Y_{e_i} to take. We should see some examples to this effect.

3. Having decided on how many applications of the rules we do in parallel and on which objects, β_i, we try in each case to find Y_β. To this end we look for each β_i, the common aspects (properties) π_j^i arising from the respective list of examples in β_i. This is a hard part and we may get some help from the Biblical text or we may have some agreed rules of how to find these π_j^i. The context of the problem will also help. See Example 3.4 below.

4. Executing the algorithm of the rule **KPR** with a view of defining the sets Y_{β_i} out of π_j^i above. Note that there may be several versions of how to execute the rule **KPR** and we may have to decide which version to use in each case.

5. Once we defined the different sets, Y_{β_i} as we indicated above by way of example, then we have to decide what to do with them. Some options are:

   5.1. Take the union

   5.2. Take the union of some of them to be chosen according to some principle, called Resonance.

   5.3. Perform some other operations.

We shall see later that we treat the sets π_j^i intensionally. So if $\pi_1^i = \pi_2^i$, we still operate with the names of the sets, i.e. π_1^i, π_2^i, and not identify them as one set. How this is done will become apparent from the examples.

Methodological Question

What are the principles actually employed by the Talmud?

To extract these we go over the case studies in the Talmud where **KPR** rules are employed (sugiyot **KPR**) and see how they fit. As there are several of these with some possible interpretations, we can find the interpretations that fit a single version of the formal **KPR** schema.

This will achieve (if indeed found to fit) two objectives.

1. Give us a formalisation of the correct **KPR** rules of the Talmud

2. Resolve problems raised by Talmudic scholars through the ages.

In our paper [4] we have systematically gone through major **KPR** studies in the Talmud and the results were amazingly consistent and confirmed our model as well as resolved Talmudic problems with respect to **KPR**.

EXAMPLE 3.4 (Royal Party). The context of this example is the imaginary world of children's stories about Kings, Princes and Princesses. These children's stories are stylised and well known to many children all over the world. They include stories like Rapunzel, Snow White and the Seven Dwarves, the Princess and the Pea, Sinbad the Sailor, Goldilocks, Ali Baba and the Forty Thieves, etc, etc. In short, all the 'night-night' stories children hear before they go to bed.

The King of some Town decides to throw a ball in honour of his daughter, the Princess. He tells his ministers to invite important people such as Princess

A and Magicians B and C and local girls G1 and G2 and Prince E and King F, and in fact anyone who may be of importance. This is an instance of KPK in the context of children's stories. What do we know about common features of Princes, Princesses, Magicians and girls in these stories?

1. All princesses are beautiful, looking for a suitable husband and totally useless (from our point of view).

2. Princes are valiant but some are 'dark'.

3. The magicians can be good, dressed in white or evil, dressed in black.

So the additional invitees could be honest nice maidens friendly with the princess.

If this story is set in modern times and the Queen of England is throwing a reception, then probably:

1. Princesses are engaged in charity

2. 'Magicians' are politicians

3. Princes are probably some sort of playboys.

So the additional invitees could be celebrities from television and Hollywood.

EXAMPLE 3.5. This is essentially a Talmudic example (from Tractat Hulin 65–66) cast in modern terms.[2] Imagine a situation where there is a credit crunch and general economic problems. Companies are going bust and the government is interested in supporting them. Such a situation existed in 2008/2009 and in fact the government supported the banking sector by buying shares in ailing banks. One such example is the Royal Bank of Scotland (RBS) where the UK government bought over 70% of its shares for over 100 billion dollars. Now imagine that the US government wants to help companies by allowing them to pay their corporation tax, not in cash, but in their own shares. This is a welcome form of help. The question is what kind of shares the government would accept and from what kind of companies? The government uses KPK to identify such companies.

General principle K_1
Official government text: companies showing signs of recovery.

Examples P
Official government text: Companies like e_1 = Microsoft or companies like e_2 = Goldman-Sachs, or companies like e_3 = South Texas Oil or a set like E_1 = any international houshold American brand name.[3]

Second General rule K_2
Official government text: Anything like the above.

---

[2] The **KPR** are essentially Talmudic and do not necessarily exactly apply to modern legal conventions or modern common sense reasoning. However, in this modern example we get identical results to the Talmud.

[3] e.g. Coca-Cola.

	U many employees	A International company	B credit crunch problems	C strong potential growth
e_1 = Texas Oil	+	+	-	-
e_2 = Goldman-Sachs	+	+	+	+
e_3 = Microsoft	+	+	-	+
E_1 = American brand	+	+	+	+

Figure 3.5.

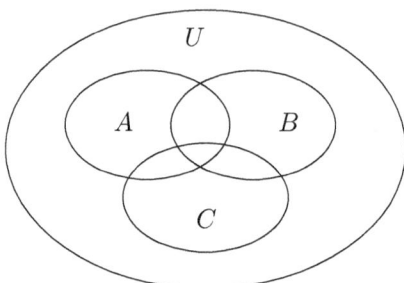

Figure 3.6.

The way the examples are formulated hints that we want to do the rule KPK separately on each of Microsoft, Goldman-Sachs, and Texas Oil, which are individual companies. We extract some π_j^i from them and then maybe we use the set E_1 = American brand name companies, in some special way.

The next step is to identify the properties (aspects) π_j^i for each e_i. We offer the following table for our particular example, see Figure 3.5.

In this example we chose companies in such a way that the aspects π_j^i have the same structure as the ones of the Talmudic examples.[4] We thus have the Talmudic example cast in modern terms.

Here each e_i has $k(i) = 4$ aspects. (The function k gives the number of aspects we use.)

The sets U, A, B, C have a meaning and therefore we can draw a Venn diagram for them. In this particular case we get the same sets or their complements at play for each e_j and so we can use the same schematic Venn diagram, see Figure 3.6. Let $\bar{X} = U - X$, then:

For Texas Oil, look at $U, A, \bar{B}, \bar{C}$.
For Goldman-Sachs, look at U, A, B, C.
For Microsoft, look at $U, A, \bar{B}, C$

We have $A \subseteq U$ because such international companies have many employees. We also have $U \subseteq E_1$ since this entire set up is for subsets of E_1.

We use the following KPK rule as our example.

---

[4] Hulin page 66 deals with types of insects we are allowed to eat. Nowadays these are not considered attractive to eat.

3. LOGICAL ANALYSIS OF THE TALMUDIC RULES

The result of applying KPK to an element e is to take the set of all elements that have two features in common with e, i.e. $\varphi(k) = 2$ in our case, see Figure 3.8. If k is the number of features then $\varphi(k)$ is the number of features we use to identify the elements of the target set we want to define. The function φ is part of the **KPR** rule we use. See Table of Figure 3.8.

So from the table we get:

For Texas Oil we get

$$\pi_{\text{Texas}} = (A \cap \bar{B}) \cup (A \cap \bar{C}) \cup (\bar{B} \cap \bar{C}) \cup (U \cap A) \cup (U \cap \bar{C}) \cup (U \cap \bar{B})$$

For Goldman-Sachs we get

$$\pi_{GS} = (A \cap B) \cup (A \cap C) \cup (B \cap C) \cup (U \cap A) \cup (U \cap B) \cup (U \cap C)$$

For Microsoft we get

$$\pi_{\text{Mic}} = (A \cap \bar{B}) \cup (A \cap C) \cup (\bar{B} \cap C) \cup (U \cap A) \cup (U \cap \bar{B}) \cup (U \cap C)$$

We now look at the syntactical description of the sets in terms of $\pm A, \pm B, \pm C, \pm U$ and apply a process which we call *Resonance*.

Take a set X, e.g. $X = B$. If B appears in one element (e.g. Goldman-Sachs) and $\bar{B}$ in another (e.g. Google) then ignore it and delete the disjunct from both.

We get new disjunctions $\pi^*_{\text{Texas}}, \pi^*_{GS}, \pi^*_{\text{Mic}}$, after applying the resonance deletion process. These are:

$$\pi^*_{\text{Texas}} = U \cap A$$
$$\pi^*_{GS} = U \cap A$$
$$\pi^*_{\text{Mic}} = U \cap A$$

Let $\pi_{\text{resonance}}$, the result of the resonance operation, be $\pi^*_{\text{Texas}} \cup \pi^*_{GS} \cup \pi^*_{\text{Mic}} = U \cap A$.

Therefore the relevant aspects in all the items e_1, e_2, e_3 are U and A. And, since $\varphi(4) = 2$, we take all elements having two aspects in common, i.e. we take $U \cap A$.

So we are left with A and U, with $A \subseteq U$. Note that if we did not have E_1, we would have stopped here and the answer/result of the algorithm would have been $A \cap U$. Now that we have E_1 (i.e. we are also given a set and not just individuals) we need to continue. First we view E_1 as a constraint and second we view E_1 as another aspect.

So we need to do **KPR** process on $E_1, E_1 \cap U, E_1 \cap A$.

A says we want an international/multi-national company. Now E_1 the set American brand comes into play. We want $A \subseteq U$ which is also an $E =$ American brand. Thus the result of our considerations is that there are three concentric aspects $A \subseteq U \subseteq E_1$ (see Figure 3.7).

Consider the black box complex individual $\beta = \{e_1, e_1, e_3, E_1\}$. We now apply KPK to this β and get

$$Y = (A \cap U) \cup (A \cap E_1) \cup (U \cap E_1) = U \cap E_1$$

The next definition will give the general algorithm we used.

DEFINITION 3.6 (Formal definition of Talmudic **KPR**). The reader should compare with Example 3.5 step by step.

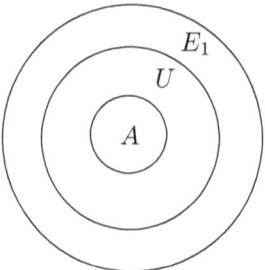

Figure 3.7.

1. An instance of **KPR** involves a general rule K_1, a list of specific instances given as individual $e_1, \ldots, e_m$ and a list of sets $E_1, \ldots, E_n$ (these are specific instances given as sets) and a concluding rule K_2. K_1 is called the first rule and K_2 is called the second rule. Note that we view the above intensionally as syntactically defined element $e_1, \ldots, e_m$ and sets $K_1, E_1, \ldots, E_n, K_2$. K_1 and K_2 contain intensionally all of $e_1, \ldots, e_m$ and $E_1, \ldots, E_n$.

It could be that some of these syntactical entitites have the same extensions but to **KPR** we see them as intensionally distinct.[5] The idea of **KPR** rules is to define sets around the examples $e_1, \ldots, e_m$ and $E_1, \ldots, E_n$. The algorithm extracts intensional properties from these items, say $D_1, \ldots, D_k$ the number k may also be determined by the rule, and tells us what degree of resemblance to these intensional sets D_i we want to use to define our target set Y.

The degree of resemblance is $\varphi(k)$ and we have $x \in Y$ iff x is in at least $\varphi(k)$ of the sets D_i.

The Talmudic algorithm for the application of KPK is first to look for defining asepcts for *each* of the items $e_1, \ldots, e_m$. So the Talmudic algorithm tells us to apply KPK in principle to each of the individual items separately. We use context and textual analysis to find the defining aspects for e_i. Call them $\pi_1^i, \ldots, \pi_{k(i)}^i$. This list is context dependent and finding it has no algorithm. It is not part of the abstract KPK algorithm. The KPK rule says that when we agree on $k(i)$ aspects for e_i then we look at the intensional set

$$A_i = \{x | x \text{ is an intensional member of at least } \varphi(k(i)) = n \text{ sets}\}$$

i.e.

$$A_i = \bigcup_{\substack{i_1 \neq i_2 \neq \ldots \neq i_n \\ \text{pairwise different} \\ \text{numbers} \leq k(i)}} \bigcap_{r=1,\ldots,n} \pi_{i_r}^i$$

---

[5] This is well known in philosphy. For example evening star, morning star are extensionally the same but intensionally different.

	Priority to first K	Priority to last K
K_1PK_2	$\varphi(k(i)) = k(i)$	$\varphi(k(i)) = 2$
PK_2	$\varphi(k(i)) = 1$	$\varphi(k(i)) = 1$
K_1P	$\varphi(k(i)) = k(i) + 1^7$ (formally this means e_i only)	$\varphi(k(i)) = k(i) + 1$ (formally this means e_i only).
P_iKP_2	$\varphi(k(i)) = 2$	$\varphi(k(i)) = k(i)$

Figure 3.8.

If $\varphi(k(i)) = 1$ then the set $A_i = \{e_i\}$.

We need to say what is $\varphi(k(i))$. This depends on the version of the **KPR** rule employed and on whether K_1, K_2 appear or not. It also depends on the priority we give to K_1 over K_2 or K_2 over K_1.[6]

The following table, Figure 3.8 summarises the options.

2. Having done this for each i, we retain the syntactic definition of A_i, and we need to continue and do what we call *Resonance*.

Resonance can be applied when for all $i, k(i)$ is the same, say $k(i) = k$.

So

$A_i\ =\ $ syntactical union of all possible syntactical intesections of $\varphi(k)$elements.

Assume that for $i \neq j$ we have in A_i an intersection of the form $\pi \cap z$, and in A_j we have a syntactrical intersection of the form $\pi \cap \bar{z}$.

Then we delete both $\pi \cap z$ and $\pi \cap \bar{z}$ from A_i and A_j respectively. Thus we get new unions after resonance is repeatedly applied for all possible cases. Call them A_i^R.

$A_i^R = $ union of less intersections obtained from A_i after resonance.

The rationale for doing this is as follows:

In A_i, we want elements sharing $\varphi(k)$ features with e_i. One possiblity is the set $\pi \cap z$, a disjunct in A_i.

We also have $\pi \cap \bar{z}$ as a disjunct in A_j. This means z is not an important feature in the context of π. Hence the element of

$$\pi = (\pi \cap z) \cup (\pi \cap \bar{z})$$

have $\varphi(k) - 1$ features and that is not enough according to our rule, and so we delete it.

---

[6]In Hebrew:
K_1 prior to K_2: Klal Kama Davka
K_2 prior to K_1: Klal Batra Davka.

[7]If we are given $k(i)$ properties of e_i and we seek all elements x which share $k(i) + 1$ properties with e_i then the only x we can safely admit is e_i itself.

This resonance deletion process leaves us with a reduced list $\eta^i_j, j = 1, \ldots, n_i)$ where $n(i) \leq k(i)$.

We now form the sets $B_i = \bigcup_{j \leq n(i)} \bigcap_{r \neq j} \eta^i_j$.

Having found B_i we take only those B_i such that

$$B_i \subseteq \bigcap_{i=1}^{m} E_i$$

Let $D_1, \ldots, D_s$ list the successful B_i which are syntactically different. We now have a list of aspects $D_1, \ldots, D_s$ which we view as aspects of a black box 'ideal' individual.

$$\beta = \{E_1, \ldots, E_n, e_1, \ldots, e_m\}.$$

We apply the KPK rule using $\varphi(s)$ and now define the final set Y, the result of the entire KPK process as

$$Y = \bigcup_{\substack{i_1 \neq i_2 \\ \neq \ldots \neq i_{\varphi(s)} \\ \text{all pairwise different}}} \bigcap_{r = i_j, j=1, \ldots, \varphi(s)} D_r$$

If there are no E_i at all, we take $Y = D_1 \cup \ldots \cup D_s$.

4 Concluding discussion

We saw that **KPR** define sets basically by examples and make use of our (context dependent) common sense to identify the target set.

We stressed two features of this rule:

1. Its simplicity

2. Its open texture, the way it can change with context.

The reader may have doubts about the simplicity, looking at the example and definition in Section 3. The procedure may seem complex because we are describing it mathematically, but on the human intuitive level it is simple.

A further point about open texture. Here the open texture arise from properties of individual agents, not from the meaning of predicates. We have abundant examples of predicate open texture in legal reasoning and legal concepts. This is not the same as dependence on individuals. Take for example the concept 'response in reasonable time' with regard to public institutions.

We can interpret 'reasonable time' differently at different circumstances. But if we define it by example, e.g.
$e_1 =$ police dial 999,
$e_2 =$ hospital ambulance service
$e_3 =$ job enquiries at the post office.
then we are relying on the adaptability of these items to circumstances, which

may be different from the common sense perception of the public of 'reasonable time' under the same circumstances.

A final remark about the range of **KPR** rules. Suppose nowadays we want to use this rule to define a set. How do we go about it and what are the ideal conditions for its use?

First we may agree on a different table from that of Figure 3.8. Second, we may be more specific about what rules can be used for K_1 and K_2.

Consider the term mug (a general term for some kind of drinking cup).

It does not seem reasonable to use **KPR** to give a definition of the set of elements considered as mugs. We do have a common sense understanding of what a mug is. It seems more likely that I define the kind of mug I personally like by using KPK. I start with $K_1 =$ mug and give some examples $e_1, \ldots, e_m$ of mugs I like and then conclude with $K_2 =$ say 'anything big and easy to hold in one hand'.

We guess what we are saying is that **KPR** is most successful in defining subsets of sets which are already intuitively (and using common sense) perceived by the man of the street; by using KPK we further limit this already well understood set.

CHAPTER 4

OBLIGATIONS AND PROHIBITIONS IN TALMUDIC DEONTIC LOGIC

Introduction

This chapter examines the deontic logic of the Talmud. We shall find, by looking at examples, that at first approximation we need deontic logic with several connectives:

$O_T A$ Talmudic obligation

$F_T A$ Talmudic prohibition

$F_D A$ Standard deontic prohibition

$O_D A$ Standard deontic obligation.

In classical logic one would have expected that deontic obligation O_D is definable by

- $O_D A \equiv F_D \neg A$

and that O_T and F_T are connected by

- $O_T A \equiv F_T \neg A$

This is not the case in the Talmud for the T (Talmudic) operators, though it does hold for the D operators. We must change our underlying logic. We have to regard $\{O_T, F_T\}$ and $\{O_D, F_D\}$ as two sets of operators, where O_T and F_T are independent of one another and where we have some connections between the two sets.

We shall list the types of obligation patterns appearing in the Talmud and develop an intuitionistic deontic logic to accommodate them. We shall compare Talmudic deontic logic with modern deontic logic.

1 Motivating Talmudic deontic logic TDL

This chapter is written for researchers in Deontic Logic and Contrary to Duties who would like to know how things stand in Talmudic logic. It is an expanded version of [5]. To set the scene for this chapter, we give some short background material.

The simplest and historically first logical system offered for dealing with obligation is Standard Deontic Logic **SDL**, which is the modal logic **KD** for an operator $O_D A$ reading 'A is obligatory'. The semantics for O are models of the form (S, R, h), where $R \subseteq S^2$, h is the assignment to the atoms, assigning each atom q of the language a subset $h(q) \subseteq S$, and R satisfies $\forall x \exists y x R y$.

This system was too simple and researchers in the community offered systems with dyadic modalities $O_D(A/C)$, reading 'A is obligatory in the context C'. This was a response to contrary to duty examples which could not be properly modelled by the unary O_D.

One such famous example is the Chisholm set:[1]

1. It ought to be that a certain man goes to assist his neighbour.

2. It ought to be that if he does go he tells him he is coming.

3. If he does not go he ought not to tell him he is coming.

4. He does not go.

If we use H for 'help' and T for 'tell', we have two options to formalise this set, either with $O_D X$ (unary) or with $O_D(X/Y)$ dyadic.

clause	monadic	dyadic
1.	$O_D H$	$O_D(H/\top)$
2.	$H \to O_D T$	$H \to O_D(T/H)$
3.	$\neg H \to O_D \neg T$	$\neg H \to O_D(\neg T/\neg H)$
4.	$\neg H$	$\neg H$

The following sums up the spirit of the research of the deontic community.

1. Find reasonable logical systems involving various monadic or dyadic modal operators with possible world or preferential semantics in which various linguistic deontic sets can be consistently and adequately formalised.

2. Emphasise the CTD examples and calibrate your logics to deal with various problems associated with them.

The community lays stress on the theory of CTDs as distinctly characteristic to deontic logic, which sets it apart from being a secondary applied branch of modal logic. It is also felt that the essence of the deontic area is the possibility of violations and hence the core of deontic logic as a discipline distinct from modal logic is its theory of CTD.

For our purpose a contrary to duty system is a set Δ of formulas of the form $\{\delta_1, \ldots, \delta_n\}$ where

$$\delta_i = O(X_i/Y_1 \wedge \ldots \wedge Y_{k(i)}).$$

Given a consistent set

$$\theta = (E_1, \ldots, E_k)$$

we consider the set

$$\Delta_\theta = \{X_i | \delta_i(X_i/Y_1 \wedge \ldots Y_{k(i)}) \in \Delta \text{ and } \theta \vdash Y_j, j = 1, \ldots, k(i)\}$$

---

[1]The translation of (1)–(4) must give four consistent and logically independent sentences adequately representing the linguistic text.

4. OBLIGATIONS AND PROHIBITIONS IN TALMUDIC DEONTIC LOGIC

Δ_θ is the set of obligations triggered by the context θ. Δ_θ may be an inconsistent set and part of any CTD logic is to "recommend" a consistent subset $\Delta_\theta^{con} \subseteq \Delta_\theta$. The "logic" has to deal coherently and in a compatible manner with common sense with the relationship between pairs of the form $(\theta, \Delta_\theta^{con})$ and $(\theta', \Delta_{\theta'}^{con})$. As far as we know, no comprehensive theory of this form exists. See references [86; 87; 50; 51; 27; 55].

In contrast with the above, The Talmud, being a religious code of law, given to us by God in the Bible, has two types of deontic rules: action obligations and action prohibitions. Both types represent the will of God for us to obey. This is why at a first logical approximation we need two independent deontic operations O_T and F_T (the subscript 'T' stands for 'Talmudic') as well as the standard deontic Obligation O_D and prohibition F_D.

There are some points we need to make clear. The variables X that go into the connectives $O_T X, F_T X, O_D X$ and $F_D X$ denote actions like work, lift, steal, wear Tefilin (Tefilin is something men wear when they offer morning prayers during week days), etc. and not lack of action like resting, not stealing, etc. When we negate them and write $\neg X$, we denote lack of action.

We are not going to discuss how to determine what is considered action and what is to be considered inaction. This is a separate issue. We assume it is always clear, for any candidate formulas A and $\neg A$, which is the action formula and which is the inaction formula.

One might think that we can model obligations and prohibitions using only one deontic operator O, letting OX represent obligations and $O\neg X$ represent prohibitions. However this is not correct. Our obligations and prohibitions can apply either to X or to $\neg X$. See examples below under the heading "Type 3: Strong obligation/prohibition'. So $O_T X$ is a Biblical obligation to take action X. $O_T \neg X$ is a Biblical obligation not to take action X. $F_T X$ is a Biblical prohibition to take action X and $F_T \neg X$ is a Biblical prohibition not to take action X (i.e. we are prohibited from choosing not to take action X). So $O_T X$ is not equivalent to $F_T \neg X$. So if X = wear Tefilin, then having an obligation to wear it is not the same as being prohibited from not wearing it. So in some cases God requires us to obey both i.e. $O_T X \wedge F_T \neg X$. The reader should recall intuitionistic logic where $\neg\neg A$ is weaker than A, so the negation used in these commands have intuitionistic flavour. (In fact, the Talmudic system will be modelled in intuitionistic modal logic.)[2]

If we look at this situation as logicians, we can say we have here three pairs

---

[2] In Talmudic logic we have that $\neg\neg F_T(A)$ is not equivalent to $F_T(A)$. The first is only a weak prohibition, a recommendation for good behaviour in the eyes of God, while the second is a full fledged strong prohibition. This is reflected in our use of intuitionistic logic as a basis.

The perceptive reader might say that perhaps we could obtain a similar result without the use of intuitionistic logic, by considering explicit permissions which are distinct from the negation of a prohibition.

More specifically, we introduce an additional modal operator P, with the axiom $F \to \neg P$, but without the axiom $\neg P \to F$. In that case, the negation of permission may correspond to a weak prohibition, but without requiring intuitionistic logic for this purpose.

However introducing another independent operator is too strong and does not manifest the intention that $\neg\neg F_T(A)$ is only a recommendation of $F_T(A)$. Furthermore the idea of explicit permissions is not compatible with Talmudic thinking. God never said in the Bible "you are allowed to do this". He only delivered to us Obligations and Prohibitions. See

of modal operators, each pair being of the form (Necessity of the form NX and Possibility of the form $PX = \neg N \neg X$). The pairs are $(N_i, P_i), i = 1, 2, 3$ as follows.

1. $O_T X$ and $\neg O_T \neg X$

2. $F_T \neg X$ and $\neg F_T X$

3. $O_D X$ and $\neg F_D X = \neg O_D \neg X$.

Since the Talmud gives no connections between O_T and F_T, we have to represent them as two pairs $\{N_1 X = O_T X, P_1 X = \neg O_T \neg X\}$, and $\{N_2 X = F_T \neg X, P_2 X = \neg F_T X\}$.

This can be made clearer when we consider the operational differences between $O_T A$ and $F_T A$ and $F_D A$.

1. If you obey $O_T A$ then God rewards you. You are also obliged to spend 20% of your income to enable yourself to fulfil your obligation.

2. If you violate $F_T A$, and actually do the forbidden A, then you will be punished (by God and or by law/society). Also you should devote 100% of your income to enable yourself to avoid doing A.

Therefore for the same X, if the Bible says $O_T X$ then 1. applies and if the Bible says $F_T \neg X$, which in practice means the same to us, then 2. applies.[3]

$F_D A$ says it is forbidden to have A for whatever reason, without going into the fine tuning of why this is so. It may arise from a Biblical $O_T \neg A$, or from $F_T A$ or from some related $F_T Y$ or whatever.

For example, in Type 1A: Obligation with deontic prohibition below we have O_T (wear Tefilin during prayer). From this it follows that F_D (pray without wearing Tefilin).

However we do not have a direct Biblical prohibition F_T (pray without Tefilin), and therefore if one actually does pray without wearing Tefilin, there is no punishment from God.

Note that we do not necessarily have any connections like

$$O_T X \to \neg F_D X$$

and

$$F_T X \to F_D X.$$

If we had them we could have derived

$$O_T X \to \neg F_T X.$$

However we know that there is no such axiomatic connection in Talmudic logic. The reason for that is as we mentioned earlier, O_T and F_T are in general generic

---

Section 5.1 for further discussion.

[3] A main difference between biblical obligation and prohibition and ordinary traditional Deontic obligation and prohibition is that violation of a biblical prohibition would imply a sanction whereas fulfilment of the corresponding biblical obligation implies a reward. This in an important dimension, and will be further discussed in Section 5.1

4. OBLIGATIONS AND PROHIBITIONS IN TALMUDIC DEONTIC LOGIC

and possibly conflicting, and it is the Rabbis who decide day-to-day how to apply the commands in any given situation.

It is possible also to have both $F_T X$ and $O_T X$ for the same X (even though on the surface this seems contradictory) because X may be a generic kind of predicate and it is expected that the Rabbis will decide for each situation **s** which obligation/prohibition applies. In fact, in many cases the Bible gives recipes (more precisely there are indirect hints in the Biblical text but the main derivation of recipes is done in the Talmud) for making such decisions. In our model these recipes are part of the (nonmonotonic) mechanisms of conflict resolution.

It is the job of the Rabbis to make decisions (according to some principles) how to resolve conflicts between obligations and prohibitions when applied to any particular situations.

The emphasis of Talmudic Deontic Logic is therefore on

1. Deciding what are the Biblical $O_T X, F_T X$. (This has been done: there are 613 master ones, though opinions differ as to which are included among these 613.)

2. Deciding which Biblical $O_T X, F_T Y$ apply to any new arising situation **s**.

3. Resolving possible conflicts between applicable rules for any **s**.

The role of CTDs is not central to the Talmudic system, nor is the theoretical maintainance of consistency. The Biblical rules are known to cause conflict and established procedures and recommendations and institutions for conflict resolution and practical day-to-day decision making are also given by the Bible.

Note that there are differences between this decision making process and precedents and legislation in law. We shall not go into that here. See, however, Section 5.3.

The following table, Table 4.1, compares Talmudic Deontic ideas with their modern counterparts.

To compare CTDs, let us look at some examples from the Bible.[4]

EXAMPLE 4.1 (Chisholm variant 1).

1. You ought to have a ceremonial meal during the Passover festival.

2. If you have your meal you ought to say prayer (blessing, grace).

3. If you do not have the meal you ought not say the prayer (blessing).

4. You do not have the meal.

(1)–(3) are Biblical obligations. We formalise them using dyadic modalities.

1. $O_T M$ (or $O_T(M/\top)$)

2. $M \to O_T B$ (or $M \to O_T(B/M)$)

---

[4] The Talmud interprets the Bible. So when we say Talmudic logic, this includes Biblical logic.

	Deontic community	Talmud	Comments
Sources of obligations and prohibitions	common sense, law, moral code	Bible/God	It took hundreds of years to study and summarise the Talmudic obligations and prohibitions. 613 major types were finally agreed upon by the end of the middle ages, though as we already mentioned, opinions differ as to which are included among these 613.
Formalisation	Monadic or dyadic operators, preference or possible world models.	Two levels O_T, F_T, and O_D, F_D. The handling meta-logic is some kind of time action logic	Modern deontic logic is a well developed area. This chapter is a first attempt in formalising Talmudic deontic logic
Status of CTD	central	marginal	The Talmud views CTD as just more conditional obligations
Conflict resolution	Recognised but not central yet. The community is beginning to address the problem.	central	Deontic community recognises the problem of inherited conflicting CTDs. They emphasise consistency. Talmud expects inconsistency even of original obligations. Emphasises methods of resolving conflicts.
Status of violations	Violations are expected, that is why CTDs are central, but there is no reward for obeying a CTD.	Obeyance is expected	Talmud emphasises punishment for violations and reward for obeyance.

Table 4.1.

3. $\neg M \to F_T(B/\neg M)$

4. $\neg M$.

Note that the Bible is explicit about $F_T(B/\neg M)$ and does not say $O_T(\neg B/\neg M)$. The Bible says generally "Do not use the name of God in vain", which applies to this case as well!

> Exodus 20:7
> You shall not take the name of the LORD your God in vain, for the LORD will not leave him unpunished who takes His name in vain.

We do *not* have the equivalence $O_T(\neg x/z) \equiv F_T(x/z)$.

Compare the above with the following.

EXAMPLE 4.2 (Chisholm variant 2).

1. We are obliged to eat meat from sheep at passover.

    > Exodus 12:21
    > Then Moses called for all the elders of Israel and said to them, Go and take for yourselves lambs according to your families, and slay the Passover lamb.

2. If we eat meat we should slaughter the sheep humanely.

3. If we do not eat meat we should not slaughter the sheep.

4. We do not eat meat.

The translation is as follows (E is Eat and H is sheep):

1. $O_T(E/\top)$.

2. $E \to O_T(H/E)$.

3. $\neg E \to F_D(H/\neg E)$

4. $\neg E$

Note that in (3) we used F_D because the Bible is not explicitly prohibiting killing animals for no reason but the prohibition follows from Rabbinical practical rulings.

Thus the reward from God for obeyance is different in the two cases. Note that it is easier to avoid the Chisholm paradox for examples 1.1 and 1.2 since our logic language is more refined.

The rest of this section will give examples of the major existing types of Talmudic obligations and prohibitions and formalise the examples in terms of O_T, F_T and F_D. The reader should note that we may have less or different paradoxes for the Talmudic system, which has more operators and so more fine distinctions can be made. Furthermore if in ordinary deontic logic we allow more operators to stand for strong moral (parallel to Talmudic) obligations and prohibitions, then we might find that some paradoxes disappear. Although we have not given yet to the reader the axiom system and semantics for these operators, we have given enough of their intuitive meaning and this should suffice for our initial formalisation.

Let us now briefly describe the eight types of obligations and prohibitions available in the Talmud.

We shall also give a preliminary intuitive formalisation in terms of O_T, F_T and F_D (note that O_D is definable from F_D, so we do not need it). In the sequel, we distinguish Types 1A, 1B and 1C. They all arise from the same Biblical Talmudic obligation O_T. The differences between them is practical implementations, as summarised in Table 4.2.

Type 1A. Obligation with deontic prohibition

As an example, we have to respect and honour our parents (this is one of the Ten Commandments), so we have O_T (Respect Parents). If we do not respect our parents, there is a violation. See Table 4.2 item 1A. The Bible says respect your parents so that you will live long and prosper. It does not threaten punishment if you do not.

> Deuteronomy 20:8
> Honor thy father and thy mother, that thy days may be long upon the land which the LORD thy God giveth thee.

Perhaps a modern example will help. We all read some Harry Potter books. The newspapers reported that the author J. K. Rowling gave her father copies of the first edition of her books, signed and dedicated by her. The idea was that he was supposed to keep them. The father needed money and so he sold them. We formalise the intention/convention by $O_T$keep $\wedge$ $F_D\neg$keep.

He is not supposed to sell them because he is expected to keep them.

Type 1B. Weak obligation

There is an obligation to live in the land of Israel. The question is whether from this obligation there is a deontic prohibition on living outside Israel. The answer is no, according to a minority opinion. Now if you do not live in Israel, there is no violation. See Table 4.2, item 1B. This is a unique case where the weak obligation is some sort of recommendation. You get a reward if you do it but there is no violation if you do not do it.

Type 1C. Prohibition arising from positive obligation

We need to let the land rest every seven years. As part of this the fruits of trees on the seventh year are allowed to be eaten by anyone, not just the owners of the tree, but are not allowed to be sold or traded with. This is to stop the temptation for farmers to work the land and trade the produce.

We write this as

$$F_D(\text{trade fruit of tree})$$

We *do* want you to eat the fruit and not to sell them. We do not require in practice to eat the fruit. The Talmudic O_T eat is not enforced. I.e. you have no actual obligation to eat the fruit only not to sell them.

Leviticus 25:1-7

God spoke to Moses at Mount Sinai, telling him to speak to the Israelites and say to them: When you come to the land that I am giving you, the land must be given a rest period, a sabbath to God. For **six years you may plant your fields, prune your vineyards, and harvest your crops, but the seventh year is a sabbath of Sabbaths for the land**. It is God's sabbath during which you may not plant your fields, nor prune your vineyards. Do not harvest crops that grow on their own and do not gather the grapes on your unpruned vines, since it is a year of rest for the land. [What grows while] the land is resting may be eaten by you, by your male and female slaves, and by the employees and resident hands who live with you. All the crop shall be eaten by the domestic and wild animals that are in your land.

Leviticus 25:20-22

And if ye shall say: 'What shall we eat the seventh year?' behold, we may not sow nor gather in our increase'; then I will command My blessing upon you in the sixth year, and it shall bring forth produce for the three years. And ye shall sow the eighth year, and eat of the produce, the old store; until the ninth year, until her produce come in, ye shall eat the old store.

To sharpen and clarify the distinctions between Type 1A and Type 1C, note that during Sukkot, the feast of Tabernacles, we must eat our meals inside the Sukkah, a temporary hut you build in your garden. However if you do eat outside the Sukkah, no punishment is due. It is not clear how to formalise it. Opinions differ, it is either of Type 1A or of Type 1C. The book *Minhat Hinuch* says that if we adopt Type 1A, then if one uses a stolen Sukkah one has not fulfilled his obligation, since he committed a violation in the process, however, if we adopt the view that the Type is 1C, then he has fulfilled his obligation.

Compare with Type 2. For a prohibition of Type 2, of the form $F_T X$, if we violate it and do perform X we get punished! We do not get punished if we violate Type 1A or Type 1C.

Table 4.2.

$O_T X$	If you do X	If you do $\neg X$
Type 1A, in this case we also have $F_D \neg X$ and consequently $O_D X$	You obeyed the will of God. God rewards you in Heaven	You committed violation. You will have to face the consequences in Heaven.
Type 1B, in this case we do not have $F_D \neg X$.	as above	The incident is not recorded in Heaven
Type 1C, in this case we only have $F_D \neg X$ without having $O_T X$	Your obeyance is not recorded in Heaven	You committed violation. You will have to face the consequences in Heaven.
Comment	If you obey 1A by committing a violation which harms other people, then obligation of type 1A is not fulfilled (you are still considered as having committed violation of 1A) but even under these circumstances an obligation of type 1C is fulfilled. See the book *Minhat Hinuch*.	

Type 2. Full prohibition

The Bible forbids the eating of pork.

F_T (eating pork), and we do not have $O_T(\neg$ eat pork).

> Leviticus 11:7-8
> And the pig, because it is parts the hoof and is cloven-footed but does not chew the cud, is unclean to you. You shall not eat any of their flesh, and you shall not touch their carcasses; they are unclean to you.

Type 3. Strong obligation/prohibition

This has the structure

$$O_T \neg X \wedge F_T X$$

An example of this is the Biblical obligation/prohibition about work on the Sabbath (seventh day). We have, for X = doing work, an obligation not to do work and also a prohibition on working. So this is a very strong demand from God!

Another example, if you have a house with accessible roof you must install a railing to the roof to prevent people falling off the roof. This can be interpreted as a typical safety rule. Its status is that of a weak obligation introduced for good practice. If you obey it, you will earn the good will of God. There is also prohibition on being without a railing. So if you do not obey it, there is no punishment. We formalise this by writing

$$O_T \text{ Rail and } F_T \neg \text{ Rail.}$$

To quote the Bible:

> Deuteronomy 22:8
> When you build a new house, you must build a railing around the edge of its flat roof. That way you will not be considered guilty of murder if someone falls from the roof.

> Note that in the Sabbath example the Obligation is on lack of action and the prohibition is on action and in the roof example the obligation is on action and the prohibition is on lack of action.

2 Contrary to Duties

Type CTD I. Obligation with positive contrary to duty

You should not steal and if you steal you should return what is stolen. We can write:

1. $F_T S$
2. $(S \to O_T R)$

or maybe the dyadic formalisation:

2a. $S \to O_T(R/S)$

Type CTD II. Temporal chain of CTDs

This example is from the Bible.

1. You should not rape a woman.
2. If you do rape a woman you must marry her.[5]
3. If you marry the woman you raped you can never divorce her.

We write this as

$$F_T R \wedge (R \to O_T(M/R)) \wedge (R \wedge M \to F_T(D/R \wedge M))$$

To quote the Bible:

> Deuteronomy 22:28-29
> If a man happens to meet a virgin who is not pledged to be married *and rapes her* and they are discovered, *he shall pay the girl's father fifty shekels of silver. He must marry the girl, for he has violated her. He can never divorce her as long as he lives.*

---

[5]Assuming she is not married. If she is married, the guy is in really serious trouble! If she is not married but does not want to marry the guy, he has to pay compensation only.

Type CTD III. Fine tuning required

Let us give some more examples of Contrary to Duties from the Talmud. These examples require further fine tuning and their delicate formalisation is postponed.

1. This is the mainstream example we mentioned before, which we recall here for comparison, that we should not steal but if we do steal we have an obligation to return the stolen property to its rightful owner. (This is a 'repairing' CTD.)

2. We have an obligation to pray three times a day. A morning prayer, an afternoon prayer and an evening prayer. The time for the afternoon prayer is from noon to sunset. The evening prayer should be done after sunset but before sunrise. The rules governing this are as follows:

    (a) It is obligatory to pray the afternoon prayer between noon and sunset.

    (b) If one was not able, due to circumstances beyond his control, to offer the afternoon prayer before sunset one can still fulfill the obligation by offering the afternoon prayer 13 minutes after sunset. (This is called 'make up'.)

    (c) If time has passed and no afternoon prayer was offered then one can offer the evening prayer twice, to make up for the afternoon prayer.

3. Another example is the Yevama example. If a woman becomes a widow without children and her deceased husband has an unmarried brother, then the brother has a duty to marry the widow to continue the family line. If the brother does not want to do that, he has the duty to give the widow a special 'divorce' document to enable her to be free to marry. (This is a 'way out', it is not a CTD or a 'making up'.)

4. A fourth example is the reading of the Book of Esther during the Purim festival. The obligation is to read it standing, not sitting. This is the a priori obligation. But if the reading was done sitting down, it does a posteriori discharge the reader from his obligation. The Talmud makes a distinction between our obligations before the event ('*Lechatchila*') and what is required after the event ('*Bede'eved*').

5. There are many more cases, for example where the same action violates several prohibitions and obligations, some of them contradictory. These are solved in practice (see Section 3).

REMARK 4.3. The prayer examples and the Yevama example, are very interesting. They hint to a type of contrary to duties which fulfill the original obligation and are not necessarily just secondary obligations, which kick into action when the original obligation is violated. The CTD can actually cancel the original violation. It is not a disjunction. We do not have the disjunctive option of either reading the Book of Esther standing or sitting. We should a priori try to read it standing but if we read it sitting the original obligation to read it sitting is discharged. In comparison, if I steal a book and then return it, I am still in violation of the 'do not steal' obligation. The difference is whether the obligation relates to the process or to the resulting state (after the process).

Let us further remark about the logic involved is the nature of the CTDs in the Talmud. There should be more emphasis on resolving conflicting obligations and prohibitions. The system is built for people to use and live by day-by-day. So the most important feature of the logic is to resolve conflicting obligations and prohibitions arising from a multitude of CTD all triggered by past actions. For this again we need a labelled system. Let us give a modern example to show what we mean and thus realise that ordinary deontic logic has not fully addressed such problems.

EXAMPLE 4.4. Suppose our starting point is that we have the following:

1. There should be no fence.
2. There should be no dog
3. If there is a dog there should be a fence
4. If there is a fence it should be white
5. If there is a dog and a fence it should be high
6. If there is a fence and it is not white it should be low

Some stubborn rebellious landlord does the following sequence of actions

(s1) get a dog

(s2) build a fence

(s3) paint the fence green.

He now decides to be a good boy and asks for our recommendation of what to do about his violation. Should he at least get a builder and modify the fence and make the fence high or low? How do we proceed?

First let us label his actions by the violations he performed, and ask at each stage what our recommendation would have been. Then we ask if there is a simple case of reverse actions (e.g. get rid of the dog) which will restore consistency. Then we decide what to recommend.

So this is a special case of controlled revision see [53; 54].[6]

---

[6]The following is the labelled history of actions violations. "+" means obeyance, "−" means violation.

(s1) label $[(-b)]$
(s2) label $[(-b), (+c), (-a)]$
(s3) label $[(-b), (+c), (-a), (-d)]$.

If he makes the fence low we will get also $(+f)$ and $(-e)$, and if he makes the fence high we will also have $(-f)$ and $(+e)$.

On the basis of the above history of labels we make a decision.

Controlled revision applies when we start with a theory Δ_0 and have a series of inputs $A_1, A_2, A_3 \ldots$. At stage n we have Δ_n, and when we revise to accommodate A_{n+1} we must

In anticipation of formulating a formal system for Talmudic logic, let us say that we probably need to extend **SDL** by allowing labelled formula and include a revision operator $*A$ (A revised) in the object language.

The reader should be aware that the Talmudic way of resolving conflict is different and new to the traditional methods. So there is novelty in that.

Note that Talmudic CTDs have special features as discussed in Remark 4.3. We can write OX and the contrary to duty saying that if in practice you have done X' then we consider OX as having been obeyed. So we can write OX and $\neg X \to OX'$ and if X' then there is no violation of OX.

EXAMPLE 4.5. To give you a glimpse of Talmudic style conflict resolution consider the following two obligations

1. you should always be seen wearing a black suit at official receptions

2. you must always wear a dark blue dinner suit at evening formal dinners.

You get a conflict when invited to an evening do with Her Majesty The Queen. What to wear black or dark blue? Modern non monotonic logic will say rule 2 is more specific, so it has priority. Talmudic reasoning also accepts that the more specific norm may have priority, but in this case we have another simple option: Talmudic style conflict resolution will say that in the evening in electric light dark blue looks black. So there is no conflict! Note that this is not a logical solution but a practical one.

Note that we can give a practical solution to Example 4.4 by recommending a low fence. Since the fence is painted green, it blends with the grass and plants and can be considered as not violating the obligation that there should be no fence, but only in this case!

3 Discussion: Talmudic deontic logic?

The perceptive reader might wonder what kind of (Talmudic) logic we have here. We possibly have the ordinary deontic logic **SDL** for the operators $\{O_D, F_D\}$ and we have two new completely unrelated Talmudic modalities O_T and F_T. We also have lots of examples for them. So where is the logic?

Our answer to this is twofold:

1. Consider a modal, possibly intuitionistic, logic with three separate **KD** modalities generated by O_T, F_T and O_D and study the correct axioms governing them.

2. We can equivalently regard $O_T X$ and $F_T X$ not as modalities but as labels. So each wff X will have several possible labels.

   (a) neither $O_T X$ nor $F_T \neg X$
   (b) $O_T X$ only

---

remember the entire history of revisions and revise accordingly.
So, for example, if $\Delta_0 = \{A, A \to B\}$ and we get $\neg B$, we revise and get $\Delta_1 = \{\neg B, A \to B\}$. If we now get input B, we ordinarily may revise and get $\Delta_2 = \{B, A \to B\}$. But in controlled revision we remember the history, so we know that we took out A and hence we bring it back and revise to $\Delta_2^{\text{controlled}} = \{A, A \to B\}$.

4. OBLIGATIONS AND PROHIBITIONS IN TALMUDIC DEONTIC LOGIC

(c) $F_T \neg X$ only

(d) both $O_T X$ and $F_T \neg X$

So the logic would be standard deontic logic applied to labelled formulas. This approach also goes well with the fact that O_T and F_T obligation and prohibition carry reward or punishment for obeyance and violations respectively. So the labels can be used to indicate that information as well. Modal systems with labels exist in the literature primarily as Gentzen or tableaux systems and there is work by D. Gabbay and others in this direction [46; 52]. So it should not be difficult to tailor a suitable Talmudic labelled variant of **SDL**. Our guess is that the system should also be intuitionistic, as we have already mentioned earlier.

We now address the problem of formulating an axiom system and semantics for Talmudic deontic logic.

Our first task is to understand the data better. We say that various prohibitions and obligations come in the Talmud from a divine Biblical source (annotated by O_T and F_T). We also know that we may have conflicting obligations and prohibitions emanating possibly directly from the divine source or because of a history of violations and the triggering of contrary to duties. We need to understand how to move from the T operators to the D operators. Once we understand how the Talmud does this, we can construct a logic.

So, before we offer a logic, we need to record and understand this body of data, and the way the Talmud handles conflict resolution.

To focus our thoughts, let us consider an artificial, but familiar example. (Compare with Example 4.4 and Footnote 6.)

EXAMPLE 4.6.

1. There should not be a fence.

2. There should not be a dog

3. If there is a dog there should be a fence

4. There is a dog

Let us pretend that the above are Talmudic obligations and prohibitions, given to us as follows:

1. F_T (fence)

2. F_T (dog)

3. dog → O_T (fence)

4. dog.

Notice that in whatever Talmudic logic we are going to formulate, we may not get the traditional paradox because although we can derive O_T (fence) ∧ F_T (fence), we have two different independent operators involved.

The Talmud is practical and so it needs to tell us what to do in this case.

Imagine a man comes to the Rabbi with a dog and says "Advise me; fence or no fence?".

The data is

1. F_T (fence) — a direct prohibition.

2. O_T (fence) — an obligation arising after a violation of an F_T prohibition.

A decision needs to be made.

We use O_D to indicate practical obligations, the ones which are the results of the Talmudic rules for conflict resolution which enable us to move from the T operators to the D operators and thus equip us with the tools of making day to day practical decisions. This answer is independent of A, as there is a general rule that $O_T(A)$ is stronger than $F_T(A)$ for any A.

Let us say the Rabbi tells our man to do a fence, (i.e. O_D (fence)), then we have the following decision table, Table 4.3.

Table 4.3.

	$F_T A$
$O_T A$	$O_D A$

Here we ignored the fact that $O_T A$ is a result of a CTD violation. Table 4.3 says simply that if there is a conflict between $F_T A$ and $O_T A$, then you do A, i.e. $O_D A$ is the answer.

Let us make this example more complicated. Let us add another obligation to maintain a well kept garden and the contrary to duty that if we do not do so, then we have to have a fence.

So we add to our example

5. O_T (well kept garden)

6. ¬ well kept garden → O_T (fence)

7. ¬ well kept garden.

Now the conflict is between two cases of O_T (fence) (later in the formal system we shall add an index to the T operators to enable us to represent several different uses of them) and one case of F_T (fence).

It is important to note that the Talmud regards contrary to duties as context dependent obligations and prohibitions and gives them equal standing as any other obligations and prohibitions. This is compatible with the dyadic view of contrary to duties, where we write $O_T(X/Y)$ and $F_T(X/Y)$. The Talmud even numbered all existing obligations and prohibitions; there are 248 generic obligations and 365 generic prohibitions, some of them are CTDs and some are not. So really we should write $O_{(1,T)}, \ldots, O_{(248,T)}$ and $F_{(1,T)}, \ldots, F_{(365,T)}$. So any single specific situation may potentially fall under 613 conflicting obligations and prohibitions. In our example for the single question of having a fence the number is 3.[7]

---

[7] For a discussion of why it is necessary to use 613 labelled modalities, see Section 5.2.

In fact, we shall find that the correct modelling of all obligations and prohibitions in the Talmud is by dyadic operators, $O_T(X/Y)$ and $F_T(X/Y)$, where Y is a context. The contrary to duties are cases where there is a violation and therefore the context changes to include the violation details. This also explains why the Talmud does not pay special attention to contrary to duties. All obligations and prohibitions are context dependent anyway!

The next step for us is to document a full conflict resolution table as practiced by the Talmud. If we take the dyadic view of the Obligations and prohibitions

$$O_{(1,T)}(X_1/Y_1), \ldots, O_{(248,T)}(X_{248}/Y_{248})$$

and

$$F_{(1,T)}(U_1/V_1), \ldots, F_{(365,T)}(U_{365}/V_{365}),$$

we get conflict between several obligations and prohibitions in contexts Z common to several Y_i and V_j. It is in such cases that the Talmud offers conflict resolution. The interesting aspect of the Talmudic conflict resolution is that it does not depend on the context Z or on how many previous violations were committed in the way to the context Z but it depends purely on the form $O_T(A)$, or $O_T(\neg A)$ or $F_T(A)$ or $F_T(\neg A)$ of the conflicting participants where A denotes the action discussed.

A close inspection of the Talmud reveals that the underlying logic should be intuitionistic based possibly on decided atomic facts. So doing this for our dog example, we have, (we are simplifying and not counting multiple instances of O_T and F_T, for example $O_{(i,T)}$, as above.).

Fact in question: $A =$ dog.
We want to decide

$$\text{fence} \vee \neg \text{ fence}$$

In our dog example, the Rabbi can tell the man one of the following options:

1. O_D (fence): you must have a fence

2. O_D ($\neg$ fence): you must not have a fence

3. $\neg\neg O_D$ (fence): I can only recommend that the decent thing to do is not to have a fence

4. $\neg\neg O_D(\neg$ fence): I recommend the decent thing to do is to have a fence

5. $\varnothing$: no decision, no comment, do whatever you want.

Considering the general case, there are twelve options and these options are listed in Table 4.4. This table is intuitionistic. Note that A itself, being a fact, is classical, i.e. $\neg\neg A \equiv A$ holds. Note that A is the action of having a fence.

We now form two 12×12 tables indicating how to resolve conflicts between the elements of Table 4.4. Table 4.5 indicates the conflict resolution in terms of the T operators, and Table 4.6 indicates, on the basis of Table 4.5, what should be done in practice. We use the intuitionistic operator $O_D A$ in Table 4.6. Thus Table 4.5 and Table 4.6 together give the Talmudic conflict resolution strategy.

Table 4.4. List of 12 possibilities for Talmudic obligations and or prohibitions for A

1.	$F_T(A)$	A is prohibited
2.	$\neg F_T(A)$	A is not prohibited
3.	$F_T(\neg A)$	Not doing A is prohibited
4.	$\neg F_T(\neg A)$	There is no prohibition on not doing A
5.	$\neg\neg F_T(A)$	A is not prohibited but the right mode of behaviour is not to do A, i.e. weak prohibition of A
6.	$\neg\neg F_T(\neg A)$	$\neg A$ is not prohibited but the right mode of behaviour is not to do A, i.e. weak prohibition of $\neg A$
7.	$O_T(A)$	A is obligatory
8.	$\neg O_T(A)$	A is not obligatory
9.	$O_T(\neg A)$	$\neg A$ is obligatory
10.	$\neg O_T(\neg A)$	$\neg A$ is not obligatory
11.	$\neg\neg O_T(A)$	A is not obligatory but good mode of behaviour is to do A
12.	$\neg\neg O_T(\neg A)$	$\neg A$ is not obligatory but good mode of behaviour is not to do A

For example entry $(1,3)$ of Table 4.5 is $F_T(A)$ pitted against $F_T(\neg A)$, and by P6 (b) below, $F_T(A)$ wins, and so in Table 4.5 we put "1" in box $(1,3)$, namely we put "$F_T(A)$" in box $(1,3)$. Then in Table 4.6 we put in $O_D(\neg A)$, to indicate what we do in practice.

Table 4.5. Conflict resolution table for the T operators of Table 4

	1	2	3	4	5	6	7	8	9	10	11	12
1	1	1	1	1	1,5	1	7	1	1,9	1	1	1,12
1		2	3	2,4	5	6	7	2,8	9	2,10	11	12
3			3	3	3	36	3,7	3	9	3,10	3,11	3
4				4	5	6	7	4,8	9	4,10	11	12
5					5	5	7	5	5,9	5	11	5,12
6						6	6,7	6	9	6	6,11	12
7							7	7	9	7	7,11	7
8								8	9	8,10	11	12
9									9	9	9	9,12
10										10	11	12
11											11	12
12												12

We now describe the Talmudic principles behind the construction of Table 4.5 and Table 4.6.

4. OBLIGATIONS AND PROHIBITIONS IN TALMUDIC DEONTIC LOGIC

Table 4.6. Conflict resolution table for T operators of Table 4 and their D operator result

	1	2	3	4	5	6
1.	$O_D(\neg A)$	$O_D(\neg A)$	$O_D(\neg A)$	$O_D(\neg A)$	$O_D(\neg A)$	$O_D(\neg A)$
2.		$\neg O_D(A), \neg O_D(\neg A)$	$O_D(A)$	$\neg O_D(A), \neg O_D(\neg A)$	$\neg\neg O_D(\neg A)$	$\neg\neg O_D(A)$
3.			$O_D(A)$	$O_D(A)$	$O_D(\neg A)$	$O_D(A)$
4.				$\neg O_D(A), \neg O_D(\neg A)$	$\neg\neg O_D(\neg A)$	$\neg\neg O_D(A)$
5.					$\neg\neg O_D(\neg A)$	$\neg\neg O_D(\neg A)$
6.						$\neg\neg O_D(A)$
7.						
8.						
9.						
10.						
11.						
12.						

	7	8	9	10	11	12
1.	$O_D(A)$	$O_D(\neg A)$	$O_D(\neg A)$	$O_D(\neg A)$	$O_D(\neg A)$	$O_D(\neg A)$
2.	$O_D(A)$	$\neg O_D(A), \neg O_D(\neg A)$	$O_D(\neg A)$	$\neg O_D(A), \neg O_D(\neg A)$	$\neg\neg O_D(A)$	$\neg\neg O_D(\neg A)$
3.	$O_D(A)$	$O_D(A)$	$O_D(\neg A)$	$O_D(A)$	$O_D(A)$	$O_D(A)$
4.	$O_D(A)$	$\neg O_D(A), \neg O_D(\neg A)$	$O_D(\neg A)$	$\neg O_D(A), \neg O_D(\neg A)$	$\neg\neg O_D(A)$	$\neg\neg O_D(\neg A)$
5.	$O_D(A)$	$\neg\neg O_D(\neg A)$	$O_D(\neg A)$	$\neg\neg O_D(\neg A)$	$\neg\neg O_D(A)$	$\neg\neg O_D(\neg A)$
6.	$O_D(A)$	$\neg\neg O_D(A)$	$O_D(\neg A)$	$\neg\neg O_D(A)$	$\neg\neg O_D(A)$	$\neg\neg O_D(\neg A)$
7.	$O_D(A)$	$O_D(A)$	$O_D(\neg A)$	$O_D(A)$	$O_D(A)$	$O_D(A)$
8.		$\neg O_D(A), \neg O_D(\neg A)$	$O_D(\neg A)$	$\neg O_D(A), \neg O_D(\neg A)$	$\neg\neg O_D(A)$	$\neg\neg O_D(\neg A)$
9.			$O_D(\neg A)$	$O_D(\neg A)$	$O_D(\neg A)$	$O_D(\neg A)$
10.				$\neg O_D(A), \neg O_D(\neg A)$	$\neg\neg O_D(A)$	$\neg\neg O_D(\neg A)$
11.					$\neg\neg O_D(A)$	$\neg\neg O_D(\neg A)$
12.						$\neg\neg O_D(\neg A)$

(P0): The entries in Table 4.6 uses "$O_D(A)$", "$O_D(\neg A)$", "$\neg O_D(A)$", "$\neg O_D(\neg A)$", "$\neg\neg O_D(A)$" and "$\neg\neg O_D(\neg A)$". When we write "$\neg O_D(A), \neg O_D(\neg A)$" as a single entry, we mean that no decision is made, no comment. The table is symmetrical, so we give only the entries above the diagonal.

(P1): Items 1, 3, 7 and 9 are ordinary Biblical norms.

(P2): Items 5, 6, 11 and 12 are not demands (norms) from God, but it would please God if we adopt them. In many practical cases the Rabbis and the courts force people (legislate) to adopt them.[8]

(P3): Items 2, 4, 8 and 10 mean that there is no relevant normative obligation or prohibition regarding A.

(P4): In any conflict between items in (P1) and items in (P2) and (P3), (P1) should win.

(P5): In any conflict between items in (P3) with items in (P1) or (P2), (P3) should *not* win.

(P6): In conflict between items in (P1) itself, the following are the rules:

(a) O_T is stronger than F_T, i.e. we always prefer positive norm, so O_T wins and therefore Table 4.5 gives O_T and Table 4.6 gives O_D see, for example, entry $(1, 7)$. The result is therefore O_D.

(b) In any conflict between $O_T A$ and $O_T \neg A$ or in any conflict between $F_T A$ and $F_T \neg A$, we always prefer to do nothing, hence $O_T(\neg A)$ and $F_T(A)$ respectively win, and therefore the entry in Table 4.6 is $O_D \neg A$.

Note that we need to use a mechanism to determine for each case A and $\neg A$ which one is the action and which none is the negation of action. So for example if we have $O_T(\text{sleep})$ and $O_T(\text{be awake})$ our mechanism needs to determine which one we consider action and hence call it A and which one the lack of action and call it $\neg A$. We assume that it is always clear to us which option between A and $\neg A$ is the action

(P7): When there is conflict inside group (P2), there is no clear cut rule. It is reasonable that, since O_T is stronger than F_T, we also should have that $\neg\neg O_T$ is stronger than $\neg\neg F_T$.

---

[8]To give an example, suppose I find a lost item in the street, say a handkerchief. There are two possibilities to consider

1. The owner does not bother to come back looking for it.
2. The owner will not give up and come back for it (monogrammed handkerchief).

Legally in case 1 my obligation to seek the owner does not exist since the owner has given up. In comparison in the second case I must pick up the handkerchief and find the owner or give it to the police.

However, even in the first case, it is recommended and even legislated that I try and find the owner (e.g. give it to the police), even though the owner has abandoned the handkerchief , i. e. there is no O_T obligation to return the handkerchief, but nevertheless the Talmud recommends that I return the handkerchief. Our notation for this is $\neg\neg O_T$.

Similarly it is reasonable to resolve conflict between $\neg\neg O_T A$ and $\neg\neg O_T \neg A$ or $\neg\neg F_T A$ and $\neg\neg F_T \neg A$ by choosing the "lack of action" option, i.e. $\neg\neg O_T \neg A$.

(P8): Conflicts among (P3) are meaningless. All is open and possible.

4 Intuitionistic standard deontic logic

In Section 3 we analysed the conflict resolution method in the Talmud for the operators O_T and F_T and how they relate to O_D.

Our conclusion from Example 4.6 is that we need 248 different $O_T(X/Y)$ operators and 365 different $F_T(U/V)$ operators. This should not alarm the deontic logician because in the dyadic approach, we have an infinite number of operators $O_A(X)$, one for each wff A. The difference between dyadic deontic logic and the Talmudic ones is that the Talmudic operators are generic, and apply to an ever growing open texture context situations Y and V. Let us simplify and begin by giving an Intuitionistic Standard Deontic Logic with one unary (not dyadic) O_T and one unary F_T, just to be able to compare ordinary classical **SDL** with the intuitionistic version of it. Remember also that once we fix the context Z of conflict, the dyadic operators become monadic (relative to Z), so our monadic logical machinery is applicable anyway.

We are now ready to address axiom systems and semantics.

Our strategy is to first give the operators O_T, F_T and O_D (we don't seem to need F_D!) suitable semantics and see whether Table 4.6 can be derived from some semantic principles. In formal logic this means that the system for O_D would be a nonmonotonic intuitionistic modal logic derived in some way from a monotonic intuitionistic modal logic for $\{O_T, F_T\}$. Note that this is a sound policy, as in the area of nonmonotonic logic, the classification of nonmonotonic logics is done in terms of variations on an underlying monotonic base logic.

The reader should beware that our system for O_D must be derived nonmonotonically from the system for $\{O_T, F_T\}$. If we look at Table 4.6, we see that for example, the conflict between $O_T A$ and $F_T A$ is resolved as $O_D A$. We must not be tempted and to simply write the axiom

$$O_T A \wedge F_T A \to O_D A$$

and similarly write more rules for each box in the table.

This would lead to contradictions because the logic we need is nonmonotonic.

To see this note that if we have $O_T(A)$ alone we get $O_D(A)$, and if we have $F_T(A)$ alone we get $O_D(\neg A)$. However if we have both of them we get $O_D(A)$. A monotonic logic would give us pragmatic oddity, $O_D(A) \wedge O_D(\neg A)$. For this reason we use Remark 4.4 below to define the semantics for O_D. Semantically when we have A we have the set of all worlds where A holds and hence we know the totality of all T operators it satisfies and hence we can make a decision based on all the data about A.

We begin with a semantical presentation of an intuitionistic modal logic with O_T^i and F_T^j $i = 1, \ldots, 248$ and $j = 1, \ldots, 365$. For simplicity, since all the operators are independent, we shall deal with a system with only two O_T and two F_T operators, and the usual intuitionistic connectives $\neg, \wedge, \vee, \to, \top, \bot$.

So we have O_T^1, O_T^2 and F_T^1 and F_T^2.

We need two of each because of entries in Table 4.6. For example entry $(1,3) = (F_T A, F_T \neg A)$ really means $(F_T^1 A, F_T^2 \neg A)$, where the two prohibitions F_T^1 and F_T^2 contradict. Similarly, entry $(7,9) = (O_T^1 A, O_T^2 \neg A)$.

DEFINITION 4.7. A model has the form $\mathbf{m} = (S, \leq, I_O^i, I_F^i, a, h), i = 1, 2$ where $(S, \leq, a)$ is a partially ordered set of worlds and $a \in S$ is the actual world and I_O^i, and I_F^i $i = 1, 2$ are functions associating a nonempty set of worlds with each $t \in S$.

We have
$$t \leq s \Rightarrow I(t) \supseteq I(s)$$
for each I.

For each atomic q, $h(q) \subseteq S$ is an assignment to the atoms. We have
$$t \leq s \Rightarrow t \in h(q) \rightarrow s \in h(q).$$

Satisfaction is defined as follows:

1. $t \vDash q$ iff $t \in h(q)$
2. $t \vDash A \wedge B$ iff $t \vDash A$ and $t \vDash B$
3. $t \vDash A \vee B$ iff $t \vDash A$ or $t \vDash B$
4. $t \vDash A \to B$ iff for all $t \leq s$, $s \vDash A$ implies $s \vDash B$
5. $t \vDash \neg A$ iff for all $s, t \leq s \Rightarrow s \nvDash A$
6. $t \vDash F_T^i A$ iff for all $s \in I_F^i(t)$, $s \nvDash A$
7. $t \vDash O_T^i A$ iff for all $s \in I_O^i(t)$, $s \vDash A$
8. $t \vDash \top$ and $t \nvDash \bot$
9. $\mathbf{m} \vDash A$ if $a \vDash A$.

DEFINITION 4.8. We offer the following axiom system **ISDL**

1. Axioms and rules for intuitionistic logic for $\{\neg, \wedge, \vee, \to, \top, \bot\}$.
2. $O_T^i A \wedge O_T^i(A \to B) \to O_T^i B$
3. $F_T^i(A \vee B) \leftrightarrow F_T^i A \wedge F_T^i B$
4. $\vdash O_T^i \top, \vdash F_T^i \bot, \vdash \neg O_T^i \bot$ and $\vdash F_T^i \top$
5. $\dfrac{\vdash A \to B}{\vdash O_T^i A \to O_T^i B}$
6. $\dfrac{\vdash A \to B}{\vdash F_T^i B \to F_T^i A}$

THEOREM 4.9. **ISDL** *is complete for the proposed semantics.*

Proof.

4. OBLIGATIONS AND PROHIBITIONS IN TALMUDIC DEONTIC LOGIC

1. Let S be the set of all complete consistent theories (Δ, Θ). Completeness means that for each A, $A \in \Theta$ or $A \in \Delta$ and consistency means that for no $A_i \in \Delta, B_j \in \Theta$ do we have $\vdash \bigwedge A_i \to \bigvee B_j$. We know that every consistent theory (Δ, Θ) can be extended to a complete and consistent theory (Δ', Θ'), with $\Delta \subseteq \Delta', \Theta \subseteq \Theta'$.

2. Define $(\Delta_1, \Theta_1) \leq (\Delta_2, \Theta_2)$ iff $\Delta_1 \subseteq \Delta_2$

3. Define $(\Delta', \Theta') \in I_O^i((\Delta, \Theta))$ iff for all $O_T^i X \in \Delta$ we have $X \in \Delta'$.

4. Define $(\Delta', \Theta') \in I_F^i((\Delta, \Theta))$ iff for all $F_T^i X \in \Delta$ we have $X \in \Theta'$)

5. Lemma: If $O_T^i X \in \Theta$ then for some $(\Delta', \Theta') \in I_O^i((\Delta, \Theta))$ we have $X \in \Theta'$.
   Proof. Consider $(\{Y | O_T^i Y \in \Delta\}, \{X\})$. We claim this theory is consistent. Otherwise for some $O_T^i Y_i \in \Delta$, we have
   $$\vdash \bigwedge Y_i \to X$$
   Hence
   $$\vdash \bigwedge O_T^i Y_i \to O_T^i X$$
   and we get $O_T^i X \in \Delta$, a contradiction.
   Extend the above set to a complete consistent theory (Δ_1, Θ_1) and this theory is what we need.

6. If $F_T^i X \in \Theta$, then for some $(\Delta_1, \Theta_1) \in I_F^i(\Delta, \Theta)$ we have $X \in \Delta_1$.
   Proof. Consider
   $$(\{X\}, \{Y | F_T^i Y \in \Delta\}.$$
   We claim this set is consistent. Otherwise for some $F_T^i Y_i \in \Delta$, we have
   $$\vdash X \to \bigvee Y_i.$$
   Hence $\vdash F_T^i \bigvee Y_i \to F_T^i X$ and hence
   $$\vdash \bigwedge F_T^i Y_i \to F_T^i X$$
   and hence $F_T X \in \Delta$ a contradiction.
   Extend the above set to a complete consistent theory (Δ_1, Θ_1) as needed.

7. **Lemma**
   Let $h(q) = \{(\Delta, \Theta) | q \in \Delta\}$. Then in the model $(S, \leq I_O, I_F, h)$ we have for each A $(\Delta, \Theta) \vDash A$ iff $A \in \Delta$.
   Proof.
   By induction on A

REMARK 4.10. We now add O_D to our model. Semantically we define a neighbourhood $\mathcal{N}(t)$ for each $t \in S$ and let $t \models O_D A$ iff $\{s | s \models A\} \in \mathcal{N}(t)$.

We define $\mathcal{N}(t)$ according to Table 4.6.

Let
$$+A = \{s | s \models A\}$$
$$-A = \{s | s \not\models A\}.$$

We compare the sets $\pm A$ with the sets $I_O^i(t)$ and $I_F^i(t)$, $i = 1, 2$ and decide according to Table 4.6 whether to admit $+A$ into $\mathcal{N}(t)$.

Note that because O_T and F_T are intuitionistic, the intuitionistic condition below is fulfilled for O_D as well, namely

$$t \leq s \to \mathcal{N}(t) \subseteq \mathcal{N}(s)$$

Therefore

$$t \models O_D A \land t \leq s \Rightarrow s \models O_D A \text{ holds.}$$

Note that the definition of the logic for $\{O_T, F_T, O_D\}$ is semantic. We take a model of $\{O_T, F_T\}$ and add to it $\mathcal{N}$ and make it a model of O_D.

Before we continue we need to make an important remark. Suppose a person embarks on a sequence of actions, just doing whatever he wants for a while. He may find himself in a state where a sequence of obligations and prohibitions has been triggered and some of these may be conflicting. In fact an obligation to do some A may have been triggered several times in different contexts for different reasons and similarly the obligation to do $\neg A$, as well as the prohibition to do A and the prohibition to do $\neg A$.

The big question now is what to do? In other words do we have $O_D A$ or do we have $O_D \neg A$?

We propose to use Table 4.6 for this purpose.

We need to check the coherence of Table 4.6, namely that we get a clear answer for each subset $\pm A$ whether it should be a member of $\mathcal{N}(t)$. This belief follows from conditions (P1)–(P8), especially (P4)–(P8) which clearly set out conflict resolution rules once we understand the semantic properties of O_D we can try to axiomatise it.

If it turns out that we do not have a unique answer in each case we need an expanded new table resolving conflicts between 4 operators at a time and not just two at a time. In fact Remark 4.11 below shows that the table does give unique answers. Before we systematically do all the cases, let us explain the method by giving two examples.

Take for example the triple set $\{1 : O_{1,T}(A), 2 : O_{2,T}(\neg A), 3 : F_{1,T}(A)\}$, and let us combine them in different orders and see whether we get the same outcome.

Case 1: 2 and 3 give 2 as a winner, see (P6), and now that we have 2, we carry on; 2 and 1 give 2 again by (P6) and the resolution is $4 : O_D(\neg A)$

Case 2: 1 and 2 give 2 and 2 and 3 give 2 and the resolution is again 4

Case 3: 1 and 3 give 1 and 1 and 2 give 2 and the resolution is again 4.

This is because according to Table 4.6, 2 is the strongest.

So the answer is 4 no matter at what order we combine them.

4. OBLIGATIONS AND PROHIBITIONS IN TALMUDIC DEONTIC LOGIC   141

Indeed this always true that we get a single answer for any group of 3 or 4 items. The Talmud however, does not always agree with the table. As we shall see in Remark 4.11 below, the table is only a very good approximation. Let us look at another example: Consider the triple $\{O_{1,T}(A), F_{1,T}(\neg A), O_{2,T}(\neg A)\}$, Table 4.6 will give the clear cut result $O_D(\neg A)$. However the Talmud in this case decrees that the combined power of $O_{1,T}(A), F_{1,T}(\neg A)$ together (which yields according to the usual priorities $O_T(A)$), is stronger than $O_{2,T}(\neg A)$, and so the result should be $O_D(A)$. This clearly shows that Table 4.6 is only an approximation of the way the Talmud combines obligations.

REMARK 4.11 (Coherence of Tables 4.5 and 4.6). The more complex situations for Table 4.5 are the cases of three conliciting prohibitions and obligations. We divide the cases into four classes:

Class 1: One O_T and two F_Ts.
We have two subcases. First we take two F_Ts and compare with O_T or first we take $\{O_T, F_T\}$ and comapre with the second F_T.

Case 1.1: $F_{1,T}(A), F_{2,T}(A)$ and $\{O_T(A)\}$.
In this case O_T is stronger according to entry $(1,7)$ of Table 4.5.

Although our Table 4.5 gives a clear cut answer for this triplet case, the Talmud contains a discussion about whether the answer is acceptable. Some Talmudic scholars express the opinion that two $F_T(A)$ can aggregate and be stronger than one $O_T(A)$. Other scholars accept the answer of Table 4.5 as the correct one.

So to sum up: The table yields $O_T(A)$ as the result for the triplet and thus records $O_D(A)$ in entry $(1,,7)$. In contrast, the opinion which aggregate would like to have $F_T(A)$ as the winner for this case and would therefore recommend $O_D(\neg A)$. But to aggregate we need a new (three dimensional) table, dealing with triplets.

Case 1.2 $F_{1,T}(\neg A), F_{2,T}(A)$, and $O_T(A)$.

Case 1.3 $F_{1,T}(A), F_{2,T}(\neg A)$, and $O_T(\neg A)$
In both cases, by (P6) we get the same result, namely that O_T wins. In case 1.2 $O_T(A)$ wins, and in Case 1.3 $O_T(\neg A)$ wins.

Class 2: Two O_Ts and one F_T.
Here we have $O_{1,T}, O_{2,T}$ pitted against F_T. This case is discussed explicitly in the Talmud, and there is an explicit ruling in the Talmud that $O_{1,T}$ is the winner.

Indeed Table 4.5 and (P6) give the same result.

Case 2.1: $O_{1,T}(\neg A), O_{2,T}(A)$, and $F_T(A)$.
Here the answer is immediate, $O_{1,T}(\neg A)$ is the winner. So Table 4.6 gives the answer $O_D(\neg A)$.

Case 2.2: $O_{1,T}(A), O_{2,T}(\neg A)$, and $F_T(\neg A)$.
This is a clear cut case. The answer is $O_D(\neg A)$. However the intermediate calculations using (P6) have one interesting feature.

When we combine $O_{1,T}(A)$ with $F_T(\neg A)$, we notice that they are not in conflict, but they agree. So (P6) has nothing to say about this. We do need however, a formal answer for the result. Is $O_{1,T}(A)$ the formal winner, or is $F_T(\neg A)$ the formal winner?

Fortunately, when pitted against $O_{2,T}(\neg A)$ we get that $O_{2,T}(\neg A)$ is the winner in either case and so the final answer is $O_D(\neg A)$.

So the table gives us a unique answer $O_D(\neg A)$, however, the Talmud does not accept this result. The Talmud rules that $O_{1,T}(A)$ must win.

This ruling means the Talmud is doing some aggregation and thus gets a different result from (P6) and from Table 4.5.

We can say that the Talmud aggregates $O_{1,T}(A)$ and $F_T(\neg A)$ which agree and reinforce each other into something stronger, call it $FO_T(A)$, and this wins against the third $O_{2,T}(\neg A)$. Thus $O_D(\neg A)$ is the answer the Talmud wants, contrary to Table 4.5.

We can formally add FO_T as a new operator and extend Table 4.4 with 6 additional options:

13. $FO_T(A)$
14. $\neg FO_T(A)$
15. $FO_T(\neg A)$
16. $\neg FO_T(\neg A)$
17. $\neg\neg FO_T(A)$
18. $\neg\neg FO_T(\neg A)$

We can now write a new Table 4.5, containing 18×18 entries.

However, the Talmud is not clear about some of the entries of such a new table. For example, we do not know the Talmud's view of the strength of $FO_T(\neg A)$.

So we leave Tables 4.4, 4.5 and 4.6 as they are and note that mathematically Table 4.5 is coherent and as far as our logic is concerned, we are formally OK.

Class 3: Three O_Ts.
Here there is a conflict between two $O_T(X)$ and one $O_T(\neg X)$. We distinguish two subcases.

Case 3.1: $O_{1,T}(A), O_{2,T}(A)$, and $O_{3,T}(\neg A)$.
In this case $O_{3,T}(\neg A)$ is always the winner according to Table 4.5. The question to ask is do we want to aggregate $O_{1,T}(A)$ and $O_{2,T}(A)$ and make their combined force stronger than $O_{3,T}(\neg A)$?

Indeed, some Talmudic scholars adopt this view, and liken our case to that of Case 1.2, where contrary to Table 4.5, there is the view of two F_Ts being stronger (when combined) than one O_T.

4. OBLIGATIONS AND PROHIBITIONS IN TALMUDIC DEONTIC LOGIC   143

Case 3.2: $O_{1,T}(\neg A), O_{2,T}(\neg A)$, and $O_{3,T}(A)$.
In this case it is clear that $O_T(\neg A)$ wins according to all combiantions using Table 4.6 and (P6).

Class 4: Three F_Ts.
This case is completely parallel to Class 3 with similar results.

Case 4.1: $F_{1,T}(A), F_{2,T}(A)$ and $F_{3,T}(\neg A)$.
In this case (P6) gives that $F_{3,T}(\neg A)$ is the winner. Here again some scholars might want to aggregate the two $F_T(A)$, with similar discussion to Case 3.1.

Case 4.2: $F_{1,T}(\neg A), F_{2,T}(\neg A)$, and $F_{3,T}(A)$.
In this case it is clear that $F_T(\neg A)$ is the winner.

This concludes our examination of triplets and we verified that Table 4.5 gives a clear unique answer in each case independent of the order of combination. We noted during our examination that some scholars might want to aggregate, in which case a new table needs to be agreed upon.

Our Table 4.5 is mathematically coherent for triplets. We now ask: How about sets of four? (P6) and Table 4.6 is coherent for the Talmud itself does not discuss such cases, and only some later Talmudic scholars raise some examples. We have evidence of discussions of the case of three O_Ts and one F_T.

Case 5: $O_{1,T}(A), O_{2,T}(A), O_{3,T}(\neg A)$, and $F_T(A)$.
Table 4.6 and (P6) give us the unique answer $O_D(\neg A)$. However, if we start with a choice of triplet and allow for aggregation (which is not according to Table 4.6, we get two possible answers.

1. If we start with $\{O_{1,T}(A), O_{2,T}(A), O_{3,T}(\neg A)\}$ then $O_{1,T}(A)$ and $O_{2,T}(A)$ aggregate and win and then the winning combined $O_T(A)$ continues to win against $F_T(A)$.
So the result would be $O_D(A)$.

2. If we start with $\{O_{1,T}(A), O_{3,T}(\neg A), F_T(A)\}$ then $O_{3,T}(\neg A)$ and $F_T(A)$ aggregate and win against $O_{1,T}(A)$ and continue to win further against $O_{2,T}(A)$, and the result would be $O_D(\neg A)$.
This means that the aggregation point of view is not coherent!

Case 6: $O_{1,T}(\neg A), O_{2,T}(\neg A), O_{3,T}(A)$, and $F_T(\neg A)$.
In this case Table 4.5 yields the clear cut $O_D(\neg A)$ without any dependence on the order of combination. This case differs from Case 5 in the sense that also different choice of triplets to start with give us the same answer as well, namely $O_D(\neg A)$, even if we consider disagreements on triplets. So the aggregation point of view comes out coherent in this case.

Summary: In the case of 4, we see that those who want to aggregate for the case of 3 are still not coherent for the case of 4. So the only way to remain coherent for all cases is to follow (P6) and Table 4.5.

REMARK 4.12. We make an interesting remark about the case of two O_Ts and one F_T. This is Case 2.2, where the Talmud aggregates and disagrees with Table 4.5 and (P6). However, there is some Talmudic discussion that does not seem to recognise Table 4.5.

The discussion is about how many violations occur in each case. Consider the case
$$O_{1,T}(\neg A), F_{1,T}(A), \text{ and } O_{2,T}(A).$$
This is Case 2.1. According to Table 4.6, and a God fearing man should follow $O_D(\neg A)$. Suppose a man decides to do A; we ask how many violations did the man commit? (God punsihes for violations!) We might say he violated both $O_{1,T}(\neg A)$ and $F_{1,T}(A)$. This man, however, might argue that he committed only one violation, becuase if we start with the pair $\{O_{2,T}(A), F_{1,T}(A)\}$ the winner is $O_{2,T}(A)$ and so $F_{1,T}(A)$ being the loser according to the Talmud (as reported in (P6) and Table 4.5), is out of the picture and hence cannot be violated.

On the other hand, if we start with $\{O_{1,T}(\neg A), O_{2,T}(A)\}$, then the winner is $O_{1,T}(\neg A)$, which agrees with $F_{1,T}(A)$ and so $O_D(\neg A)$ is what our man should have followed and by doing A he violates both $O_{1,T}(\neg A)$ and $F_{1,T}(A)$.

There is a disagreement among scholars with regard to the number of violations in this case, which can be explained by the order in which the triplet is applied.

In contrast to the above, in the case of $\{O_{1,T}(A), F_{1,T}(\neg A), O_{2,T}(\neg A)\}$ (this is Case 2.2), we saw here that according to Table 4.5 and (P6), $O_T(\neg A)$ wins, but we saw that the Talmud rules that $O_T(A)$ should win, by constructing the aggregated norm $FO(A)$.

Now assume a man does $\neg A$. Here we cannot explain the opinion(of some Talmudic scholars) that $F_{1,T}(\neg A)$ was not violated using an argument concerning the order of combining the norms, because $F_{1,T}(\neg A)$ is aggregated!

We can say that $\neg A$ is a lack of action and claim that one cannot violate in principle any $F_T(\neg A)$, but one can violate $F_T(A)$. However, this does not look convincing. We will ot go into this any further.

Anyway, this remark gives the reader a taste of what is involved in Talmudic argumentation about violations.

REMARK 4.13. Let us give quick comparisons with the traditional view of obligations and contrary to duties, as described in for example [1,2].

1. Talmudic obligations are generic meta-level and are open texture.

2. The Talmud uses independent obligations and prohibitions.

3. The Talmud regards contrary to duties as obligations/prohibitions arising in some context, and considers them of equal standing with original prohibitions/ obligations. Furthermore, it lists formally 613 such norms, including 248 generic obligations and 365 generic prohibitions,some of them are CTDs and some are not.

4. The Talmud provides rules and tables for conflicts between these 613 norms. It looks only at the form of the norm as in Table 5 or similar

tables and does not look at the content nor consider how the norm was activated by how many violations of how many other norms. Compare this divine approach with [1] which tries to determines logically when an obligation OA can pass on to a contrary to duty context OB. The considerations involve A and B.

5 Concluding remarks

This section will clarify some key points, as promised in the footnotes.

5.1 Reward and punishment

In ordinary Deontic logic and general legal and ethical systems, it is accepted that the difference between obligations and prohibitions manifests itself in the question of whether we are required to take active action or a deliberate lack of action. In comparison in Talmudic thinking the difference between obligations and prohibitions is something different. A biblical obligation is a requirement from a man to better himself and a prohibition is a requirement from a man to make sure he does not decline and deteriorate. The question of whether these requirements are fulfilled and obeyed by a man through his taking action or maintaining lack of action is not important.

The biblical obligation to observe the Sabbath as a holy day is achieved through lack of action (lack of doing any work). This means that the state of a man of not doing work on the Sabbath is a positive state, it makes him a better man, and we are required to achieve this state. In comparison, the biblical prohibition in Leviticus Chapter 19, verse 16 says

> Thou shalt not go up and down as a talebearer among thy people; neither shalt thou stand idly by the blood of thy neighbour: I am the LORD.

The Prohibition

> Neither shalt thou stand against the blood of thy neighbour

is the Good Samaritan Rule, requires us not to stand idle when our neighbour needs our help. It being a prohibition does mean that the Bible views the lack of helping as a negative state (and does not view the act of helping as a positive state, not according to this verse). This means that the Bible views helping and saving your neighbour in need is an elementary requirement, a *natural state for man*, and so obeying this rule does not lead to spiritual betterment but the lack of obeyance of this prohibition can lead to spiritual deterioration.

In comparison, in the case of the Sabbath, the Bible view that *natural elementary state for man* is to go to work on the Sabbath day, and the obligation to refrain from working on the Sabbath day is a requirement intended for the spiritual betterment from the natural state.

Traditional legal and ethical systems do not offer an objective definition of *man's natural state*. So in such systems they have only the distinctions between taking actions and maintaining lack of action. In Talmudic biblical law on the other hand the requirement for the betterment of man's state is given in the

Bible as an obligation and the requirement not to deteriorate to a worse state is given as a prohibition.

An example from general legal debate is the problem addressed by Robert Nozick [82; 83] regarding Seduction and Blackmail. What is the difference between the two? On the face of it, in both cases one tries to make his neighbour do something. In the case of seduction, we offer our neighbour a reward for taking the action and in the case of blackmail, we offer him punishment in case of his not taking the action. Here again we see that there is a natural state. Any requirement which is not compatible with it is blackmail and any legitimate requirement which is compatible with it is seduction. If I say to a man that if he does a job for me I shall pay him , this is seduction, because in the natural state I need not pay him. But if I say to the man that if he does not do the job for me I shall beat him up, this is blackmail. The reason for that is that not to be beaten up is an elementary right and natural state and he deserved this right even if he does not do the job for me.

How do we define the dividing line between elementary rights and such that are not? We cannot deal with this here.

The Bible indicates this distinction by the way it presents the obligations and prohibitions. If the requirement is written in the Bible as an obligation(to do an action or to maintain lack of action) then the requirement is compatible with what the Bible regards as a natural state and intends to better it, and if the required is a prohibition, then doing (or lack of doing) what is prohibited is not compatible with the natural state and causes deterioration.

We can now understand why the Bible offers a reward for fulfilling obligations and gives no reward for obeying prohibitions, while also it does not punish for not fulfilling obligations and does punish for disobeying prohibitions. The explanation is that reward is forthcoming to those who better themselves, and if they do not better themselves why punish them? On the other hand if a man deteriorates he should be punished and if he avoids deterioration why should he be rewarded?

We discuss this issue at length in the second part of our book [6].

5.2 Why 613 Talmudic operators?

We now explain why we need so many Talmudic modal operators, 248 for obligations and 365 for prohibitions. Why not have just one operator for obligations and one for prohibitions, as in standard Deontic logic?

The basic claim is that as we go through our daily life we may end up in a situation where several different biblical Obligations and prohibitions apply (coming from different sources in the Bible). For example every seventh year we must let our fields rest and we are not allowed to plough our fields. A man may plough his field on the Sabbath on the seventh year, thus he is violating two explicit prohibitions. We can have similar situations with obligations. We may end up in a situation where we have conflicting obligations.So we may have, for example

1. An obligation to do A

2. A prohibition to do A

3. Another obligation (for a different reason) to do A

4. Another obligation not to do A.

How do we represent and handle such a situation?

According to our model such situations exist only in the normative plane, in the language of the operators O_T and F_T. To indicate possible different source we need indeed 248 different O_Ts and 365 different F_Ts, to reflect what exists in the Bible.

So we represent the above situation as

1. $O_{(1,T)}(A)$

2. $F_{(1,T)}(A)$

3. $O_{(2,T)}(A)$

4. $F_{(3,T)}(\neg A)$

For the practical level, what one is actually supposed to do in any given situation? We make a decision and represent this by one operator O_D. If the decision in the case of (1)–(4) above is to do A, we write $O_D(A)$, and if the decision is not to do A, then we write $O_D(\neg A)$.

The decision what to do is done by Tables 5 and 6 and Remark 4.11.

5.3 Comparison with legislation in law

We have already remarked that the general charcteristics of Talmudic legal system is different from the general ones. This follows mainly from the fact that in general legal systems we do not have obligations in the sense of Section 5.1.

We may have laws about what to do and what not to do but not in the normative sense of Section 5.1. An ordinary legal system does not give reward for acting according to the obligations of the law; it only imposes punishment on violations of the law. Therefore there cannot be any serious distinction in general law between violation of an obligation to do something and a violation of a prohibition to do something.

In contrast, in the Talmud, such distinctions are central. An obligation is a command to better yourself and a prohibition is a command to stop yourself from deterioration, as discussed in Section 5.1. It is therefore natural that there would be different status to obligations and to prohibitions. God rewards you for obeying his obligations and either God or a local court will punish you for violating a prohibition. This is also why the Talmud requires special rules in cases of conflicts between obligations and prohibutions. We do not get too many such rules in general legal systems.

The distinctions between the normative level (O_T, F_T) and the practical level (O_D) is of course applicable also in general ethical and legal systems, and may even help resolve some legal paradoxes.

For more details, see our book [6].

5.4 Comparison with preference based models

This section will compre our results with three central papers on preference based models for obligations, namely Carmo and Jones [36], Cholvy and Garion [35], and Tore and Tan [97].

To do this successfully and avoid a lengthy presentation of the theoris of these papers, we chose an example addressed by all and use it to show the diffreneces between our chapter and their papers.

Consider the dog example:

(a.) There ought to be no dog.

(b.) If there is no dog, there ought not be a warning sign.

(c.) If there is a dog, there ought to be a warning sign.

We begin by listing the models we can form out of the propositions "dog" and "sign". These are:

$$w_1 = \text{dog} \wedge \text{sign}$$
$$w_2 = \text{dog} \wedge \neg \text{sign}$$
$$w_3 = \neg \text{dog} \wedge \text{sign}$$
$$w_4 = \neg \text{dog} \wedge \neg \text{sign}.$$

A preferential model for obligation will give a preference relation on the worlds and will derive the obligations from the preference.

Let $w \gg w'$ mean w is better than w'. For example, something reasonable compatible with (a)–(c) is:

$$w \gg w_1 \gg w_2$$

and

$$w_4 \gg w_3.$$

We can argue about what what the status of w_3 is in relation to w_2 or w_1.

The Talmudic view, as we saw, is looking at what world state we are, say w_2, and checking what obligations and prohibitions are activated in this state. In this case it would be no dog and yes sign. The Talmud gives rules to decide what to do in practice. The obligations and prohibutions activated at w_2 may be conflicting. (We might remove the dog and put up a sign!)

The preferential approach would largely ask the agent to move to a better preferred world if he can. Carmo and Jones, for example, distinguish between ideal obligation O_i (our O_T?) and actual obligation O_a (our O_D?).

There is another feature put forward by Carmo and Jones and others and this is the question of whether the agent controls the possibility of change? The agent may not be able or willing to remove the dog or put up a sign. The Talmud recognises this possiblity but does not take it into consideration in connection with the question of whether there is a violation. The Talmud always counts as violation if the state is not as it should. So if there is a dog and no sign there are violations. The Talmud might say if the sign is too expensive then the obligation is not valid, but if signs are not available at all then there is still violation.

4. OBLIGATIONS AND PROHIBITIONS IN TALMUDIC DEONTIC LOGIC

Carmo and Jones and, to some extent, Cholvy and Garion, may say that if the agent is unable to execute an obligation then either there is no obligation any more or maybe at least there is no violation. The Talmud does not make such connections.

The Torre and Tan paper presents a system of obligations based on preference and defines

α should be done if β is done is true iff

1. No $\neg \alpha \wedge \beta$ state is preferable to $\alpha \wedge \beta$ state and

2. The preferred β states are α states.

The Talmud does not use preferences to define its obligations but decrees 613 types of prohibitions and obligations.

To sum up: The above discussion shows that the preferential approach is completely different in flavour from the Talmudic approach. The preferential approach wants the agent to move to a better preferred world. So we need to look how the worlds are organised, see where we are and decide where to go.

The Talmudic approach gives obligations and prohibitions which are triggered by the state of the world you are in. These may be conflicting. There are rules to tell you what to do. You are not moving to a better world but making yourself better.

CHAPTER 5

CONTRARY TO TIME CONDITIONALS IN TALMUDIC LOGIC

Preliminaries

We consider conditionals of the form $A \Rightarrow B$ where A depends on the future and B on the present and past. We examine models for such conditional arising in Talmudic legal cases. We call such conditionals Contrary to Time (CTT) conditionals.

Three main aspects will be investigated:

1. Inverse causality from future to past, where a future condition can influence a legal event in the past (this is a man made causality).

2. Comparison with similar features in modern law.

3. New types of temporal logics arising from modelling the Talmudic examples.

    We shall see that we need a new temporal logic, which we call Talmudic Temporal Logic (**TTL**) with linear open advancing future and parallel changing past, based on two parameters for time.

1 Introduction: orientation and motivation

The Talmud is a body of legal debate and interpretations going on for hundreds of years. It contains debates and various case studies on contrary to time conditionals. We try and model in logic the intuitive way of thinking in the case studies we find in the Talmud and try and export our findings to the modern logic, AI and law community.

Having some possible logics in mind (arising from our Talmudic modelling) we begin our exposition in this section by motivating them with a variety of modern as well as Talmudic examples. We then continue in Section 2 with a short focussed introduction to temporal logic and show what temporal patterns are charateristic to the Talmud. In Section 3 we give some pure Talmudic examples. If the modern point of view is different from the Talmudic one, we highlight and discuss the differences. Section 4 explains through examples our new backward causality temporal logic and Section 5 presents the logic formally.

In Section 6 we offer a general discussion and compare our logical system with the important work of Guido Governatori and Antonino Rotolo on Changing Legal Systems: Abrogation and Annulment. We conclude in Section 7.

Let us begin.

There are four types of CTT conditionals in Talmudic logic. The pattern is

General pattern
φ at time t on the condition that ψ at time $t + s$.

Pattern 1
Objectively ψ at t has a truth value, except that we do not know it yet. We will know the value at $t + s$. See Example 5.1.

Pattern 2
Objectively ψ is an event, which may happen or may not happen, at $t + s$. See Example 5.3.

Pattern 3
Objectively, ψ is a future non-deterministic event of choice. See Example 5.4.

Pattern 4. Backward causality
ψ at $t + s$ is actually the backwards temporal (legal) cause for φ at t.

This is characteristic to the Talmud and does not exist in modern legal systems. See Examples 5.5 and 5.6.

EXAMPLE 5.1 (Pattern 1: Sale of a company). Consider the following scenario for the sale of a company: Smith sells his business to Jones on 1 January 2010. The exact amount for the sale (say x) will be determined by the company's performance during 2009. So x is defined to have value on 1 January 2010 according to the profits and growth as announced and calculated on 31 December 2010 for the period 1 January–31 December 2009. Say if growth and profits exceed 10%, the price is $x = k$ pounds, otherwise $x = 0.8k$ pounds. Such conditions are common in business. It is also common that accountants take their time in evaluating company performance, as tax returns are done a year backwards. Note that on January 2010 all the information existed about the company's 2009 performance, except that we did not know it at the time.

We have to be careful here to distinguish whether the agreement is that the purchase price is $0.8k$ and an additional $0.2k$ is paid if performance exceeds 10% or whether the performance determines the purchase price. The difference may matter for the purpose of taxation.

Smith and Jones agree that if growth is less than 1% then the sale is off, i.e. the question of whether on 1 January 2010 the company is sold or not depends on future information we get about the 2009 performance. If the performance is low, then there is no sale.

REMARK 5.2 (Discussion of Example 5.1). We need to address the following in view of Example 5.1

1. Adequate logical language to describe such phenomena, and all relevant distinctions. We call this area Contrary to Time (CTT) conditionals.

2. Identify exactly our intuitions and options for evaluating such cases.

3. See what extensions to the language in (1) are needed to model legal rulings for such cases.

There are definitely legal points which need to be clarified for this case; for example, we may ask who owns and runs the company during the year

2010? Suppose we agree that Smith continues to run the company. Suppose Mr Smith is negligent in running the company during 2010 and as a result of his mismanagement the company incurs serious losses. Can Mr Jones ask for compensation? The loss of a good company he bought? Smith can claim that there was no sale! However, had the company been sold outright on 1 January 2010 and Mr Smith was just acting as interim director, then certainly he would have been found negligent and been asked to pay compensation!

Let us compare the above sale example with a different example.

EXAMPLE 5.3 (Pattern 2: The Princess's Marriage). The King of a certain kingdom has a beautiful daughter ready to be married. To find her a husband, her father made a call to all young princes from other kingdoms to come and compete for her hand in marriage. Many came. The King said that the bravest prince who wins the test shall marry her. The test is to overcome and kill the big monster known to reside in the mountains. Some princes said that perhaps they are not qualified in bravery for such a competition. They asked "can other members of their family do the killing for them"? The King agreed that if a brother or father of the candidate does the job and slays the monster then the candidate wins.

The King was very careful in setting up this competition. He made each candidate give his daughter a ring and sign a copy of a proper set of marriage papers with the condition that the marriage becomes immediately valid if the candidate slays the monster in the future.

The candidates went to the mountains looking for the monster. Many perished in the mountains, and many were killed by the monster. Eventually one of them came back after many months with the head of the slain monster. This candidate (actually it was the brother of the candidate which qualified the candidate) now claimed the validity of the marriage and declared himself married to the princess from day 1! He was told that during all these months the princess fell ill and died!

The prince said that he is now a widower, since the marriage was valid retrospectively, and that he inherits all the princess's estates.

There are questions to be clarified about this story.

1. What is the status of the princess before the monster is slain? I.e. from the time she signed the marriage papers until the time someone killed the monster?

2. What is the status of the princess in the period if no one slays the monster? (All candidates perished.)

3. What is the status of the princess in the period if two princes cooperated and slay the monster? (The princes may have been in a position where they had to cooperate to survive an attack by the monster.) Who is married to the princess now? None?

4. If the princess died in the period, should not the deal be immediately cancelled?

Clearly we need a formal language to talk about such examples and represent what is involved.

Let us tentatively write

$\alpha(x) = x$ is a prince qualified to compete for the princess.

$\beta(x, y) = y$ is a brother or father of x

$\varphi(t, x, m) = x$ kills the monster at time t.

$\Psi(s, x, y) = x$ marries y at time s.

EXAMPLE 5.4 (Pattern 3: Insurance example). We now give a common day to day example of insurance. A car policy can be viewed as a temporal statement of the form:

$\mathbb{P}$: car stolen $\Rightarrow$ we pay

where by 'stolen' we mean any other damage as well.

The policy has validity of 12 months, say 1.1.2010–31.12.2010. Let us represent this by

$$[1.1.2010\text{–}31.12.2010] : \mathbb{P}$$

During January 2011, the policy needs to be renewed. The usual practice is that the policy can be renewed any time in January 2011 and the validity of the renewal policy would be from 1.1.2011–31.12.2011. So assume that the date of renewal (i.e. payment for the year 2011) is 20 January 2011. What is the situation of insurance coverage on 15 January 2011?

Assume the customer had no intention of renewing his policy. So he was not going to pay anything during January 2011. Then on 15 January 2011, the car was stolen. He needs to hurry and pay the premium by 31 January 2011 and his car will be insured on 15 January 2011. The insurance company cannot say that he paid because the car was stolen and otherwise he would not have paid. This is irrelevant.

So we see again we have three periods here, as in Figure 5.1.

EXAMPLE 5.5 (Pattern 4).

1. A man gives his wife legal divorce papers at time t, on the condition ψ that she does not drink alcohol for 12 months (until $t = s$).

    The condition is that if the wife does drink during the period, the divorce is annulled. This can be viewed as an instance of backward causality (man made by Talmudic law).

    The problem arises if the wife does not drink but she dies in six months. Is the divorce valid, or is it invalid?

    She certainly did not drink in the first six months and will certainly not drink afterwards (being quite dead).

    If the divorce is valid, she died free and her brother inherits. If it is not valid then she died married to her husband and he inherits.

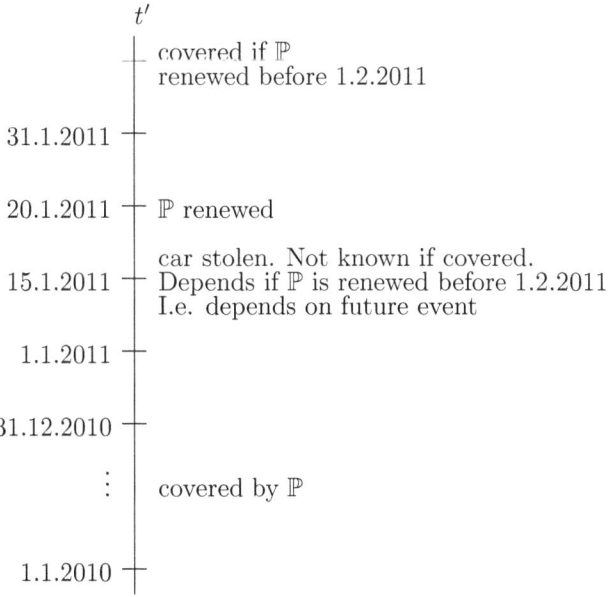

Figure 5.1.

2. Another modern example of this pattern is the following.

   John lives in a flat right next to rock musician Terry and his singer wife. John is much bothered by the noise Terry makes every night playing his music. One November (time t), John gave Terry $1000 cash to be Terry's at time t, on condition that Terry plays no music until after the New Year (time $t + s$).

   Three days later (after t), Terry died. John wants his cash back. Terry's wife said, here dead husband certainly is not going to play music. The condition would certainly be fulfilled. The Talmud sees this as a backward causality case. There are three options:

   (a) Since Terry is not available at time $t + s$, the deal is off.
   (b) The money becomes Terry's (or his heirs) at time $t + s$ only and not before.
   (c) Since we know for sure that Terry will not play music (him being dead) the money goes to Terry (or his heirs) already at the time of death.

EXAMPLE 5.6 (Pattern 4). This is a naughty example. John gives a divorce to his wife Mary at time t on the condition that she has sex with Terry at time $t + 1$.

The question we ask is are we going to allow this type of condition?

Is the condition inappropriate? Does Mary commit adultery if she has sex with Terry at time $t + 1$?

One can say that if she does have sex at time $t+1$ with Terry, then the condition of the divorce is fulfilled, Mary is divorced from time t, and so at $t+1$ there is no adultery.

However, the Talmud takes the view that Mary should not have sex with Terry at time $t+1$. If she does do that then she committed adultery and also she is divorced from time t (having fulfilled the condition).

We ask ourselves, what kind of temporal model explains these (and other rulings)? We shall see that we need a new type of logic for backwards causality.

EXAMPLE 5.7 (Divorce variations). The following examples illustrate possible logical connections between the original action and the condition it relies on

1. **Physically possible but legally forbidden condition**
   A man a signs divorce paper to his wife b on the conditions that she has sex with another man c.

   The ruling is that if she does have sex with c then the divorce is valid.

   Note that there is a fine point here. It is sinful to have sex with c while she is married to a and therefore she cannot fulfil the condition without initially sinning. Once she has sex with c then she is retrospectively divorced and therefore there is no sin.

   Compare with Example 5.11 below. (Origin and ruling in *Jerusalem Talmud and Shulhan Aruch, Even Ha-ezer*, 153-518.)

2. **Legally impossible condition**
   In *Gittin* 84–1, there is a variation of the above example, where a gives divorce to his wife on the condition that she marries c (rather than the condition of having sex with c). In this case the ruling is that she can get married to c and the marriage is legal.[1]

   The puzzling question arises that when she wants to marry c, the condition is not fulfilled yet and so she is still married to her husband a and so she cannot have a legally valid marriage to c. So how can she ever fulfill the condition? And why the ruling is that she can marry c?

   The answer is that the condition itself, because of the above considerations, is not legally consistent and so she was originally divorced without (the legally inconsistent) condition.

   Thus if an action is taken with an inconsistent condition it is deemed that the action was taken without that condition, as opposed to ruling that no action is taken (because there is something wrong with the condition).

3. **Logically looping condition**
   In *Gittin* 83–1 we have the example that a divorces his wife on the condition that she does not marry c.[2]

   As long as the woman does not marry c, her divorce from a is valid and she is divorced and can marry anyone she wants. If she marries c however,

---

[1] In practice such condition is not allowed because it looks like legalised wife swapping.
[2] c may have been b's "friend", and the husband insisted on this condition.

she violates the condition and therefore her divorce from a is not valid retrospectively, and so she is still married to a. But then, if this is the case, her marriage to c is not valid because she is still married to a!

But if her marriage to c is not valid then she has not violated the condition of her divorce from a, and therefore she is indeed divorced and therefore her marriage to c is valid, etc., etc., and we are in a loop!

4. **Condition that one of the partners dies**
   These are cases where a gives divorce to b on the condition that x dies, where x is one of $\{a, b\}$.

   Such circumstances arise when for example a is a soldier who might die in battle and would like to ensure that in the event of his death, his wife b is retrospectively free from the time he has left for the battle. This was the custom in Biblical times, as reported in *Shabat* 56-1 The case where the condition is the death of the wife is in *Yoma* 13-1.

   In both cases the ruling is that the divorce is valid

   There is also a lengthy detailed discussion of such cases in *Gittin* 72-1 and in *Kidushin* 60-1.

   In this discussion there is a need to clarify whether some specific "conditions" fall under the case of backwards causality conditional actions or cases of the use of the Iota operator.

2 Language for contrary to time with examples

This section begins in subsection 2.1 with a survey of known results outlining our conceptual options in formulating an applied temporal logic. It is a focussed introduction directed at the needs of this chapter. The reader already familiar with temporal logic might also benefit from reading this subsection, as we offer a general point of view. The reader will also appreciate better our new and novel temporal logic of section 5, against the background of this section. There will be further discussion in Section 6. We then continue in subsection 2.2 to present the temporal patterns which occur in the Talmud. We shall then continue in Section 3 and present and analyse some examples from the Talmud. All of this is in preparation for our presentation of a temporal logic for backward conditional to be given in sections 4 and 5.

2.1 Choice of language

There are in the literature two main options here:

1. Semantically based languages where we have a flow of time with branching future and a temporal language to talk about it. This we call **Traditional Temporal Logic**.

   There are many variations of such systems, depending on the flow of time, the operators used and the number of time indices used.

2. A syntactically based language where the future does not exist yet and we only have various syntactical formulas talking about it. The future

formulas can be made true by our actions but there is no future (branching or not) in which they can be semantically evaluated.

A future statement of temporal logic can be understood in two ways: the declarative way, that of describing the future as a temporal extension; and the imperative way, that of making sure that the future will happen the way we want it. Since the future has not yet happened, we have a language which can be both declarative and imperative. This we call **Executable Temporal Logic**.

Our own new **TTL** will emerge as a new third approach, capable of handling backwards causality in time. It is a completely new approach, but can be viewed as some sort of a variation of the executable family.

We now give more details on (1) and (2) above.

Traditional Temporal Logic

When deciding on how to model temporal phenomena, the first step is to decide on the flow of time. In most applications time is taken to be acyclic (non circular) with the past linear (no ambiguity or branching of the past) but with the future being branching to allow for the fact that the future is not determined.

We start with a flow of time $(T, <), T$ is the set of moments of time and $<$ is the earlier later relation. We have that $(T, <)$ satisfies the following axioms.

1. $<$ is transitive and irreflexive.

2. For every t, the set $T_{<t}$ is linearly ordered by $<$

$$T_{<t} = \{x | x \leq t\}.$$

Figure 5.2 shows that $(T, <)$ can be a tree, branching into the future with linear past.

Additional axioms on $(T, <)$ are needed to ensure the tree property. For our purpose, we need not insist on trees.

There are two points of view we can adopt when considering the flow of time.

1. The external view, where we stand outside time and look at the entire history like God viewing the history beneath us. In this case there is no fundamental difference between future and past. There is only one actual real linear flow of time, the real history as it happened, and if we have a branching flow then the real history must be marked in the flow as what actually happened. See Figure 5.2.

2. The internal view, where we see ourselves as ordinary mortals residing at some point in history, and the future is truly branching, because it has not happened yet, and all we have is our linear past.

Once we decide on how we view history, we need a language to talk about it. Again we have two options:

OPTION 1: Use a global language to talk about time in absolute sense. This is like using a global clock dates and saying for example

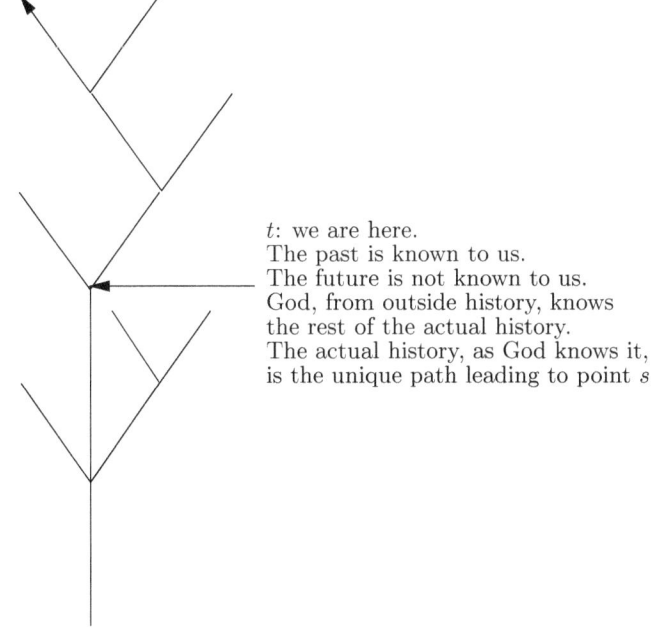

Figure 5.2.

In the year 701 BC, Sennacherib king of Assyria attacked all the fortified cities of Judah and captured them

OPTION 2: We use temporal markers relative to where we are (e.g. tomorrow, yesterday, when we got married) or markers of any kind. This is how the Bible does it:

> Kings 18:13-15 In the fourteenth year of King Hezekiahs reign, Sennacherib king of Assyria attacked all the fortified cities of Judah and captured them. So Hezekiah king of Judah sent this message to the king of Assyria at Lachish: I have done wrong. Withdraw from me, and I will pay whatever you demand of me. The king of Assyria exacted from Hezekiah king of Judah three hundred talents of silver and thirty talents of gold. So Hezekiah gave him all the silver that was found in the temple of the LORD and in the treasuries of the royal palace.

OPTION 3: Use a mixed approach, as may be convenient for the application at hand.

We shall use Option 3.

We consider a two sorted predicate logic with atoms of the form

$$P(t, x_1, \ldots, x_n).$$

The first coordinate variable t is a time variable ranging over $(T,<)$. The other variables $x_1,\ldots,x_n$, range over a variable domain D_t. We consider such $P(t,x_1,\ldots,x_n)$ as facts. We can quantify over t and x_i, and write formulas like

$$\forall x \varphi(t,x) \text{ for } \forall t \varphi(t,x).$$

It may be the case that some atomic predicates are independent of time. In this case we write $\alpha(x_1,\ldots,x_n)$ without a time variable and understand that they are either true for all time or are false for all time. So if $\forall t P(t,x) \vee \forall t \neg P(t,x)$ holds we can write it as $P(x)$.

We allow for the *Iota* operator $(\iota x)\varphi(x)$ and the $(\iota t)\varphi(t)$, meaning

"the unique x (or t) such that $\varphi(x)$ (or $\varphi(t)$) holds."

Iota can be used only when such a unique element can be proved or assumed to exist.[3]

Let the above language be called temporal **L**. It is a two sorted language. The atomic wffs of **L** are either $P(t,x_1,\ldots,x_n)$ or $t < s$.

L is closed under the classical connectives and the quantifiers $\forall t$ and $\forall x$, and the *Iota* operator $(\iota x)\varphi(x)$.

A model for **L** is a flow of time $(T,<)$ and a classical domain D_t associated with each $t \in T$.

We have an assignment h giving for each atom P a set of tuples $(t,x_1,\ldots,x_n)$ where $x_i \in D_t, i = 1,\ldots,n$.

For simplicity, let us assume that $D_t = D$ for all t. This assumption simplifies the model because we do not have to deal with $\varphi(t,x)$, when $x \notin D_t$. Of course, in real life, people are born and die and the domain changes. But also in real life we talk about dead people and yet unborn children and we refer to them and interact with "them" and do things with them and so we can allow for a predicate $\lambda(t,x)$, saying x is alive in time t. So x can be either live or a dead person or a person to be born.

Our basic statements have the form

$$s : \varphi(t_1,\ldots,t_k,x_i,\ldots,x_k).$$

reading

at time s $\varphi(t_1,\ldots,t_k,x_1,\ldots,x_k)$ is claimed to hold.

φ a complex formula, e.g.

$$\varphi = P_1(t_1,x_1) \wedge P_2(t_2,x_2).$$

---

[3]We can formulate a formal language for the Iota based on the temporal logic of the current chapter enriched with the Iota symbol. We shall have to allow for $(\iota \tau)\phi(t,\tau)$ and for $(\iota t)\phi(t,x)$ to be formed independently of any semantical condition. This means that we have to give denotation to these expressions also in the case where there exists more than one element satisfying ϕ and for the case where there exists no element satisfying ϕ.

There are several options in the literature of what to assign to the Iota expression in such cases, but as far as we know, there is no discussion in the context of temporal logic. The classical options are to make the Iota expression undefined or to assign an arbitrary element to it. In temporal logic it is better to view the Iota elements as a non existent free element which may come into existence, should a unique element show up.

There is no need for us to pursue this course of action. It is too complex. Our paper [7] and chapter 6 below avoid the use of the Iota by using quantum superposition models.

This gives rise to a two dimensional logic.

Note that we use two indices for time. The t_1, t_2 time indices are according to Option 1 and the s index which is the second dimension, is according to Option 2.

Time s, the second dimension, is where we are (Option 2) and from time s, we are talking like gods (Option 1) about other times t_i.

First note that we have to assume that for atomic sentences, all observers at s agree on the past. Thus to express this formally we need to make the assignment h depend on s. Thus $h_s(P)$ gives a set of tuples $(t, x_1, \ldots, x_n)$ meaning

According to s, $P(t, x_1, \ldots, x_n)$ holds.

Our condition becomes, for $t \leq s$

- $(t, x_1, \ldots, x_n) \in h_s(P)$ and $s \leq s' \Rightarrow (t, x_1, \ldots, x_n) \in h_{s'}(P)$.

h_s may not agree on future predictions.

So if $s < s' < t$ we may have

$(t, x_1, \ldots, x_n) \in h_s(P)$ but
$(t, x_1, \ldots, x_n) \notin h_{s'}(P)$.

Executable temporal logic

We explain the idea of executable temporal logic. Imagine that we are at time t and we consider the statement:

(*)   If p was true at $t - 1$ then q is true at $t + 1$ with p, q atomic.

Ordinary temporal logic will have a flow of time and an assignment, giving truth values to p and q at each moment of time. Given such a model, we can check whether (*) holds in model or or not.

The executable view is different. We imagine ourselves operationally living at a certain point in time, say time t. If we know the past (i.e. we have an assignment to the atoms for points $s \leq t$), but we do not know the future, as it has not happened yet. So we cannot check the truth of statement (*). What can we do?

We can make a note at time t to take action at time $t + 1$ and make q true. This of course is provided that q is under our control.

The reader can see why such executable views are useful to us in handling backwards causality because it involves day to day actions making wffs true forwards or backwards.

Our conditionals are certainly most compatible with the executable point of view since the conditions involved are set in the future.

2.2 Sample uses of the language

We now give some examples of the use of time in the Talmud.

EXAMPLE 5.8 (Sample contract). Consider:

s: x enters the room at t.

written
$$s : E(t, x, \text{room}).$$

Reading: At time s, it is said that the element x entered the room at time t. We distinguish two cases:

Case 1 $t \leq s$. This is a statement about the present or the past. It has no prediction.

Case 2 $t > s$. This is a statement about the future.

We may use, at time s, the statement $E(t, x, \text{room})$ to identify a person at time s and say something about this person.

We can say

> s: the person x who (will enter) entered the room at time t, is now (at time s) in prison.

Using the *Iota* symbol, we write
$$s : P(s, (\iota x) E(t, x, \text{room}))$$

To be able to say that and use the *Iota* symbol we need the condition that exactly one person entered the room at time t.

If $t > s$, we are identifying the person by what is going to happen to him. So at time s, $s < t$ we cannot yet be sure whom we are talking about. We can only be sure at time $s < t$ that exactly one person will enter the room at time t. We are saying at time s that whoever this person is, he is the one we are talking about.

Some people may take the view that identifying x by a future event at time t is not acceptable for some purposes (e.g. legal inheritance documents, etc). The Talmudic approach to such examples is addressed in detail in [7].

EXAMPLE 5.9. Consider the following contract $\Psi(s, a, y)$, between individual a and individual y. Assume this document is put forward for legal approval at time s. The contract has the form $s : \Psi(s, a, y)$. It is a contract at time s between a and y. The content of the contract is spelled out by Ψ. y is a variable for an individual to be identified as follows:
$$y \in Y = \{y | \alpha(s, a, y)\}.$$

$\alpha(s, a, y)$ is a predicate identifying a set of ys. If α is timeless and does not depend on s, then we write $\alpha(a, y)$.

Furthermore from among this set of ys we further identify those ys which stand in relation β to a specific z_0. If this relationship depends on s we write $\beta(s, z_0, y)$. If this relationship is timeless we write $\beta(z_0, y)$. This z_0 is identified by future time t, i.e. $z_0 = (\iota z)\varphi(t, a, z)$. Let us assume that both α and β are timeless. So we have altogether
$$\alpha(a, y) \wedge \beta((\iota z)\varphi(t, a, z_0, y).$$

It may be that α and β and φ depend on other elements $b_1, \ldots, b_k$, with possibly $b_1 = a$. In such a case we write $\alpha(s, b_i, y)$ and we write $\beta(s, b_i, z, y)$, and also $\varphi(t, b_i, y)$.

The Talmud uses $\alpha, \beta, \varphi, \psi$ in two main forms:

1. **Conditional form**

   $$s : \varphi(t, b_i, y_0) \Rightarrow \Psi(s, b_i, y_0)$$
   and
   $$s : \neg\varphi(t, b_i, y_0) \Rightarrow \neg\Psi(s, b_i, y_0)$$

   where $t > s$ and where y_0 is a certain named individual and where $\Rightarrow$ is a possibly nonclassical strict or resource implication or an intuitionistic constructive implication. We require $\Rightarrow$ to satisfy modus ponens

   $$A, A \Rightarrow B \vdash B$$

   In Hebrew the name for this is "Tenai", meaning "condition".

2. **Choice form**
   (In Hebrew the name is "Breira", meaning "choice".)
   The form is

   $$\Psi(s, b_i, y) \equiv \alpha(b_i, y) \wedge \beta(b_i, y, (\iota z)\varphi(t, b_i, z))$$

   where y is a variable, $t > s$ and the predicate $\varphi(t, b_i, z)$ defines a unique z at time t, unique because $\exists! z \varphi$ is assumed to hold, or hoped that it will hold!

   So what is happening here is that $a = b_1$ says I want to enter in contraction relation with an element $y \in Y$.

   The identity of this element is determined by φ. β says what is the nature of the relationship that a enters with each possible y.

   Both β and φ may depend on additional elements b_i which may include $b_1 = a$ or not, i.e. we have $\varphi(t, b_i, z)$ and $\beta(z, b_i, y)$. For the purposes of comparison, note that if the conditional is expressed in classical logic we get
   Classical logic conditional:

   $$\Psi(s, b_i, y_0) \equiv \varphi(t, b_i, y_0).$$

   Parameters of importance here are the following:

   (a) does Y allow for more than one element?
   (b) Is $t > s$ or $t \leq s$? How is t defined? It may be defined or specified as $s : \gamma(t, x_i)$ in which case is there a unique t_0 known at s or only known at some later t, $s < t < t_0$?
   (c) Is a one of the b_i?

Here is an example:

EXAMPLE 5.10 (Sample choice form: Breira). a says "I will sell to one of my cousins either my Montblanc pen or my Parker pen".

The pen I sell depends on the cousin and on a third party b. There are two cousins John and Mary. If I sell to cousin John, it will be the Parker pen. If I sell to cousin Mary then which pen I sell depends on party b. The dependence on b is whether b wins the election tomorrow. The cousin of choice for sale is the one who calls me first tomorrow to ask about the sale. Here $\alpha(a, y)$ is

> "y is cousin to a" (i.e. $y =$ John or $y =$ Mary).

$\beta(z, y)$ is

> "a sells Montblanc to z if b wins and $z =$ Mary and a sells Parker to z if z is cousin John".

3 Introducing temporal Talmudic logic (TTL)

In this section we discuss our advancing future–changing past model, capable of handling conditionals.

We begin with methodological remarks, on how we discovered Talmudic Temporal Logic. There are many examples and discussions in the Talmud about various cases of conditional actions and various legal rulings about them. This is our body of evidence. We were looking for a temporal model which can accommodate and explain all the different approaches and views of the Talmudic scholars discussing and ruling about all of these examples. What we call **TTL** is the simplest such model which can do the job.

What do we mean by a logical model? One's immediate reaction might be just to give syntax and semantics for the appropriate language and define logical consequence using the semantics. However, this is not sufficient for two reasons:

1. The Talmudic data by nature is a body of arguments, counter arguments and debates and so we would expect modelling using a proof theoretical and arugmentation system which can also model the way the debates are executed.

2. The nature of the temporal examples, as we shall see below, involves alternative histories which then disappear as time goes on, and so even if we give a many dimensional parallel histories semantic model, the natural way of defining a semantic consequence will be too weak to reflect what is really happening unless we are able to add to the language syntactical constructs explicitly talking about alternative histories. Such constructs, however, are not present in the Talmud.

In this section we introduce **TTL** using modern examples. The next section will present **TTL** as a formal logic and later we show how this model explains Talmudic examples. A very detailed discussion can be found in our companion book [8].

We begin with some preliminary distinctions

1. **Backward causation vs normative retroactivity**
   Backward causation is when the effects can precede the causes, and normative and legal retroactivity is when we legislate backwards in time. There are similarities but the concepts are not the same.

5. CONTRARY TO TIME CONDITIONALS IN TALMUDIC LOGIC

Conditional patterns 1-3 are more like normative retroactivity, while conditional pattern 4 is indeed man made backward causality.

The temporal modelling of normative retroactivity can be handled in traditional two dimensional temporal logic, as Governatori and Rotolo have admirably shown since 2005. See [64]. We offer also a logical model of parallel worlds (Fisher).

The backward causality pattern 4 does require specialised temporal modelling. Let us illustrate this distinction using item 2 of Example 5.5.

In November (time t), John gave Terry $ 1000 cash to be Terry's at time t, on condition that Terry plays no music until after the New Year (time $t + s$). Three days later (after t), Terry died. John wants his cash back.

Terry's wife said, her dead husband certainly is not going to play music. The condition would certainly be fulfilled. The Talmud debates whether this case is a a backward causality case. There are three options:

(a) Since Terry is not available at time $t + s$, the deal is off.

(b) The money becomes Terry's (or his heirs) at time t but this is clearly finalised at time $t + s$ only and not before.

(c) Since we know for sure that Terry will not play music (him being dead) the money goes to Terry (or his heirs) at time t but this is clearly finalised already at the time of death.

There are two views in the Talmud of this example:

The Fisher view: The view of Rabbi Fisher, who views this and indeed all backwards conditionals as cases similar to normative retroactivity. Fisher models these cases using parallel histories. One history in which the condition is fulfilled and one history in which the condition is not fulfilled. At time $t + 3$ it was clear which history prevailed and hence Fisher votes for option (c).

The Shkop view: The view of Rabbi Shkop is that we are dealing with a case of backward causality which the Talmud stipulated/created for us. The temporal model which explains this causality is that at time t both John and Terry progress temporally forward to time $t + s$ at which time the condition is checked. If it holds then John and Terry both jump back in a simulated time line, back to time t, finalise the deal and move again along the time line back to time $t + s$.

This means that

- John and Terry travel a simulated temporal distance of $2s + 1$.
- If one of them dies or changes his mind at real time between t and $t + s$ then the deal is off, (both have to jump back at time $t + s$).
- The deal is not finalised until after they jump back to time t in the simulated time line. So the deal is still open at real time $t + s$.

According to the above model, Shkop would support option (a) above. Some followers of the Shkop view might support (b).

The difference between Fisher and Shkop is sharpened in Example 5.6.

John gives a divorce to his wife Mary at time t on the condition that she has sex with Terry at time $t+1$.

According to Fisher, there are two parallel histories. One in which Mary has sex with Terry at time $t+1$, and one in which she does not.

If she does not have sex with Terry, she is not divorced at time t and since factually she did not have sex with Terry, she did not commit adultery.

If she does have sex with Terry then we are at the history where she fulfils the condition and so she is divorced from time t, and so in this history, having sex with Terry at time $t+1$ is not adultery.

So in either case, Mary did not commit adultery.

The Shkop model behaves differently. Mary moves in time from t to $t+1$. If she does not have sex with Terry at time $t+1$, the condition is not fulfilled and there is no divorce. If she does have sex with Terry at time $t+1$, she and John jump back in simulated time to point t and conclude the divorce then, and then continue back to $t+1$. The divorce is valid at real time t through backward causality, but in the simulated time at $t+1$ before she jumped back she had sex with Terry while she was still married and so in the simulated time she committed adultery!

Let us consider another example, suggested to us by the referee. Consider the following simple case: one states at time t that some X should hold at $t-1$ if condition Y holds at time t. Here, such a provision simply changes things from t onwards as if they were changed in the past, but the past is not in fact changed, because this is impossible: This is normative retroactivity and it has only a counterfactual character. This is the Fisher view of parallel histories. Changing our view of the past without actually changing the past is something that happens in the law, for example, when tax law states in 2011 an increase of 10% of the tax rate starting from 2009 thus obtaining, e.g., an overall tax rate of 40%. This does not mean that from 2011 onwards the tax legislation of 2009 stated that the rate was 40%: if this were the case, those who paid in 2009 and 2010 only the 30% of their annual income (as it was required at that time) are tax dodgers, which is not. Here, all taxpayers are only required to pay in 2011 two extra amounts: 10% of their annual incomes in 2009 and 2010; such extra payments work as requested, i.e., as if taxpayers had paid 40% in 2009 and 2010. However, for comparison, if backward causality is allowed here and the 2009 legislation was done conditional on some future condition, then we would have a debate between the Shkop view and the Fisher view in this case.

To explain more sharply the theological roots of the difference between Rabbi Shkop and Rabbi Fisher, consider the following:

Man creates social states (ownership, marriage, legal death, tax obligations, etc) by agreement and legislation. Some of these states (marriage for example) are done by the blessing and permission of God. Shkop believes that God also allowed for these states to be subjected to backwards causality (as God has perhaps done in Physics). Fisher does not believes that and accepts only parallel histories and normative retroactivity.

By the way in modern law, retroactivity in legislation is not the same as retroactivity in contract law. This distinction is crucial in most modern legal systems. In the Talmud they are treated the same.

2. **The role of presumptions in the legal domain**
   The referee suggested a slightly more complex example, where the lawmaker states at time t that some X should hold at $t - x$ if condition Y occurs at time $t + y$. Should X hold at any moment of time from $t - 1$ to $t + y - 1$? Here we need more than one temporal dimension. (Note that this idea was already explored by Governatori and colleagues: see [64])
   If our temporal viewpoint is time t, and we model the situations as

   $$t : [Y \text{ holds at } t + y \Rightarrow X \text{ holds at } t - x]$$

   then we cannot derive (X holds at $t - x$) (from the perspective of real time t', for any t' between $t - x$ and $t + y - 1$.

   Things may be different in the law, since here legal presumptions apply.

   Consider nother example by the referee, a sales contract. If I sell now to you my house A on the condition that you will be selling your own house B in a month to anyone else, the law presumes that you are the owner of A, but this presumption can be rebutted (and the legal effect retroactively cancelled) if you do not meet the condition. This is an example of a conditional contract, which could be modelled, in traditional two dimensional temporal logic. Such distinctions are central in most modern legal systems.

   The Talmud does handle this type of consideration, and in a very fine tuned way. We have a companion book [8], of over 600 pages, unfortunately in Hebrew, dealing with such issues, in chapters 26–28, pages 505–585. The current chapter concentrates on modelling the main features of backward causality, which give rise to a novel temporal logic.

We now begin describing our logic in more detail. First we need to clarify some concepts. Consider the following statements.

1. The vase is broken into two pieces.

2. Mary is married.

3. John's income is from employment on a sea-faring ship. (Therefore is tax free!)

Statement 1 is a physical statement. It is not a legal or social convention statement. One has a bit of leeway in understanding what "two pieces"means and if one piece is very small we might say that the vase is "chipped", not broken. We might even argue, in the case of a slightly bigger piece, whether

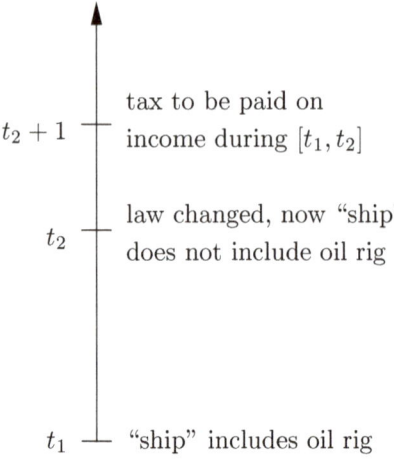

Figure 5.3.

we can still say "chipped", or say "broken". The difference may be important for insurance purposes. Do we replace the vase or do we fix it? It may even be the case that the insurers stipulate that "broken" means, as far as they are concerned, broken into 3 pieces or more, but now we are into the legal domain.

Statement 2 is a statement of legal and social agreement. Society and the law allows for a marriage action **a** to take place, provided certain preconditions $\mathbb{C}_\mathbf{a}$ do hold and the result of which we get the truth of the legal predicate x is married to y. x is married is $\exists y(x$ is married to $y)$.

Being a legal predicate, the marriage status can be changed by a divorce action **b**. Again, given preconditions $\mathbb{C}_\mathbf{b}$ we can make true the predicate x Divorce y. We have that if x Divorce y holds at time t, then $\neg(x$ is married to $y)$ holds at t.

This is different from "broken" predicate. No action can "$\neg$ break". We can "glue" the pieces but what we get is "broken but glued" or "broken (leg) but healed", etc.

Statement 3 is also a legal statement. Here one can legally change the meaning of "employment on a ship". In fact the British definition included working on an oil rig. To increase taxation the government changed the meaning into "moving ship", thus excluding oil rigs.

Such a move can cause a lot of resentment because it involves backward taxation as Figure 5.3 shows

The British tax system would claim that this is not backwards legislation as the tax assessment is done at $t_2 + 1$. However, for the legislation not to be backwards one should adopt the meaning of "ship" as it was at $[t_1, t_2]$ for the purpose of tax paid at $t_2 + 1$ on the period $[t_1, t_2]$.

We understand that countries like Austria, never legislate backwards. It is taboo! So the new definition of "ship" will be applied only to employment after t_2!

Let us summarise what we need for our logic. We need to allow for time dependent predicates of legal and social nature generated by actions. We write them as follows:

- $t \vDash P(x_1,\ldots,x_n)$ if action **a** is taken by $x_1,\ldots,x_n$ at time t satisfying the pre-conditions $\mathbb{C}_\mathbf{a}$.

- $t \vDash \neg P(x_1,\ldots,x_n)$ if either no action **a** was taken in the past or a cancelling action **b** was taken at t, with preconditions $\mathbb{C}_\mathbf{b}$.

It is with this sort of predicates we want to present our logic **TTL**.

EXAMPLE 5.11. Two security agents meet in a bar having a beer and discussing their profession. Say Microsoft chief security officer **m** and Google chief security officer **g**. **m** boasts to **g** that his methods are impregnable. **g** admits **m** is good but not perfect. **m** challenges **g**. He says:

> I have a laptop in my office which is security protected. I shall clear the disk drive and leave it on the internet. At 18.00 hours it will be security protected and I shall call you and give you this laptop to be immediately yours on the condition that you break into it within 30 minutes.

m cautions **g** that he had better not trip any alarms because it is illegal to hack into the system.[4]

We have here three periods of time

1. Before 18.00

2. From 18.00 to 18.30.

3. After 18.30

During period 2 it is not clear who owns the laptop.

After 3, the situation clarifies. There are two approaches of how to model the situation.

1. *The Fisher approach*[5]

    From 18.00–18.30 we have two parallel histories. One in which the laptop belongs to **m** and **g** is unable to hack into it and second in whch the laptop belongs to **g** (from18.00) and **g** was able to hack into it. At 18.30 we know which history is real. At period 3, after 18.30, there is only one history.

    Note that according to Fisher, no crime has been committed by **g**. Even if he managed to hack into the laptop, this made the laptop his from 18.00 and there is no crime to hack into one's own laptop.

    Furthermore, even if **m** dies between 18.00 and 18.30, the deal is on — nothing changes!

---

[4]According to British law **m**, by making the offer to **g** is already giving him permission to hack into the laptop.

We can change the example a bit. **m** sells the laptop to **a**. **a** makes the condition that if anyone hacks into it between 18.00–18.30 then the deal is off. Now **m** gives the laptop to **g** under the condition that **g** hacks into it between 18.00–18.30. Now **g** would commit a crime.

[5]Rabbi Shlomo Fisher, 1932–.

Also if **m** changes his mind at 18.15, he cannot cancel the deal. Ownership of the laptop has already been (conditionally) transferred at 18.00!

2. *The Shkop approach*[6]
   This view says that the deal is completed and actually executed at 18.30. Hence

   (a) **g** commits a crime in hacking into the laptop because at the time of hacking the laptop was not yet his.

   (b) If **m** dies at 18.15 or changes his mind and cancels, then the deal is off as he (**m**) is not there to execute the deal at 18.30.

How do we model Shkop's view? We need dual time t and τ:

$$t = 18.00, \ldots, 18.15, \ldots, 18.30, \ldots, 19.00$$
τ = simulated time in minutes.
We start at $\tau = 0$ at $t = 18.00$, continue to $\tau = 30$ at $t = 18.30$ and immediately go back to $t = 18.00$,[7]
At $\tau = 30$ **m** and **g** complete the deal, then carry on to $t = 18.30, \tau = 60$ and continue to eternity with t and τ.

Think of it as that both **m** and **g** jumping instantly back from time $t = 18.30$ to $t = 18.00$ using a time machine and completing the deal. Their personal time is τ. They live through history again and are back at $t = 18.30$ with their personal time τ being 60 minutes.

With τ, we remember that crime was committed at $\tau = 30$. If **m** dies at 18.15 then he cannot go back at 18.30 ($\tau = 30$) to the beginning ($t = 18.00, \tau = 30$), to complete the deal.

REMARK 5.12 (Semantic discussion of the Fisher approach). Let us appreciate the difficulties in modelling the Fisher approach. The Fisher view gives rise to a temporal history without memory. If you go with time to infinity then there is only one linear past without any memory that it could have been otherwise. It cannot be modelled by branching time with one infinite branch being the real history because it allows for memory of alternatives.

EXAMPLE 5.13 (Iterated conditions). Once we allow conditional legal actions of the form **a** at t conditional on **b** at $t+s$, we should be able to iterate. Figure 5.4 shows such a case.

The story is as follows: John gives Mary a pen to be her property immediately at time t on the condition that she buys some shares at time $t+s$. At time $t+s$ Mary approaches Terry who has shares and he is willing to sell Mary his shares to be hers immediately on the condition that Mary does his garden on $t+s+r$.

The first comment we make is that we consider we have two actions here:

1. Action **a** starting at time $x = t$ with condition at time $x + s$.

---

[6] Rabbi Shimon Shkop, 1869–1939.
[7] At $\tau = 30$ there is a discontinuous jump from $t = 18.30$ back to $t = 18.00$.

5. CONTRARY TO TIME CONDITIONALS IN TALMUDIC LOGIC

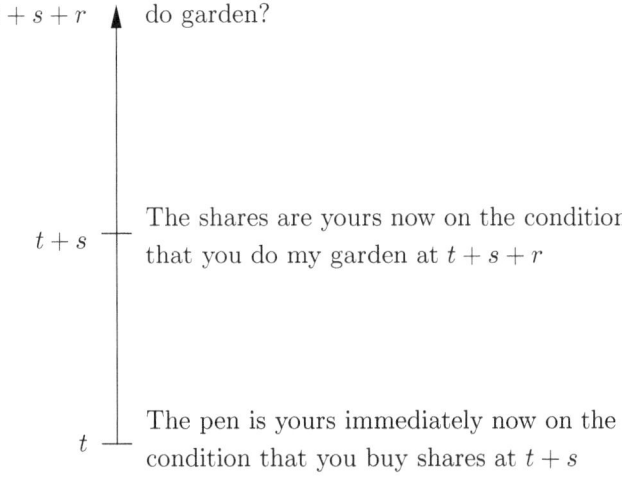

Figure 5.4.

2. Action **b** starting at time $y = t + s$ with condition at time $y + r$.

According to Fisher we have two conditional actions which are chained by making basically $y = x + s$.

According to Shkop, we also have two actions which are chained by making $y = x + s$. However according to Shkop the actions retain their identity as distinct actions in the sense that each action has its own τ. So action **a** has τ and action **b** has τ'.

According to Fisher, we have two parallel histories. See Figures 5.5, 5.6. The real history is decided on time $t + s + r$.

According to Shkop, Figure 5.4 turns into Figure 5.7 as follows.

We start with action **a** at t and $\tau = 0$. At $t + s$ we have $\tau = s$. We want to jump back using our time machine and be again at t but with $\tau = s$. We ask ourselves: where are the shares? Do we have them at time $t + s$ (with $\tau = s$)? Can we jump back? Is the matter of the shares decided at $t + s$ so that we can jump back and conclude the deal if Mary bought the shares or cancel it if Mary does not have the shares? The answer is that we don't know yet, it depends on action **b**. Well, we have the shares but on the condition of Mary doing the garden at $t + s + r$.

OK then. We cannot jump back with τ at $\tau = s$, because we have to wait for action **b** to play itself out with its own τ'.

So action **a** does not jump back to t, action **a** has to wait for action **b**. So both action **a** and action **b** proceed together to time $t + s + r$.

So now $\tau = s + r$ and $\tau' = r$ and both actions are sitting at time $t + s + r$. Action **a** is waiting for action **b** to jump with its τ' back to time $t + r$ and decide the matter of whether Mary buying the shares is successful. So τ' jumps back to time $t + r$ and decides the matter of Mary's owning the shares (depending on her doing the garden at time $t + s + r$) and then τ' goes back to time $t + s + r$. By this time $\tau' = 2r$. While τ' was jumping back τ was sitting at $t + s + r$,

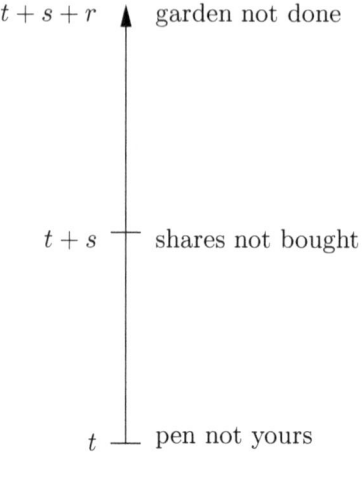

Figure 5.5.

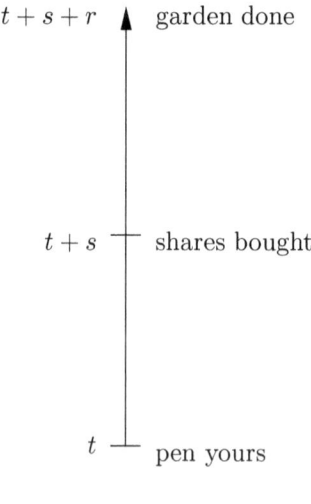

Figure 5.6.

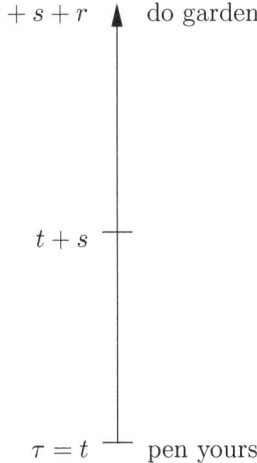

Figure 5.7.

with $\tau = s + r$, waiting for an answer from **b**. The changes in τ' have nothing to do with τ. It is an internal action **b** simulation.

Once action **a** gets an answer from **b** it jumps back to time t, decides whether the pen belongs to Mary and proceeds back to time $t+s$. At this time $\tau = (s+r)+s$. Now it is known whether the condition **b** holds so τ jumps back to t and proceeds straight back to $t+s+r$. By this time $\tau = (s+r)+(2s+r) = 3s+2r$.

Notice that in this case action **a** is equivalent to a new action **a'** comprised of the giving of pen at time t on the condition of buying shares at $t+s$ with a final decision time of doing the garden on $t+s+r$.

The following is the scenario for action **a'**.

The τ count starts with $\tau = 0$ at at t! See Figure 5.7.

The situation clarifies and the deal is executed on time $t+s+r$ with $\tau = s+r$. At that time we go back to t to execute the deal and $\tau = s+r$ carries on through history again back to time $t+s$ where another jump back is done to time t and then we go straight to time $t+s+r$ with $\tau = (s+r) + (2s+r) = 3s+2r$.

EXAMPLE 5.14 (Logical loop). Let us analyse now case 4 of example 5.7.

> Time $t = 0$: a gives divorce to b on the condition that she never marries c
> Time $t = s$: [b has married c before time s] or [b has not married c before time s]

Analysis according to Fisher:
We have two parallel histories beginning at $t = 0$ and ending at $t = s$. At $t = s$ a decision is made as to which history is real.

History 1:
[At $t = 0$, b is divorced from a] and [at $t = s$, b has not married c before time s]
History 2:

[At $t = 0$, b is not divorced from a] and [at $t = s$, b has married c before time s].

Obviously History 2 is legally inconsistent and therefore History 1 prevails.

Analysis according to Shkop:
Start at $t = 0$ and $\tau = 0$. Continue to $t = s$ and $\tau = s$.

Case 1:
If b has not married c up to s then carry on with t and τ to $s + 1$ and repeat the case analysis.

Case 2:
If b has indeed married c then assume s is the first time this is done. Jump back to $t = 0$ and $\tau = s$ and cancel the divorce. Continue forward from this point (i.e. $t = 0$ and $\tau = s$) and reach any $t = r$ and $\tau = s + r$ for any r. b can never marry anybody at $\tau = s + r$ since she is already married to a since $\tau = s$.

EXAMPLE 5.15 (Two actions). Let us have two actions. One giving the laptop at $t = 18.00$ and the other giving the pen also at $t = 18.00$. What do we do?

We need two τ counts. One for the laptop, τ_1 and one for the pen, τ_2. In fact, during a normal history with many actions and many chains, we have as many τs counting simulated time.

REMARK 5.16 (Analysis of chains). We now want to analyse Example 5.13 and prepare ourselves for Example 5.18.

Let us start with action **b** of Example 5.13. This action starts at an abstract time y (which was instantiated as $y = t + s$) trying to make the predicate $P_\mathbf{b} =$ "Mary owns shares" true at y.

The truth value of the predicate was not clarified until time $y + r$. At this time the final predicate $Q_\mathbf{b} =$ "Mary doing the garden" was the one whose truth value clarified the status of the starting predicate $P_\mathbf{b}$.

Taken in the abstract, the relevant parameters of action **b** are as follows:

1. Starting time y

2. Predicate involved is $P_\mathbf{b}$

3. Stretch of the action, namely the duration until the predicate $Q_\mathbf{b}$ is to be determined, is r (i.e. it goes from y to $y + r$)

4. The final predicate which clarifies the state of the predicate $Q'_\mathbf{b} = Q_\mathbf{b}$, at the same time $y + r$.

Let us now do a similar analysis for action **a**.

1. Starting time is x

2. Predicate involved is $P_\mathbf{a}$, ("Pen belongs to Mary at time x")

3. Stretch is s, with predicate $Q_\mathbf{a}$ at time $x + s$

4. The final predicate which clarifies the status of $Q_\mathbf{a}$ is $Q'_\mathbf{a} = Q_\mathbf{a}$ also at time $x + s$.

How do we make a chain of these two abstract actions? We equate the final predicate of **a** with the initial predicate of **b** and say at what time. In example 5.13 we did the following:

1. Let $Q'_\mathbf{a} = P_\mathbf{b}$
2. For the time let Equation (x, y) be: $y = x + s$

This chaining resulted in a new action, which we called **a**':

1. Starting time is x
2. $P_{\mathbf{a}'} = P_\mathbf{a}$
3. Stretch is s with $Q_\mathbf{a} = P_\mathbf{b}$
4. Final predicate $Q'_\mathbf{a}$ is $Q_\mathbf{b}$ at time $x + s + r$.

Note that we could have chosen a different equation for the combination of **a** and **b**, we could have chosen $y = x + s - 1$. In this case we would have got a new action, say **a**'' with stretch $s + r - 1$.

In practice, when combining actions such as **a** and **b**, one does not write any equation between x and y. When x and y are realised in a real time model, they get specific time values, and the equation is determined automatically. Example 5.18 below is such an example.

The exact formal definitions of action combination is worked out in Section 6.

REMARK 5.17. Note that we are dealing here with a single condition $Q_\mathbf{a}$ for the action **a**. In other words the conditional is of the form:

- $P_\mathbf{a}$ now at time t, on the condition that $Q_\mathbf{a}$ later at time $t + s$.

For example

- The pen is yours immediately now at time t, on the condition that you buy shares at $t + s$.

We have only one atomic condition and no more. So we are not addressing multiple conditions of the form:

- $P_\mathbf{a}$ now at time t, on the condition that for $i = 1, \ldots, k$ we have $Q(i, \mathbf{a})$ holds later at time $t + s_i$.

For example we are not dealing with:

- The pen is yours immediately now at time t, on the condition that you buy shares at $t + s$ and put your computer on Ebay at $t + r$.

There is no technical difficulty in addressing multiple conditions, it is just that such examples do not appear in the Talmud in this form.

The Talmud can have conditions of the form:

- The pen is yours immediately now at time t, on the condition that you DO NOT sell your shares BEFORE time $t + s$.

This has the formal form:

- $\neg P_\mathbf{a}$ now at time t, on the condition that $Q_\mathbf{a}$ holds at a time r such that $t < r < t + s$

or equivalently

- P_a now at time t, on the condition that $Q_\mathbf{a}$ holds at all times r such that $t < r < t + s$.

We may have some difficulties with chaining such conditions. Obviously we have no problems chaining if maintaining that $Q_\mathbf{a}$ holds at all times r such that $t < r < t + s$ is enabled by some condition **b** executed after time s. However what if for each $r, t < r < s$ we need to promise a separate condition $\mathbf{b}(r)$ to ensure that $Q_\mathbf{a}$ holds at r?

This would fall under item (2) of Definition 5.23 below.

EXAMPLE 5.18 (Cross chain dependency). We start with the chain action of Figure 5.6. This is the chain action discussed already in Example 5.13 and Remark 5.16. We now want to chain into it a new action **c**.

The laptop is yours at $t - 1$ provided the pen is yours at $t + s + \frac{r}{2}$ (of Figure 5.6).

We have two actions here to be synchronised. See Figure 5.8.

We start counting $\tau_1 = 0$ at $t - 1$. We get to time $t + s + \frac{r}{2}$ with $\tau_1 = 1 + s + \frac{r}{2}$ and ask "Is the pen yours?".

Well, at this time there is the τ_2 counting of the pen. τ_2 counting at $t + s + \frac{r}{2}$ is at $\tau_2 = s + \frac{r}{2}$. We have to wait another $\frac{r}{2}$ for τ_2 to get to $s + r$ and τ_1 to get to $1 + s + r$. The real time is now $t + s + r$. Then τ_2 has to go back to t to complete the pen deal and advance back to time $t + s$, double back to t and then proceed to $t + s + r$. This takes $\tau_2 = 3s + 2r$ minutes.

Note that τ_1 does not change, it does not care what τ_2 does. So τ_1 is equal $(1 + s + r)$. When τ_2 reaches time $t + s + r$ it "informs" τ_1 that the pen deal is done. Now τ_1 jumps back to $t - 1$ to complete his deal. The jumping is from real time point $t + s + r$. τ_1 advances another simulated time from $t - 1$ $t + s + \frac{r}{2}$ where the deal is supposed to be done and then jump back to t to clinch the deal and then proceed straight to $t + s + r$ because the real time $t + s + r$ is where τ_1 is. He can now confirm the deal is done. This brings us to

$$\begin{aligned}\tau_1 &= (1 + s + r) + (1 + s + \tfrac{r}{2}) + (1 + s + r)\\ &= 3 + 3s + \tfrac{5}{2}r.\end{aligned}$$

Note that $\tau_2 = 3s + 2r$ as calculated in Example 5.13.[8]

From $t + s + r$ real time τ_1 and τ_2 continue to tick.

EXAMPLE 5.19 (Contrary to duties in the Talmud). These have been analysed in [9; 5]. Some of them are temporal, what we called Type CTD III.

You should not steal, and if you did steal, you have an obligation to return or pay for the stolen object. If you do return the stolen object, the violation is cancelled retrospectively. This is why the Talmud does not recommend immediate

---

[8]Note that what we call τ_2 here is called τ in Example 5.13, it is the τ of action **a'** at that example.

5. CONTRARY TO TIME CONDITIONALS IN TALMUDIC LOGIC

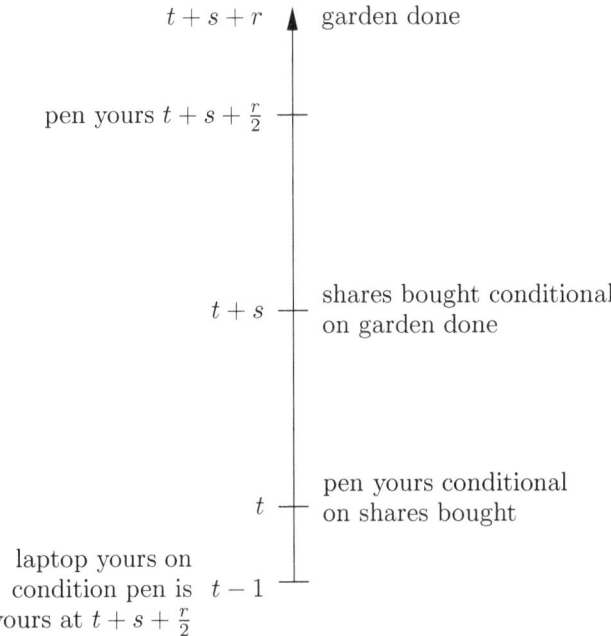

Figure 5.8. Right hand side = pen ownership conditions; left hand side = laptop ownership conditions

punishment for stealing because the action might be cancelled retrospectively in the future by returning the object.

We make two relevant comments here.

1. In the case of stealing, Rabbi Shkop agrees with the Fisher model. So his Shkop model applies only to conditional actions and not to Contrary to Duties.

2. Since the stealing can be cancelled retrospectively in the future, one might adopt the view of habitually stealing objects and then cancelling the action by returning the objects stolen, and so he has no sin, but lots of "temporarily stolen" objects, which he returns again and again.

   This is reminiscent of the case where a person has no income and no tax to pay, because he only borrows the money at the beginning of a tax year to return it at the end of the tax year, only to immediately borrow it again at the beginning of the next tax year.

   There is an extensive discussion in the Talmud of how to deal with such cases.

4 Talmudic temporal logic

We begin with the definition of Talmudic action system. In order to present it properly, let us start with existing simple action systems of artificial intelligence.

In ordinary artificial intelligence an action for a certain language **L** has the form $\mathbf{a} = (\alpha_\mathbf{a}, \beta_\mathbf{a})$, where $\alpha_\mathbf{a}$ is the precondition of the action and $\beta_\mathbf{a}$ is the post condition of the action, $\alpha_\mathbf{a}$ and $\beta_\mathbf{a}$ are in the language **L**.

We can be more specific about this form. Let t be a moment of time (in which the action takes place) and let $x_1, \ldots, x_n$ be the individuals involved in the action. We can write $\alpha(x_1, \ldots, x_n), \beta(x_1, \ldots, x_n)$ as the preconditions and post condition of the action and write $\mathbf{a}(x_1, \ldots, x_n)$ to indicate that the action $\mathbf{a}$ involves the individuals $x_1, \ldots, x_n$.

We can now write $\mathbf{Exec}(t, \mathbf{a})$ to indicate that the action $\mathbf{a}$ was executed at time t.

In ordinary AI there are no backward causal actions and so all we have is the above. We can specialise it a bit, like asking that $\beta_\mathbf{a}$ be an atomic predicate.

Note that the preconditions and post-conditions are not time dependent.

DEFINITION 5.20 (Classical action temporal logic).

1. The language of classical action temporal logic has the following components:

    1.1. Variables and constants for time points $t_1, t_2, \ldots, \mathbf{t}_1, \mathbf{t}_2, \ldots$

    1.2. Variables and constants for domain elements, $x_1, x_2, \ldots, \mathbf{d}_1, \mathbf{d}_2, \ldots$.

    1.3. The classical connectives and quantifiers for two sorted logic.

    1.4. A set of n-place action names with domain variables or constants of the form $\mathbf{a}(x_1, \ldots, x_n)$

    1.5. A unary existence predicate $E(x)$, x domain variable.

    1.6. An execution predicate of the form $\mathbf{Exec}(t, \mathbf{a}(x_1, \ldots, x_n))$.

    1.7. The earlier–later predicate $t < s$ for time variables.

    1.8. n-place atomic time + domain predicates $P(t, x_1, \ldots, x_n)$ with t time variable and x_i domain variables.

    1.9. We define traditionally the usual notion of a time domain formula $\varphi(t_1, \ldots, t_k, x_1, \ldots, x_n)$ using the atomic predicates in 1.5, 1.6, 1.7, 1.8 and the connectives and quantifiers in 1.3.

    1.10. We associate with each action $\mathbf{a}(x_1, \ldots, x_n)$ two formulas $\alpha_\mathbf{a}(t, x_1, \ldots, x_n)$ and $\beta_\mathbf{a}(t, x_1, \ldots, x_n)$ as defined in 1.9. We assume $\beta_\mathbf{a}(t, x_1, \ldots, x_n)$ is atomic as defined in 1.8. The variables in $\alpha_\mathbf{a}$ and $\beta_\mathbf{a}$ are as indicated. We call $\alpha_\mathbf{a}$ the precondition for $\mathbf{Exec}(t, \mathbf{a}(x_1, \ldots, x_n))$ and $\beta_\mathbf{a}$ the post-condition. Note that $\alpha_\mathbf{a}, \beta_\mathbf{a}$ and $\mathbf{Exec}$ have the same variables $(t, x_1, \ldots, x_n)$.

2. A model $\mathbf{m}$ has the form $\mathbf{m} = (T, <, \mathbb{A}, D, h)$ where $(T, <)$ is a flow of time, say linear flow, $\mathbb{A}$ is the set of actions and D is a domain of elements. $T, \mathbb{A}$ and D are pairwise disjoint. h is an assignment giving to each n-place predicate P a subset $h(P) \subseteq T \times D^n$. For each n-place action $\mathbf{a}(x_1, \ldots, x_n)$ and each $d_1, \ldots, d_n \in D$ and each $t \in T$ we have $h(\mathbf{Exec}(t, \mathbf{a}(d_1, \ldots, d_n)) \in \{0, 1\}$.

The truth value of a wff $\varphi(x_1,\ldots,x_n)$ is defined by induction in the traditional manner.

$$\begin{aligned}
\mathbf{m} &\vDash P(t,x_1,\ldots,x_n) \text{ iff } (t,x_1,\ldots,x_n) \in h(P) \\
\mathbf{m} &\vDash \mathbf{Exec}(t,\mathbf{a}(x_1,\ldots,x_n)) \text{ iff } h(\mathbf{Exec}(t,\mathbf{a}(x_1,\ldots,x_n))) = 1 \\
\mathbf{m} &\vDash \text{the connectives and quantifiers in the traditional manner}
\end{aligned}$$

We require some integrity constraints to hold, for example

- $\mathbf{m} \vDash \mathbf{Exec}(t,\mathbf{a}(x_1,\ldots,x_n)) \to \alpha_\mathbf{a}(t,x_1,\ldots,x_n) \wedge \beta_\mathbf{a}(t,x_1,\ldots,x_n)$

- $\mathbf{m} \vDash \beta_\mathbf{a}(t,x_1,\ldots,x_n)$ iff $\exists s \leq t[\mathbf{m} \vDash \mathbf{Exec}(s,\mathbf{a}(x_1,\ldots,x_n))$ and for all u, $s \leq u \leq t$ and all $\mathbf{b} \in \mathbb{A}$ such that $\beta_\mathbf{b} = \neg \beta_\mathbf{a}$ we have $\mathbf{m} \nvDash \mathbf{Exec}(u,\mathbf{b}(x_1,\ldots,x_n))$

- Note that the pre-conditions of actions do not change with time. So, for example, if a foreign language is requied for a PhD it is always a requirement.

EXAMPLE 5.21 (Conditional actions). Now that we have a more exact formalism for actions, let us reconsider the examples of Section 3. Consider Example 5.11. We have to specify more precisely the pre-conditions and post-conditions of each action.

1. *Action x gives laptop ownership to y.*
   Preconditions:

   - x owns the laptop
   - y is allowed to own the laptop
   - a document is written transferring ownership
   - x and y exist and sign document

   Postconditions

   - x does not own the laptop
   - y owns the laptop
   - document exists

2. *Action y hacks into x's laptop undetected.*
   Preconditions:

   - laptop exists
   - y exists

   Postconditions:

   - y logged onto laptop
   - no alarms triggered.

In the Shkop model of the conditional of Example 5.11, we said that at time 18.30 both agents **m** and **g** go back in time to 18.00 and conclude the deal. The question is which of the pre-conditions of the action of "give laptop ownership" we require to hold at 18.30?

Obviously **m** and **g** need to exist at 18.30.[9] Do we also require that the document exists? What if at 18.15 the document was destroyed? Well, this depends on the legal system. In the Talmud, for example, to have an effective divorce agreement, the document must exist! Another question is do we need the original document, or can a new one be drawn at 18.15 if the original one was destroyed? Obviously we need to specify, when we make a conditional of the form

Action **a** at t if Action **b** at $t + s$

which pre-conditions of Action **a** should hold at $t + s$ before we "jump" back (in the Shkop model).

For this reason we present the pre-conditions of any action **a** as a pair of formulas

$$\mathbb{C}_\mathbf{a} = (\alpha_\mathbf{a}, \gamma_\mathbf{a})$$

Both have to hold in order for the action to be executed. However, $\gamma_\mathbf{a}$ is the one that passes on to the future if we make **a** conditional on some future **b**. So for example in the laptop case,

$\alpha_\mathbf{a} =$ document signed and exists, x owns the laptop and y allowed to own laptop

and

$\gamma_\mathbf{a} =$ x and y exist.

REMARK 5.22.

1. It stands to reason to say that all pre-conditions of actions **a** are always pure and unconditional. Otherwise we put them as conditionals for **a** itself. So to make it clear, if the ownership of the laptop by **m** is itself conditional on **c**, then **m** can give the laptop to **g** only if he makes the action conditional on the condition **c** as well as any other conditions he may wish to add.

2. We have seen in Example 5.11 that preconditions of actions can be ignored and the results of the illegal action can be used for backwards causality. Also not all the postconditions of the action need to be recorded but only those relevant to the backwards causality. Therefore the facts of interest to our models are

    • whether an action can be executed, legally or not
    • what post conditions are relevant

---

[9] Note that in the case that one of them dies exactly at 18.30, this still counts as "existing" at 18.30, for the purpose of the model. This follows from Talmudic rulings in such cases. So, according to Shkop, the Talmud requires them to exist at all moments of time up to but not necessarily including the end time 18.30.

- what preconditions can, if not satisfied, block the execution of the action.

3. We can also assume that the "condition" is a state caused by some action. It could be a state of "being married to c" caused by the action of conducting the marriage ceremony, in which case if the woman is already married to a with a different from c, and so the action has no consequence. It could also be the state of "having executed a marraige ceremony with c" in which case the state is achieved by the action, even if the woman is already married to a.

DEFINITION 5.23 (Linear chain of conditional actions, preliminary version).

1. *Level 0 (no condition) actions*
   These have the form $\mathbf{a}(\mathbb{C}_\mathbf{a}, \beta_\mathbf{a})$ where $\mathbb{C}_\mathbf{a} = (\alpha_\mathbf{a}, \gamma_\mathbf{a})$ are the pre-conditions and $\beta_\mathbf{a}$ is the post-condition. We assume that if $\mathbf{a}$ is used in conditionalised form then $\alpha_\mathbf{a}, \gamma_\mathbf{a}$ will be required to hold at different times, as discussed in (2) below.
   Level (1) actions
   These have the form
   $\mathbf{a}$ at t if $\mathbf{b}$ at all u such that $t < u \leq s$ and $\varphi(t, s, u)$,
   where $\mathbf{a}$ and $\mathbf{b}$ are level (0) actions and where t, s are temporal constants $t < s$ and φ a temporal statement about the interval $[t, s]$. We allow for s to be infinity $s = \infty$. For example $\varphi(t, s, u) \equiv (s = u)$ or $\varphi(t, s, u) \equiv (t < u \leq s)$ or $\varphi(t, s, u) \equiv (t < u)$.
   Level $(n+1)$ actions
   These have the form
   $\mathbf{a}$ at t if $\mathbf{b}$ at all u such that $\varphi(t, s, u)$
   where $\mathbf{a}$ is a level one action and $\mathbf{b}$ is level $(n+1)$ action.

   The above defines simple linear chains.

2. *General inductive clause*
   The general definition is as follows:

   Let $\mathbf{a}$ and $\mathbf{b}$ be any conditional action already defined, then:

   $\mathbf{a}$ at t if $\mathbf{b}$ at all u such that $t < u \leq s$ and $\varphi(t, s, u)$
   is also an action where $t < s$

5 Comparison with the literature

In this section we discuss in what way our contribution is innovative, and compare our work with the key paper [64] of Governatori and Rotolo.

Let us imagine a reader who says the following: "I have not found in this chapter anything really new. The idea of having more than one temporal dimension was technically explored in the AI and Law community since 2005 by Governtori, Rotolo and others. Section 4 presents a two-sorted language interpreted in discrete-linear-time semantic structures. Actions are standardly described using preconditions and postconditions. The operator

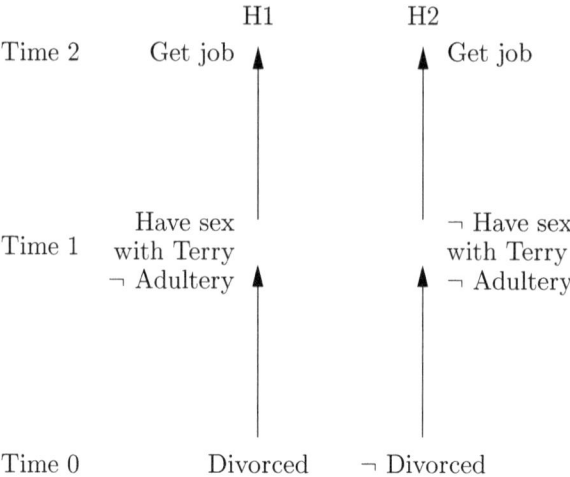

Figure 5.9. Fisher model

Exec looks somehow new, but its semantic interpretation is trivial: Exec statements are true when 1 is assigned to them. Its substantial semantics characterization are given by the constraints: the first relates, as expected, Exec with pre- and post-conditions, the second reframes the well-known law of inertia (introduced for example in Kowalski and Sergot's Event Calculus); since states the idea that β holds at any time t if no terminating actions occurred (but we could also have states-of-affairs blocking the persistence) before it. What's really innovative and new in this picture? One could think of the logic as something close to a temporalisation of FOL plus action symbols".

These are harsh words but very far from the truth as we shall now discuss.

We start with the story of Example 5.6 as discussed at the beginning of Section 3 and modify it a bit.

We start at time $t = 0$ when John gives a divorce to his wife Mary on the condition that she has sex with Terry at time 1. Suppose further that at time 2 Mary gets a teaching job at Church school, on the condition that she is a virtuous woman in her private life.

Let us analyse this example and see whether traditional temporal logic can handle it. We have already discussed the case of time 0 and time 1 of this example from both the Fisher and Shkop points of view at the beginning of Section 3. The following are the results

1. The Fisher model requires paralled histories. We can have up to 4 parallel histories corresponding to two conditions. In our case we have only 2, as in Figure 5.9.

    We have seen that according to Fisher, Mary does not commit adultery even in the case when she has sex with Terry. Therefore according to Fisher, Mary always gets the job.

2. According to Shkop, we get two histories as well, shown in Figure 5.10.

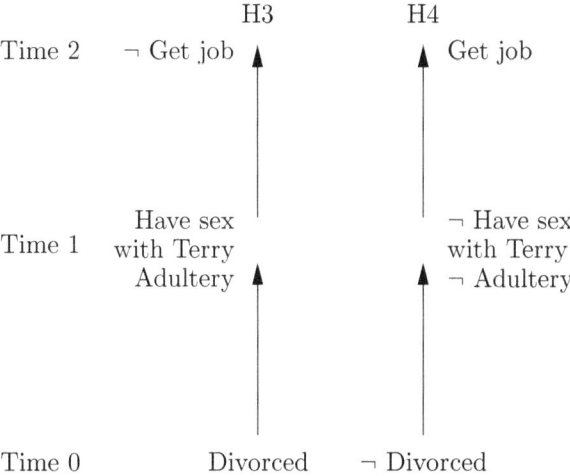

Figure 5.10. Shkop model

Here we also get different histories, but they are calculated differently.

The calculation of the truth value of the various predicates is the key difference between Fisher and Shkop. If the time line has n conditions, according to Fisher there are 2^n parallel histories and as we move along the time line we eliminate more and more of them, until we emerge with one.

There is no possibility of loops, it is a straightforward process of elimination, as more and more information comes in as time progresses.

According to Shkop the calculation is different. We also have in this case 2^n possibilities, two for each condition, but the calculation of the truth values of the predicates involves a complex algorithm of simulated time (one simulated time for each condition) and the algorithm may loop, as we see in Example 5.7 (divorce variations) item 3. The loop arises because of the backward causality which is allowed in the Shkop model. According to Shkop in the history H3 there is Adultery and Mary does not get the job.

To appreciate the conceptual significance of the involvement of these algorithms, consider traditional temporal logic and the way it is presented. We start with a set Q of atoms, some temporal connectives with their truth tables and a flow of time $(T, <)$. Let us take say a one dimensional connective $\Box$, meaning "always in the future", and write $\vDash$ for satisfaction and say:

$$t \vDash \Box \varphi \text{ iff } \forall s(t < s \to s \vDash \varphi).$$

To give a model, we need to give an assignment h, giving truth values to each atom $q \in Q$, at each moment of time t.

So we write $h(t, q) \in \{0, 1\}$. h is arbitrary.

Now suppose we want to be awkward and so instead of giving you h, we say to you, for each $q \in Q$, let $\mathbf{f}_q$ be a function $\mathbf{f}_q : T \mapsto \{0, 1\}$. We say to you there is an infinite set of equations $\mathbb{E}$ on the functions $\mathbf{f}_q, q \in Q$. Solve it and you get your assignment h. This will seem to you just an exercise in mathematics.

From the logical point of view all we need is the assignment h. Using h we have a model and we can go on with our logic evaluation. The equations $\mathbb{E}$ which we use to calculate h, are not part of the logic.

Well, Fisher and Shkop say, no, this is not the case. $\mathbb{E}$ is the logic. Fisher and Shkop do not use connectives. The main thrust of their models is their algorithm. The conditions "φ now if ψ in future" is not a counterfactual logical connective but a condition (equation) for calculating the assignment h of the semantic model.

This is why when we view the model we need to use the executable view as discussed in Section 2.1. This view is best for calculating h.

Fisher and Shkop say that temporal modelling is done by the choice of algorithms for calculating h and not necessarily by choice of connectives as traditionally is the case.

Let us get some support for this view from the logical analysis of the language. Consider the sentence "**John is tall**". We can write it in predicate logic as $\varphi =$ **Tall (John)**. Is φ true? Predicate logic gives truth values to atomic wffs by assigment. However, in real life, the truth value of **Tall(John)** is calculated. The thrust of the models for φ is how we calculate!

So our innovative system and idea is that we say the algoithm for computing the assignments is part of temporal logic and that certain algorithms can model backward causality in time. We believe this is quite innovative.

Let us now compare our model with that of Governatori and Rotolo. We saw above that our message is that we model temporal phenomena also by the algorithms governing the assignment h and that our temporal logic offers certain algorithms.

Implicit in our approach is that it is semantical.

One can take a proof theoretical approach. Instead of giving an assigment h to each atom q at time t, we give a logical theory Δ_t and define

$$h(t,q) = 1 \text{ iff } \Delta_t \vdash q$$

or to use traditional satisfaction notation:

$$t \vdash A \text{ iff } \Delta_t \vdash A.$$

Governatori and Rotolo use a proof theoretical approach and introduce two dimensions (and more) to model norm change. They have to do that since norms and norm change and legislation, etc., are proof theoretical. Their modelling task is not easy, as we may have repeated norm changes of different sorts and different temporal validity. They use defeasible temporal logic and many dimensions (in fact every trick in the trade) to present in [64] a quite sophisticated system.

The proof theoretical approach is not new. Gabbay used it in [59] in his time action model. However, Governatori and Rotolo make quite clever and justified logical moves in their drive to model legal norm change.

Their system can simulate the Fisher approach without difficulty, this is because the Fisher approach does not allow for loops. So we have several possible histories (which can be presented proof theoretically as [64] would like them) and as time progresses, all but one hsitory are eliminated. This can be handled like norm change.

We don't think, however, that one can simulate proof theoretically the Shkop approach. The history $H3$ of Figure 5.10 would be a problem. There is no way one can say proof theoretically at the same time that

$\Delta_1 \vdash$ have sex with Terry
$\Delta_0 \vdash$ divorced if have sex with Terry at 1

and

$\Delta_1 \vdash$ adultery.

We need the Shkop algorithm with the simulated time τ to get this conclusion. Such algorithms can have loops as we have seen, and so even if we (following Governatori and Rotolo) proof theoretically use an additional metamodal logic to talk about fixed point solutions of such loops, we get more and more complicated systems which are less and less intuitive.

This ends our comparison with [64].

By the way, Shkop does offer a way of resolving loops and so his approach covers all potential problems. He puts forward the following Shkop principle:

- If at time t, taking action **a** causes a loop (because of backwards causality) which makes action **a** invalid, then it is forbidden to take action **a**.

Consider the loop of item 3 of Example 5.7.

John divorces his wife Mary at time $t = 0$, on the condition that she does not marry Terry. Now since she is divorced, she asks "Can I take the action at time $t = 1$ and marry Terry"? The precondition for this action is that she is free and indeed the precondition holds. So let us simulate and apply the Shkop principle. If she marries Terry, her divorce at time $t = 0$ is not valid, hence at time $t = 1$, the precondition for taking the action of marrying Terry becomes invalid, so she cannot take the action. The Shkop principle says that she cannot take the action. See chapter 7 below about the Shkop principle.

The above considerations can be considered as further support for our innovative models. It can be generalised and expanded in new directions.

We do have loops in international law, where a person falls under several jurisdictions. It may be that each jurisdiction sends the case to the other. The Shkop principle can be used there. It is quite intuitive and reasonable.

6 Conclusion

We introduced in this chapter the Talmudic Temporal Logic, capable of modelling the Talmudic examples. The logic was motivated and introduced semantically. It is a new innovative system as explained in Section 5, and compared with the major work of Governatori and Rotolo, [64]. We are not going to develop its formal properties, proof theory, completeness, its relation to other logics, etc., etc. This is the subject for another, pure logic paper and is not essential for applying logic to modelling legal reasoning.

Note however that our model does "export" to general logic new ideas about temporal causality.

Some of our examples in this chapter dealt with entities defined using the future. These are studied extensively in chapter 6 where we show that the Talmud exports to general logic a new type of public announcement logic with quantum superposition semantics.

CHAPTER 6

FUTURE DETERMINATION OF ENTITIES IN TALMUDIC PUBLIC ANNOUNCEMENT LOGIC

Preliminaries

Ordinary dynamic action logics deal with states and actions upon states. The actions can be deterministic or non-deterministic, but it is always assumed that the possible results of the actions are clear cut.

Talmudic logic deals with actions (usually legally meaningful actions which can change the legal status of an entity) which depend on the future and therefore may be not clear cut at the present and need future clarifications.

The clarification is modelled by public announcement which comes at a later time after the action has taken place.

The model is further complicated by the need to know what is the status of formulas at a time before the results of the action is clarified, as we do not know at which state we are in. Talmudic logic treats such states much like the quantum superposition of states and when clarification is available we get a collapse onto a pure state.

The Talmudic lack of clarity of actions arises from applying an action to entities defined using the future, like the statement of a dying man on his death bed:

> **Let the man who will win the jackpot in the lottery next week be the sole heir in my will now**

We need to wait a week for the situation to clarify.

There is also the problem of legal backwards causality, as this man, if indeed he exists, unaware of his possible good fortune, may have himself meanwhile donated all his property to a charity. Does his donation include this unknown inheritance?

This chapter will offer a model and a logic which can represent faithfully the Talmudic reasoning in these matters.

We shall also see that we get new types of public announcement logics and (quantum-like) action logics. Ordinary public announcement logic deletes possible worlds after an announcements. Talmudic public announcement logic deletes accessibility links after an announcement. Technically these two approaches are similar but not equivalent.

1 Introduction and orientation

This chapter offers a new variant of public announcement logic arising from the logical modelling of the Talmudic approach to the legal status of entities defined by future conditions.

We present and discuss the Talmudic legal options in Example 6.1. We ask the reader to accept that our analysis and presentation of these Talmudic options is correct, (see our monograph [65] on the subject) and focus our analysis on what kind of logic is required to formalise these options.

Readers more interested in logic as applied to law are invited to read up to section 3 of this chapter and further consult [65] and [11].

Readers interested in formal logic and in traditional public announcement logic are invited to continue to read sections 4 and 5 of this chapter and to consider our system as a new variant (hopefully of some merit) of traditional public announcement logic. We note that such a logic has applications not only in formalising Talmudic reasoning but also to general modern legal reasoning as well. Our strategy is as follows:

(A) First we give the reader a general impression of what kind of a new logic to expect.

(B) Then we give a motivating example allowing us to present and discuss the Talmudic approaches requiring a new logic.

(C) The remainder of Section 1 is devoted to a semi-formal discussion of the logical components required.

(D) Sections 2–3 describe the new logic in a semi formal manner. Section 4 is more aimed at the formal logician and formally describes Propositional Talmudic public announcement logic TPK.

(E) Section 5 compares the new logic with traditional public announcement logic.

(F) The Appendix collects various technical results, to which we can refer in the appropriate places in the chapter.

Our starting point is the Kripke semantics for predicate modal logic **K** with expanding domains. This semantics has models of the form $\mathbf{m} = (S, R, \mathbf{m}_t), t$ in S, where S is the set of possible worlds, R is a binary relation on S and for each t in S, $\mathbf{m}_t$ is a classical model. We require that whenever tRs holds then the domain D_t of $\mathbf{m}_t$ is a subset of the domain D_s of $\mathbf{m}_s$.

The traditional way of adding a public announcement feature to such models is to allow for operators of the form $\lfloor \phi \rfloor$, where ϕ is a formula of the language, which takes a model $\mathbf{m}$ to a model $\mathbf{m}_\phi$, whose set of possible worlds is $S_\phi = \{t \in S \mid t \vDash \phi\}$.

Let us isolate the two features we are going to change in this semantics

(a) The kind of classical models $\mathbf{m}_t$ we are going to use is going to be special and the embedding of the domain of $\mathbf{m}_t$ in the domain of $\mathbf{m}_s$ (for the case of tRs holding) is also special. This restricts the class of models of the semantics.

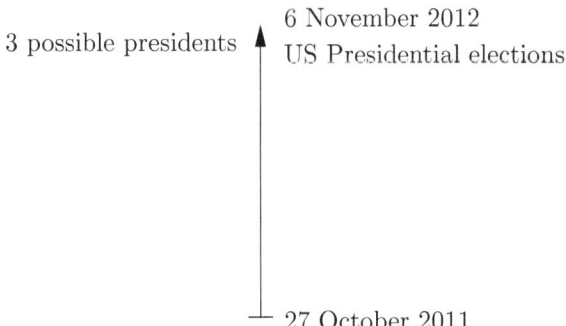

Figure 6.1. Donation

(b) While traditional public announcement operators take out points elements of S, the Talmudic public announcement operators take out elements of R. These two operations are not exactly equivalent (see Appendix B4).

(c) Note that the changes in (a) and in (b) above are orthogonal and independent of each other. So once we explain the change (a) for the classical models (which we call Talmudic classical models), we can explain the new Talmudic public announcement logic of change (b) on the propositional level only.

We now motivate the need for above changes via an example.

EXAMPLE 6.1 (Presidential elections). Warren Buffet and Bill Gates give a gift on 27 October 2011 of a total of 50 billion US dollars to the candidate who wins the presidential elections (see Figure 6.1). They put the money in an account in the Bank of America. We assume for simplicity that there are at this date 3 candidates running and so we can assume that by 6 November 2012 we know who wins. The question arises what is to be done with this donation in the period between 27 October 2011 and 6 November 2012, (see Figure 6.2).

The legal question we ask, under the above circumstances, who has control of the money in the periods between 27 October 2011 to 6 November 2012 and in the period after 6 November 2012?

Talmudic scholars in their debates of how to handle the above case and similar cases put forward five different approaches. Some of these approaches can be formalised in traditional linear temporal logics and traditional public announcement logic. Others, however, do require the new semantics with the new (a) and (b) features mentioned above. The following are the five Talmudic approaches:

1. Reject such an action, do not accept the money. The money still belongs

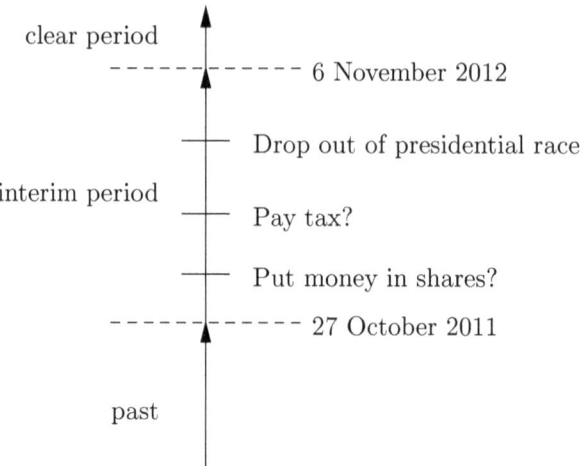

Figure 6.2. Election time line

to Bill Gates and Warren Buffet. There is no legal way to accept such a condition.

2. The money belongs to all 3 candidates as a block entity, even after the president is known. This means that a partnership is formed on 27 October 2011, involving the three candidates and this partnership owns the money, and this partnership continues even after 6 November 2012. It is irrelevant who becomes president in 6 November 2012.

   This approach for the case, creates a new entity, the partnership. We are familiar with this in modern life, but there are other examples, which require a quantum superposition of the elements involved.

3. We assume parallel histories from 27 October 2011 to 6 November 2012. We have a parallel history for each candidate, in which history he gets the money on 27 October 2011 and proceeds to win the elections on 6 November 2012. Which history is true will become clear in November 2012.

4. We have (2) until 6 November 2012, and the correct history afterwards This means that the legal partnership of all 3 candidates controls the money from 27 October 2011 until 6 November 2012 and after 6 November 2012, the president among them takes sole ownership of whatever money is left and takes control.

5. Nothing happens in the period 27 October 2011 to 6 November 2012. The money is frozen and cannot be touched. We have uncertain unclear situation during this period. Once clarified in November 2012, the clarification is effective retrospectively from 27 October 2011

Let us now have a short discussion:

6. FUTURE DETERMINATION OF ENTITIES

- First we discuss the difference between (3) and (5).

  In 3, one of the candidates gets the money from 27 October 2011. We don't know who he is until 6 November 2012. So, for example, let us say that candidate no 1 donates some of the money to a charity in January 2012. If candidate no 1 becomes president, the donation stands, because it is his history that is true and he was the owner of the money at the time of the donation. It can be taxed for example by the gift laws in force in January 2012. If candidate no 1 does not become president, then in the real history, as clarified on 6 November 2012, he was not the owner of the money and there is no donation. To secure the donation it would be wise to have all candidates approve it.

  In 5, the candidate who becomes president gets the money on 6 November 2012 retrospectively from 27 October 2011. So let us say that candidate no 1 donates some of the money to a charity in January 2012. Even if candidate no 1 becomes president, the donation does not stand because at the time of the donation, he was not the owner of the money. He became owner retrospectively on 6 November 2012. The candidate can, if he still wants to, donate the money again on 6 November 2012 and then it is taxed for example by the gift laws in force on 6 November 2012. The perceptive reader may ask, in what way is this retrospective ownership different from the straightforward case of ownership beginning on 6 November 2012? Well, suppose the winning candidate divorces his wife on January 2012. The retrospective ownership of the money may count for the divorce settlement.[1]

- Second we discuss a chain situation. Suppose one of the candidates is the favourite of the opinion polls. He goes ahead and promises the money to other banks who give credit to other companies and a long chain is created. If the unexpected happens and he is not elected president, then we ask in what state are we left in 6 November 2012? This is not so much a practical problem but a logical problem. In the model we may think we are at one state in one time line and the public announcement tells us we are in a different time line, how do we identify logically in the semantics where we are supposed to be?

There are two components in this example which call for new logical features:

(i) The second Talmudic approach (item 2 above), requires the creation of new entities. The presidential example requires the creation of a partnership, which is a well known procedure, but other cases may require the creation of a quantum superposition of elements. We now briefly explain.

Suppose a man marries one of identical twin sisters and then on his way back from church has an accident and loses his memory. Suppose each of the twin sisters claims she is the wife. There is no way of telling which

---

[1] It may be interesting to compare the above 5 Talmudic approaches with British Law. British law requires the money to have a clear cut owner at any moment of time. So the only way to give money in such a case of future uncertainty, is to set up a trust on 27 October 2011, with clear instruction to give the money to the winner on 6 November 2012.

is which, we have to wait for the man to gain his memory and hopefully clarify.

We cannot say for any of the sisters that she is married or not married. The Talmud treats them as a quantum superposition of two entities (using modern terminology). This is not a partnership. You cannot form a partnership to marry a man. We may have other problems, like are each considered married for tax allowance or not, do we give each all the tax allowance or half of it?

(ii) The modelling of the clarification details, which require some form of public announcement logic, which may be newly defined or may already be available in the literature.

Section 2 models (i) and Section 3 models (ii).

It is by now clear that we need to construct a special logic to model the Talmudic approaches (2) and (5) of Example 6.1

The Talmudic logic we are going to construct is comprised of several components, some known to us already and some are new. The Talmudic system is then used to model certain aspects of reasoning in the Talmud.

The fragments of the logics we are going to use to combine and construct our final Talmudic logic system are as follows:

1. Some aspects of modal **K** action logic.

2. Some aspects of public announcement logic.

3. Some aspects of the logic of time.

4. Some aspects of (quantum-like) superposition and collapse.

We begin by explaining the effects of these components.[2]

Imagine a modal **S5** logic of the form (S, t),[3] where S is the set of possible worlds and $t \in S$ is the actual world. Suppose we perform an action **a** in the world t which moves us from the world t to the world s where s is the world where the post condition of the action holds. Schematically we have Figure 6.3.

---

[2] For the convenience of the reader, who might not be familiar with one or more of these components, we are including a short exposition in the Appendix.

[3] We use the letter "t" for the actual world, even though it is usually reserved for time points. In our intended models (after actions are clarified) time is linear and discrete and time points are the results of the application of linear sequences of actions, and so the worlds are the times. This is done in Definition 6.14 below.

6. FUTURE DETERMINATION OF ENTITIES

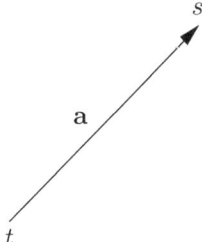

Figure 6.3. Change of state following an action

The model after the action is (S, s). To be specific, consider a model $\mathbf{m}_t$ with three element domain $D = \{a, b, c\}$ and a unary predicate $\lambda x P(x)$.[4] Assume that
$$\mathbf{m}_t \models \neg P(a) \wedge \neg P(b) \wedge \neg P(c).$$
The action **a** is to make P hold for exactly one of the elements.
So if we describe the action **a** as

$$\text{execute ``}\exists!xP(x)\text{''}$$

then it is non-deterministic and can have three outcomes:

$$s_1 \models P(a) \wedge \neg P(b) \wedge \neg P(c)$$
$$s_2 \models \neg P(a) \wedge P(b) \wedge \neg P(c)$$
$$s_3 \models \neg P(a) \wedge \neg P(b) \wedge P(c)$$

If we must have perfect clarity we must execute one of the options above, i.e.

either   execute "$P(a)$"
or   execute "$P(b)$"
or   execute "$P(c)$"

So far we have a very simple action logic, where actions **a** performed in one world t take us to a clear cut unique world s.

Let us now complicate the situation. Suppose the action was done in such a way that it is not clear whether the result is world s_1 or s_2 or s_3, as in Example 6.1, where the money is given at time m at state t to the candidate from among $\{a, b, c\}$ who wins at time m'. So at time m it is not clear whether we moved to state s_1 (a is the winner) or to s_2 (b is the winner) or to s_3 (c is the winner). We represent this situation in Figure 6.4.[5]

---

[4]The reader should note that we are dealing with finite domains and therefore the logics involved are propositional, not predicate logics.

The universal quantifier can be rewritten as a conjunction over all elements of the domain and the existential quantifier can be rewritten as a disjunction over all elements of the domain.

So because our work looks like a first-order logic, it makes it easy to express superposition of elements but at the same time since the logic is really propositional, we need not worry about the well known difficulties in the treatment of first-order modal/epistemic/deontic/temporal logics.

[5]Let us be more specific here. Suppose I ask my agent, (from Mrs Renton matrimonial

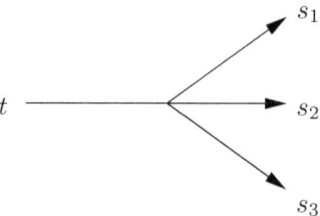

Figure 6.4. Lack of clarity

We are not necessarily saying that the action is non-deterministic and allows for several possible outcomes (with some probability) as they do in Agent Theory and Dynamic Logic. We are thinking that perhaps it wasn't clear exactly what happened or that the action was interrupted or any other reason for us to have to wait until the matter clarifies. So time is always linear to us, the branching occurs because of lack of clarity. When all is clear all the branching will disappear.

This is why we use special notation, see Figure 6.5.

So we expect a clarification, a public announcement, telling us where we are. Figure 6.6 describes the situation all in terms of public announcement.

In Figure 6.6, the arrows are schematic, they do not take time. In the Talmud, the models are temporal and the arrows take time. Figure 6.7 shows what happens in time in the Talmud.

To make the example real, let us recall our presidential Example 6.1, for the candidates a, b and c. There is some lack of clarity on 27 October 2011 which clarifies at time 6 November 2012.

In this case our predicate is $P(x) = $ "x is the sole owner of the money".

So the clarification takes time and it is at this point that the temporal aspect comes in.

We need to address the following problems:

1. Analyse the nature of the (Talmudic) action which can give rise to the lack of clarity at time 1.

    1.1 Identify parameters in the action which cause the lack of clarity.

    1.2 Determine what are the possible results of this lack of clarity.

    By possible results we mean that if action **a** is applied to model $\mathbf{m}_t$ and action **a** has component α causing lack of clarity, what is the list of possible models $\mathbf{m}^\alpha_{s_1}, \ldots, \mathbf{m}^\alpha_{s_n}$ which can result.

---

services) to go and arrange for my engagement to one of the three candidates $\{a, b, c\}$. I leave it to my agent to decide who is most suitable. The interview is scheduled for Monday. In this case one of them is engaged to me on Monday, though I may not know which one it is until the following Friday. Another possible scenario is that I give my agent a ring and ask him to arrange for my engagement to one of $\{a, b, c\}$ on Monday. The agent gives the ring to all three of them and says he will inform them later which one he chooses. In this case on Monday one of them is engaged but for each one of $\{a, b, c\}$ we cannot say she is engaged.

6. FUTURE DETERMINATION OF ENTITIES

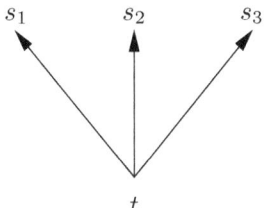

Non-deterministic action **a**

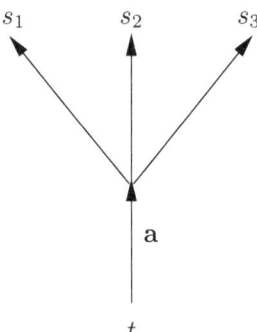

Deterministic action **a** in need of clarification

Figure 6.5. Non-deterministic action

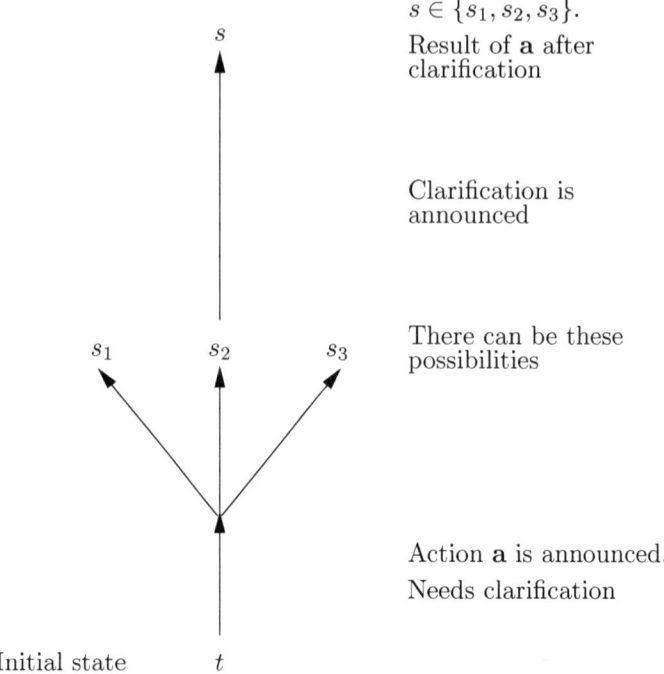

Figure 6.6. Public announcement clarification

We await clarification as to which $\mathbf{m}_{s_i}^\alpha$ does result. Note that in Figure 6.7 the possible results of action **a** on $\mathbf{m}_0$ are $\mathbf{m}_1$ or $\mathbf{m}_2$ or $\mathbf{m}_3$. These are all classical models. Note that we cannot adopt the view that we are, at time 1, after the execution of the action, either at model $\mathbf{m}_1$ or at model $\mathbf{m}_2$ or at model $\mathbf{m}_3$. To see this, think of predicate P to mean being infected. So as a result of the action, either a or b or c were infected. At time 2, we would like to put all infected people into isolation. Common sense says we need to isolate all three elements $\{a, b, c\}$. This action cannot be justified when applied to the situation in each of the models $\mathbf{m}_1$, $\mathbf{m}_2$ or $\mathbf{m}_3$. Clearly the result of the lack of clarity puts us in a new model $\mathbf{m}_4$. The Talmud allows (because of the lack of clarity) additional models which are some sort of (quantum-

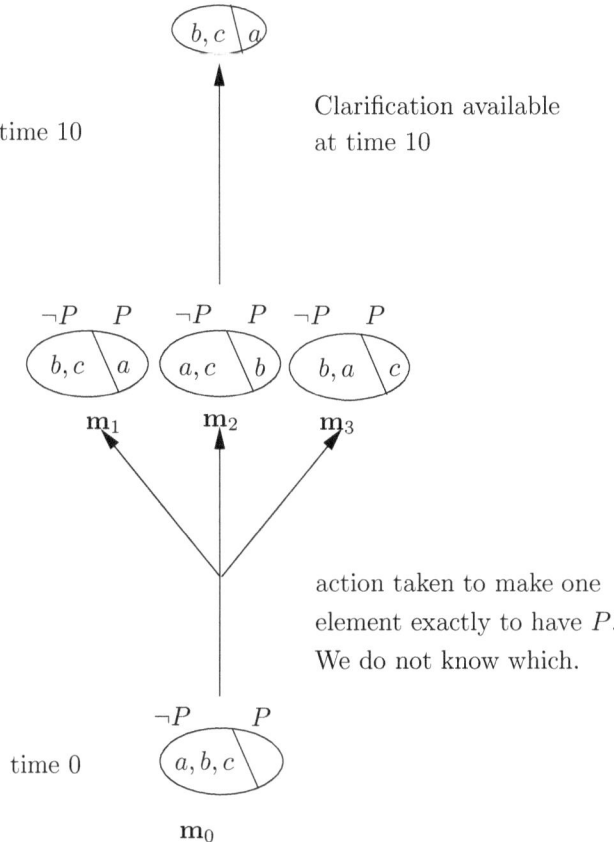

Figure 6.7. Time action in the Talmud

like) superposition models,[6] which are different from the classical models. So we will have to define some new Talmudic models of our logic.

1.3 We ask: can the situation be clarified? Do we treat these "unclear" actions as a new type of actions, and a new type of action logic?

Furthermore, if we have new superposition models, how does the old action **a** apply to the new model?

2. Once we have clarity at some later time, do we apply it backwards from

---

[6]It should be noted that the quantum-like superposition is itself the model here — and not a logicized form of quantum mechanics as attempted in some forms of "quantum logic". For a survey of attempts at conveying the logical form of a quantum-mechanical state (physical, mathematical) or logicize vagueness and fuzzyness, [34]. The Superposition principle is what makes the Hilbert spaces and their subsets into (quantum mechanically) more than classical [34, p. 207]. Quantum mechanics deals with different sorts of fuzziness, the "sharp kind" — where "events are sharp, while all semantic uncertainties are due to the logical incompleteness of the individual concepts, that correspond to pure states of quantum objects." (such as determination of Hamlet's height — [34, p. 245] and an "unsharp" vagueness where the predicate itself is not well defined (the honor of Brutus). See also [92] for general reading.

time 1?

If not, what is the status (where are we? at which world? at which model?) at times the intermediate times, during which there was not yet clarity?

We can see that we need to develop at least 3 new logics, maybe 4 logics.

(a) A modal public announcement logic where the identity of the actual world has several options and the public announcement narrows down these options or moves the actual world to a new set of options.

(b) A temporal logic where one can move from time t to time $t+1$ by taking an action.

(c) A combination of the two models where the need for public announcement logic arises from lack of clarity in the action at time t which is clarified by public announcement at a future time.

(d) A new type of classical Talmudic logic.

We noted already that in the Talmud the lack of clarity in actions comes from using the future to identify the elements to which the action is applied. So we need a Talmudic theory of individual objects.

Thus Talmudic law has inherent situations of vagueness and underdetermination, emerging from a role a contingent future plays in the very definition of Halakhic states.[7]

(e) We need a model of backwards causality, as the future identification of such entitites has influence into the past, see [11].

So our logic will have the above components put together as required by the Talmud.

Summary

The situation in Figure 6.6 arises in the Talmud when an action is taken relating to an individual x whose identity is determined at a future time. Therefore

1. Start with a model t

2. Action **a** is performed on the x such that $\varphi(x)$ is true in the future.

---

[7]Within deliberations of the jurisprudential system of Halacha (Talmudic Law), Halakhic State may refer to a state of affairs in a civil, economic (*Mamonot*) or criminal law (*Nefashot*). It can also denote an evoked condition of ritual impurity (*Tumah*) or the status of a sacrificial animal (*Korban*), agronomical produce with an intermediary status between personal and consecrated property (*Trumot U'Maasrot*). All of these realms of Halacha and more have a possibility-spectrum within them, and the Halakhic state is normally the result of human action taken, or an evolved physical situation, with a predefined Halakhic meaning attached to them. In short — a Halakhic state denotes the definition, the status of an object, person or occurrence in accordance with Halacha as it pertains to personal, public, secular and religious laws (all falling under different purviews of Halakha, Talmudic Law). A popular term in the modern special school dedicated to Talmudic study, the Yeshiva (the Brisk-Yeshiva style of learning), is Chalut, sometimes pronounced *Chalus* or *Chalos* — literally "aplication", short for "application of a law".

3. Therefore action **a** is not completely clear. We need to wait until the identity of x is revealed in time. The possibilities are s_1, s_2, s_3.

4. This is the clarification we are waiting for. We are, of course, in difficulty in the interim period until the clarification is revealed. We stress again that the action takes place at time t with the intention that its effect takes place immediately at t. The action needs to be clarified so we wait. When clarified, we still want the result of the action to take place at the original time t!

5. The Talmudic debate on such cases involves five approaches, as outlined in Example 6.1. To model two of these approaches we need new kind of semantics involving quantum like superposition of elements and possibly a new type of public announcement logic.

2 Introducing Talmudic classical models

We saw in the previous section that there can be a lack of clarity about the result of applying an action to a classical model. We presented schematically this lack of clarity in Figure 6.7.

Classical model theory can handle the fine distinctions required by Figure 6.7.

Our starting model is model $\mathbf{m}_0$ in Figure 6.7 and after action **a** we move to a triple option

$$\{\mathbf{m}_1, \mathbf{m}_2, \mathbf{m}_3\}.$$

Thus we can say that an extended classical model is a set of several classical models, i.e. an S5 modal model.

The Talmud looks at additional options for a model, call it a "Quantum-like" model $\mathbf{m}_4^Q$, where the predicate P is spread over the vector element (a, b, c). So in this model we have

(*) $\qquad\qquad \neg P(a) \wedge \neg P(b) \wedge \neg P(c) \wedge P(a,b,c)$[8]

We say "Quantum-like" because this possibility is actually identical to the quantum superposition idea.

We therefore need to do two things:

1. increase our stock of basic models;

2. Specify how our old actions apply to the new models of (1).

Let us allow for products of models.

Consider a model

$$\mathbf{n} = \mathbf{m}_1 \times \mathbf{m}_2 \times \mathbf{m}_3.$$

---

[8]The predicate P is one place, the vector element (a, b, c) is a single element, so we should write

$$P((a,b,c)).$$

We abuse notation and write

$$P(a,b,c).$$

The elements of **n** are vectors (x, y, z), x from $\mathbf{m}_1, y \in \mathbf{m}_2$ and $z \in \mathbf{m}_3$. We identify the old elements a, b, c as the diagonal (pure state) vectors

$$\begin{aligned} \bar{a} &= (a, a, a) \\ \bar{b} &= (b, b, b) \\ \bar{c} &= (c, c, c) \end{aligned}$$

take the element

$$\bar{x} = (x_1, x_2, x_3)$$

Let $\|\mathbf{n}\|_i = \mathbf{m}_i$, the ith component of **n**. Similalry $\|\bar{x}\|_i = x_i$. We can define

$$\mathbf{n} \vDash P(\bar{x}) \text{ iff for all } i \text{ we have } \|\mathbf{n}\|_i \vDash P(\|x\|_i).$$

So, for example, we have

$$\mathbf{m}_1 \times \mathbf{m}_2 \times \mathbf{m}_3 \vDash P(a, b, c)$$

but

$$\mathbf{m}_1 \times \mathbf{m}_2 \times \mathbf{m}_3 \vDash \neg P(a, a, a) \wedge \neg P(b, b, b) \wedge \neg P(c, c, c).$$

This is an "implementation" of (*) above.[9]

Note that the product is ordered. a is chosen from $\mathbf{m}_1$, b from $\mathbf{m}_2$ and c from $\mathbf{m}_3$, i.e. each x is chosen from the model where $P(x)$ is made true.

We can now replace Figure 6.7 by Figure 6.8.[10]

We can therefore give the following definition:

DEFINITION 6.2 (Talmudic classical models).

1. Let $\mathbf{m}_i$ be a classical models over the same domain D for the same language **L**.

2. A basic Talmudic model for **L** is any product $\mathbf{m}' = \prod_{i=1}^{n} \mathbf{m}_i$ over the domain D^n. Define satisfaction by

   $$\mathbf{m}' \vDash \varphi(\bar{x}) \text{ iff for all } i \ \mathbf{m}_i \vDash \varphi(x_i), \text{ where } \bar{x} = (x_1, \ldots, x_n).$$

An ordinary classical model **m** over domain D can be canonically embedded in any product $\mathbf{m}'$ of the form above over D^n by the mapping of any $a \in D$ to $\bar{a} = (a, \ldots, a) \in D^n$.

---

[9]This construction is generic. It always works no matter what the actions do or in what language they are defined, because all we need is to add to our model several additional accessible worlds which are the possible results of the action as well as the product of all of these worlds. It may be the case that if all our actions can be described by a first order formulas then we might be able to describe the entire operation in traditional modal logic. For example in the above particular case we may be able to write something like

$$(\bigwedge_{i=1}^{n} \Diamond Px_i) \wedge \bigwedge_{i=1}^{n} \Box(Px_i \to \bigwedge_{j \neq i, j=1}^{n} \neg Px_j) \wedge \Diamond \exists y(\psi(y) \wedge P(y)) \wedge \bigwedge_{i=1}^{n} (y \neq x_i)).$$

We need also say that the world where y is has y acting as a superposition of all the x_i using the wff $\psi(y)$, and maybe we can say that in first order logic or maybe not.

[10]Note that according to Remark 6.4 below, we shall take $\mathbf{m}_0$ here and not $\mathbf{n}_0$ as in this figure. The two are equivalent.

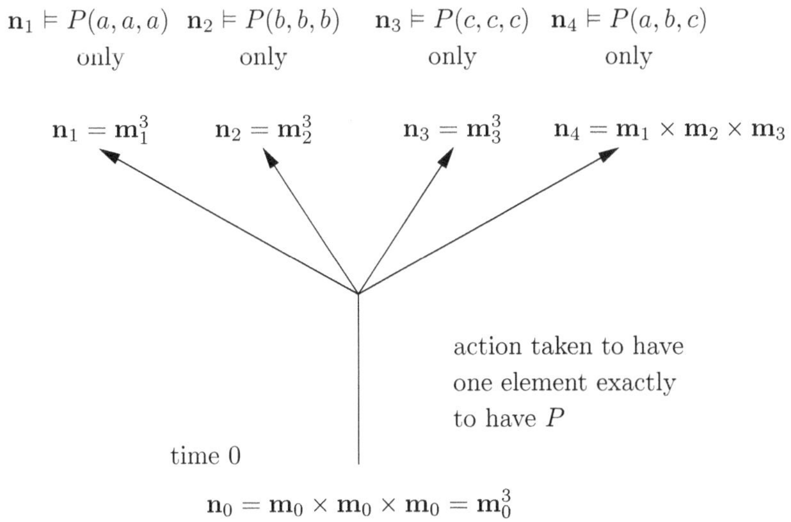

6. FUTURE DETERMINATION OF ENTITIES

$\mathbf{n}_1 \vDash P(a,a,a)$ only $\quad \mathbf{n}_2 \vDash P(b,b,b)$ only $\quad \mathbf{n}_3 \vDash P(c,c,c)$ only $\quad \mathbf{n}_4 \vDash P(a,b,c)$ only

$\mathbf{n}_1 = \mathbf{m}_1^3 \quad \mathbf{n}_2 = \mathbf{m}_2^3 \quad \mathbf{n}_3 = \mathbf{m}_3^3 \quad \mathbf{n}_4 = \mathbf{m}_1 \times \mathbf{m}_2 \times \mathbf{m}_3$

action taken to have one element exactly to have P

time 0

$\mathbf{n}_0 = \mathbf{m}_0 \times \mathbf{m}_0 \times \mathbf{m}_0 = \mathbf{m}_0^3$

Figure 6.8. Talmudic classical models

3. The process can be iterated, since the model $\mathbf{m}'$ is itself also a classical model, we can assume in the product of item 2 above the factors $\mathbf{m}_i$ are themselves products $\mathbf{m}'_i$ and form the further product $\mathbf{m}''$.

DEFINITION 6.3 (Embedding of Talmudic models). Let $\mathbf{n}$ be a classical Talmudic model of the form $\mathbf{n} = \prod_{i=1}^{r} \mathbf{m}_i$, where each $\mathbf{m}_i$ is an ordinary classical model for the same language based on the same domain D.

Let $\mathbf{n}_1, \ldots, \mathbf{n}_k$ be k such models, i.e. $\mathbf{n}_j = \prod_{i=1}^{r} \mathbf{m}_i^j$, where each $\mathbf{m}_i^j$ is a classical model based on the same domain D. Note the "r" is fixed for all models. We define the diagonal embedding of $\mathbf{n}$ into $\mathbf{n}^* = \prod_{j=1}^{k} \mathbf{n}_j$.

1. Each element $\bar{a}$ in the domain of $\mathbf{n}$ is mapped onto $(\bar{a}, \ldots, \bar{a})$ in $\mathbf{n}^*$.

We also have $\mathbf{n}^* \vDash \varphi(\bar{x})$ iff for each j, $\mathbf{n}_j \vDash \varphi(\|\bar{x}_j\|)$.

REMARK 6.4. Consider again Figure 6.8. In this figure $\mathbf{n}_0 = \mathbf{m}_0^3$ is embedded into $\mathbf{n}_1, \ldots, \mathbf{n}_4$. If we were to conform to what is suggested in Definition 6.3, we would take $\mathbf{m}_0$ in the figure and not $\mathbf{m}_0^3$. This simplifies the presentation and complexity of our models. Note that $\mathbf{m}_0$ and $\mathbf{m}_0^3$ are basically the same model since satisfaction is achieved coordinatewise!

DEFINITION 6.5 (Connection between models). Assume $(x, \{x_1, \ldots, x_n\}) \in \mathcal{R}$ and assume $\mathbf{m}_x^0$ is a Talmudic classical model associated with x. Let D_x be its domain. We now say what models we associate with $x_1, \ldots, x_n$. We need to assume an action $\mathbf{a}$ which when applied to $\mathbf{m}_x$ yields k possible outcomes

$$\mathbf{m}_x^1, \ldots, \mathbf{m}_x^k.$$

Let $\mathbf{n}$ be any product

$$\mathbf{n} = \prod_{j=1}^{k} \mathbf{n}_i$$

where $n_i \in \{m_x^1, \ldots, m_x^k\}$ and let $z \in \{x_1, \ldots, x_n\}$.
Then we can take the model $\mathbf{n}$ to be the model at z, i.e. $\mathbf{m}_z = \text{def}.\mathbf{n}$.
Clearly we can embed $\mathbf{m}_x$ into $\mathbf{m}_z$ as in Definition 6.3.

3 Talmudic public announcement models

We recall our plan to define a variant of predicate modal $\mathbf{K}$ with public announcement features suitable for modelling the Talmudic examples. The components are first the classical Talmudic models which are to be used as the model in each world and the way they embed into one another, and second the nature of the public announcements which deletes arcs. The former we addressed in the last section, and the latter we are going to address in this section. It is sufficient to treat the propositional case.

DEFINITION 6.6 (Talmudic $\mathbf{K}$ frame). A Talmudic $\mathbf{K}$ frame has the form $(S, \mathcal{R}, \mathbb{P})$ where

1. $S \neq \varnothing$ is a set of possible worlds

2. $\mathcal{R}$ is a multi-valued accessibility relation of the form $x\mathcal{R}Y_x$, where $Y_x = \{x_1, \ldots, x_{n(x)}\}$,

   reading: one of x_i in Y_x is accessible to x but we do not know which one and we await a public announcement clarification. We require that the set $Y_x = \{x_1, \ldots, x_{n(x)}\}$ is unique in its $\mathcal{R}$ relation to x. This requirement reduces the relation $x\mathcal{R}Y_x$ to a binary relation R on S. We can define

   - xRy iff def. y is an element of the unique Y_x such that $x\mathcal{R}Y_x$ and conversely, given a binary relation R on S define
   - $x\mathcal{R}Y$ iff $Y = \{y | xRy\}$.

   We say that $(S, \mathcal{R})$ is a tree if for any y in S there is at most one x in S such that y is in Y_x and $x\mathcal{R}Y_x$ holds, (i.e. xRy holds).

   We call $(n(x)$, for x in S the accessibility branching parameter of x.

3. $\mathbb{P}$ is a set of public announcements of the form

$$\alpha = (x, \{x_1, \ldots, x_{n(x)}\}, y), y \in \{x_1, \ldots, x_{(n(x)}\}$$

   where

$$(x, \{x_1, \ldots, x_{(n(x)}\}) \in \mathcal{R}$$

   reading:
   I hereby announce that y is the element accessible to x.

   Given α, let $\|\alpha\|$ be $(x, \{x_1, \ldots, x_{n(x)}\})$.

   The above is a deterministic public announcement, because it chooses exactly one $y \in \{x_1, \ldots, x_{n(x)}\}$. The public announcement can be non-deterministic if it chooses a subset Y of $\{x_1, \ldots, x_{n(x)}\}$. It therefore has the form $\alpha = (x, \{x_1, \ldots, x_{n(x)}\}, Y)$, Y is a subset of $\{x_1, \ldots, x_{n(x)}\}$. If we allow Y to be empty, this means that we announce that x has no accessible points. This corresponds to the announcement that the action at x failed to execute. See Appendix B4 for the significance of allowing such an announcement. This capability allows us to delete points, not just arcs, because we can delete all access to a point.

4. For a given α and $\mathcal{R}$, let $\mathcal{R}_\alpha$ be
$$\mathcal{R}_\alpha = (\mathcal{R} - \|\alpha\|) \cup \{(x, Y)\}$$
where $\alpha = (x, \{x_1, \ldots, x_{n(x)}\}, Y)$.

5. Let $\bar{t} = (t_1, \ldots, t_n)$ be a sequence of points in S. We define by induction the notion of $\bar{t}$ being a legitimate sequence from t_1 to t_n.

   5.1. (t_1, t_2) is a legitimate sequence if for some $T_2 \subseteq S$ we have $(t_1, T_2) \in \mathcal{R}$ and $t_2 \in T_2$. (This means $t_1 R t_2$ holds.)

   5.2. $(t_1, \ldots, t_{n+1})$ is a legitimate sequence if (t_1, t_2) and $(t_2, \ldots, t_{n+1})$ are legitimate.

6. A legitimate sequence $(t_1, \ldots, t_m)$ is said to be *clarified* if $(t_i, \{t_{i+1}\}) \in \mathcal{R}$, for $i = 1, \ldots, n-1$.

7. Let $\alpha_1, \ldots, \alpha_k$ be public anouncment from $\mathbb{P}$. Let $\bar{t} = (t_1, \ldots, t_n)$ be a legitimate sequence from t_1 to t_n. We say that $\alpha_1, \ldots, \alpha_k$ clarify $\bar{t}$ if $\bar{t}$ is clarified in $\mathcal{R}_{\alpha_1, \ldots, \alpha_n}$.

DEFINITION 6.7 (Talmudic **K** models and Talmudic **K** syntax). We can derive Talmudic **K** models from Talmudic **K** frames of Definition 6.6 as follows:

1. Let the set of possible worlds S^* be the set of all legitimate sequences of the frame. Obviously S^* depends on CR.

2. Let the accessibility relation $R_\mathcal{R}^*$, which is also dependent on $\mathcal{R}$, be defined by $\bar{t} R_\mathcal{R}^* \bar{t}'$ iff for some s in S we have $\bar{t} = (t_1, \ldots, t_n)$ and $t' = (t_1, \ldots, t_n, s)$.

3. With each $(t_1, \ldots, t_n)$ in S^*, we associate a classical Talmudic model $\mathbf{m}_{(t_1, \ldots, t_n)}$, and denote the the domain of this model by $D_{(t_1, \ldots, t_n)}$. We further assume that for any $(t_1, \ldots, t_n, s)$ in S^*, the model $\mathbf{m}_{(t_1, \ldots, t_n, s)}$ is a product of models with domain $D_{(t_1, \ldots, t_n)}$, where the product is as defined in Definition 6.2, and we further assume that $\mathbf{m}_{(t_1, \ldots, t_n)}$ is embedded in $\mathbf{m}_{(t_1, \ldots, t_n, s)}$ as in item 2 of Definition 6.2.

4. We define the syntax of the language. We have atoms, the classical connectives and modal operators as follows:

   - a necessity operator $[N]$.
   - for $\alpha = (x, \{x_1, \ldots, x_n(x)\}, Y)$ being a public announcement, define the operator $[\alpha]$.

Let $[N]$ be a necessity operator and A a formula.

Define

$[N]A$ holds at x in $(S^*, R_{\mathcal{R}}^*)$ iff for all y such that $xR_{\mathcal{R}}^*y$, we have that A holds at y. $[N]$ is an ordinary necessity operator on the accessibility relation $R = R_{\mathcal{R}}^*$.

$[\alpha]A$ holds in $(S^*, R_{\mathcal{R}}^*)$ at x iff (If x is a legitimate sequence in $(S^*, R_{(\mathcal{R}_\alpha)}^*)$ then A holds at x in $(S^*, R_{(\mathcal{R}_\alpha)}^*)$).

5. Note that the syntax depends on the particular semantics and contains elements from the semantics.

REMARK 6.8. Note that Definition 6.7 is not adequate for the purpose of modelling Talmudic behaviour. The problem is with clause 4. Suppose our starting point is t_1 and we have a legitimate sequence $\bar{t} = (t_1, \ldots, t_n)$ and assume that t_2 is chosen from the set $T_2 = \{t_2, s\}$ such that $(t_1, T_2) \in \mathcal{R}$. Further suppose that it is clarified that the correct new state after t_1 should be s. Clause 4 does not apply to this public announcement because $\bar{t}$ *is no longer a legitimate sequence. So we do not have a semantics for this case.*

We must provide a new legitimate sequence to replace $\bar{t}$.

So what is this new legitimate sequence?

The answer is not clear because we cannot say the obvious, namely that it is $\bar{t}' = (t_1, s, t_3, \ldots, t_n)$, because this $\bar{t}'$ may not be a legitimate sequence.

Since a legitimate sequence indicates a possible world where we reach at a certain time after having embarked from our starting point t_1 at time 1, then if the public announcement clarification literally cancels that sequence, we need to know where we are going to be after the announcement!

This question still needs still to be addressed. We shall do this in Section 4 leading to Definition 6.14 and we shall further give full discussion and comparison in Section 5.[11]

REMARK 6.9. We quickly compare our Talmudic public announcement models frames with the traditional one. See Appendix B and [37, Chapter 4]. A more detailed comparison and discussion is done in Section 5 and Appendix B4.

1. Traditional public announcement logic operates as follows. We have a modal **K** model (S, R, t) and we are at node t. We announce a wff φ such that $t \vDash \varphi$. We move to the new model $(S_\varphi = \{s | s \vDash \varphi\}, R, t)$.[12]

2. Talmudic public announcment logic we have $(S, \mathcal{R}, t)$. We announce α and we move to $(S, \mathcal{R}_\alpha, t)$.

---

[11]The perceptive reader might say maybe we should have defined the relation in item (4) slightly differently, for example as follows: sR^*s' iff there exists a legitimate sequence from s to s'. This means in terms of R that s' can be reached from s in the transitive closure of R. This will not help because the public announcement may cancel arcs used to reach s itself. Furthermore when the model is a tree, each node has a unique legitimate sequence leading up to it and we are back to the earlier definition. We would still have a problem.

[12]If φ is announced and it is not true at t then we do nothing.

3. In traditional (say predicate model **K** with increasing domains) public announcement logics the models $\mathbf{m}_t$ associated with t are classical models.

4. In Talmudic public announcement logic the models $\mathbf{n}_t$ associated with t are products, as in Definition 6.2.

   Furthermore, the assignment is not arbitrary but respects the geometry of $(S, \mathcal{R})$ the details of what this means was defined in Definitions 6.3 and 6.5.

DEFINITION 6.10.

1. Let $(S, \mathcal{R}, \mathbb{P})$ be a deterministic Talmudic **K** frame. A subset $\mathbb{P}_0 \subseteq \mathbb{P}$ is said to be consistent if for no $\alpha, \beta \in \mathbb{P}_0$ do we have

$$\alpha = (x, \{x_1, \ldots, x_n\}, y) \text{ and}$$
$$\beta = (x, \{x_1, \ldots, x_n\}, z) \text{ and}$$
$$y \neq z.$$

2. Let $\mathbb{P}_0$ be consistent, then define $\mathcal{R}_{\mathbb{P}_0}$ to be

$$\mathcal{R}_{\mathbb{P}_0} = \mathcal{R} - \{\|\alpha\| | \alpha \in \mathbb{P}_0\} \cup \{(x,y) | (x, \{x_1, \ldots, x_{n(x)}\}, y) \in \mathbb{P}_0\}.$$

   Note that in the above we abuse notation and identify (x,y) with $(x, \{y\})$.

3. $\mathbb{P}$ is said to be a properly clarifying set[13] iff for every maximal consistent subset $\mathbb{P}' \subseteq \mathbb{P}$ we have that $\mathcal{R}_{\mathbb{P}'}$ is a binary relation, namely we have:

   for every x there exists a uniqe y such that $(x, \{y\})$ is in $\mathcal{R}_{\mathbb{P}'}$.

We now introduce time into our models. Our concept of time is discrete and time ticks discretely as we move from one state to another by executing some action. So Figure 6.9 is a classic discrete flow of time

The problem arises when the actions involve the need for clarification. Then we get Figure 6.10.

Note that in Figure 6.10 we move from t to s by executing action **a**. Now because of lack of clarity about action **a**, we might end up at states $s_1, \ldots, s_n$. We now apply action **b**. We therefore must apply **b** to each of the states $s_1, \ldots, s_n$. We thus get the possible states $r_1^i, \ldots, r_m^i$. Note that the same action **b** is applied to each option $s_1, \ldots, s_n$ and that the resulting split is to m options for each s_i (i.e. m depends on **b** only and not on i). This is a design assumption motivated by the Talmud and not by any technical reason!

Also note that our system must tell us how to apply **b** to cases where the models at state s_i are new superposition models.

---

[13]The notion of properly clarifying set is not technically used in the chapter. We have to mention it because our starting point is a linear sequence of events, like the one in Figure 6.9, which because of lack of clarity, becomes branching, like the one in Figure 6.10. We therefore need to define formally, for the sake of conceptual completeness, when a public announcement system restores clarity.

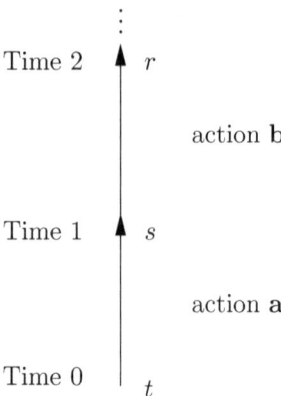

Figure 6.9. Time and actions sequence

EXAMPLE 6.11 (How to apply actions to superposition models). Let us go and take another look at Figure 6.8. Suppose we have another predicate $\lambda x P_1(x)$, which we want to apply to one of the elements in $\{a, b, c\}$. Suppose in the initial model $\mathbf{m_0}$ we have

$$\neg P_1(a) \wedge \neg P_1(b) \wedge \neg P_1(c).$$

We can easily apply first say $P(a)$ and then go on and apply say $P_1(b)$. The result is the model with

$$\neg P_1(a) \wedge P_1(b) \wedge \neg P_1(c) \wedge P(a) \wedge \neg P(b) \wedge \neg P(c).$$

Now if the P-application is not clear, then we get the four options of Figure 6.8. We now want to apply the $P_1(b)$ action. Since we have four optional models $\mathbf{n}_1, \mathbf{n}_2, \mathbf{n}_3$ and $\mathbf{n}_4$, we will have to say that we apply $P_1(b)$ to each one of them. What we do in the case of $\mathbf{n}_1$–$\mathbf{n}_3$ is clear. We apply $P_1(b, b, b)$ to each. But what do we do in the case of $\mathbf{n}_4$? Well, you may think what is the problem? In $\mathbf{n}_4$ let us apply $\mathbf{b}$ and have

$$P(a, b, c) \wedge P_1(b, b, b).$$

This formulation might be sufficient, but now suppose that we have the integrity constraint

(IC) $\neg \exists x [P(x) \wedge P_1(x)]$.

Now in this case we cannot apply $P_1(b, b, b)$ to $\mathbf{n}_2$. But can we apply it to $\mathbf{n}_4$?

Does $P(a, b, c) \wedge P_1(b, b, b)$ violate the integrity constraint?

We can say no, (a, b, c) and (b, b, b) are not the same x or we can say that the property P is superimposed also on b in (a, b, c) and therefore we adopt the view that we cannot apply $P_1(b)$.

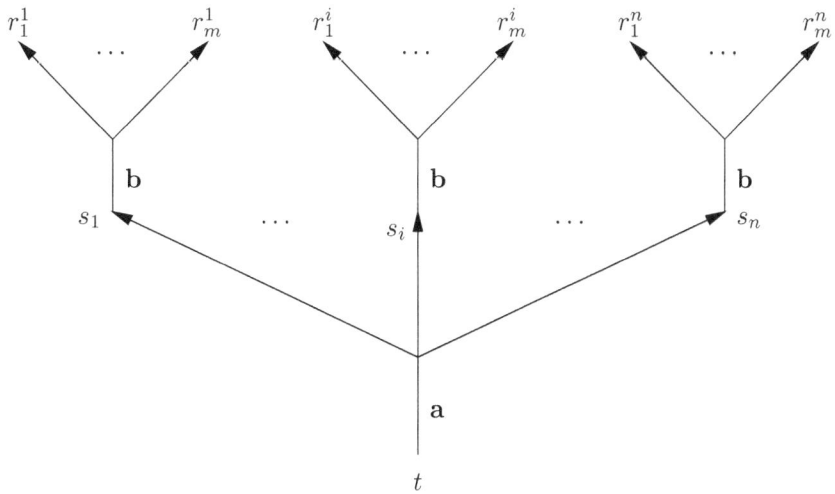

Figure 6.10. Lack of clarity in time and actions sequence

The formal approach would have to accept that (a,b,c) and (b,b,b) are not the same x, however further axioms may come into play for some predicates, for example

$$P(a,b,c) \to P(a,a,a) \bigwedge P(b,b,b) \bigwedge P(c,c,c).$$

The Talmud might have additional constraints for some P and P_1.[14]

We can say do not apply $P_1(b)$. We can also say apply $P_1(b)$ and retract if the clarification for P chooses $P(b)$.

EXAMPLE 6.12 (Talmudic views, Example 6.1 refined). We are now ready to revisit the Talmudic opinions about the situation in Figures 6.7 and 6.8. Think of the action taken at time 1 as legally endowing entity x from among the set $\{a,b,c\}$ with the legal status $\lambda x P(1,x)$ such as ownership of an account with 50 billion dollars in it. The action was not clear and the available options for clarification are that either $P(a)$ or $P(b)$ or $P(c)$ or the partnership (superposition) of all three elements, which we formalise as $P(\{a,b,c\})$. Denote the respective models for these options as $\mathbf{n}_1, \ldots, \mathbf{n}_4$.

The simplest story we can give is that we want to confer status P now at time 1 on the x such that $x \in \{a,b,c\}$ and x wins the elections to take place at time m.

Obviously we need to wait for time m to clarify the situation. Meanwhile, the following can happen:

1. Nothing happens at time m.
2. a wins at time m.

---
[14]For example the constraint might be that one cannot hold public office and be fraudulent at the same time, and also hold the view that if one is involved as a partner in a legally registered partnership which is fraudulent, then one is to be considered fraudulent as well.

3. b wins at time m.

4. c wins at time m.

5. a dies at time 2.

6. a and b die before time m.

7. Some of the parameters involved are cancelled, e.g. no elections, donation is cancelled etc.

Obviously from the logical point of view we get lack of clarity[15] because we define at time $t = 1$ an entity using the Iota $ix\varphi(x)$, where φ is a predicate dependent on time m.

Formally we have

($\sharp$) $\qquad\qquad [y \in \{a,b,c\} \wedge [y = ix\varphi(m,x)] \rightarrow P(1,y)$

The question is: Do we accept such definitions?

These are called *Breira (choice)*[16] in the Talmud.

We have the following Talmudic positions, as we already mentioned in Example 6.1.

1. We do not accept such definitions. Nothing happens. Reject i.e., making such a conditional proposition is not logically coherent and carries no sense.

2. We do not accept such definitions but nevertheless something does happen. We move to the quantum model $\mathbf{n}_4$ *immediately* from time 2, and even at time m if a specific y is found, we still remain with model $\mathbf{n}_4$.

   Of course, if say c dies at time 2 then from time 3 the superposition may be on $\{a,b\}$ only, but not necessarily. For example if it is not clarified to which of $\{a,b,c\}$ I am married, then if c dies then I may be considered a widower, so the superposition (a,b,c) still continues. In fact, in legal and every day life elements never die, we still talk about them. In the UK it is possible for parents to register their unborn child to Beavers (the youngest age group in the Scouting movement) on the expectation of the child's coming existence.

   To be quite clear, this position says that even when there is clarity at time m that $P(a)$ should hold, we still stick with the (quantum-like)

---

[15] This problematic feature of future indeterminates has been recognised in classical aristotelian logic and was treated along the lines of binary truth values that apply to all times, [1]. In pp. 140-142 the different explanations for the status of the predicate of a future (and later past) event in Aristotelian logic.

[16] Breira (literaly 'determination'/'resolution') is an underdetermined or uniquely future-oriented choice defining a Halakhic (Talmudic legal) state, that differs from a regular condition (Tenai). Breira is chiefly discussed in Trachtate Gittin 25a, 74a concerning divorce law, and Trachtate Eruvin 37b regarding definitions of extended 'personal space' in holidays (allowing for motion beyond the default degrees of freedom). A more involved case appears in Trachtate Beitza 10a, in the context of deciding on a specific fowl for the holiday feast. For a treatment of classic logical attributes of Breira, [72].

superposition $P(a,b,c)$. So if at time $m+1$ we want to execute $P_1(b)$, with the constraints
$$\neg \exists x(P(x) \wedge P_1(x))$$
we still reject the action because the superposition on b remains. See Example 6.11.

3. We do accept such definitions. We think of parallel histories and wait for time m for clarification to find the y (if it exists) and $P(y)$ holds from time 1.

4. We accept the definition, however the clarification is effective only from time m. At the intermediate times, times 2 to $m-1$, the model is the (quantum-like) superposition model $\mathbf{n}_4$. Again if c dies the superposition is reduced. Even after time m when we look back and ask what model was at time 2? We will say $\mathbf{n}_4$.

5. We accept the definition and the clarification is effective from time m. Thus the winner has property P only from time m.

REMARK 6.13 (Methodological comments). The perceptive reader must have noticed that so far we defined semantic models to help us understand Talmudic reasoning. We gave Kripke type semantics but did not give any corresponding formal syntax. This is not needed in principle. Think for example of Situation semantics, pioneered by Jon Barwise and John Perry in the early 1980s, this was a purely semantic attempt to provide a solid theoretical foundation for reasoning about common-sense and real world situations. No axiom system was necessary. Only a sharpening of concepts using formal semantics of logic.

So to explain the various opinions and nuances of the great Rabbis about lack of clarity in action and time the semantics is sufficient, and the various distinctions can be written in English in the metalevel. No need to introduce modal operators and further write the distinctions in the language of the operators and prove a completeness theorem.

Nevertheless, this new Talmudic semantic does inspire new types of logics and we shall present some in Section 4.

4 Propositional Talmudic public announcement logic TPK

We now introduce propositional public announcement logic based on **K** inspired (see Remark 6.13) by the Talmud. We first need to motivate the formal design of the system.

4.1 Motivation

Consider a state t at time 1. To have a concrete example, assume John owns a certain book. John performs an action **a** depending on the future. He gives the book either to Tracy or to Mary, provided that next week, at time 7, a coin is flipped. If it lands heads then the book is Mary's (action $\mathbf{a}_1$ at state s_1) and if lands tails, then it is Tracy's (action $\mathbf{a}_2$ at state s_2).

Now consider another action:

$$\mathbf{b} = \text{Tracy writes her name in the book.}$$

Its precondition is that $\alpha = $ Tracy owns the book.

Its postcondition is

$$\beta = \text{Tracy's name is in the book.}$$

The question is: Can Tracy perform action $\mathbf{b}$ at time 2?

Well, if at time 7 Tracy wins, then the action $\mathbf{b}$ at time 2 is OK, but if not then the precondition of the action is not fulfilled and so $\mathbf{b}$ cannot be performed. However, at time 2 we do not know who owns the book. So one of two scenarioes can be allowed to happen at time 2:

1. $\mathbf{b}$ is not allowed to be executed.

2. $\mathbf{b}$ is tolerated, i.e. it can be executed anyway and a risk is taken.[17]

Note that no matter what the policy is, it is a symmetrical policy, as Figure 6.11 shows, with respect to states $\{s_1, s_2\}$.

1. Either $\mathbf{b}$ cannot be executed, neither at s_1 nor at s_2; or

2. $\mathbf{b}$ is tolerated both at s_1 and at s_2.

The important feature of Figure 6.11 is that action

$$\mathbf{b} = \text{Tracy writes her name on book}$$

is tolerated even if its precondition does not hold. This is because the states $\{s_1, s_2\}$ are regarded as some sort of superposition single entangled state $s_1 \times s_2$. So either $\mathbf{b}$ can be applied to all of them or to none of them.

The technical importance of this observation can be seen in Figure 6.12.

In Figure 6.12 the two actions $\mathbf{a}$ and $\mathbf{b}$ are not clear and require clarification. $\mathbf{a}$ can be $\mathbf{a}_1$ or $\mathbf{a}_2$ and $\mathbf{b}$ can be $\mathbf{b}_1$ or $\mathbf{b}_2$. Suppose Tracy uses disappearing ink which holds for a maximum of 3 days. So there are two possibilities:

1. Tracy's name is permanently on the book.

2. Tracy's name is not permanently on the book.

Suppose at time 7 we discover that Mary is the owner. This is the public announcement. Suppose that at time 7 we are at node x, because we chose the path $(t, \mathbf{a}_2, s_2, \mathbf{b}_2, r_2, \ldots, x)$ at our own best guess and risk.

The public announcement says we should have gone to $(t, \mathbf{a}_1, s_1, \ldots)$. So where are we now? We are not at x. If we allow for $\mathbf{b}$ to be executed at s_1 as well as at s_2, with the same possible options, then we can continue the same continuation path from a_1

To do this we must pair the unclear states r_1, r_2 which are the result of the lack of clarity when $\mathbf{b}$ is executed on s_1 with r'_1 and r'_2, which are the result of $\mathbf{b}$ executed at s_2.

---

[17]The Talmud deals with situations like this, where there is a doubt. The Bible requires us to be strict and so we should not tolerate Tracy writing her name on the book. The situation of flipping a coin is not under her control. Suppose for comparison that the book is given to Tracy on condition that at time 7 she cleans her flat, and if she does not do so then the book goes to Mary. Tracy can argue at time 2 that she is in control and at time 7 she will indeed clean her flat. So her action at time 2 of writing her name in the book, may be tolerated.

6. FUTURE DETERMINATION OF ENTITIES   211

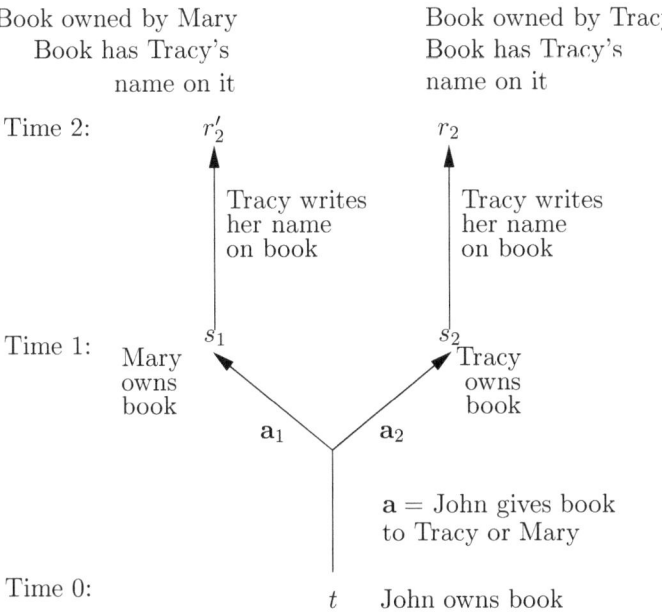

Figure 6.11. Actions which are tolerated

We can thus continue

$$(t, \mathbf{a}_2, s_1, \mathbf{b}_2, r'_2, \ldots, y)^{18}$$

So what are the formal assumptions we need on our formal modelling?

1. Any action $\mathbf{a}$ has the lack of clarity that it might be $\mathbf{a}_1, \ldots, \mathbf{a}_k$. When in state t we perform action $\mathbf{a}$, then we might be in any of the states $s_1(t, \mathbf{a}_1), \ldots, s_k(t, \mathbf{a}_k)$.

2. Any other unclear action $\mathbf{b}$, which might be $\mathbf{b}_1, \ldots, \mathbf{b}_m$ can be applied to any of $s_i(t, \mathbf{a}_i)$ resulting in $r_j(s_i(t, \mathbf{a}_i), \mathbf{b}_j)$ $1 \leq j \leq n$.

    The number of outcomes m is fixed and depends on $\mathbf{b}$ only, and not on $s_i(t, \mathbf{a}_i)$.

3. The m outcomes for each $s_i(t, \mathbf{a}_i)$ are matched and the listing indicates the matching. Thus for each $1 \leq j \leq n$ $r_j(s_1(t, \mathbf{a}_1), r_j(s_2(t, \mathbf{a}_2), \ldots,$

---

[18]Note that we can use simpler notation. The points in Figure 6.12 can be identified by the actions leading to them. Thus we can write

$$\begin{aligned} s_1 &= t\mathbf{a}_1 \\ s_2 &= t\mathbf{a}_2 \\ r_1 &= t\mathbf{a}_2\mathbf{b}_1 \\ r_2 &= t\mathbf{a}_2\mathbf{b}_2 \\ r'_1 &= t\mathbf{a}_1\mathbf{b}_1 \\ r'_2 &= t\mathbf{a}_1\mathbf{b}_2. \end{aligned}$$

We shall use this notation in Section 4.2.

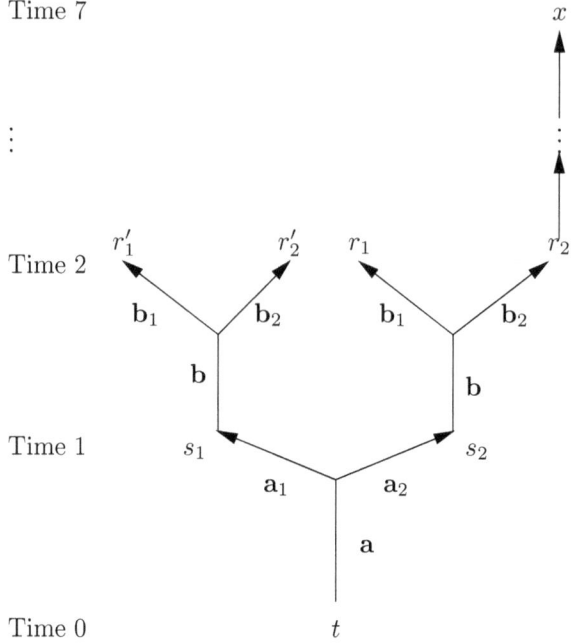

Figure 6.12. Technical view of tolerated actions

$r_j(s_k(t, \mathbf{a}_k))$ are matched because they are all obtained by the application of action $\mathbf{b}_j$.

Note that two matched states need not be the same. In Figure 6.11, r_1 is matched to r_2', but in r_2 Tracy owns the book and in r_2', Mary owns the book. The states are matched because both are the result of the action $\mathbf{b}$ of Tracy writing her name on the book in permanent ink.

The notation we use is

$$(t, \mathbf{a}_i, s_i, \mathbf{b}_j, r_j, \ldots)$$

4.2 Preliminary formal discussion

We now semi-formally motivate and explain our system. Let $\mathbf{A}$ be a set of actions. Let s_0 be an initial state. If the actions are all deterministic then we can move from state to state by applying the actions. The following is a simple run:

$$s_0 \mathbf{a} \mathbf{a}' \mathbf{a}'' \ldots$$

The state arising from s_0 after the application of action $\mathbf{a}$ is $s_1 = (s_0 \mathbf{a})$, etc, etc.

Actually what we have here is a deterministic automaton, where the states are sequences of actions applied to s_0 and the alphabet are the actions.

Now assume that the actions $\mathbf{a} \in \mathbf{A}$ have some ambiguity to be clarified at a later stage (i.e. after more actions are applied). So applying $\mathbf{a}$ could be any of $\mathbf{a}_1, \ldots, \mathbf{a}_{k(\mathbf{a})}$, where $\lambda \mathbf{x} \mathbf{k}(\mathbf{x})$ gives us the number of possibilities for $\mathbf{x}$.

Then when we apply say $s_0\mathbf{aa'a''}$ we can get any one of the states

$$\{s_0\mathbf{a}_i\mathbf{a}'_j\mathbf{a}''_r\}$$

where $1 \leq i \leq k(\mathbf{a}), 1 \leq j \leq k(\mathbf{a}')$ and $1 \leq r \leq k(\mathbf{a}'')$.

If at this point there is a public announcement that $\mathbf{a}$ is indeed $\mathbf{a}_1$, then part of the ambiguity is resolved and our options are now

$$\{s_0\mathbf{a}_1\mathbf{a}'_j\mathbf{a}''_r\}$$

We are now ready to define the model. We do this in stages.

1. A model has the form $(S, \mathbf{A}, s_0, \rho, h)$ where $\mathbf{A}$ is a set of actions and S is a set of elements of the form

$$\alpha = (s_0\mathbf{a}^1_{j_1}\mathbf{a}^2_{j_2}\ldots\mathbf{a}^m_{j_m})$$

where $1 \leq j_i \leq k(\mathbf{a}^i), \mathbf{a}^i \in \mathbf{A}$ and $1 \leq \mathbf{k}(\mathbf{a}^i)$.

We also allow for $\alpha = (s_0)$.

2. Let R_1 be the relation $\alpha R_1 \beta$ iff $\beta = \alpha * (\mathbf{a}_j)$ for some $a \in \mathbf{A}$ and $j \leq \mathbf{k}(\mathbf{a})$, where $*$ denotes concatenation of sequences. Let R be the transitive closure of R_1.

3. We need the notion of a node x is at a distance n from (s_0).

   - (s_0) is at a distance 0 from itself.
   - If α is at a distance n from (s_0) then $\alpha * (\mathbf{a})$ is at a distance $n+1$.
   - The distance is actually the time, since we are applying the actions in sequence, one after the other.

4. We now define ρ. Let $\alpha = \beta * (\mathbf{b}_j) * \gamma$ where we have that $\mathbf{b}_j$ is one option from among $\{\mathbf{b}_1, \ldots, \mathbf{b}_{\mathbf{k}(\mathbf{b})}\}$.

   We are at point $\alpha = \beta * (\mathbf{b}_j) * \gamma$. At this point there is a public announcement that the correct meaning of action $\mathbf{b}$ taken at the β level was $\mathbf{b}_1$ and not $\mathbf{b}_j$. So we actually should have been at $\beta * (\mathbf{b}_1)$ and subsequent actions γ would bring us to $\beta * (\mathbf{b}_1) * \gamma$.

   If the public announcement says b_1, i.e. $j = 1$, then it is a confirmation that we are at the right place. The procedure still works.

   Now suppose we take action $\mathbf{e}$ and apply to our current state. Without the public announcement we move to $\beta * (\mathbf{b}_j) * \gamma * (\mathbf{e})$.

   However, the public announcement says we should be at $\alpha' = \beta * (\mathbf{b}_1) * \gamma$ and so we should move to $\alpha' * (\mathbf{e}) = \beta * (\mathbf{b}_1) * \gamma * (\mathbf{e})$.

   Thus the effect of the public announceent at α is to send us to $\alpha' * (\mathbf{e})$ which is $\beta * (\mathbf{b}_1) * \gamma * (\mathbf{e})$.

   We draw the function ρ as in Figure 6.13. Ordinary arrows $\rightarrow$ indicate R and double arrows $\twoheadrightarrow$ indicate ρ.

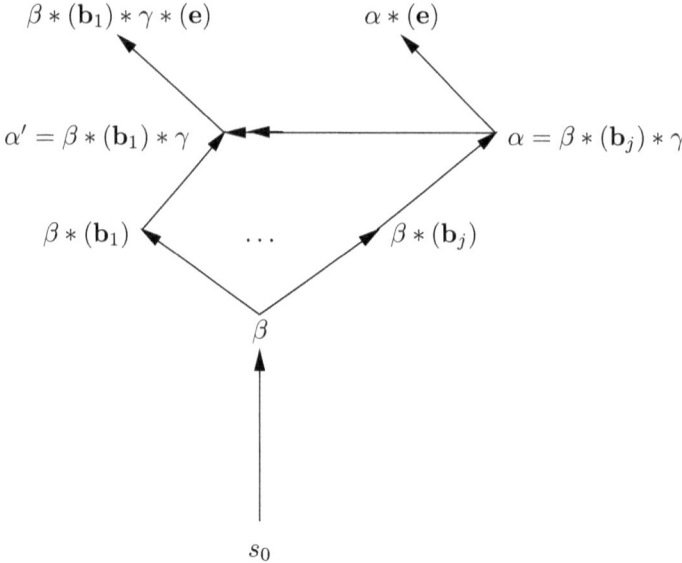

Figure 6.13. The function ρ

The relation ρ between α and α', identifies the public announcement uniquely. Note that α and α' are at the same distance from (s_0).

Actually there is a problem. What if the public announcement says that actually $\mathbf{b}_j$ was the correct choice? How do we express that? We will have to let ρ take us to $\beta * (\mathbf{b}_j)$. The perceptive reader might ask, why not be consistent and let ρ take us to $\beta * (\mathbf{b}_1)$ in all cases and the case where $\mathbf{b}_1 = \mathbf{b}_j$ will sort itself automatically?

The problem with that is that we need to identify where we are going to be when we apply the next action $\mathbf{e}$, in our example we need to identify $\beta*(\mathbf{b}_1)*\gamma*(\mathbf{e})$. We are using ρ to help us so we let ρ point to $\beta*(\mathbf{b}_1)*\gamma$.[19]

The very next paragraph does public announcement without action symbols, using just accessibility relation, and and the problem of identifying where we should be is crucial.

Let us now look at this differently. Assume $x\rho y$. Since (S, R) is a tree, let z be the unique maximal first point below both x and y. Note that if y itself is below x then z is the predecessor of y. Let u be the next point in the direction of x and v the next point in the direction of y. Again

---

[19] The pure minded reader may object to our approach. He will say that we can still identify where to go. Let ρ take us to the point $\beta * (\mathbf{b}_1)$, which is the conceptually correct clarification point. We now know two points

(a) where we are, namely $\alpha = \beta * (\mathbf{b}_j) * \gamma$
(b) the clarified action $\alpha = \beta * (\mathbf{b}_1)$.

From the above two items we can identify γ and go to $\alpha' = \beta * (\mathbf{b}_1) * \gamma$.
  This is true but only because points are identified by sequences of actions. We do not have this luxury in the general case.

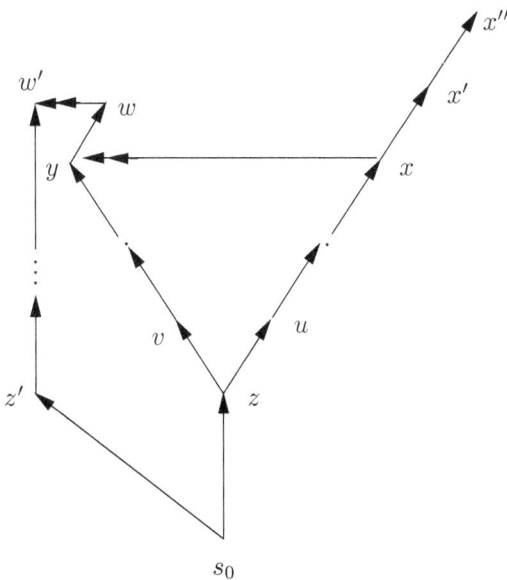

Figure 6.14. Public announcement and ρ

note that if y is below x then $u = v = y$. Then the public announcement at x says that u is clarified and really should be v. Again, if y is below x then the public announcement says that u was the correct choice.

We can write the public announcement in the form $x\rho y$ and we identify the point z as its *target base*.

Figure 6.14 describes the situation.

Note that whenever $x\rho y$ holds and x is at distance n from the root s_0, then y is at distance $n+1$, unless y is below x.

Note that Figure 6.14 clarifies a further point. In this figure there is another public announcement namely $w\rho w'$. This one says that z should have been z'. Note that the public announcements need not come in the same order as the order of the ambiguities. (z, z') came before (u, v) but was clarified after. This can be a bit problematic because once we go through z' we do not pass through z any more. So we had better require that the clarifications come in order. In the notation where points are described by actions as in Figure 6.13, the order is not important and is not confusing because it is the actions that are clarified.

Note also that if we have another public annuncement sending say w' to an extension of x' of x (i.e. $w'\rho x'$) then a previous public announcement will be reversed.

We can require coherence and stability and not allow such reversals!

5. We have one more point to discuss. Imagine we have had a clarification as in Figure 6.14, where we had $x\rho y$. Take the branch of history from z

to x. This is not the real history because we are moving to point y.

However this history is real past for anyone living along the path from z to x.

To make it real to the reader assume the action taken at z was the marriage of John and Mary using a priest who has been ambiguously ordained. John and Mary continued as a married couple from z up to x when it was announced that the priest was not properly ordained and therefore the marriage is null. So John and Mary move to point y and their history (path z to y) does not include marriage. We must allow them to remember as part of their past also the path z to x.[20]

Thus when we create a temporal model out of R and ρ, we must take the above into account!

4.3 Formal TPK

In view of the discussion in the previous two subsections, we are now ready to present our Talmudic public announcement logic.

DEFINITION 6.14 (Deterministic **TPK** model).

1. A deterministic **TPK** model has the form $(S, R_1, R, \rho, s_0, h)$ where (S, R_1, s_0) is a tree with root s_0 and successor relation R_1 and where R is the transitive closure of R_1.

2. ρ is a functional relation satisfying the following properties

    2.1. $\forall xyz(x\rho y \wedge x\rho z \rightarrow y = z)$[21]

    2.2. If $x\rho y \rightarrow y \neq s_0$.

    2.3. $x\rho y \wedge \neg y R x \wedge y \neq x \rightarrow D(y) = D(x)$, where D is the distance from the root, $D(s_0) = 0$ and whenever $uR_1 v$ then $D(v) = D(u) + 1$.

    2.4. Let $x \in S$ and let zRx. We say the successors of z are publicly clarified to be v, where $zR_1 v$ holds, if we have $x\rho y$, with vRy.

    We require the property of coherence:

    - If $\{zR_1 v_1$ and $zR_1 v_2$ and [z is publicly clarified at x_1 to be v_1] and [z is publicly clarified at x_2 to be v_2]$\}$ then $v_1 = v_2$.

    2.5. Let z be any point, then there exists an x, such that zRx and the successors of z are publicly clarified at x.

    2.6. Since every z has a unique successor which is publicly clarified at some point, this means that there exists a path $\pi = (s_0, s_1, \ldots)$ such that for every $0 \leq i, s_{i+1}$ is the uniquely clarified successor of s_i. Note that this is why we call the model deterministic.

---

[20]The perceptive reader, familiar with the key paper of Governatori and Rotolo [64], might wonder whether this is just a case of revision. It is not. It is a case of backwards causality of [11] We have compared and discussed the Governatori and Rotolo work in Section 5 of [11].

[21] 1. There may be no z such that $x\rho z$.

2. This condition is for deterministic actions only, otherwise ρ is just a binary relation.

6. FUTURE DETERMINATION OF ENTITIES 217

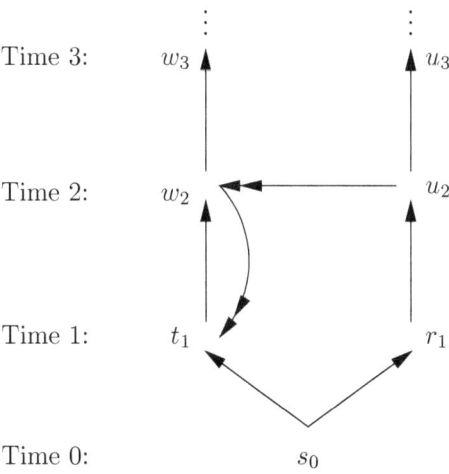

Figure 6.15.

2.7. Note that if we define, for x in S, the set T_x to be $\{y|xR_1y\}$ and let $\mathcal{R}$ be defined as the set of all pairs (x, T_x), we get a frame in the sense of Definition 6.6. We can also define the public announcements correctly from ρ using item 2.4.

3. We now define a temporal relation $<$ on the model. We use the notion of legitimate sequence of worlds

   3.1. (s_0) is a legitimate sequence.

   3.2. Assume $(s_0, \ldots, s_n)$ is a legitimate sequence leading to s_n.

   Case 1. $\neg \exists x [s_n \rho x]$.
   In this case let w be any point such that $s_n R_1 w$, then $(s_0, \ldots, s_n, w)$ is a legitimate sequence.

   Case 2. For some y we have $(s_n \rho y \wedge \neg y R s_n)$.
   In this case let w be any point such that yR_1w, then $(s_1, \ldots, s_n, w)$ is a legitimate sequence.

   Case 3. For some y $s_n \rho y \wedge yRs_n$.
   Then this case is like Case 1.

   3.3. Define $x < y$ iff there exists a legitimate sequence $(s_0, \ldots, s_i, x, s_{i+2}, \ldots, y)$.

REMARK 6.15 (Axiomatic formulation of **TPK**). It may be of interest to the reader to see how we can design syntax and axioms for the deterministic semantics of Definition 6.14. The models involve the tree relation R_1 and the functional relation ρ. Each one of these would require a modality to control it. To motivate the syntax, let us give an illustrative figure, Figure 6.15.

In this figure, we start at state s_0 and apply action **a**. Action **a** is not clear. It either takes us to state t_1 or to state r_1. We then apply more clear-cut actions **b**, which takes us to w_2 from t_1 and to u_2 from r_1 and then action **c** which takes us from w_2 to w_3 and from u_2 to u_3.

At time 1, we can either be at t_1 or at r_1. At time 3 we can either be at w_3 or at u_3.

Suppose at time 2 the nature of action **a** is clarified (publicly announced). It is clarified that t_1 is the correct successor. If we are at u_2 then we should be at w_2.

This is indicated by the double arrow (ρ relation $u_2 \twoheadrightarrow w_2$).

If we are at w_2, then we are at the correct place. This is indicated by the double arrows $w_2 \twoheadrightarrow t_1$. We now have several legitimate sequences of states:

1. $s_0 r_1 u_2 w_3 \ldots$

2. $s_0 t_1 w_2 w_3 \ldots$

We also have the tree relation sequences

3. $(s_0 r_1 u_2 u_3)$ (not a legitimate sequence)

4. $(s_0 t_1 w_2 w_3)$

We need connectives in the syntax that will give us complete control to describe the properties of the semantics and axomatise it.

The following is a possible choice.

1. Modality $\Box$ to follow the tree relation

    - $t \vDash \Box A$ iff for all s such that $tR_1 s$ we have $s \vDash A$

2. Yesterday operator for $\Box$

    - $t \vDash YA$ iff the R_1 predecessor of $t \vDash A$.
    - If $t = s_0$ then $YA = \bot$

3. Modality corresponding to ρ (i.e. the double arrow relation).

    - $t \vDash \boxminus A$ iff for all s such that $t\rho s$ we have $s \vDash A$.

4. Yesterday relation for $\boxminus$.

    - $t \vDash \mathbb{Y} A$ iff for the s such that $s\rho t$ we have $s \vDash A$ and if no such s exists then $\bot$.

5. Time constants D_n. $t \vDash D_n$ iff the distance of t from s_0 is n.

I think we have enough operators in the syntax to describe the semantics. We can write axioms and attempt to prove completeness.

It is not our purpose in this chapter to put forward pure technical results, but we are giving enough details for the interested reader.

EXAMPLE 6.16. In Figure 6.14 we have $z < x < w$.

REMARK 6.17. To obtain a non-deterministic model we allow ρ in Definition 6.14 to be a general binary relation. To explain how this works consider Figure

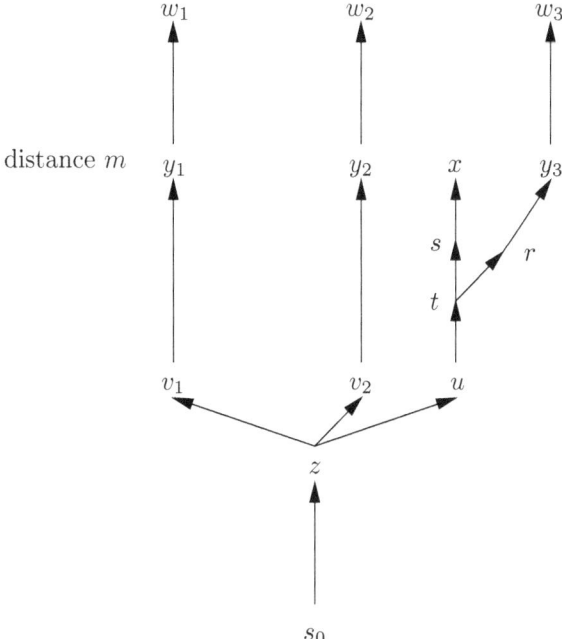

Figure 6.16. Non-deterministic model

6.16. The points y_1, y_2 and x are at distance m from t and they are all on different paths separating at z.

The points x and y_3 are also at distance m but they are on paths separating at t. So the path $s_0, \ldots, z, \ldots, u, \ldots, t, s, \ldots, x$) made a choice of u over v_1 and v_2 and s over r.

If we let $x\rho y_3$ we are saying r is a correct non-deterministic choice and if we let $x\rho y_1 \wedge x\rho y_2$ we are saying that v_1 and v_2 are the right non-deterministic choice.

Note that by saying $x\rho y_3$ we are also implying that u is a correct non-deterministic choice, because only through u can we get to r.

However, we can also take the view that $x\rho y_3$ says that only as long as we can go through u, then r is the correct choice.

5 Discussion and Comparison with traditional public announcement logic

REMARK 6.18. We begin by comparing Definitions 6.6 and 6.7 and Remark 6.8 with Definition 6.14.

Consider the following Figure 6.17. Ignore the double arrows, and consider only single arrows.

The arrows represent the relation R_1 for the set of nodes S.

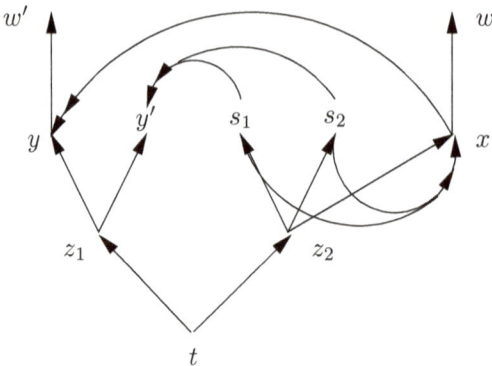

Figure 6.17.

Define the relation $\mathcal{R}$ (according to Definition 6.6) as follows:

$$t \, \mathcal{R} \, \{z_1, z_2\}$$
$$z_1 \, \mathcal{R} \, \{y, y_1\}$$
$$z_1 \, \mathcal{R} \, \{s_1, s_2, x\}$$
$$x \, \mathcal{R} \, \{w\}$$
$$y \, \mathcal{R} \, \{w'\}$$

We used the obvious recipe

(*) $\qquad\qquad\qquad \alpha \, \mathcal{R} \, \{\beta | \alpha R_1 \beta\}$

Consider the following public announcements in the sense of Definition 6.6:

(a_1) $(t, \{z_1, z_2\}, z_1)$

(a_2) $(z_1, \{y, y'\}, y)$

(a_3) $(z_2, \{s_1, s_2, x\}, x)$.

We now have a model frame in the sense of Definition 6.6. To turn this into a proper model we need to say what are the worlds and which worlds we assign to atoms. Let us do that. The worlds are the legitimate sequences, which are really the points in the graph, because the graph is a tree. This is in full agreement with Definition 6.7.

Now assume we live at the world s_1.

Our public announcements establish that the real sequence is (t, z_1, y, w'). So where does s_1 collapse to?

Obviously, if we have all the public announcements (a_1)–(a_3), then s_1 collapses to y. However, if we only have (a_1), then where does s_1 go to? (The other public announcements (a_2)–(a_3) may come later.) So our model lacks full information. This is what we have already remarked in Remark 6.8. Now consider the double arrows $s_1 \twoheadrightarrow y'$, $s_2 \twoheadrightarrow y'$, $x \twoheadrightarrow y$. These double arrows, when read according to Definition 6.14, all express the public announcement (a_1), but they also say more than that, they also say where s_1, s_2 and x are supposed to go to, in the event that public announcement (a_1) is put forward! There are provisions in Definition 6.14 (items 2.3 and 2.4) which ensure that this extra information does not contradict itself.

Furthermore, the double arrows also tell us at what time and place the public announcement is made. So the possible additional double arrow $s \twoheadrightarrow w'$ for example (which is not shown in Figure 6.17) not only tells us the public announcement (a_1) and where w is to go to (to w') but it also tells us that (a_1) was announced at time 4 (4 is the distance of w from the origin t.

REMARK 6.19. We now compare in more detail the Talmudic public announcement logic with the traditional public announcement logic as described in [37].

Assume we have modal operators $[\varphi]$ for φ a wff and $[\alpha]$ for α a nondeterministic public announcement statement in the sense of Definition 6.6. We have, in a model (S, R, t).

- $t \vDash [\varphi]A$ iff If $t \vDash \varphi$ (i.e. $t \in S_\varphi$) then $t \vDash A$ in the model $(S_\varphi, R \upharpoonright S_\varphi, t)$ where $S_\varphi = \{x | x \vDash \varphi\}$.

For comparison we have according to Definition 6.6

- $t \vDash [\alpha]A$ iff If t is a legitimate sequence in $(S, \mathcal{R}_\alpha)$ then $t \vDash A$ in $(S, \mathcal{R}_\alpha, t)$.

Both definitions move from a larger model (S, R) to a smaller model either made smaller by φ or by α.

So if we require that the Kripke frame (S, R) is a tree (every point y in S has a unique predecessor x such that xRy) and allow for any subset $T \subseteq S$ to be definable by a formula φ, the two definitions are essentially the same otherwise they are not, see Appendix B4 for exact results.

In both cases the public announcement is metalevel and outside the model and we require that the point of evaluation t is not destroyed by the public announcement.

The refinement of Definition 6.14 is different

1. It is object level

2. It ties the announcment to a time and place.

3. It allows for the evaluation world to be destroyed by the announcement and displaces us and sends us to another world.

4. It has a backward effect in that it allows us to define $<$ as in Definition 6.14, item (3).

Appendices
Appendix A: A convenient view of modal logic K

We view modal logic **K** as a time action logic, which is more convenient for our purpose.

Modal logic K

Modal logic **K** is formulated in the language of classical logic with the added unary operator $\Box$. The set of theorems is generated by the following axioms schemes:

1. All substitution instances of classical truth functional tautologies.
2. $\Box(A \to B) \to (\Box A \to \Box B)$
3. $\dfrac{\vdash A}{\vdash \Box A}$

The logic is complete for Kripke models of the form (T, R, Ω, h), where (T, R, Ω) is a tree with root Ω and h is an assignment giving for each atom q of the language a subset $h(q) \subseteq T$.

Note that actually modal **K** is complete for the class of finite trees.

Satisfaction is of the form $t \vDash A$, where $t \in T$ and A a wff and is defined recursively as follows:

- $t \vDash q$ iff $t \in h(q)$ for q atomic.
- $t \vDash A \wedge B$ iff $t \vDash A$ and $t \vDash B$
- $t \vDash \neg A$ iff $t \nvDash A$
- $t \vDash \Box A$ iff for all s such that s is an immediate successor of t in the tree we have that $s \vDash A$.
- A holds in the model (T, R, Ω, h) iff $\Omega \vDash A$.
- **K** is complete for this semantics in the sense that we have for any A:
  (*) A is a theorem of **K** iff A holds in every model.

Time action view of K

We now want to view this tree semantics for **K** as a time-action model. We first describe the tree (T, R, Ω) using successor functions. Let $\mathbb{R} = \{\mathbf{r}_1, \mathbf{r}_2, \ldots\}$ be a set of unary successor functions capable of operating on Ω. We thus form all element sequences of the form

$$t = \Omega \mathbf{a}_1 \mathbf{a}_2 \mathbf{a}_3 \ldots \mathbf{a}_n$$

We define tRs to hold iff for some $\mathbf{a} \in \mathbb{R}$ we have $s = t\mathbf{a}$.

We call such models $\mathbf{m} = (\mathbb{R}, R, \Omega)$ *time action models*. We regard Ω as the initial state, the elements of $\mathbb{R}$ as actions $\mathbf{a} \in \mathbb{R}$ moving us from any state t to a new state $t\mathbf{a}$. Such a view is consistent with agent theory, if we regard as part of any state also the sequence of actions generating this state.

Figure 6.18 shows a time action model.

Time comes into the model if we take the view that time moves one unit when we perform any action.

So at time 0 we are at the initial state Ω.

If at time n we are at the state t and we apply action $\mathbf{a}$ then we move to time $(n+1)$ and to state $t\mathbf{a}$.

Note the following

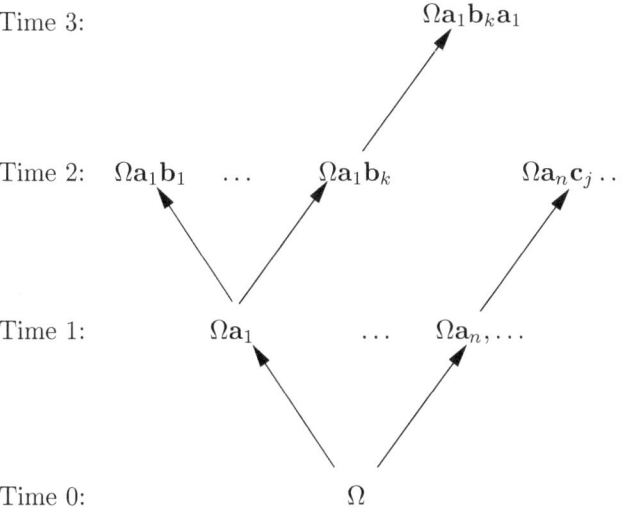

Figure 6.18.

(a) Actions **a** are deterministic and uniquely take a state t to the unique state $t\mathbf{a}$.

(b) The meaning of $t \models \Box A$ is that at state t any action **a** when applied will take us to a new state $t\mathbf{a}$ in which A holds.

(c) To do proper justice to this view, we need to specify the actions through their pre-conditions and post-conditions and present Ω as a compelte theory Δ_Ω defining the initial state. When we apply any action **a** to state Ω, we need a revision operator $*$ taking us from Δ_Ω to the theory of the new state $\Delta_{\Omega \mathbf{a}}$. Let $(\alpha_\mathbf{a}, \beta_\mathbf{a})$ be the precondition and post condition respectively of the action **a**. Then we have

$$\Delta_{\Omega \mathbf{a}} = \Delta_\Omega \text{ if } \Delta_\Omega \nvdash \alpha_\mathbf{a}$$
$$\Delta_{\Omega \mathbf{a}} = \Delta_\Omega * \beta_\mathbf{a} \text{ if } \Delta_\Omega \vdash \alpha_\mathbf{a}$$

The upshot of the above is that technically an assignment h into the model which is arbitrary in the traditional case of modal **K** corresponds to assigning $\Delta_\Omega, (\alpha_\mathbf{a}, \beta_\mathbf{a})$, and $*$ to the time action system.

Of course we can always take a tree model for traditional modal **K** and take the successor functions $\mathbf{r}_n$ and pretend they are actions and pretend that some $*$ exists such that for each t,

$$\Theta_{t\mathbf{r}_n} = \Theta_t * \beta_{\mathbf{r}_n}$$

where $\Theta_t = \{\varphi | \varphi \text{ does not contain } \Box \text{ and } t \models \varphi\}$.

If we do this we need the extra coherence condition that

$$\Theta_t = \Theta_s \Rightarrow \Theta_{t\mathbf{r}_n} = \Theta_{s\mathbf{r}_n}$$

which means in terms of the assignment h:

- for all atoms $q(t \vDash q \Leftrightarrow s \vDash q) \Rightarrow$ for all atoms $q(t\mathbf{r}_n \vDash q \Leftrightarrow s\mathbf{r}_n \vDash q)$.

The reader can read more about modal logic in [33] and generally about time action logic in [60]

Appendix B: Public announcement logic

Modal jump operators

We begin with modal logic **K** with a jump operator. This is done as follows. We add to the language a unary operator JA. We add to the semantics of modal **K** a unary function $\mathbf{f}$ from $T \mapsto T$. So our models have the form $(T, R, \mathbf{f}, \Omega, h)$, where (T, R, Ω, h) is a tree model as before and $\mathbf{f}$ a unary function. We have

$$t \vDash JA \text{ iff } \mathbf{f}(t) \vDash A.$$

A well known jump operator in temporal logic is **Tomorrow**A.

Let $\mathbf{m}_i = (T_i, R_i, \Omega_i, h_i)$ be a family of models for $i \in I$. We can define a *fibring jump* operator through a function $\mathbf{g} : I \mapsto I$ as follows, $t \in T_i$

$$t \vDash_i JA \text{ iff } \Omega_{\mathbf{g}(i)} \vDash_{\mathbf{g}(i)} A.$$

In this statement we write $t \vDash_i A$ to mean satisfaction in modal $\mathbf{m}_i$.

The function $\mathbf{g}$ can be more general. We can assume T_i are all pairwise disjoint. So when we write $t \vDash A$, for $T \in \bigcup_i T_i$ then there is a unique i such that $t \in T_i$, and so we know to evaluate $t \vDash A$ as $t \vDash_i A$.

Now let $\mathbf{g} : \bigcup_i T_i \mapsto \bigcup_i T_i$. We can let

$$t \vDash JA \text{ iff } \mathbf{g}(t) \vDash A.$$

It is important to adopt the convenient point of view towards the operator J. We start with a model $\mathbf{m}$ and whenever we apply JA at a point t, we move to a new model $\mathbf{m}_{\mathbf{f}(t)}$. Thus the operator J moves us from one model to another.

Traditional public announcement logic

Such logics involve operators of the form J_φ, φ a wff, basically declaring publicly that φ is true. This is done in the context of interacting agents with knowledge operators and the public announcements are made by the agents to contribute to common knowledge.

Let $\mathbb{A}$ be a set of agents and for each $a \in \mathbb{A}$ let $\mathbb{K}_a$ be a knowledege operator. This is a **K** modality satisfying the following additional axioms:

- $\mathbb{K}A \to A$, knowledge is true
- $\mathbb{K}A \to \mathbb{K}\mathbb{K}A$, positive introspection
- $\neg\mathbb{K}A \to \mathbb{K}\neg\mathbb{K}A$, negative introspection

For a detailed example involving the famous muddy children, see [73].

We start with an initial Kripke model for $\{\mathbb{K}_a | a \in \mathbb{A}\}$ of the form $\mathbf{m} = (S, R_a, h), a \in \mathbb{A}$ where S is the set of possible world and R_a are relations $R_a \subseteq S \times S$ satisfying the suitable conditions for $\mathbb{K}_a$ axioms. When we use

the public announcement jump operator J_φ, φ a wff, we move to a model $\mathbf{m}_\varphi$ where
$$\mathbf{m}_\varphi = (S_\varphi, R_a^\varphi, h^\varphi)$$
where
$$S_\varphi = \{t \in S | t \vDash \varphi\}$$

$$R_a^\varphi = R_a \upharpoonright S_\varphi$$

$$h^\varphi = h \upharpoonright S_\varphi.$$

We have the condition

$$t \vDash_\mathbf{m} J_\varphi A \text{ iff } (t \vDash_\mathbf{m} \varphi \Rightarrow t \vDash_{\mathbf{m}_\varphi} A) \qquad (\sharp)$$

This definition makes sense in the context of knowledge.

If φ is announced as true, we need consider only worlds in which φ holds. So we move from one model to another as more and more information is announced.

Public announcement logic for time-action modal K

How do we introduce the public announcement operators $J_\varphi A$ into our modal logic **K**, where we have the interpretation of time-action for the nodes $t = \Omega \mathbf{a}_1, \ldots, \mathbf{a}_n$?

We can start by adopting a technical approach, but this will not work. Let us see why. Start with a time action model

$$\mathbf{m} = (T, R, \Omega, h).$$

Let φ be any wff. Let $T_\varphi = \{t \in T | t \vDash \varphi\}$.

$$\mathbf{m}_\varphi = (T_\varphi, R \upharpoonright T_\varphi, \Omega, h \upharpoonright T_\varphi).$$

We can first try to define the semantical condition for the operator $J_\varphi A$, as follows. Assume $t = \Omega \mathbf{a}_1, \ldots, \mathbf{a}_n$. Define $t_0 = \Omega$, $t_{i+1} = t_i \mathbf{a}_{i+1}$ for $0 \leq i \leq n-1$. This makes $t = t_n$.

We let

$$t \vDash_\mathbf{m} J_\varphi A \text{ iff } \bigwedge_{i=0}^{n} t_i \vDash_\mathbf{m} \varphi \Rightarrow t \vDash \mathbf{m}_\varphi A. \qquad (\sharp 1)$$

The reasons for trying to use Condition ($\sharp 1$) and not ($\sharp$) is as follows. We start with state Ω and apply actions $\mathbf{a}_1$ and $\mathbf{a}_2$ to get to $t = \Omega \mathbf{a}_1 \mathbf{a}_2$. If there is public announcement J_φ and $\Omega \mathbf{a}_1 \vDash \neg \varphi$, then even though we may have that $\Omega \mathbf{a}_1 \mathbf{a}_2 \vDash \varphi$, we could not have legitimately reached $t \mathbf{a}_1 \mathbf{a}_2$ in the first place. So our condition ($\sharp 1$) is really conceptually the same as the traditional one ($\sharp$) given our time-action interpretation of modal **K**.

This attempt is not satisfactory. It is not fully compatible with the idea that a public announcement gives us more information about the model and becasue of that information we get a smaller model. Our time action model is generated from the initail state Ω (whose theory is Δ_Ω) via actions of the form $\mathbf{a} = (\alpha_\mathbf{a}, \beta_\mathbf{a})$ and a revision process $*$.

Thus
$$\Delta_{\Omega \mathbf{a}} = \Delta_\Omega * \beta_\mathbf{a}$$
$$\Delta_{\Omega \mathbf{ab}} = (\Delta_\Omega * \beta_\mathbf{a}) * \beta_\mathbf{b}$$

The information that φ must be true must be in tune with the way the model is generated and therefore must affect the initial Δ_Ω, say we have

$$\Delta_\Omega^\varphi = \Delta_\Omega * \varphi$$

and must affect all subsequent action sequences, say recursively

$$\Delta_{t\mathbf{a}}^\varphi = \Delta_t^\varphi * (\beta_\mathbf{a} * \varphi).$$

This is one possible way of doing it. However, the Talmud is concerned with a different type of the need for public announcement. In the Talmud, we address lack of clarity in the action $\mathbf{a}$ itself. Let $\mathbf{x}$ be an action variable where $\mathbf{x} \in E_\mathbf{x}$

$$E_\mathbf{x} = \{\mathbf{e}_1, \ldots, \mathbf{e}_k\}.$$

So we apply action $\mathbf{x}$ at t but we don't know whether we applied $\mathbf{e}_1$ or $\mathbf{e}_2, \ldots,$ or $\mathbf{e}_k$.

Thus after a sequence of further actions, say $\mathbf{b}_1, \ldots, \mathbf{b}_m$, we might be at any of the following k posisble points, denoted by $\mathbf{s}(\mathbf{x}) = t\mathbf{x}\mathbf{b}_1, \ldots, \mathbf{b}_m$.

$$s_1 = t\mathbf{e}_1\mathbf{b}_1, \ldots, \mathbf{b}_m$$
$$\vdots$$
$$s_k = t\mathbf{e}_k\mathbf{b}_1, \ldots, \mathbf{b}_m$$

A public announcment will have the form, say $J_{\mathbf{x}=\mathbf{e}_1}$ announcing at a later time that the action $\mathbf{x}$ taken in the past was $\mathbf{x} = \mathbf{e}_1$.

How such situations can arise and how to handle them is what is discussed in this chapter.

Comparing arc deletion with point deletion

This appendix compares formally the traditional public announcement logic and the Talmudic one. The comparison will be on two levels:

1. The Technical level; comparing expressive power.

2. The conceptual level; our view of what we are doing.

Technical comparison

Basically we will be comparing deleting points from a Kripke model with deleting arcs.

Consider the Kripke model of Figure 6.19. We have $S = \{t, s\}$. $R = \{(t,t), (t,s), (s,t), (s,s)\}$.

We have $t \vDash q$ and $s \vDash \neg q$.

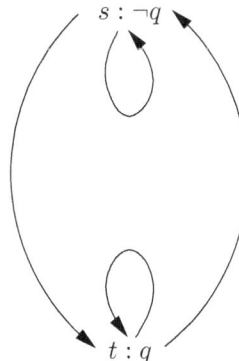

Figure 6.19. A simple model

This model can also be viewed as a Talmudic model with $\mathcal{R}$ if we also understand $t\mathcal{R}\{t,s\}$ and $s\mathcal{R}\{t,s\}$. Thus Figure 6.19 gives rise to both models (s, R) and $(S, \mathcal{R})$.

Traditional public announcement has the modal form of either $[q]$ or $[\neg q]$ for the model (S, R). Talmudic public announcment has the updates of the form $[\alpha]$ where α can be:

$$\alpha_1 = (t, \{t,s\}, t)$$
$$\alpha_2 = (t, \{t,s\}, s)$$
$$\beta_1 = (s, \{t,s\}, t)$$
$$\beta_1 = (s, \{t,s\}, s).$$

We have
$[\alpha_1]$ takes out the arc $t \to s$
$[\alpha_2]$ takes out the arc $t \to t$
$[\beta_1]$ takes out the arc $s \to s$
$[\beta - 2]$ takes out the arc $s \to t$.

We turn $(S, \mathcal{R})$ into a temporal model if we choose a starting point and start moving along the arcs.

Start at point t at time 1. We imagine we take action **a** because of lack of clarity we don't know whether action **a** takes us to t or to s. Taking us to s means action **a** worked. Taking us to t (remaining at t) emans action **a** did not work.

Similarly action **a** can be applied at s. Understand action **a** as saying:

leave this world

Figure 6.19 shows where we can be as time ticks on.

We now check what options we have for public announcement.

The traditional case

Assume we are at t. Since $t \vDash q$, the public announcement $[\neg q]$ will have no effect and $[q]$ will delete point s from the model and we are left with $S_{[q]} = \{t\}$ and $R_{[q]} = \{(t,t)\}$. See Figure 6.21

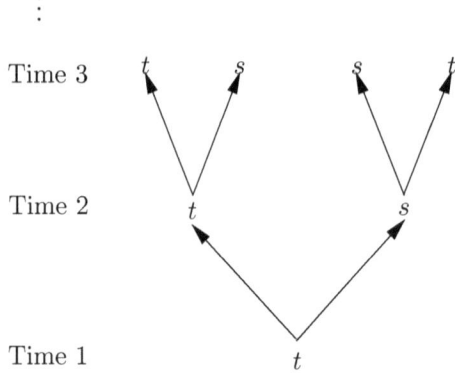

Figure 6.20. Time in the simple model

Figure 6.21. Result of traditional public announcement

The Talmudic case

Again assume we are at t. The public announcements in this case can take out any combination of arcs, one from each node. We get the models of Figure 6.22.

Item 1 of Figure 6.22 corresponds to Figure 6.21. In general Talmudic public announcement cannot disconnect all arrows emanating from a point, it is uspposed to clarify which arrow is the correct one. So one arrow must remain. So in case of the model of Figure 6.23 Talmudic public announcement cannot disconnect/delete the arrow $t \to s$, but traditional public announcement can delete s by announcing $[q]$.

If we allow the announcement of deletion of any number of arcs, including the possibility of deleting all arcs emanating from a point (which says that the action did not take place at all), then arc deletion is stronger than point deletion, because we can achieve point deletion by using arc deletion. We can delete all arcs leading to a world and thus effectively delete the world.

REMARK 6.20. Talmudic deletion of arcs can be simulated in traditional public announcement logic if we add auxiliary worlds and have nominals. Let us illustrate the procedure by doing it to the frame of Figure 6.19. Consider Figure 6.24.

The procedure goes as follows: Given a **K** Kripke frame (S, R) for the modality $[N]$, let S_R be a set of new points of the form $S_R = \{x_{ts} | (t, s) \in R\}$.

Define R_0 to be $R_0 = R \cup \{(t, x_{ts}), (x_{ts}, s)\}$.

Let $S_0 = S \cup S_R$.

Let φ be any wff fo the modal logic with $[N]$. Translate every occurrence of $[N]$ in φ by $[N][N]$. Thus we obtain φ_0 from φ. For any assignment h_0 into

6. FUTURE DETERMINATION OF ENTITIES   229

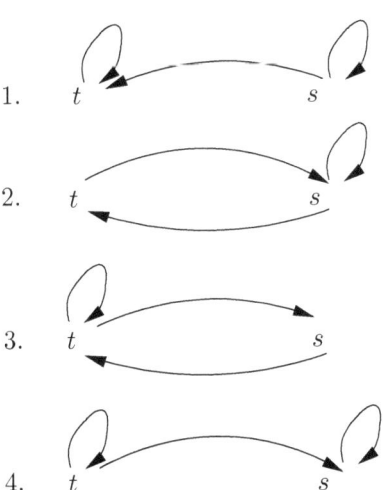

Figure 6.22. Results of Talmudic public announcement options

Figure 6.23. A model with one arrow only

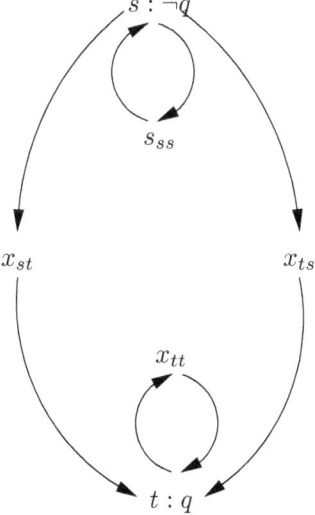

Figure 6.24. Model with auxiliary points for arcs

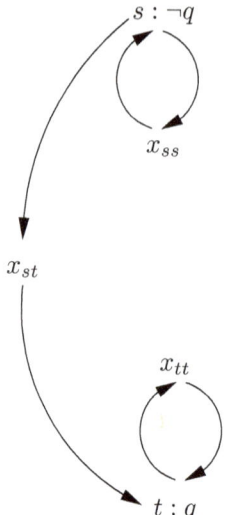

Figure 6.25. Model with $t \to s$ deleted

(S_0, R_0), let $h = h_0 \upharpoonright S$. Then we have for any $t \in S$

(*) $t \vDash_h \varphi$ iff $t \vDash_{h_0} \varphi_0$.

(*) means that we can operate in (S_0, R_0, h_0) instead of in (S, R, h).

To simulate arc deletion, we need nominals.

Let $\mathbf{n}_{ts}$ for $(t, s) \in R$ be a nominal for the point $x_{t,s} \in S_0$. Let $\mathbf{n}_R$ be a nominal for S_R. We thus have

$$y \vDash \mathbf{n}_{ts} \text{ iff } y = x_{ts}$$
$$y \vDash \mathbf{n}_R \text{ iff } y \in S_R$$

Given a model (S, R) we can now simulate public announcement fo arcs and nodes in (S, R) using (S_0, R_0) as follows

1. Deleting nods using φ in (S, R), i.e. the modality $[\varphi]$ is translated as $[\varphi_0 \vee \mathbf{n}_R]$ in (S_0, R_0).

2. Deleting an arc $t \to s$ in (S, R) is translated as $[\neg \mathbf{n}_{ts}]$ in (S_0, R_0).

To see how this works, let us delete the arc $t \to s$ in Figure 6.19. We get the frame of item 1 of Figure 6.22. The translation procedure applied to this figure would yield Figure 6.25.

It is clear that if we apply the traditional public announcement $[\neg \mathbf{n}_{ts}]$ to Figure 6.24 we get as a result the frame of Figure 6.25.

Conceptual comparison

Conceputally the Talmudic view is different from the traditional view of public announcement logic. To highlight the differences, let us do traditional public

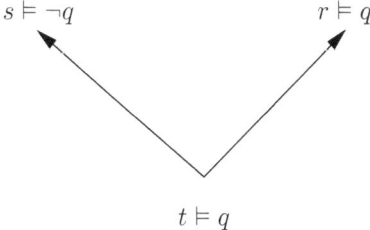

Figure 6.26. We are at s and we delete s, where do we go?

announcement logic (deleting points) from a Talmudic point of view. Consider Figure 6.26. Assume we are at point s and we announce publicly $[q]$.

According to traditional public announcement logic, we cannot proceed, because where we are is the world s, and we have $s \vDash \neg q$. However, if we adopt a Talmudic point of view, we can proceed. The Talmudic view would delete point s by deleting the arc $t \to s$ and move to point r, the new world to be at.[22] So for traditional public announcement logic, to be able to conceptually be compatible with the Talmudic one, its models must have the capability of deleting the evaluation point and moving to a new point. So we must have an additional function $\mathbf{f}$ such that the following two conditiosn hold

1. for each $x \in S$ and each $E \subseteq S, \mathbf{f}(x, E) \in S$

2. if $x \in E$ then $\mathbf{f}(x, E) = x$ and if $x \notin E$ then $\mathbf{f}(x, E) \in E$. Thus $\mathbf{f}(x, \varnothing)$ is not defined!

So our models have the form (S, R, h), where h is an assignment to the atoms and $\mathbf{f}$ is as above. Let φ be a formula which is true at some world in S. Then we define the pubic announcement truth condition to be as follows:

$x \vDash [\varphi]A$ in $(S, R, \mathbf{f}, h)$ iff $\mathbf{f}(x, S_\varphi) \vDash A$ in the model $(S_\varphi, R \upharpoonright S_\varphi, \mathbf{f} \upharpoonright S_\varphi, h \upharpoonright S_\phi)$,

where
$$S_\varphi = \{y \in S | y \vDash \varphi\}.$$

Note that $\mathbf{f} \upharpoonright S_\varphi$ gives values in S_φ, because for any $E \subseteq S_\varphi$ and $y \in S_\varphi$, $\mathbf{f}(x, E)$ is either y (if $y \in E$) or some $z \in E$. In either case $\mathbf{f}(x, E) \in S_\varphi$.

REMARK 6.21. This view can be promising because of its connection with the conditional. Consider the conditional $\varphi \Rightarrow A$. Take the traditional reading for $t \vDash \varphi \Rightarrow A$. This holds if A holds in the most similar worlds to t, where φ is true. So if $t \vDash \varphi$, then we want that $t \vDash A$. If $t \vDash \neg\varphi$, then we want A to hold in the best similar world to t in which φ holds. But we can now understand the function $\mathbf{f}(t, S_\varphi)$ as giving us the most similar world to t from among the worlds in which φ holds.

So there is a resemblance to conditionals.
We have for conditionals:

---

[22]This is because the branching at t into worlds r and s comes from lack of clarity of where we are supposed to be, following the execution of some action. We can be either at s or at r, and deleting s clarifies that we should be at r.

- $x \vDash \varphi \Rightarrow A$ iff $\mathbf{f}(x, S_\varphi) \vDash A$ in $(S, R, \mathbf{f})$.

and in comparison, we have for our public announcement the similar condition:

- $x \vDash [\varphi]A$ iff $\mathbf{f}(x, S_\varphi) \vDash A$ in $(S_\varphi, R \restriction S_\varphi, \mathbf{f} \restriction S_\varphi)$

As you can see, the definitions are very similar.

CHAPTER 7

THE HANDLING OF LOOPS IN TALMUDIC LOGIC, WITH APPLICATION TO ODD AND EVEN LOOPS IN ARGUMENTATION

1 Background

The Talmud is a body of arguments and discussions about all aspects of the human agent's social, legal and religious life. It was completed over 1500 years ago and its argumentation and debates contain many logical principles and examples very much relevant to today's research in logic, artificial intelligence, law and argumentation.

In a series of books on Talmudic Logic, the authors have studied the logical prinicples involved in the Talmud, one by one, devoting a volume to each major principle

We have just finished writing Volume 5, entitled *Resolution of Conflicts and Normative Loops in the Talmud*, and the present chapter describes how the Talmud deals with even and odd loops and compares the results with open issues in argumentation.

For other English papers corresponding to previous books, see [3; 12; 5; 11; 5; 7] and of course earlier chapters of this book which make use of them.

We start by looking at two typical loops, as in Figures 7.1 and 7.2.

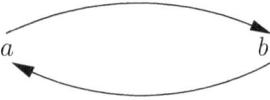

Figure 7.1.

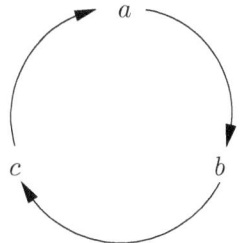

Figure 7.2.

We need to give some definitions.

An abstract network has the form (S, R), where S is a set of abstract nodes (arguments) and $R \subseteq S^2$ is the attack relation. Traditional research looks at extensions, these are subsets of S satisfying certain conditions (formulated in terms of R). Given (S, R) there may be several possible extensions of several types. In our case, for example, Figure 7.1 has three complete extensions $\{a\}, \{b\}$ and $\varnothing$, and Figure 7.2 has only one extension $\varnothing$.

Current research in argumentation, which relates to such loops and which connects with Talmudic logic, has two aspects:

1. Giving new definitions of extensions which can apply to abstract argumentation networks containing loops and allow us to get some new extensions other than "all undecided".

2. Adding extra information to the argumentation network which helps resolve the loops or help choose an extension.

The extra information one can add to the nodes of the network can be valuations or preferences among nodes. Mathematically one can look at valuations only, as preferences can be derived from them.

When we add valuations, we add a function $V : S \mapsto U$ where U is a value domain, giving some value to each $x \in S$.

V can be used in two extreme ways:

(a) Use V in the definition of extensions, by modifying the network or by disregarding and removing attacks, etc.

(b) Calculate the extensions without using V (i.e. ignoring V) and then using V to choose one's favourite extension or modify existing extensions and create new modified extensions.

(c) There is a third way, highly recommended by some members of the community, which is to use V in combination with the internal structure of the argument. (Note that V is not definded on arguments here but on components of arguments).

(a) is supported by Leila Amgoud and Trevor Bench-Capon.

(b) is supported by the 1500 years old Talmudic logic and recently by a 2010 paper by Toshiko Wakaki, [99].

(c) is supported by Henry Prakken in a 2010 paper [88].

The (b) and (c) approaches maintain consistency while (a) is problematic. See a critique by Martin Caminada [31]. We are grateful to Martin Caminada for providing us with the above information, as well as sending us his critique of aproach (a).

Our plan for this chapter is very simple. In Section 2 we present the notion of Shkop extension to an abstract network (S, R) and compare it with Baroni's and his colleagues [19; 20] CF2 extensions.[1]

In Section 3 we discuss some counter examples by Martin Caminada. In Section 4 we conclude the chapter. In a follow-up paper, yet to be written, we

---

[1] Rabbi Shimon Shkop, 1860–1930. A Talmudic scholar analysing many logical principles in the Talmud.

7. THE HANDLING OF LOOPS IN TALMUDIC LOGIC

give examples of how the Talmud offers valuations to resolve loops of odd and even types and how the Talmud chooses extensions.

2 Shkop extensions

We begin with a motivating Talmudic example, the dates are all in the same year, say 2010.

EXAMPLE 7.1 (The divorce). Jane is married to John. She develops some feelings for Frank and wants a divorce from John. Frank is a rich man and promises to compensate John generously if he cooperates. We now have the following temporal sequence:

Jan 01: John gives divorce papers to Jane. The divorce is conditional on Jane marrying Frank by the 31st of March. Such conditional divorces are allowed in the Talmud. If Jane marries Frank before 31st March then all is well. If Jane does not marry Frank by 31st March then the divorce papers, the beginning, from January 01 are nullified and the divorce is not valid from Jan 01. This is Talmudic legal backwards causality.

Feb 01: Jane takes her divorce papers and marries Terry. This marriage is valid because Jane's divorce papers are valid. Jane can still potentially fulfill the condition mentioned in the divorce papers; she can still divorce Tery and marry Frank.

31st March: Jane, without getting a divorce from Terry, goes and marries Frank.

There is no doubt that Jane is a naughty girl! Frank is a bit paranoid, asking John to give Jane a conditional divorce.

Now we seem to have landed in a logical loop.

Let us build up an argumentation network based on this story.

The base logic is classical temporal logic. The base theory in the logic is the following:

1. If x is married to someone then x cannot marry someone else.

2. If x is married to y at time t then x continues to be married to y until there is a divorce or death.

3. (a) A divorce can be given at time t, conditional on an action taken at time $s > t$.

   (b) If the action is not taken at time s then there is backward causality and the divorce is not valid from time t.

   (c) If the action is taken at time s then the divorce is valid at time t.

   (d) At any time $t', t \leq t' < s$, the divorce given at time t on a condition to be fulfilled at time s, is considered valid at time t' as long as there is the reasonable possibility, as seen from time t', that the condition will be fulfilled at time s.

4. **Fact**: John gave a divorce to Jane on January 01, conditional on Jane marrying Frank by March 31.

5. **Fact**: Jane married Terry on Feb 01.

6. **Fact**: Jane married Frank on March 31, without ever getting a divorce from Terry.

7. **Note**: It is possible for x to give a divorce to y at time t on the condition that y marries z ($z \neq x$) at time $s > t$.

    One might argue that at time s, we have a problem:

    y is still married to x therefore y cannot marry z. It is only when y marries z at time s that y is divorced from x at time t and is therefore able to marry z at time s.

    Since we allow for such conditions, we regard marrying z at s and enabling the divorce at t as simultaneous.

    The answer is that the condition of marrying z is not an enabling condition for the divorce papers but a nullifying condition. If it is not fulfilled the divorce papers are nullified.

We now consider the following arguments seen from the temporal point of view of March 31.

DJJ- John's divorce from Jane on January 01 is not valid.
The reasoning in this argument from base data goes as follows:

On February 01, the divorce was valid because there was the possibility of fulfilling the condition of the divorce, from Rule (3d). Therefore the marriage to Terry (Fact (5)) is valid and does not nullify the divorce, since Jane can still divorce Terry and marry Frank (Rule (3d)).

Therefore at the time March 31, when Jane married Frank without divorcing Terry, her marriage to Frank was not valid (Rules (1) and (2)). Hence, since the condition of the divorce was not fulfilled, the divorce is not valid.

MJT+ Jane's marriage to Terry on Feb 01 is valid.
The argument goes as follows:

Since Jane got a conditional divorce from John and the condition can still be fulfilled her divorce stands and she can marry Terry.

MJF+ Jane's marriage to Frank is valid.
the argument for that is as follows:

Assume the marriage to Frank is not valid. Then Jane's divorce from John is not valid. Hence her marriage to Terry is not valid. But then Jane has a conditional divorce from John and she is not married to Terry, therefore she is free to marry Frank and the marriage is valid. Therefore since ¬**MJF+** → **MJF+**, we conclude **MJF+**.

7. THE HANDLING OF LOOPS IN TALMUDIC LOGIC

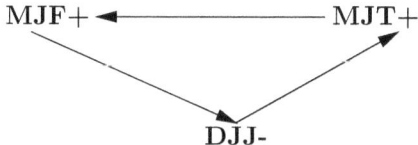

Figure 7.3.

We now get the argumentation loop presented in Figure 7.3.

It is clear that we have an odd loop here and the only Dung extension is ∅, being all undecided. However, life must go on and we need a resolution as to whom Jane is married to! Is she married to John, to Terry or to Frank?!

Here we introduce the intuitive Rabbi Shkop principle:

Shkop principle

If by assuming $x =$ in, we deduce that $x =$ out, then surely x must be out.

Let us apply this to our example. We have three possibilities for the choice of x, see Figure 7.3.

1. $x = \mathbf{DJJ}-$

2. $x = \mathbf{MJT}+$

3. $x = \mathbf{MJF}+$

We reason against the direction of the attack arrows. This reasoning is done later on, see Example 7.6 below for the calculation.

We get three extensions for each one of the choices of x:

1. Marriage to Frank is valid.

2. Divorce not valid — Jane is married to John.

3. Marriage to Terry is valid.

Commonsense dictates that we should not test the validity of the divorce because at the time (and here we make use of the temporal sequence) we did not know what Jane was going to do. Similarly we should not test the validity of the marriage to Terry because Jane could still have divorced him. So the only test is that of the validity of marriage to Frank. This test gives by the Shkop principle that $\mathbf{MJF}+ =$ out and therefore the network looks like Figure 7.4, (see also Example 7.6 below for a detailed analysis).

Figure 7.4 has the extension:

$$\begin{aligned} a &= \text{in} \\ \mathbf{DJJ}- &= \text{in} \\ \mathbf{MJT}+ &= \text{out} \\ \mathbf{MJF}+ &= \text{out} \end{aligned}$$

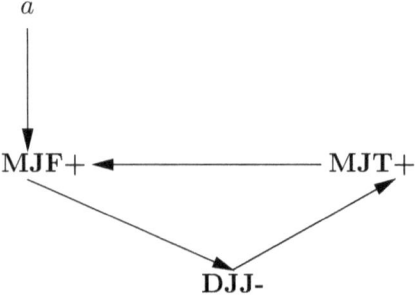

Figure 7.4.

In the above considerations we kept the temporal aspects in the metalevel. We can include these aspects in the object level. We time stamp each argument and each attack arrow, according to the way the story unfolds. If we do this we get Figure 7.5.

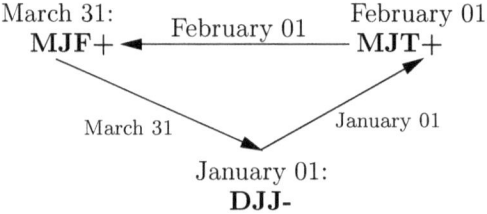

Figure 7.5.

Obviously the loop occurs on March 31. So we have to do the Shkop test on the March 31 argument, which is **MJF+**.

In general we can talk about Shkop temporal argumentation frames of the form $\mathbf{N} = (S, R, \mathbf{T})$, where (S, R) is an ordinary network and $\mathbf{T}$ is a time stamping function:

$$\mathbf{T}: S \cup R \mapsto \text{Time axis}.$$

For any choice of time t we look at the network

$$\mathbf{N}_t = (S_t, R_t),$$

where

$$S_t = \{a \in S | \mathbf{T}(a) \leq t\}$$
$$R_t = \{(x, y) \in R | \mathbf{T}(x, y) \leq t\}$$

Given $a \in S$ with $\mathbf{T}(a) = s$, we check according to Shkop the test $a = 1$? in the network $\mathbf{N}_s = (S_s, R_s)$.

Let us now be a bit more formal about Shkop extensions. Our aim is to offer the argumentation community the notion of Shkop semantics, and compare it

7. THE HANDLING OF LOOPS IN TALMUDIC LOGIC

with CF2 or Stage semantics. To do that, we need to generalise the intuitive Shkop principle in a sensible way.

For reasons of clear exposition, we find it advantageous to actually start from a recent paper of Martin Caminada, entitled Preferred semantics as Socratic discussion [30].

Caminada sets himself to give a game theoretic answer to the question:

Q: Given (S, R) and $a \in S$, can a be an element of some admissible extension?

His method is to assume that $a = $ in and see by Socratic discussion whether such a position can be maintained. The method is best explained by two examples.[2]

EXAMPLE 7.2. Consider Figure 7.6

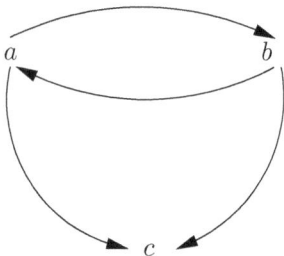

Figure 7.6.

We ask can we have $c = $ in in some extension? We proceed as follows:

1. $c = $ in, assumption

2. $b = $ out, from (1)

3. $a = $ in, from (2)

4. $a = $ out, from (1)

We get a contradiction. The assumption $c = $ in, lead us, using the attack rules and the geometry of the figure, that both $a = $ out, and $a = $ in.

Thus the answer the question about c is that it cannot be in, it must be out.

EXAMPLE 7.3. Consider Figure 7.2. Ask the question can $c = $ in? Let us check:

1. $c = $ in, assumption

2. $b = $ out, from (1)

3. $a = $ in, from (2)

4. $c = $ out, from (3)

---

[2] Appendix A offers a Tableaux algorithm for this test.

So again the answer is negative, there is no extension in which $c =$ in.

REMARK 7.4. Note that the proofs in the Caminada Socratic discussion obtain a contradiction by using the direction in the graph against the arrow. Thus if we have

$$x \to y \to z$$

and we assume $y =$ in, Caminada is allowed to deduce $x =$ out, going against the arrow, but is not allowed to deduce $z =$ out going with the arrow.

It seems that even with this restriction, the Socratic discussion is strong enough to identify all nodes a in the network for which $a =$ in is impossible.

Caminada's paper stops when we get our answers to the question of whether $a =$ in is possible or not.

Now let us use these two examples to explain what Shkop does. Shkop introduced a principle for resolving loops:

Shkop's original principle

If the test assumption $a =$ in leads to the conclusion that $a =$ out, then a must be annihilated and be out.

To implement such a principle we need some notation. Let (S, R) be a network and let the elements of S be denoted by lower case letters. Let us add for any $a \in S$ a new annihilator letter, capital A.

With the above notation, let us redo Examples 7.2 and 7.3 according to Shkop.

EXAMPLE 7.5 (Doing Example 7.2 according to Shkop). We start by testing $c =$ in in Figure 7.6.

1. $c =$ in, test assumption

2. $b =$ out, from (1)

3. $a =$ in, from (2)
   The Caminada Socratic discussion goes against the arrow and would continue

4*. $a =$ out, from (1), a contradiction, because we get both $a =$ in and $a =$ out.
   The Shkop original principle requires us to get $c =$ out for a contradiction, because our original test was for $c =$ in?. Therefore we need to go forward with the arrow using (3), as this is the only way to get back to c, and get (4) below. Going forward:

4. $c =$ out, from (3)

5. From (1)–(4) we get that c must be annihilated by the Shkop principle.

This means that we replace Figure 7.6 by Figure 7.7.

We may now feel comfortable, allowing ourselves to go both backwards and forwards with the arrow, and thus maintaining the intuitive spirit of the Shkop principle. This, however, is problematic. Caminada has shown a counter example which is problematic. We discuss this later in Section 3. So we cannot

7. THE HANDLING OF LOOPS IN TALMUDIC LOGIC

allow ourselves to prove forward with the arrow. So we need to modify the Shkop principle.

Our choice of modifying the Shkop principle is to state:

- If $a =$ in leads to a contradiction then a must be out. In deriving the contradiction, we use reasoning going backwards with the arrow only, see Appendix A. Once the contradiction is derived we introduce an annihilator for a.

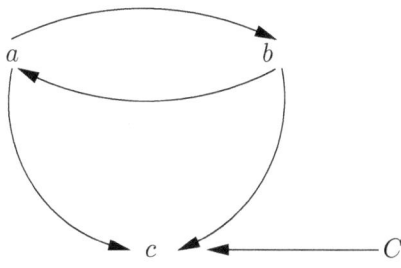

Figure 7.7.

Coming back to the argumemtation network of Figure 7.6, having tested $c =$ in?, we can continue to test $a =$ in and test $b =$ in but this will not require any more annihilators.

The Shkop extensions for Figure 7.6 are obtained by taking ordinary extensions for Figure 7.7 and ignoring the annihilators. In the case of Figure 7.6 the Shkop procedure made no difference but for Figure 7.2 it does as it resolves loops.

EXAMPLE 7.6 (Doing Example 7.3 according to Shkop). We have three tests to conduct:

Test 1: $c =$ in

Test 2: $b =$ in

Test 3: $a =$ in

Test 1

1. $c =$ in, test assumption

2. $b =$ out, from (1)

3. $a =$ in, from (2)

4. $c =$ out, from (3)

5. Using the Shkop principle c must be annihilated and Figure 7.2 replaced by Figure 7.8.

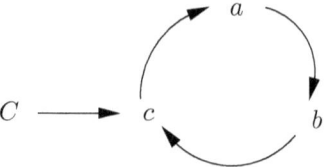

Figure 7.8.

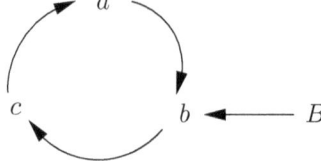

Figure 7.9.

Figure 7.8 is a new network and we can apply the Shkop test to it. We will get no more contradictions. The Dung extension for it is $\{C, a\}$.

The other tests will give us Figures 7.9 and 7.10.

The normal Dung extensions for Figures 7.9 and 7.10 are respectively $\{B, c\}$ and $\{A, b\}$.

According to Shkop, the Shkop extensions for Figure 5.1 are obtained from the normal extensions of Figures 7.8, 7.9 and 7.10 by ignoring the annihilators letters.

Thus we get the extensions $\{a\}, \{b\}, \{c\}$. Notice that these are the conflict free sets of Figure 7.2.

We ask the reader to remember this because we shall compare the Shkop extensions with Baroni's CF2 extensions.

REMARK 7.7. The reader should note that the Shkop procedure was originally intended for elements x of a network which are part of an odd loop, see Example 7.1. Once the element is found to be out by the Shkop principle, we move to a new network containing the annihilator X of x and we deal with the new network only. Shkop would never test $c =$ in ? immediately (at that moment, if we take into account the temporal aspect, see Section 4) in Figure 7.1 because c is not part of a loop. He would test $a =$ in? and $b =$ in? and find no contradiction. For the sake of mathematical completeness and generalising Shkop, we can allow the use of the Shkop principle to any x in the network. The test is similar to the Caminada Socratic discussion (see Appendix A for a Tableaux algorithm doing the same as Caminada's Socratic discussion), and if $x =$ in is found contradictory, this means that x must be out. Thus adding the annihilator X with $X \to x$ to the network will make no difference and we get an equivalent network.

We therefore put forward the Generalised Shkop Principle:

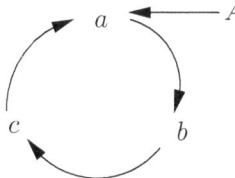

Figure 7.10.

Generalised Shkop Principle

Let (S, R) be a network and let $a \in S$. If the assumption $a = \text{in}$ leads to a contradiction (i.e. for some $x \in S$, we get both $x = \text{in}$, and $x = \text{out}$) by reasoning only backward against the direction of the arrow (as Caminada does in his Socratic discussion, or as we do in Appendix A using Tableaux) then a must be out. To ensure that a is out, we move to a new network $(S \cup \{A\}, R \cup \{(A, a)\})$, where A is a new letter, being the annihilator of a.

Note that Caminada proved in his Socratic paper that for a network (S, R) and $a \in S$ the condition:

- The assumption $a = \text{in}$ leads to a contradiction by correctly reasoning backwards against the direction of the arrow.

is equivalent to the declarative condition

- a is not a member of any admissible set.

We can therefore formulate the Generalised Shkop principle in an equivalent declarative way as follows:

Generalised Shkop principle (declarative)

Let (S, R) be a network and let $a \in S$. If a is not a member of any admissible set, then a must be out. To ensure that a is visibly out we move to a new network $(S \cup \{A\}, R \cup \{(A, a)\})$, where A is a new letter, being the annihilator of a.[3]

We are now ready to define the notion of Shkop extensions.

DEFINITION 7.8.

1. Let $\mathbf{N} = (S, R)$ be a finite argumentation network. Assume elements $y \in S$ are denoted by lower case letters. For each such y let Y be the annihilator of y.

   We define by induction the notions of

   (a) $(y_1, \ldots, y_k), y_i \in S$ is a legitimate Shkop sequence.

   (b) $\mathbf{N}_{(y_1, \ldots, y_k)}$ is a Shkop model dependent on $(y_1, \ldots, y_k)$.

---

[3]So for example the Liar paradox network $(\{a\}, \{a \to a\})$ becomes the network $(\{A, a\}, \{a \to a, A \to a\})$.

Case $k = 1$

y_1 is a legitimate Shkop sequence if y is not a member of any admissible set of (S, R) (or equivalently by Caminada [30], if the assumption $y = \text{in}$, in (S, R) leads to a contradiction using Caminada Socratic discussion). In this case let

$$\begin{aligned}\mathbf{N}_{y_1} &= (S \cup \{Y_1\}, R \cup \{(Y_1, y_1)\}) \\ &= (S_{y_1}, R_{y_1}).\end{aligned}$$

Case $k + 1$

Assume $(y_1, \ldots, y_k)$ is a legitimate sequence and assume $\mathbf{N}_{(y_1,\ldots,y_k)}$ is well defined. Let $y_{k+1} \in S$ be a point such that y_{k+1} is different from all $y_1, \ldots, y_k$. Assume that y_{k+1} is not a member of any admissible set in $\mathbf{N}_{(y_1,\ldots,y_k)}$, (or equivalently the assumption $y_{k+1} = \text{in}$, in the network $\mathbf{N}_{(y_1,\ldots,y_k)}$ leads to a contradiction using Caminada Socratic discussion). Then $(y_1, \ldots, y_{k+1})$ is a legitimate sequence and let $\mathbf{N}_{(y_1,\ldots,y_{k+1})}$ be $(S_{(y_1,\ldots,y_{k+1})}, R_{(y_1,\ldots,y_{k+1})})$, where

$$\begin{aligned}S_{(y_1,\ldots,y_{k+1})} &= S_{(y_1,\ldots,y_k)} \cup \{Y_{k+1}\} \\ R_{(y_1,\ldots,y_{k+1})} &= R_{(y_1,\ldots,y_k)} \cup \{(Y_{k+1}, y_{k+1})\}.\end{aligned}$$

2. Let $(y_1, \ldots, y_k)$ be a legitimate sequence. Let n be the number of elements of S. Then we say the rank of $\mathbf{N}_{(y_1,\ldots,y_k)}$ is $n - k$.

3. Let $(y_1, \ldots, y_k)$ be a legitimate sequence. Let $\mathbf{N}_{(y_1,\ldots,y_k)}$ e its associated Shkop network. We say $\mathbf{N}_{(y_1,\ldots,y_k)}$ or equally $(y_1, \ldots, y_k)$ is *clean* iff there are no legitimate sequences extending $(y_1, \ldots, y_k)$. Alternatively, iff for any $y \in S, y \neq y_i, i = 1, \ldots, k$, we have that the test $y = \text{in}$ does *not* lead to a contradiction.

4. Let $\mathbf{N}_{(y_1,\ldots,y_k)}$ be clean. Then we define the set of Shkop extensions of $\mathbf{N} = (S, R)$ as derived from $(y_1, \ldots, y_k)$.
Notation
$$\mathbb{E}^{\text{Shkop}}_{(y_1,\ldots,y_n)}$$
to be defined as follows.

Let E be any ordinary Dung extension of $\mathbf{N}_{(y_1,\ldots,y_k)}$ or equivalently let λ be any Caminada labelling for $\mathbf{N}_{(y_1,\ldots,y_k)}$, then $E \cap S$ (or equivalently) $\lambda \restriction S$ be an element of $\mathbb{E}^{\text{Shkop}}_{(y_1,\ldots,y_k)}$.

5. We now define the notion of all Shkop extensions of a finite network $\mathbf{N} = (S, R)$. We define the set of all Shkop extensions of $\mathbf{N}$ to be

$$\mathbb{E}^{\text{Shkop}}_{\mathbf{N}} = \bigcup_{\substack{(y_1,\ldots,y_k) \\ \text{clean}}} \mathbb{E}^{\text{Shkop}}_{(y_1,\ldots,y_k)}$$

7. THE HANDLING OF LOOPS IN TALMUDIC LOGIC

REMARK 7.9. Note that this is our definition based on the generalised Shkop principle. We can give restricted variations of it. For example, following Baroni et al. in their paper [20] of SCC recursiveness, we can first rewrite (S, R) as an acyclic ordering of maximal loops and then apply the Shkop procedure to loop elements starting from the top loops. This is like the way the CF2 extensions are calculated. We shall give a substantial example below to show you what happens.

It is now time to give some more Shkop examples.

EXAMPLE 7.10. Consider Figure 7.11

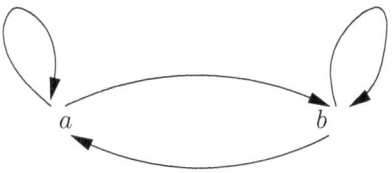

Figure 7.11.

Testing b and then testing a or testing a and then testing b will lead to the same Figure 7.12.

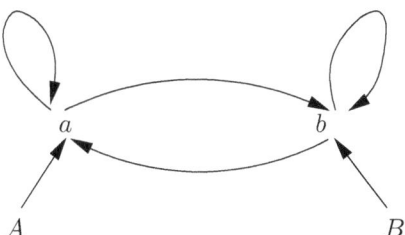

Figure 7.12.

Therefore the Shkop extension of Figure 7.11 is $\{a = \text{out}, b = \text{out}\}$.
This does not contradict the usual Dung extension of all undecided!

EXAMPLE 7.11 (Shkop compared with CF2). Consider the network in Figure 7.13. This figure appears in [63] as an example of how Baroni's CF2 semantics works. Gaggl and Woltran have a program which can compute the CF2 extensions.

The CF2 extensions for Figure 7.13 are the following:

$$\begin{aligned} E_1 &= \{c, f, h\} \\ E_2 &= \{c, g, i\} \\ E_3 &= \{b, d, e, g, i\} \\ E_4 &= \{a, d, e, g, i\}. \end{aligned}$$

The CF2 semantics would start with the top cycle $\{a, b, c\}$. They would take maximal conflict free subsets which are in this case $\{a\}, \{b\}, \{c\}$ and then arbitrarily decide on the three assignment:

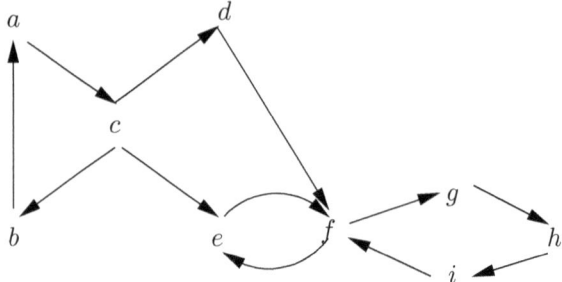

Figure 7.13.

1. $c = $ in, $b = $ out, $a = $ out

2. $b = $ in, $c = $ out, $a = $ out

3. $a = $ in, $c = $ out, $a = $ out

Having now given values to a, b and c, one can propagate the values to the rest of the network and get extensions.

For example:
If $c = $ in, then $d = e = $ out.

Therefore $f = $ in and hence $g = $ out, $h = $ in and $i = $ out.

We got ourselves an extension by breaking the loop $\{a, b, c\}$. The alternative, if we follow traditional Dung style approach is to have one extension only $=$ all undecided.

The method makes sense, it is not arbitrary, it is not just a technical device to generate extensions.

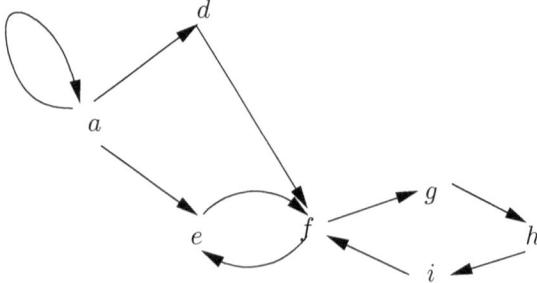

Figure 7.14.

CF2 would take maximal conflict free subsets of the loop $\{a\}$, which is the empty set, therefore d and e are in and so f is out, g is in, h is hout and i is in.

Now let us look at Shkop extensions of Figure 7.13.

Option 1
Accept the procedure where we start from the top loops. Call this top-down

7. THE HANDLING OF LOOPS IN TALMUDIC LOGIC

Shkop procedure. In this case we start from $\{a, b, c\}$ and ask, as in Example 7.6,

Test 1: $a =$ in
Test 2: $b =$ in
Test 3: $c =$ in

This will yield Shkop figures 7.15, 7.16 and 7.17.

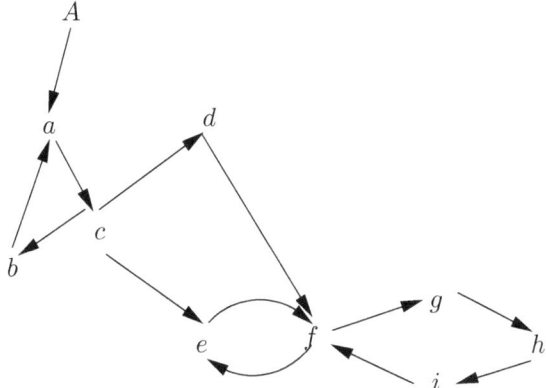

Figure 7.15.

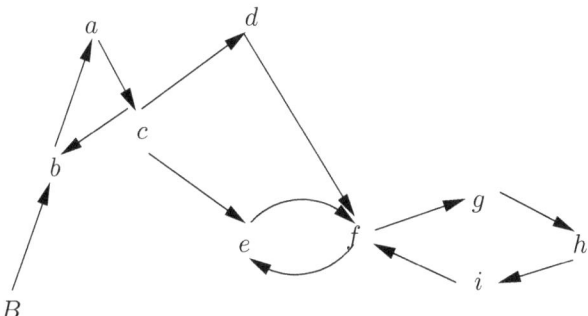

Figure 7.16.

From Figure 7.15 we get the extensions E_1 and E_2. From Figure 7.16 we get Extension E_4 and from Figure 7.17 we get extension E_3.

In the case of Figure 7.14, using the Shkop procedure on $a =$ in will give Figure 7.18.

and we get the extension $\{d, e, g, i\}$.

Let us now check what happens if we allow the Shkop process to start from any point. Let us start with $d =$ in? and then $e =$ in?. We will get that both need to be annihalated. If we carry on asking $a =$ in? or $b =$ in? or $c =$ in?

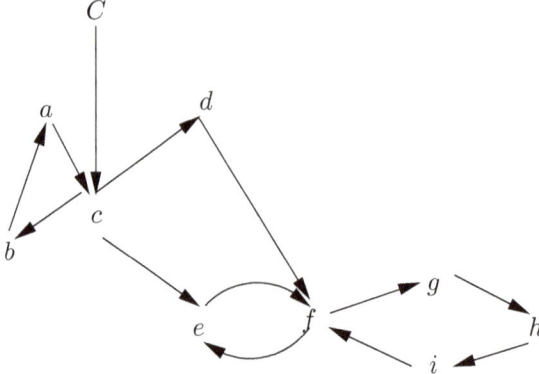

Figure 7.17.

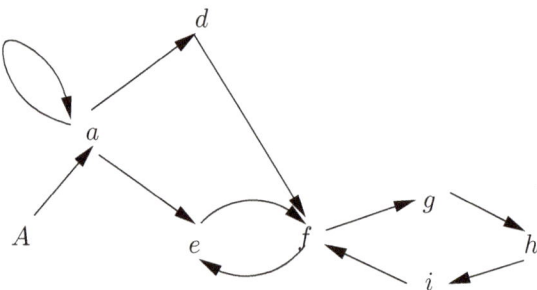

Figure 7.18.

we get the extensions

$$\{c, f, h\}$$
$$\{c, g, i\}$$
$$\{a, f, h\}$$
$$\{a, g, i\}$$
$$\{b, f, h\}$$
$$\{b, g, i\}$$

This chapter is mainly qualitative. A more mathematical exposition will need to address some open problems.

Problem 1
Under what circumstances is the top down Shkop process the same as CF2?

Problem 2
Is there a set of equations in the equational approach [61] characterising say the top down Shkop extensions?

Note that all extensions obtained by the Shkop procedure are stable. There is no undecided. Shkop kills all undecided!

REMARK 7.12. The reader may seek some meaning to the Shkop algorithm.

Figure 7.19.

For this, see the conclusion Section 4. The reader must remember that Talmudic logical argumentation and debate was conducted from the first to the end of the fifth centuries and was used in Jewish communities in the world during the following 1500 years.

Rabbi Shkop just explained the principles involved and we in this chapter are formally modelling them in terms of known abstract argumentation methods.

The principle works!

REMARK 7.13 (Comparison with stage semantics). Stage semantics is discussed in detail in [29]. It has similarities with the Shkop extensions but it is not the same. Both ignore self loops but stage semantics may ignore arguments which are not attacked by any other argument. Shkop extensions never do that.

We take our examples from [29]. Consider Figure 7.19

Stage semantics will ignore the self looping a and will have the extension $\{b\}$. The same is the case with the Shkop semantics. They both agree on $b =$ in. Stage will say $a =$ undecided while Shkop will say $a =$ out.

As a second example from [29], take Figure 7.20.[4] Shkop will not agree here with the traditional extension. According to Shkop we have

$a =$ in, $b =$ out, $c =$ out.

The traditional extension will have

$a =$ in, $b =$ out, $c =$ undecided.

Stage semantics allows for two extensions: the first one is the same as the traditional one

$a =$ in, $b =$ out, $c =$ undecided.

The second one is

$a =$ undecided, $b =$ in, $c =$ out.

Note that in the second stage a is not in, even though it has no attackers. This is rather strange. Caminada has proved, however, that every argumentation network has at least one stage extension which contains its ground extension. So it can be well behaved. Compare the stage semantics result for the network of Figure 7.20 with Example 7.14 and the considerations leading to Figure 7.21. We get the stage semantics if we go forward. Is this a coincidece? We think it is.

---

[4]In fact Pietro Baroni and Massimilano Giacomin invented this figure in order to show that CF2 semantics has some advantages above stage semantics.

3 Caminada counter examples: A discussion

Martin Caminada read an earlier version of Section 2 and gave us penetrating comments and devastating counter examples. The aim of this Section is to put forward an alternative formulation of the Shkop principle which maintains the spirit of Shkop while avoiding the counter examples of Caminada.

We need to summarise the intellectual chain of reasoning events.

(1)   The original Shkop principle, as formulated by Shkop, says as follows:

(*1)   Let $\mathbf{N} = (S, R)$ be a network. Let $x \in S$. Assume (test) $x = $ in. If one can prove that this entails $x = $ out, then surely x must be out.

Our modelling of this principle was to move to the network $\mathbf{N}_x$, as defined in Definition 7.8.

Shkop does not specify what it means "to be able to prove that $x = $ in entails $x = $ out". We adopted the Caminada Socratic method to give meaning to this notion.

(2)   Here we had a problem. Caminada's method uses reasoning against the direction of the arrow. So if we have, for example

$$y \to x \to z$$

and we test the assumption $x = 1$, then Caminada allows us to deduce $y = 0$, but we are not allowed to deduce $z = 0$.

The difficulty with this is that Shkop formulated his principle by saying "$x = $ in can prove $x = $ out".

It is the same x.

The "same x" restriction is OK for cases of pure loops of the form

$$x \to a_1 \to a_2 \to \ldots \to a_k \to x$$

We can prove $x = $ in implies $x = $ out by going backwards, but for cases like Figure 7.6 (the test case assuming $c = $ in) we cannot get $c = $ out by going against the arrow only, as discussed in Example 7.5.

Our original modification of Shkop principle was to allow forward reasoning with the arrow. However, Caminada landed a devastating counter example on this attempt (see Example 7.14 below).

We therefore reformulated the generalised Shkop principle in a safe way, as follows.

(*2)   Let $\mathbf{N} = (S, R)$ be a network. Let $x \in S$. Assume (test) $x = $ in. If one can prove a contradiction from this assumption, say that for some $y \in S$, both $y = $ in and $y = $ out are derivable, then surely x must be out, and move to $\mathbf{N}_x$

The above is equivalent to the following (in view of Caminada's Socratic paper).

(*3)   Let $\mathbf{N} = (S, R)$ and let $x \in S$. If x is not part of any extension (equivalently if there is no Caminada labelling λ with $\lambda(x) = $ in), then surely x must be out and we move to $\mathbf{N}_x$

So the Shkop extensions and Shkop semantics are obtained by systematically annihilating all points which cannot be part of an extension, as defined in Definition 7.8. This is a Draconian instrument. Note that it needs to be done in sequence, one node at a time.

EXAMPLE 7.14 (Caminada's counter example). Consider Figure 7.20

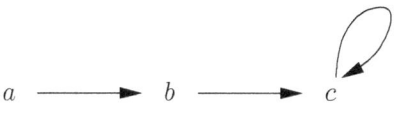

Figure 7.20.

Let us test $a = 1$? allowing reasoning both with and against the arrow. We reproduce Caminada's reasoning

1. $a = $ in, assumption

2. $b = $ out, from (1)

3. We now do case analysis for c.

   Case 3a $c = $ in
   In this case we continue

   (4a) $c = $ out, since c attacks itself.
   (5a) $b = $ in, from (4a)
   (6a) $a = $ out, from (5a)

   Case 3b $c = $ out

   (4b) $b = $ in, since $c = $ out
   (5b) $a = $ out, from (4b)

4. Since in both cases we get $a = $ out, then by the Shkop principle surely $a = $ out and we move to Figure 7.21.

   Clearly this is not acceptable.

Later on we shall modify the forward proof procedures by means of Labelled Deductive Systems and hopefully avoid the Caminada counter example.

We shall now show the idea behind this modification. Let us do the proof again, using our idea:

1. $a = $ in, assumption

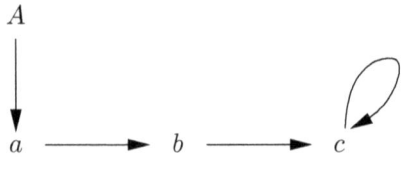

Figure 7.21.

2. $b = $ out, from (1)

3. we now have a node c which is not attacked by any node which is in, and instead of doing a case analysis, let us ask, by way of a subcomputation, can $c = $ in?

Subcomputation

- Given assumptions: $a = $ in, $b = $ out
- we test: $c = $ in.

(3.1) $c = $ in, assumption

(3.2) $c = $ out, from (3.1)

Therefore using the Shklop principle c surely must be out, and we move to Figure 7.22.

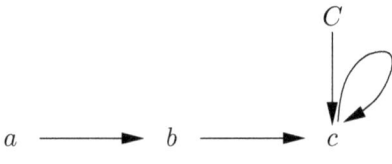

Figure 7.22.

(4) We now continue the original computation with Figure 7.22.

To make our idea crystal clear, let us present the reasoning structure as follows: (Note the network changes as we reason, so each line has to indicate which network we are dealing with).

1. Figure 7.20, $a = $ in, assumption

2. Figure 7.20, $b = $ out, from (1)

3. subcomputation in Box1

Box 1:
3.1	Figure 7.20, $c = $ in, assumption
3.2	Figure 7.22, $c = $ out, from (3.1)
3.3	Use (3.1) and (3.2) and the Shkop principle: c must be out
3.4	Exit subcomputation with Figure 7.22

4. We are now in Figure 7.22 from Box 1: we continue reasoning.

Thus the network changes as we reason along the arrows!

At present we do not know if this new computation is sound. It may be that counter examples can be found. Even if it is sound, we do not know exactly what it does. Our conjecture is that it just forces us to consider the loops first and eliminate them. At any rate, this is not crucial to our chapter, since we are happy with the General Shkop Principle and the algorithm we have in the Appendix.

4   Conclusion

The original Shkop principle is given in temporal context: Imagine a group of agents operating in time and taking actions. To execute an action **a** the pre-condition of the action $\alpha_\mathbf{a}$ needs to be fulfilled and then after the action is taken, the post-condition $\beta_\mathbf{a}$ of the action holds.

So if we start at time $t = 0$ in a certain state s and let our agents proceed with their actions then we move from state to state without any trouble and no argumentation networks arise and no loops arise.

The difference between ordinary actions and Talmudic actions is that the Talmud allows for the pre-conditions to contain future conditions and actions. Thus the enabling conditions of the actions can depend on the future and this can create loops. The Talmud also says that if the future condition is not fulfilled, then the action is nullified backwards in time (backward causality). As discussed in chapters 5 and 6.

To give a simple example, suppose that on Monday John orders a new laptop to be delivered on Friday. John gives his old laptop on Monday to a student named Tracy, free of charge, on the condition that on Friday, Tracy will configure his new laptop. Call this action **a**.

On Tuesday Tracy is ready to sell the laptop she got from John to a new buyer, Mary, for a good price, but Mary insists that on Friday Tracy transfers the contents of her old computer to the laptop she is buying. Call this action **b**.

The pre-condition for action **b** is that Tracy owns the laptop she is selling. For this to hold she must configure John's new laptop on Friday. However, if we allow action **b**, then Tracy will not be able to configure John's new laptop on Friday, because she will be busy transferring Mary's old data. If Tracy does that for Mary, then action **a** is nullified and so Tracy will not be the owner of the laptop she wants to sell and therefore action **b** is nullified.

What we get here is that if action **b** is allowed then it is nullified. The Shkop principle says that in this case do not allow action **b**.

We see here the context in which the Shkop principle operates. It is a time action model with future pre-conditions and backward causality, which progresses in time. Shkop says that any action which is about to be taken at time t which causes a chain reaction which cancels its own pre-condition at the same time t, should not be taken at time t.

We used the idea of Shkop to suggest and create the Shkop extensions for argumentation networks. These networks are not temporal but are static. We get them from the temporal action model by looking at what is happening at any certain fixed time.

This initial discussion is mainly qualitative and a more detailed modelling of the temporal aspects is forthcoming.

Appendices

5 Appendix A: Tableaux for Caminada Socratic discussion

We offer here a tableaux method designed to test, for an element x in a finite argumentation network, whether x is an element of any admissible extension. Compare also with the Verheij paper [98].

DEFINITION 7.15. Let $\mathbf{N} = (S, R)$ be a finite argumentation frame.

1. A tableaux for $\mathbf{N}$ has the form

$$\tau = (\mathbb{A}_\tau, \mathbb{B}_\tau, \mathbb{D}_\tau)$$

where $\mathbb{A}_\tau \subseteq S$ is the left inside of τ and $\mathbb{B}_\tau \subseteq S$ is the right outside of τ, and $\mathbb{D}_\tau$ is the set of elements marked to be treated in τ. $\mathbb{D}_\tau$ will be treated in the next tableau derived from τ. We have either $\mathbb{D}_\tau \subseteq \mathbb{A}_\tau$ (left treatment) or $\mathbb{D}_\tau \subseteq \mathbb{B}_\tau$ (right treatment).

2. A tableau τ is said to be closed if one or more of the following holds:

   - $\mathbb{A}_\tau \cap \mathbb{B}_\tau \neq \varnothing$
   - For some $y \in \mathbb{B}_\tau$, we have $\{x \in S | xRy\} = \varnothing$.

DEFINITION 7.16. Let $\mathbf{N} = (S, R)$ be finite argumentation frame and let $x \in S$. We define a tree $\mathbb{T}$ of tableaux for testing whether $x = $ in is possible at all, i.e. whether x can be a member of any admissible extension. The tree of tableaux will have tree relation ρ.

Step 1
Form the tableau $\tau_1 \in \mathbb{T}$, where

$$\tau_1 = (\{x\}, \varnothing, \{x\})$$

say $\{x\}$ is marked to be dealt with at this stage.

Step 2
Form the tableau $\tau_2 \in \mathbb{T}$, where

$$\tau_1 = (\{x\}, \{y|yRx\}, \{y|yRx\})$$

Say $\{y|yRx\}$ are marked to be dealt with at this stage and that $\{x\}$ has been dealt with. Let $\tau_1 \rho \tau_2$ hold.

If for some y such that yRx we have $\{z|zRy\} = \varnothing$ or if xRx then this tableau is closed. Otherwise we move to Step 3.

Step 3
Let $\mathbf{f}$ be any choice function such that for each y to be dealt with in the tableaux τ_2 of the previous step, (i.e. $y \in \mathbb{D}_{\tau_2}$), it chooses an element $\mathbf{f}(y) \in S$ such that $\mathbf{f}(y)Ry$. Form the tableaux, $\tau_3^{\mathbf{f}} \in \mathbb{T}$:

$$\tau_3^{\mathbf{f}} = (\mathbb{A}_3^{\mathbf{f}}, \mathbb{B}_3^{\mathbf{f}}, \mathbb{D}_3^{\mathbf{f}})$$

for each such an $\mathbf{f}$, where

$$\mathbb{A}_3^{\mathbf{f}} = \mathbb{A}_2 \cup \{\mathbf{f}(y) | y \in \mathbb{B}_2\}$$
$$\mathbb{B}_3^{\mathbf{f}} = \mathbb{B}_2$$
$$\mathbb{D}_3^{\mathbf{f}} = \{\mathbf{f}(y) | y \in \mathbb{B}_2 \text{ and } \mathbf{f}(y) \notin \mathbb{A}_2\}.$$

Say that all elements of $\mathbb{B}_2$ (all the ys) have been dealt with and all elements of $\mathbb{D}_3^{\mathbf{f}}$ are marked to be dealt with.

Let $\tau_2 \rho \tau_3^{\mathbf{f}}$, for all $\mathbf{f}$.

Note that $\mathbb{D}_3^{\mathbf{f}}$ may be empty.

Step 4
Let $\tau_3^{\mathbf{f}}$ be any tableau of Step 3. Construct the tableau $\tau_4^{\mathbf{f}} \in \mathbb{T}$ as follows:

$$\mathbb{A}_4^{\mathbf{f}} = \mathbb{A}_3^{\mathbf{f}}$$
$$\mathbb{B}_4^{\mathbf{f}} = \mathbb{B}_3^{\mathbf{f}} \cup \{z | \text{ for some } u \in \mathbb{D}_3^{\mathbf{f}} \text{ we have } zRu\}$$
$$\mathbb{D}_4^{\mathbf{f}} = \{z | \text{ for some } u \in \mathbb{D}_3^{\mathbf{f}} \text{ we have } zRu \text{ and } z \notin \mathbb{B}_3^{\mathbf{f}}\}.$$

We say the elements of $\mathbb{A}_3^{\mathbf{f}}$ have been dealt with and the elements of $\mathbb{B}_4^{\mathbf{f}}$ are marked to be dealt with.

Let $\tau_3^{\mathbf{f}} R \tau_4^{\mathbf{f}}$.

Inductive step type odd
We assume by induction that we have $\tau = (\mathbb{A}, \mathbb{B}, \mathbb{D})$ and the elements marked to be dealt with are all in $\mathbb{A}$, i.e. $\mathbb{D} \subseteq \mathbb{A}$ and $\mathbb{D} \neq \emptyset$. In this case proceed as in Step 3 and create τ' and let $\tau' \in \mathbb{T}$ and let $\tau R \tau'$.

Inductive step type even
We assume by induction that we have $\tau = (\mathbb{A}, \mathbb{B}, \mathbb{D})$ and all the elements to be dealt with are from $\mathbb{B}$ (i.e. $\mathbb{D} \subseteq \mathbb{B}$), and that $\mathbb{D} \neq \emptyset$.

Then proceed as in Step 4.

LEMMA 7.17. *If $\mathbf{N} = (S, R)$ is finite then after a finite number of steps the Tableaux process terminates. We reach tableaux at the bottom of the ρ-tree such that they are either closed or their $\mathbb{D}$ is empty.*

Proof. Since $\mathbb{D}$ always adds new elements either to $\mathbb{A}$ or to $\mathbb{B}$ and $\mathbb{A}$ and $\mathbb{B}$ do not decrease, and S is finite, sooner or later $\mathbb{D} = \emptyset$. ∎

LEMMA 7.18. *Let (S, R) be a finite argumentation network and let $(\mathbb{T}, \rho)$ be the tableaux for it.*

Then there exists a maximal path $\tau_1 \rho \tau_2 \rho \ldots \rho \tau_n$ of non-closed tableaux in $\mathbb{T}$, if and only if x is a member of some admissible extension E.

Proof.

1. Assume $x \in E$ and E is an admissible extension. We will define a maximal path $\tau_1 \rho \tau_2 \rho \ldots \rho \tau_n$ of non-closed tableaux in $(\mathbb{T}, \rho)$.

   Let $\tau_1 = (\{x\}, \emptyset, \{x\})$ as in Step 1 of the inductive definition of $(\mathbb{T}, \rho)$.

   Let τ_2 be as in Step 2. τ_2 is not closed, because if xRx holds, then x cannot be in any admissible extension, and if for some y, yRx and $\neg \exists z(zRy)$ hold, then x is out.

   Assume by induction that we have defined a chain $\tau_1 \rho \tau_2 \rho \ldots \rho \tau_k$ of non-closed tableaux such that for each $1 \leq i \leq k$ we have

   - If $y \in \mathbb{A}_{\tau_i}$ then $y \in E$
   - If $y \in \mathbb{B}_{\tau_i}$ then for some $z \in E, zRy$ holds.

   We now define τ_{k+1}.

   Case k is odd
   In this case we have
   $$\mathbb{D}_{\tau_k} \subseteq \mathbb{A}_{\tau_k}$$
   Let τ_{k+1} be defined in Inductive Step type odd (same as Step 3). Clearly $\tau_k \rho \tau_{k+1}$ holds. We want to show that τ_{k+1} is not closed. Since $\mathbb{A}_{\tau_k} \subseteq E$ and $\mathbb{D}_{\tau_k} \subseteq \mathbb{A}_{\tau_k}$ we have that any yRu for $u \in \mathbb{D}_{\tau_k}$ is atatcked by E and hence is out. Thus
   $$\mathbb{A}_{\tau_{k+1}} \cap \mathbb{B}_{\tau_{k+1}} = \emptyset.$$
   Also every such y is attacked by something and so τ_{k+1} is not closed.

   Case k is even
   In this case we have $\mathbb{D}_{\tau_k} \subseteq \mathbb{B}_{\tau_k}$. This means that all points of $\mathbb{D}_{\tau_k}$ are out. Moreover by construction, $\mathbb{D}_{\tau_k}$ are points attacking points in $\mathbb{A}_{\tau_{k-1}}$, and so by the admissibility of E each such point y has an attacker $\mathbf{f}(y) \in E$. Then let τ_{k+1} be $\tau_{k+1}^\mathbf{f}$ for this function $\mathbf{f}$. we have that $\tau_k \rho \tau_{k+1}^\mathbf{f}$ and $\tau_{k+1}^\mathbf{f}$ is non-closed.

   We carry on until such an n that $\mathbb{D}_{\tau_n} = \emptyset$.

2. Assume there exists a maximal path of non-closed tableaux $\tau_1 \rho \tau_2 \rho \ldots \rho \tau_n$ in $(\mathbb{T}, \rho)$. Then clearly
   $$\mathbb{D}_{\tau_n} = \emptyset.$$
   Let $E = \mathbb{A}_{\tau_n}$. We show that E is conflict free and self-defending. If xRy holds for $x, y \in E$, then at some $\tau_i, y \in \mathbb{A}_{\tau_i}$ and so $x \in \mathbb{B}_{\tau_{i+1}}$ and so τ_j will be closed, for some $j \geq i$ (the j in which x gets into $\mathbb{A}_{\tau_j}$).

   Assume for some z that $zRx, x \in E$. We need to show a $u \in E$ such that uRz. Since $x \in E$ then $x \in \mathbb{A}_{\tau_i}$ for some i. Then $z \in \mathbb{B}_{\tau_{i+1}}$ and so in $\mathbb{B}_{\tau_{i+1}} = \mathbb{B}_{\tau_i}\mathbf{f}$ we have $\mathbf{f}(z) \in \mathbb{A}_{\tau_i} = \mathbb{A}_{\tau_{i+1}}$ and $\mathbf{f}(z)Rz$.

This completes the proof. ∎

EXAMPLE 7.19. Let us check again whether $c = \text{in}$ is possible in Figure 7.6, this time using tableaux.

$$\tau_1 : (\{c\}, \varnothing, \{c\})$$
$$\tau_2 : (\{c\}, \{a, b\}, \{a, b\})$$
$$\tau_3^{\text{f}} : (\{c, a, b\}, \{a, b\}, \{a, b\}).$$

Here $\mathbf{f}(a) = b$ and $\mathbf{f}(b) = a$. τ_3^{f} is closed.

REMARK 7.20. Note that the tableaux method works for the query for several points, namely

- Can $c_1, \ldots, c_n$ all be together in some admissible set?

We simply start our tableaux with

Step 1:

$$(\{c_1, \ldots, c_n\}, \varnothing, \{c_1, \ldots, c_n\})$$

6 Appendix B: Shkop principle in temporal context

It would be helpful to the reader if we present the Shkop prinicple in its natural temporal context. Imagine a linear flow of time of the form $(N, <)$ where N is the set of natural numbers $\{1, 2, 3, \ldots\}$ and $<$ is smaller than relation. We associate with each $n \in N$, a state of the world, which we denote by Δ_n, being a classical propositional logical theory in the language with the atoms $Q = \{q_1, \ldots, q_k\}$. We imagine history as evolving. At step 1 we have only state Δ_1 as given and state Δ_2 has not been created yet. The future states are created by actions. An action has the form $\mathbf{a} = (\alpha_{\mathbf{a}}, \beta_{\mathbf{a}})$, where $\alpha_{\mathbf{a}}$ is the precondition of the action and $\beta_{\mathbf{a}}$ is the post condition, all in the same classical langauge of the states Δ.

So at state Δ_1 we might wish to take action $\mathbf{a}$. We can do that if the precondition holds, i.e. $\Delta_1 \vdash \alpha_{\mathbf{a}}$. If this is the case, then we take the action and we move to state Δ_2, which is the state at time 2. Δ_2 is connected with Δ_1 via a revision process, denoted by "$\circ$". Thus $\Delta_1 = \Delta_1 \circ \beta_{\mathbf{a}}$.

The exact nature of the revision process is not relevant to our purpose. It is sufficient to know that for any Δ and any action $\mathbf{a} = (\alpha_{\mathbf{a}}, \beta_{\mathbf{a}})$, such that $\Delta \vdash \alpha_{\mathbf{a}}$ we get a new state $\Delta' = \Delta \circ \beta_{\mathbf{a}}$.

This is a simple model which can easily be made richer and more complicated. The Talmudic twist to this model is that the Talmud allows for future *conditional actions*. Part of the precondition for allowing action $\mathbf{a}$ to take place at time n is that a related action $\mathbf{a}'$ be taken at future time $n + n'$.

For example: I give you this computer to be yours now on the condition that you clean my garden in a week's time. We have

$\mathbf{a}$ = (I own computer, you own computer)
$\mathbf{a}'$ = (Truth, you have cleaned my garden)

So if you do not clean my garden in a week, then the original action is cancelled. This is *backward causality*. We denote these conditional actions by $\mathbf{a}$ if a' within n' days.

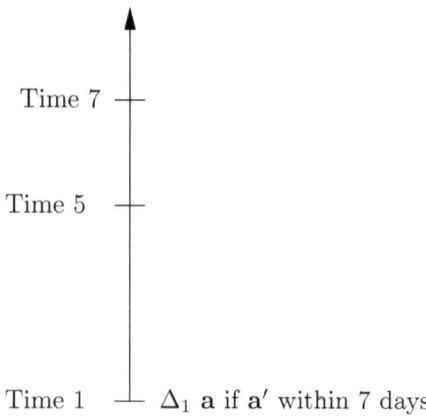

Figure 7.23.

Consider now Figure 7.23.

So action **a** can be taken at Δ_1 on the condition that action **a'** is taken at time 7. Note that time 7 has not yet happened.

Now suppose we continue to take actions and at time 5 we want to take action **b**. The precondition of action **b** holds and so we want to proceed. It could be the case that if we take action **b** at time 5, then a situation is created where action **a'** cannot be taken at time 7. If action **a'** is not taken at time 7, then action **a** at time 1 is not valid and past history is affected to the extent that at time 5 in the new history, the precondition for action **b** does not hold. The Shkop prinicple says that any action **b**, which when taken, changes history backwards in such a way that it cannot be taken (cancelling its own precondition) then **b** should not be taken!

A simple example will illustrate the idea:

EXAMPLE 7.21. On Monday, John buys a new computer to replace his old one. He gives the old computer (which is still good and fast) to his student Terry, on the condition that on Saturday, Terry comes to John's home and installs the new computer.

Terry decides to sell the computer he was given to a housewife neighbour called Mary. The precondition for the sale is that Terry owns the computer. This is OK because there is still the possibility for Terry to fulfil the condition to John and go on Saturday and install John's new computer.

Mary is prepared to buy the computer from Terry but she has her own condition. She wants Terry to come on Saturday and teach her how to use it.

We ask: can Terry sell the computer to Mary? We reason, following Shkop, that if Terry does sell the computer to Mary, he will have to spend Saturday with her and would not be able to go to John and install John's new computer. Failing to go to John on Saturday would nullify the gift of John giving Terry the old computer, which would nullify the precondition of the sale of this computer by Terry to Mary, namely Terry is not the owner of this computer.

So by selling the computer to Mary, Terry is nullifying the legitimacy of the sale!

So the Shkop prinicple applies and the sale cannot be permitted.

Let us now give another temporal argumentation model in which the Shkop principle can apply for resolving loops.

Suppose we have a sequence of argumentation networks of the form $(S_n, R_n), n = 1, 2, 3, \ldots$ such that $S_n \subseteq S_{n+1}$ and $R_n \subseteq R_{n+1}$. Thus as time passes on, (i.e. $n = 1, 2, \ldots$) we get more and more arguments and more and more attacks.

Consider time $n + 1$ and let $x \in S_{n+1} - S_n$. So x is a new argument added at time $n + 1$. So if x causes an odd loop and cannot be part of any extension, then we apply the Shkop principle, as detailed in Section 2, and annihilate it. To understand the usefulness of this principle and the temporal setup, consider Figure 7.13. We have many options for resolving the loops there. Our task is made easier if we have a temporal sequence of when each argument was put into the figure. We can follow the temporal sequence and use the Shkop principle to incrementally in time resolve the loops.

CHAPTER 8

UNCERTAINTY RULES IN TALMUDIC REASONING

Introduction

The Babylonian Talmud, compiled from the 2nd to 7th centuries CE, is the primary source for all subsequent Jewish law. It is not written in apodictic style, but rather as a discursive record of (real or imagined) legal (and other) arguments crossing a wide range of technical topics. Thus, it is not a simple matter to infer general methodological principles underlying the Talmudic approach to legal reasoning. Nevertheless, in this chapter, we propose a general principle that we believe helps explain the variety of methods used by the Rabbis of the Talmud for resolving uncertainty in matters of Jewish Law (henceforth: halacha). Such uncertainty might arise either if the facts of a case are clear but the relevant law is debatable or if the facts themselves are unclear.

A Formal Model

Roughly speaking, the principle we argue for is that, in general, halachic rules for dealing with uncertainty are not probabilistic, but rather are action rules telling us what to do.

Thus, suppose that in situation S we have that

1. If a_1 we do x_1

2. If a_2 we do x_2

3. $\neg x_1 \wedge \neg x_2$ implies y

If there is a 50% doubt about a_i we formally decide $\neg x_i$. Assume that there is such a 50% doubt. Having formally decided $\neg x_1 \wedge \neg x_2$, we now get y. This conclusion holds even if we know that $a_1 \vee a_2$ must logically hold.

Let's now consider one such model.

Our starting point is a language for describing states and actions. Our language has constants for states, $s_1, \ldots, s_k, \ldots$, constants for actions $a_1, a_2, \ldots$ and notation for sets of actions, e.g. $\mathbb{A} = \{a_1, a_2\}$.

We can take predicates like $P(s, x)$ meaning $P(x)$ holds at state s, and predicates like $\mathbf{move}(\mathbb{A}, s, s')$ reading: the set of actions $\mathbb{A}$ moves us from state s to state s'. Our axioms have the form:

$$\bigwedge_i P_i(s, x) \wedge \mathbf{move}(\mathbb{A}, s, s')) \to \bigwedge_j P'_j(s', x).$$

If state s satisfies P_i for x and we move to s' by doing $\mathbb{A}$, then s' satisfies P'_j for x.

We also have a language with meta-predicates $\Psi(P(s,x))$ reading: the property P is classified as an instance of Ψ, at the state s for the individual x.

A history $\mathbf{s}$ is a sequence of states $\mathbf{s} = (s_1, s_2, \ldots, s_k)$ such that $\mathbf{move}(\{a_i^j\}, s_i, s_{i+1})$ holds for some $j = 1, 2, \ldots, m(i)$. This means the actions $\{a_i^j\}, j = 1, 2,$ were taken at s_i and we shifted from state s_i to state s_{i+1}. We also have a language with O_T and F_T. $O_T\Psi$ means Ψ is obligatory and $F_T\Psi$ means Ψ is forbidden. For the nature of rules and character of O and F see [5].[1]

A halachic decision takes the following form. Suppose we moved along the states $s_1, \ldots, s_r$. Suppose at state s_i we have $P_{i,j}(s_i, x_i)$ holding, $j = 1, \ldots, m(i)$. Suppose actions $\{a_i^k\} = \mathbb{A}_i$, $k = 1, \ldots, n_i$, is responsible for moving us from state s_i to s_{i+1}. Then the Halacha might stipulate that $\Psi(P(s_r, x))$ holds. We write this as follows

$$(*) \quad \bigwedge_i \mathbf{move}(\mathbb{A}_i, s_i, s_{i+1}) \wedge \bigwedge_{i,j}[P_{i,j}(s_i, x_i) \text{ and } \Psi_{i,j}(P_{i,j}(s_i, x_i))] \Rightarrow !\Psi(P(s_r, x)).$$

the arrow '$\Rightarrow$!' symbolises halachic stipulation and we allow for some of the $\Psi_{i,j}$ not to appear in (*).

Thus, for example, the Bible forbids doing any work on the Sabbath. Call this $F_T\Psi_1$ where $\Psi_1(P)$ means that P is a "work" predicate. A fellow bought a complicated do-it-yourself cupboard and wants to slot all pieces together on the Sabbath. Is this considered work? Here $P(x)$ is "to slot x together" and we are asking whether $\Psi_1(P(x))$ holds. Once a ruling is given, then the ruling holds from then on, and $P(x)$ is forbidden.

Let $\mathbf{HR}(s)$ be the set of Halachic rulings of the form (*) available at state s. When we move from state s to state s', we carry the Halachic rulings with us and may add some new rules. Thus $\mathbf{HR}(s)$ is a subset of $\mathbf{HR}(s')$. When in state s' a question arises as to the status of some predicate $\Psi(P(s,x))$, we check whether some ruling of the form (*) can be instantiated to give an answer. If not we have to ask the Rabbis for a ruling and the new ruling of the form (*) is added to $\mathbf{HR}(s')$. This is how the sets $\mathbf{HR}$ grow and evolve

Majority Rules in the Talmud

In what follows we treat various uncertainty examples in the Talmud and show that the considerations involved are not probabilistic but operational rulings for the practicing individual to take action.

One of the Talmud's guiding principles for dealing with uncertainty is "follow the majority" (Hullīn 11a). As we shall see, this rule is applied in a variety of ways. Perhaps the canonical form of the rule concerns the oft-cited (e.g.,

---

[1]Note that here we use the meta-predicates Ψ as objects of obligations and prohibitions $O_T\Psi$ and $F_T\Psi$. We can use predicates $P(s,x)$ as well as meta-predicate defining themselves., i.e.

$$\Psi_{P(s,x)}(Q(s',y))$$

holds iff

$$Q(s',y) = P(s,x)$$

holds. Thus we can also have $O_T P$ and $F_T P$

Ketubot 15a) case in which an unlabeled piece of meat is found on the street in a town with p kosher butcher shops and q non-kosher butcher shops. All other considerations (such as proximity and size of the shops) being equal, the meat is deemed kosher if and only if $p > q$. We note as an aside that will be of some importance below that if $p = q$, the meat is deemed "in doubt" by this decision method and a secondary decision method must be invoked to resolve the matter.

This sounds rather straightforward. However, scattered around the Talmud we find a number of extensions of this rule as well as a number of limitations. Let's now consider the complete picture.

The Talmud (Tractate Hullin 11a) states that there are two distinct principles of "follow the majority" that cannot be inferred one from the other. The first principle is typified by the example of the meat we just considered in which the majority is said to be "present". The second principle involves what is called an "absent" majority and is typified by the following example. The milk of a cow suffering from some life-threatening illness is not kosher. Such an illness might be completely undetectable unless we slaughter the cow and perform an autopsy. Nevertheless, we can drink milk from a random cow, despite the inevitable uncertainty regarding its health, because most cows are healthy.

The Talmud does not define the difference between present and absent majorities but it is worth attempting to define that difference since there are important differences in the respective follow the majority principles. For example, the 2nd century scholar, Rabbi Meir, asserts that an absent majority does not constitute sufficient grounds to overturn an existing status quo but implies that a present majority does (Yevamot 67b). Conversely, in capital cases, where we require something approximating certainty to convict, a present majority never constitutes grounds for conviction but an absent majority might. For example, in a case that rests on establishing the identity of a defendant's mother, the fact that 99 out of 100 candidate mothers would satisfy the conditions for conviction (a present majority) is inadequate grounds to convict, but the fact that (in the absence of countervailing evidence) most apparent family relationships represent biological relationships (an absent majority) is sufficient grounds to convict.

The examples cited in the Talmud of each type of majority as well as the above rules suggests that the difference is that a present majority entails a closed set of objects the proportion of which have some relevant status is known. An absent majority entails some empirical claim regarding the proportion of a population that has some relevant status, where the claim is based on some sample. Since this sample might not be currently present, such a majority is regarded as absent. (The distinction between present and absent majorities can be fruitfully compared with the distinction between the classical interpretation of probability, motivated by gambling applications, and the frequentist interpretation of probability, motivated by insurance applications. See [13].)

Consequently, the rule that we follow a present majority is regarded as formal and procedural. It is treated identically whether the majority is 0.51 or 0.99. Furthermore, the conclusion to which it leads is never regarded as a certainty sufficient for convicting in a capital case. By contrast, an absent majority is tied to an underlying empirical claim and hence the rule that we follow an absent majority is linked to the strength that the Rabbis wished to assign to that claim. Rabbi Meir always regards empirical claims as sufficient only to yield a default rule, which in turn he regards as no stronger than a different default rule that presumes that the last known status quo continues. On the other hand, those who do not accept Rabbi Meir's view hold that a sufficiently strong empirical claim be treated as a certainty for legal purposes.

Let's now consider a simple paradox that arises in the use of the rule that we follow an absent majority.

1. Suppose that known kosher milk and known non-kosher milk (call this state s), have been inadvertently mixed. Call this action of mixing action a, resulting in a new state s'. In symbols, we have

   $\neg$ Kosher (s, unit of milk with label number i) $i = 1, 2, 3, \ldots, n$, and Kosher (s, unit of milk with label number j), $j = n+1, n+1, \ldots, m$ and action **Mix** applied to the units takes us from state s to the new mixed state s' where the numbering labels on the units is lost.

   We need a rule which will say whether Kosher (s', unit of milk without a number) is true or not in state s'.

2. The mixture is kosher if the proportion of kosher to non-kosher units milk in the mixture is greater than 60:1. This is the rule applied in his case which decides whether the milk is kosher. So the rule is

   $\bigwedge \neg$ Kosher (s, unit of milk with label number i) $i = 1, 2, 3, \ldots, n$, and $\bigwedge_j$ Kosher (s, unit of milk with label number j), $j = n+1, n+1, \ldots, m$, and $n/m < 1/61$ and action **Mix** applied to the units takes us from state s to the new mixed state s' where the numbering labels on the units is lost $\Rightarrow$ Kosher (s', units of milk without a number).

   Now suppose that

3. it is known in general that 5% of all cows are non-kosher due to various endemic illnesses, though these cannot be identified through external examination. Call this state t.

4. Now we take the combined milk of a huge herd of cows, as is common in the dairy industry. Call this action b, resulting in state t'.

We need a rule to tell us whether this milk kosher or not. The probability that less than 1/61 of this milk is non kosher is vanishingly small, so that one might think that it is non-kosher by the rule used in 2 above. Nevertheless, the vast majority of commentators do not rule this way. The principle is that by the rule that we follow an absent majority, it has already been decided (as we saw above) that each individual cow is kosher. Once that decision has been made, the matter is settled. The mixture is regarded as consisting of 100% kosher milk. Formally, the rule is as follows:

If in state s [less than 50% of cows are unhealthy] **and** [milk from unhealthy cow is non-Kosher] **and** [we take action **Mix** of all milk from any single cow at state s and thus move by **Mix** action to state s' in which the milk is mixed], **then** at s' the milk is Kosher.

We add the rule above to **HR**(s'). This rule is of the correct form (*). Let us write it more carefully: If in state s [less than 50% of cows are unhealthy]. Call this $P(s, \text{cows})$ and [milk from unhealthy cow is non-Kosher] i.e $\neg\Psi(P'(s, \text{milk}))$ (where "Kosher" = "Ψ") and [we take action **Mix** of all milk from any single cow at state s, call this **move** (**Mix**, s, s') and thus move by **Mix** action to state s' in which the milk is mixed], then at s' the milk is Kosher i. e call the mixture $Q(s'\ \text{milk})$ **then** $\Psi(Q(s'\ \text{milk}))$.

If we write the ruling only in symbols we get

$$P(s,\ \text{cows}) \bigwedge \neg\Psi(P'(s,\ \text{milk})) \bigwedge \textbf{move}(\textbf{Mix}, s, s') \Rightarrow !\Psi(Q(s'\ \text{milk}))$$

Extensions and Limitations of the Present Majority Rule

In what follows we discuss extensions and limitations on the formal decision rule that we follow a present majority. We will see that it too is quite different than what we customarily think of as probabilistic reasoning.

Suppose we have three pieces of identical meat of which one unidentified piece is non-kosher (call this state x). Using the "follow the (present) majority" rule, the Talmud states (Gittin 54b) that each of the pieces is regarded as kosher. More remarkably, the 15th century commentator Rabbi Asher (in gloss 37 to Hullin, Chapter 7) interprets this to mean that we are permitted to eat all three pieces simultaneously. Indeed, he rules that if the three pieces are liquefied, the liquid mixture can be drunk even though it is know with certainty that 1/3 of the mixture is non-kosher, far in excess of 1/61. The principle is quite clear. Once some rule has been invoked (in this case, to treat each piece as kosher), the matter is settled and can be applied even after subsequent state transitions occur such that the prior decision leads to absurd conclusions (in this case, that all the pieces can be eaten).

It is worth noting that if there are two pieces of identical meat of which one unidentified piece is non-kosher, call this state y, the majority rule is obviously inapplicable. In such case, we have an "unresolved set" and some secondary decision method must be invoked to resolve the matter. However, the secondary method invoked in the case of an unresolved set state y is different than the secondary method invoked in the case we saw above in which an isolated piece of meat is found in a town with an equal number of kosher and non-kosher butcher shops. The Talmud (Kritut 17b) does not treat an item from an unresolved set in the same way as it treats an item that is in doubt.

Another example of the present majority rule, indeed its purported source according to the Talmud (Hullin 11a), is the rule that when there is disagreement among a panel of judges, the ruling is according to the majority. The critical point to note is that in this case there is no uncertainty at all regarding facts and hence interpreting the present majority rule as a probabilistic method for resolving uncertainty regarding facts is, ipso facto, too narrow. Rather, the rule must be interpreted as concerning the treatment of mixed sets and can be stated as follows:

> Given a set of objects the majority of which have the property

P and the rest of which have the property not-P, we may, under certain circumstances, regard the set itself and/or any object in the set as having property P.

An important extension of the present majority rule applies to cases in which the set in question does not consist of objects but rather of abstract possibilities. For example, in a civil case involving a man who accuses his wife of infidelity (based solely on the uncontested fact that at the time of their marriage she was not a virgin), the Talmud (Ketubot 9a) argues on her behalf that a) it is not known if she was raped or had intercourse of her own volition and b) in either case, it is not known if the event occurred subsequent to her contracting marriage with her husband. Since the husband would prevail in the case only for one of the four possibilities in the Cartesian product, he loses the cases on grounds of the formal present majority rule.

Formally the problem is that we know that at the time s' of the marriage x was not a virgin; call this $Q(s', x)$. Call her previous state s and assume that in that state she was a virgin but it is not clear what action moved her from state s to state s'. It could have been rape (action a_1, it could have been consent, action a_2 and either case could have been before or after their engagement, $P(s, x)$ or $\neg P(s, x)$. It is clear the formal pattern is the following:

- $P_i(s, x) \wedge \mathbf{move}(a_i, s, s') \to Q(s', x)$, for $i = 1, \ldots, k + m$.

We also know that

- $P_i(s, x) \wedge \mathbf{move}(a_i, s, s') \Rightarrow !\Psi(Q(s', x))$, if $i \leq k$

and

- $P_i(s, x) \wedge \mathbf{move}(a_i, s, s') \Rightarrow !\neg\Psi(Q(s', x))$, if $k < i \leq k + m$.

We observe $Q(s', x)$ but we do not know which action a_i was taken. What is the ruling Ψ or not Ψ?

The commentators note that no claim has been made that the probabilities of her having been raped or of her having had intercourse subsequent to the contract, respectively, are precisely $\frac{1}{2}$. Rather the claim is that nothing is known about these probabilities at all (and indeed if the probabilities were known, different decision method would be invoked). Thus, the method is vulnerable to manipulation in a manner somewhat reminiscent of Bertrand's paradox. For example, we could artificially collapse the majority argument by restating the crucial issue as "infidelity or not infidelity" and, conversely, we could artificially strengthen the majority argument (to seven out of eight, rather than three out of four) by distinguishing between violent rape and statutory rape. The argument is thus seen to rest rather formally on assumptions about what categories are natural kinds (e.g., rape) and which are not (e.g., statutory rape).

Finally, we turn to a crucial limitation on the application of the present majority rule. Suppose we have a set of ten pieces of meat, nine of which are kosher and one of which is non-kosher and identifiable as such (say, by its position in the pile). Now we randomly choose a piece without paying attention to which one, and, having done so, it is no longer possible to determine if it was one of the kosher pieces or the non-kosher piece. In contrast with the canonical case of a piece of meat found in the street in which we assign a status according to the majority of the sample from which it is drawn, in this case the Talmud rules that the proportion of kosher and non-kosher pieces is irrelevant. Rather, the set is treated as an unresolved set, precisely as in the case above in which two pieces of meat, one kosher and one non-kosher, are mixed.

The principle is this. An isolated item such as one found on the street must be assigned some status applicable to an individual item, e.g., kosher or non-kosher, and hence the majority rule is invoked to resolve the matter. An unresolved set might, however, be assigned a third status appropriate to a set, namely, neither kosher nor non-kosher but, rather, mixed. An item that is taken from an unresolved mixed set simply inherits the mixed status of the set from which it is taken; it is treated like a chip off the old block. Plainly, from a probabilistic point of view, it is hard to distinguish the case of the found piece from the case of the selected piece (and although it is tempting to suggest psychological explanations, these do not hold water when the full range of examples is carefully examined).

Conclusion

We have seen that the Talmudic way of dealing with uncertainty is pragmatic and not probabilistic

1. Given a situation s arising from action x, resulting in situation s' where some uncertainty occurs, the Talmud makes a decision that sticks and allows life to continue.

2. Given a situation x which could have arisen fron one of actions $a_1, \ldots, a_n$, we may have uncertainty as to the nature of the situation depending on which action a_i gave rise to it. Again, we use a rule to make a decision.

The above rules are not probabilistic because in a sequence of actions, we draw conclusions that persist even in cases where judging the final state in isolation might have lead to very different conclusions.

Acknowledgement

This chapter is based on D. Gabbay and M. Koppel, Uncertainty rules in Talmudic logic. In *Journal of the History and Philosophy of Logic*, special issue on Judaic Logic edited by A. Schumann, 32(1), 63–69, 2011.

CHAPTER 9

DELEGATION, COUNT AS, AND SECURITY IN TALMUDIC LOGIC

Preliminaries

Delegation is a commonplace feature in our society. Individuals give power of attorney to their lawyers to perform certain actions for them (e.g. buy or sell property), institutions delegate to certain employees to sign for them (human resources send letters of appointment) and owners can grant access and administrative rights to other people in relation to their servers.

The logic behind such a system has been studied by several communities.
In philosophy this is known as "count as". X counts as Y in context C.
In law there are various rules for power of attorney.
In computer science one talks about access control and delegation.
This chapter examines the approach to delegation in Talmudic Logic.
The current approaches to delegation, mainly study three features

1. Dominance — if several primary sources delegate to secondary sources who carry on delegating then what is the dominance relationship among the chains of delegations

2. Revocation — if some sources revoke the delegation or some change their minds and reinstate, how does this propagate through the chains of delegations?

3. Resilience — if one source revokes delegation do we cancel other delegations from other sources on the grounds that we now do not trust the delegate?

In the literature systems have been constructed which either model or implement a calculus of Delegation-Revocation (Privilege calculus). Their purpose is to answer the question of whether the chain of delegation and revocations can allow an agent to perform an action and their models are chain update models.

The Talmudic approach is slightly different not only in the details of its model but also in its point view.

The Talmud not only examines[1] the procedure of the actual acts of delegation and revocation and its calculus but also includes the analysis of ordinary actions (not just chain update actions) — their elements of agency, action, deliberation

---
[1] The Talmud deals with delegation — Shlichut — in various contexts. It appears in many places across Talmudic literature, for example Tractate Kidushin, 41b-42a (basic source on the subject), Tractate Gittin 18a, 33c (on inexplicit multiple delegation).

and competence. These attributes have preconditions addressing not only acts but also delegation and revocation chains leading to the actions. The Talmud also addresses cases of delegated agents unable to execute the actions for various reasons, and the possibility of agents going mad or dying during the delegation revocation process, with their repercussions.

1 Background and orientation

Delegation is a commonplace feature in our society. Individuals give power of attorney to their lawyers to perform certain actions for them (e.g. buy or sell property), institutions delegate to certain employees to sign for them (human resources send letters of appointment) and owners can grant access and adminisrtative rights to other people in relation to their servers.

The logic behind such a system has been studied by several communities.

In philosophy this is known as "count as". X counts as Y in context C [94; 95; 76], and see [66] for a survey.

In law there are various rules for power of attorney.

In computer science one talks about access control and delegation, see for example [90].

This chapter examines the approach to delegation in Talmudic Logic.

The following are feature to be addressed:

1. The general logical context in which delegation takes place.

2. Exactly how (by what process) does agent **a** delegate to agent **b** item φ.

3. What are the rules for making chains of delegation?

4. How can delegation be revoked in a chain?

5. What happens in a delegation chain if some of the agents in the chain become insane (i.e. irresponsible or generally break down) and how to continue if such agents become sane again? What if they die (drop out permanently)?

6. What to do if some agents exceed their remit in a chain (e.g. human resources in a University sends a letter of appointment by mistake to the wrong candidate)?

7. It may be the case that several agents $\mathbf{a}_i$ capable of executing action α, each delegates to the same agent **b** to do α. Meanwhile some of these agents $\mathbf{a}_i$ go insane, some die, and some cancel the delegation. What can **b** do?

A word on methodology. The Talmud (completed at the end of the fifth century) and its later interpreters (another 5-10 centuries) is full of debate about various cases of delegation. There is no formal logic, but a dialogue-based argumentation and analysis that is true to the casuistic nature[2] of the Talmud's core object of analysis (the Mishna). This process involves various case studies

---
[2]Cf. Leib Moscovitz, Talmudic Reasoning: From Casuistics to Conceptualization, Tübingen: Mohr Siebeck, 2002.

of "hard-cases" and approaches offered by various deliberators. Finding the logic behind such extravagantly lively debate, spread over thousands of discussions is challenging: It requires find a logical model with some degrees of freedom and a mapping of the various scholars or views to parameters in the logical model. We then have to go to all places and cases in the Talmud where there is a debate and the model must explain each move in each argument in each debate in each place in a perfect match. This is possible to do because as a body of law, Talmudic debates are remarkably coherent and consistent, with much effort invested in sorting out conceptual irregularities and disagreements. A formal-logical background is called for especially where it can benefit the Talmudic scholar (in the deliberation process) as well as the benefit of formulating that the Talmud implicitly uses and can be beneficial in the development of modern logic. The Talmudic logic project is geared toward this dual goal.

2 Motivating the Talmudic system

Let $\mathcal{A}$ be a set of actions and $\mathbf{A}$ be a set of agents. We need a relation $\mathbb{R} \subseteq \mathbf{A} \times \mathcal{A}$ giving us for each agent $\mathbf{a}$ in $\mathbf{A}$ the set of all actions $\alpha \in \mathcal{A}$ such that $\mathbf{a}$ can execute α ($\mathbf{a}$ has the authority to execute α). The actions have the form $\alpha = (A_\alpha, B_\alpha)$, where A_α is the pre-conditon and B_α is the post-condition. A_α and B_α are written in some predicate language $\mathbb{L}$, to be decided according to the required strengths and specifications of Talmudic delegation structure.

An agent $\mathbf{a}$ can delegate his authority to do any action to agent $\mathbf{b}$ (there are some restrictions on agent $\mathbf{b}$, like he has to be sane and responsible and can perform actions similar to α). He must not be involved in the action α himself, and the action α must be legally meaningful). We need a relation $\mathbb{D}$ where $\mathbb{D}(\mathbf{a}, \mathbf{b}, \alpha)$ means that $\mathbf{a}$ delegated action α to $\mathbf{b}$. This can be delegated further by $\mathbf{b}$. So the relation $\mathbb{R}$ can be expanded to a relation $\mathbb{F}^*$, namely

$$x\mathbb{R}^*\alpha \text{ iff } \exists y_1, \ldots, y_k \text{ for some } k, \text{ such that } y_1\mathbb{R}\alpha \wedge \bigwedge_{i=1}^{k-1} \mathbb{D}(y_i, y_{i+1}, \alpha) \wedge y_k = x.$$

In order to model the complexities of delegation in Talmudic logic we want to realise $\mathbb{D}$ using tokens (modern papers call them certificates, see for example [15; 40] and [89]).

An agent $\mathbf{a}$ which can do α has a token $\mathbb{T}(\mathbf{a}, \alpha)$. Think of it as a copy print of $(\mathbf{a}, \alpha) \in \mathbb{R}$. If $\mathbf{a}$ wants to delegate to $\mathbf{b}$, he signs on the token, "I authorise $\mathbf{b}'$. We denote this by $(\mathbf{a}, \mathbf{b}, \alpha)$. Thus we can get the chain $(y_1, \ldots, y_k, \alpha)$. If y_k wants to execute an action α, $\alpha = (A_\alpha, B_\alpha)$, the language $\mathbb{L}$ must also enable A_α to ask y_k: do you have a token $(y_1, \ldots, y_k, \alpha)$?

So for example to sell a table t, we need the agent $\mathbf{a}$ to own t and then he can sell it to agent $\mathbf{b}$. Or we can have $(\mathbf{a}, y_1, \ldots, y_k, \text{sell table})$ and y_k can sell the table on behalf of $\mathbf{a}$. So the language $\mathbb{L}$ must contain $\mathbb{D}$, as well as the names of agents and facts about the world.

This is a language where $\alpha = (A_\alpha, B_\alpha)$ and A_α can talk about α. It is a self reflecting language.

Different delegation theories will be implemented by different properties of the tokens.

There are two main types of delegation in Talmudic logic.

1. *Power of attorney* view (Maimonides[3] view).

2. The *long arm/extended reach* view (Tur[4] view).

If **a** delegates to **b** and **b** delegates further to **c**, let us refer to **a** as the master (or principal, using modern terminology) and to **b** as the agent and to **c** as the subagent.

The *power of attorney* view is for the master to delegate to an agent to do action α.

The action is done by the agent and the result of the action is passed on to the master.

The *long arm* view is that the agent is an extension of the arm of the master, and the master is doing the action α by means of his arm extension — the agent.

So the agent "counts as" the master.

We model the difference between these two views through the properties of the token. The token is given from the master to the delegated agent and in the token there is a list of actions to be done by the agent.

The *power of attorney* view postulates a token for each agent. The *long arm* view postulates a token for each delegated action/job.

The token per agent view envisages the token as listing all the actions to be done. These include actions that the master has authority to do, as well as actions which he (the master) was originally recruited by a previous master to do (to whom he acts as an agent).

Figure 9.1 shows what this token looks like. Note also that this token allows for the master to cancel the appointment of the agent as an agent for the action (in modern terminology, the master revokes the delegation to the agent).

In the case of the *long arm* view, the tokens look like Figure 9.2

We now describe what happens when agent John Smith wants to execute an action. We check the following:

1. The *power of attorney* view checks whether action α shows in John Smith token (see Figure 9.1). Is he the master for this action? Was he appointed agent for this action by a master who has authority? Was he appointed by an agent who was himself appointed by a master? etc. All the above is supposed to be recorded in the token.

---

[3] Named here for Moses ben-Maimon, called Maimonides or Ramban (Hebrew acronym for "Rabbi Moshe ben Maimon"). For the *power of attorney* view, Cf. Rabbi Isaac Herzog, *The Main Institutions of Jewish Law, Vol. II, The Law of Obligations*, (2nd ed.) London; Soncino, 1967, pp. 141–142

[4] Jacob ben Asher, also known as Ba'al ha-Turim as well as Rabbi Yaakov ben Raash (Rabbeinu Asher), was likely born in Cologne, Germany, c. 1269 and likely died in Toledo, Spain, c. 1343. In point of fact, the *long arm/extended reach* and *power of attorney* concepts were suggested later on and used to explain the Tur. Cf. Ketzot Hachoshen (Aryeh Leib Heller-Kahane, 1745–1812), Ch. 188, ii; 244, iii.; Lekach Tov (Yosef Engel, 1858–1920), Ch. 1. In the Tur, the limits of delegation are mentioned in Even haEzer, Ch. 141 section 43, regarding the laws of divorce contracts (Gitin) and the ability of a receiving agent (Shaliach Kabala) to delegate his task.

Note by the way the English expression "The long arm of the law".

9. DELEGATION, COUNT AS, AND SECURITY IN TALMUDIC LOGIC

Owner of token:	John Smith Social Security number (SSN):	
Action	Master (who has authority over the action)	Verify nomination of owner of this token (i.e. John Smith)
1. Sell house (property ♯)	Terry Jordan owner of the house	+from Terry
2. α	a	+from a

Figure 9.1.

```
action α.
Issued by agent a
such that aℝα.
```

Figure 9.2.

2. The *long arm* view would simply check if our John Smith has the token as in Figure 9.2.

EXAMPLE 9.1. To see the difference between the two views, let us assume that the master **a** appointed **b** as an agent for him to do action α, and then lost his mind.

The *long arm* view will say the action cannot be performed because the source of the long arm, the master, is mentally incapacitated, making his *long arm/extended reach* useless, as he is without a sound mind. If we look at the token 9.2, the **a** in **a**ℝα is no longer sane.

The *power of attorney* view, the owner of the token (the agent **b**) is capable and sane, his token indicates he has the authority to take action, so he can do it!

Let us take a very simple example from practice. The manager of a company delegates to a secretary to delete certain sensitive files from the server, just before a shareholders' meeting is about to take place. The secretary goes to the meeting and intended to do the action afterwards. During the stormy meeting, the manager resigned and discussions were ongoing about appointing a new manager. The *long arm* view would say the secretary cannot delete the files because she is the long arm of the manager who is no longer in power, he resigned. The *power of attorney* view says that the secretary has a power of attorney, he/she should do the action and delete the files.

EXAMPLE 9.2 (Cancellation and reinstatement).

1. Both views allow for cancellation (the modern term is revocation). The master cancels either the token of Figure 9.1 or of Figure 9.2, depending on the view.

2. Both views agree that if the master becomes sane again (the manager

of Example 9.1 gets reinstated) the action can take place without the need for doing again the formal appointment of delegation (i.e. the secretary need not ask the reinstated manager to reconfirm his instructions to him/her).

EXAMPLE 9.3 (The delegated agent becomes insane). Suppose the agent goes crazy, and then becomes sane again (goes through a mental breakdown for a while). Can he/she continue being an agent and execute the action?

According to the *long arm* view he can. He got the token, he is now sane, so he can do it. Similarly according to the *power of attorney* view. He got the token.

There is a difference however in the view about pre-condition A_α of α.

The *long arm* view says A_α must check the sanity (capability) of both the master who controls the long arm and the agent, who is the arm. Both have to be functional.

The *power of attorney* view needs the functionality check in A_α of the agent only. The agent carries the token, he is supposed to execute the action!

We now examine how, according to each view, an agent can nominate a subsgent for himself.

The *long arm* view treats this very simply. The agent has a token as in Figure 9.2. So he just passes this token on to his subagent. All very simple. The subagent is now the long arm of the master. The agent is no longer in the picture. We may have a long chain of such nominations. So a by-product of this view is that the master can cancel the nomination of his long arm agent at the end of the chain, no matter how long the chain is.

The *power of attorney* view would have to say that the subagent is delegated from the agent and not from the master. Thus the token must record this information. It must record the chain of delegations from agent to agent. A by-product of this view is that the master cannot cancel the nomination of the subagent. The subagent was nominated by the agent not by the master! The master can cancel the nomination of the agent but if the agent has already nominated a subagent then the nomination of the subagent stands! Figure 9.3 shows what the token looks like.

Owner of token: John Smith. SSN:

Action	Master a	who nominated John	confirm nomination from Levy not retracted	Who nominated Levy	Confirm nomination from Terry not retracted
sell house: address	Terry Jordan	+Levy =c	+confirm	+Terry =b	+confirm
α	a	c	+	b	(negative, a retracted the nomination

Figure 9.3.

3 Technical definitions of the logical model

3.1 Preliminary discussion

The framework in which we are working involves agents and actions, with a relation $\mathbb{R}$ between agents **a** and actions α, saying whether agent **a** can execute action α ($a\mathbb{R}\alpha$). α has preconditions A_α and postconditions B_α.

To this model we add the delegation component, in which agent **a** can delegate to agent **b** the execution of action α. We wrote this as $\mathbb{D}(\mathbf{a}, \mathbf{b}, \alpha)$.

Thus any model of delegation needs to be based on a model for agents and actions. Since our primary interest is in modelling delegation we can take a simple basic model of agents and actions, without any fine refinements (coming from a sophisticated multi-agent theories), provided that this agent-action model is rich enough to allow us to express all the delegation features we need to model.

DEFINITION 9.4. Let **A** be a finite set of agents and $\mathcal{A}$ a finite set of actions. By a basic multi-agent system we mean a tuple of the form $\mathfrak{M} = (S, \mathbf{R})$, where S is a non-empty set of states and $\mathbf{R} \subseteq (S \times S) \times \mathbf{A} \times \mathcal{A}$.

When $(t, s, \mathbf{a}, \alpha) \in \mathbf{R}$, we draw it graphically as in Figure 9.4. The figure means that at state t agent **a** can execute action α which moves the system to state s.

It may be that agent **b** can also execute α at state t but not agent **c**. So we write Figure 9.5.

where $\mathbf{E} \subseteq \mathbf{A}$ is the set of agents which can execute α at state t.

Thus
$$\mathbf{E} = \{\mathbf{x} | (t, s, \mathbf{x}, \alpha) \in \mathbf{R}\}.$$

We need to require that the execution of α is deterministic, i.e.

- $(t, s, \mathbf{x}, \alpha) \in \mathbf{R}$ and $(t, s', \mathbf{y}, \alpha) \in \mathbf{R}$ impies $s = s'$.

We believe that this simple model is good enough for our purposes.

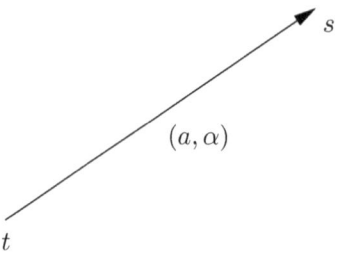

Figure 9.4.

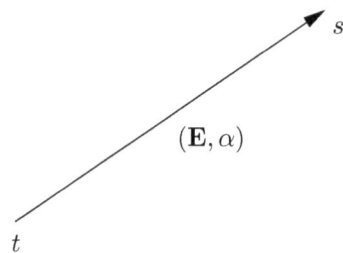

Figure 9.5.

REMARK 9.5. Note that we ignored the representation of the preconditions A_α and postconditions B_α of actions α. This we can do because we use a set of states. If A_α does not hold at state t then the action cannot be taken. If it is taken then B_α holds at state s.

Thus to complete the model, we take $(S, \mathbf{R})$ and associate with each $t \in S$, a model $\mathbf{m}_t$ of the language $\mathbb{L}$ of the preconditions and postconditions, so that we can write $t \vDash A_\alpha$ or $s \nvDash B_\alpha$, etc.

Thus our final models have the form

$$\mathfrak{M} = (S, \mathbf{R}, \mathbf{m}_t), t \in S.$$

The above does not deal with delegation yet. We now examine our options for modelling delegation.

It is convenient to list the views and types of delegation we encountered in Section 2.

Type 1. **a** delegates to **b** action α in any context (state), e.g. "sell my house".

Type 2. **a** delegates to **b** action α only in certain contexts, e.g. "sell my house when the Euro is over 1.30 to the dollar".

Type 3. Preconditions and postconditions of actions involve delegation considerations, even though the action itself is not a delegation action.

For example, when **a** delegates to **b** action α then when **b** wants to execute α, part of the precondition of α is that agent **a** is sane and alive.

View 1. Agent **b** is the long arm of agent **a**.

> In this case if we are at state t, we move to state s after the execution of the action (either by **a** or by **b**).

View 2. Agent **a** gives Talmudic power of attorney to agent **b** for example, to buy a house for him from agent **c** or to collect a debt for him from agent **c**.

> In this case the execution of the action may result in an intermediate state. In the case of buying a house there is no intermediate state, but in the case of collecting a debt, where agent **c** also owes money to agent **b**, there is an intermediate state. We view the sequence of actions to be that the money first goes in the hands of agent **b**, who then passes it to agent **a**. So if we start at state t we move to t' and then to s, unlike the long arm delegation, where we move from t to s directly.

Option 1: The fibred (combined) option

This option puts a delegation program or logic next to a model $\mathfrak{M}$ for agents and actions. The program is used to update the relation $\mathbf{R}$ in $\mathfrak{M}$.

Let Δ be a database of all the delegation tokens in the system. The model becomes

$$\mathfrak{M} = (S, \mathbf{R}^\Delta, \mathbf{m}_t), t \in S.$$

When an agent delegates an action to another agent, the delegation database Δ is updated to Δ' and $\mathfrak{M}$ changes to

$$\mathfrak{M}' = (S, \mathbf{R}^{\Delta'}, \mathbf{m}_t), t \in S.$$

So the update system of Δ communicates with $\mathbf{R}$ of $\mathfrak{M}$.

Thus logically modelling such a system requires the logical modelling of communication between a program and a logic.

Since the updating system is independent of $\mathfrak{M}$, many researchers use Δ only as models of delegation and do not mention $\mathfrak{M}$ at all. This may not be possible if the systems interact. For example, part of the precondition of action α may be that it is not performed through delegation. The prime minister of a country or a King, for example, cannot freely delegate some actions associated with his position. A wife having difficulties giving a child to her husband cannot, nowadays, delegate the job to her maid, as was the custom in Biblical times.

Another example is when the delegations comes as a result of an action α in the real world is the following. If I run over the parents of a small child then by law the court becomes delegates for his interests. So here the delegation is a postcondition of my actions.

In such cases, where there is interaction between the delegation system and the preconditions and postconditions of ordinary actions, the next integrated model is a better option.

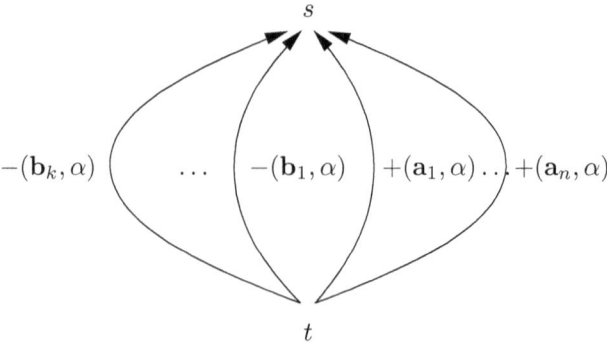

Figure 9.6.

Option 2: The integrated model

This model views the delegation details (certificates, tokens, etc.) as part of the state $t \in S$, and the act of delegation is viewed as just another action modifying the state. So in this integrated model, m_t talks not only about facts, but includes the details of each delegation certificate/token ever issued. The precondition of actions must include that the action is executed by an agent who has the valid delegation token for the action.

A variety of models can be constructed under this option, but they all have the drawback that the delegation part gets a bit lost as a separate system. We could save the uniqueness of the delegation part by separating delegation actions from ordinary actions and add temporal like connectives to the model which can chain correctly the delegation actions, etc., etc. If we do that well, we will be back to Option 1, hidden inside Option 2 under the guise of additional connectives.

Option 3: Reactivity model for the *long arm* view of the Tur

We now intuitively explain the components of this model. It is an integrated model which uses reactivity to separate delegation actions from ordinary actions in a natural way. For reactive Kripke models see [62].

It is best suited when there is intereaction between delegation and post and preconditions of actions or where there are delegations which are valid only in certain contexts (states).

If delegations involve just agents and actions then Option 1 may be best.

First we decide that we keep the agent action model as it is, with the states describing pure facts, with no mention of delegation. So the relation $\mathbf{R}$ can be represented as in Figure 9.5. So there is no mention of delegation in this figure. We are going to add delegation into it. We need to write Figure 9.5 more explicitly. Consider Figure 9.6.

This Figure contains some information as Figure 9.5. We just wrote the information explicitly. We have $\mathbf{E} = \{\mathbf{a}_1, \ldots, \mathbf{a}_n\}$ and $\mathbf{A} - \mathbf{E} = \{\mathbf{b}_1, \ldots, \mathbf{b}_k\}$.

The action α can be executed by $\mathbf{a}_1, \ldots, \mathbf{a}_n$ and so we have the arrows $t \to s$ annotated by $+(\mathbf{a}_i, \alpha), i = 1, \ldots, n$. The action α cannot be taken by $\mathbf{b}_1, \ldots, \mathbf{b}_k$ and so we have the arrows $t \to s$ annotated by $-(\mathbf{b}_j, \alpha)$.

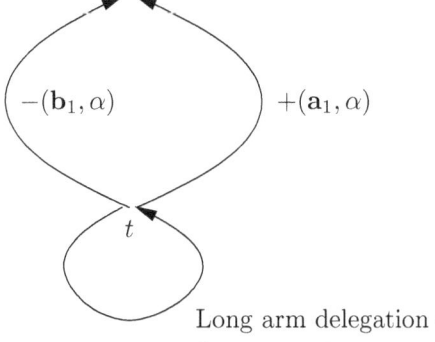

Long arm delegation of action α from a_1 to b_1

Figure 9.7.

It would be easier to replace the relation **R** by its characteristic function $\mathbf{F_R}$. We have

$$\mathbf{F_R}(t, s, \mathbf{a}, \alpha) = 1 \text{ iff } (t, s, \mathbf{a}, \alpha) \in \mathbf{R}.$$

From now on we regard **R** as such a function (by abuse of notation).

We begin discussing delegation for the *long arm* view of the Tur:

Now suppose we perform an action of delegation. Agent $\mathbf{a}_1$, who can perform action α, wants to delegate to agent $\mathbf{b}_1$, the execution of α at state t. Agent $\mathbf{b}_1$ cannot perform action α at state t before the delegation (i.e. we have $+(\mathbf{a}_1, \alpha)$ and $-(\mathbf{b}_1, \alpha)$ before the delegation) but after delegation $-(\mathbf{b}_1, \alpha)$ is updated and changed to $+(\mathbf{b}_1, \alpha)$.

How do we represent this using reactive arrows? When we perform the delegation action, we remain at state t, since in our model, the states represent facts about the world and do not contain any token/certificate delegation information.

Figure 9.7 represents this move for $\mathbf{a}_1$ and $\mathbf{b}_1$.

We represent Figure 9.7 by the reactive Figure 9.8.

The reactive double arrow is written as

$$(t \to_{(\mathbf{a}_1, \mathbf{b}_1, \alpha)} t) \twoheadrightarrow_\lambda (t \to_{(\pm(\mathbf{b}_1, \alpha))} s).$$

λ is a label indicating the nature of the delegation/revocation double arrow. As $\mathbf{a}_1$ moves from t to t along the arrow, he triggers the double arrow which sends a signal λ to $t \to_{\pm(\mathbf{b}_1, \alpha)} s$. Let us assume that $\lambda =$ switch. Then if the annoation of $t \to s$ is "+", it turns into "-" and if it is "-" it turns it into "+". thus the double arrow is a switch!

Let us look at Figure 9.9.

Again, let us assume that $\lambda_1 = \lambda_2 = \lambda_3 =$ switch. Suppose $\mathbf{a}_1$ goes along the path

$$t \to_{(\mathbf{a}_1, \mathbf{b}_1, \alpha) \text{ and } (\mathbf{a}_1, \mathbf{a}_2, \alpha)} t \to_{(\mathbf{a}_1, \mathbf{b}_1, \alpha) \text{ and } (\mathbf{a}_1, \mathbf{a}_2, \alpha)} t$$

and then $\mathbf{a}_2$ continues along the path $t \to_{(\mathbf{a}_2, \mathbf{b}_1, \alpha)} t$.

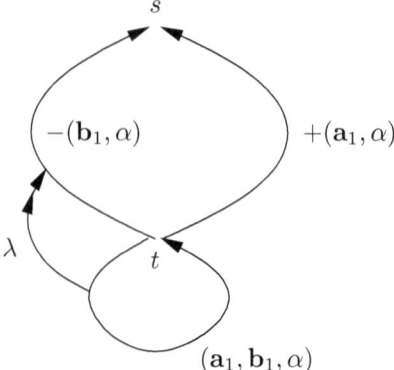

Figure 9.8.

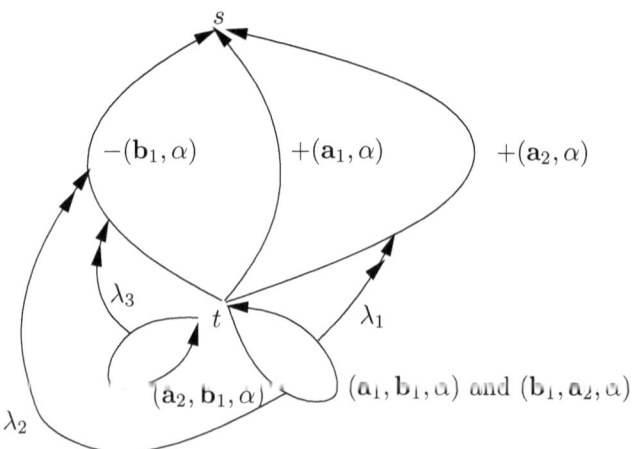

Figure 9.9.

The total movement is

$$t \to_{(\mathbf{a}_1,\mathbf{b}_1,\alpha)\ and\ (\mathbf{a}_1,\mathbf{a}_2,\alpha)} t \to_{(\mathbf{a}_1,\mathbf{b}_1,\alpha)\ and\ (\mathbf{a}_1,\mathbf{a}_2,\alpha)} t \to_{(\mathbf{a}_2,\mathbf{b}_1,\alpha)} t$$

The first $t \to_{(\mathbf{a}_1,\mathbf{b}_1,\alpha)\ and\ (\mathbf{a}_1,\mathbf{a}_2,\alpha)} t$ switches $-(\mathbf{b}_1,\alpha)$ into $+(\mathbf{b}_1,\alpha)$. We consider that legitimate because we do have in the Figure $t \to_{+(\mathbf{a}_1,\alpha)} s$.

This same first movement also revokes the right of $\mathbf{a}_2$ to execute α. So it switches $+(\mathbf{a}_2,\alpha)$ into $-(\mathbf{a}_2,\alpha)$. Now $\mathbf{a}_2$ cannot delegate α because his ability to execute α was revoked by $\mathbf{a}_1$. Fortunately, $\mathbf{a}_1$ went again through $t \to_{(\mathbf{a}_1,\mathbf{b}_1,\alpha)\ and\ (\mathbf{a}_1,\mathbf{a}_2,\alpha)} t$ and switched back to $+(\mathbf{a}_2,\alpha)$ and $-(\mathbf{b}_1,\alpha)$. Now $\mathbf{a}_2$ can go through his arc $t \to_{(\mathbf{a}_2,\mathbf{b}_1,\alpha)} t$ and switch on $+(\mathbf{b}_1,\alpha)$.

In the general case, where $\lambda_1, \lambda_2, \lambda_3$ can be general labels, not necessarily "switches", we need to collect the labels and decide whether the target arc (which is hit by several labels) is supposed to be on ("+") or not ("-").

For example, assume that

λ_1 = switch
λ_2 = dominant delegation
λ_3 = switch

So as we move along

$$t \to_{(\mathbf{a}_1,\mathbf{b}_1,\alpha)\ and\ (\mathbf{a}_1,\mathbf{a}_2,\alpha)} t$$

the arc $t \to_{+(\mathbf{a}_2,\alpha)} s$ is switched to $t \to_{-(\mathbf{a}_2,\alpha)} s$ and the arc $t \to_{-(\mathbf{b}_1,\alpha)} s$ is changed to dominant $t \to_{+(\mathbf{b}_1,\alpha)} s$.

As we continue along

$$t \to_{(\mathbf{a}_1,\mathbf{b}_1,\alpha)\ and\ (\mathbf{a}_1,\mathbf{a}_2,\alpha)} t$$

the arc $t \to_{-(\mathbf{a}_2,\alpha)} s$ changes back to become $t \to_{+(\mathbf{a}_2,\alpha)} s$ as it is hit by λ_1 but the arc $t \to_{+(\mathbf{b}_1,\alpha)} s$ does not change as it is hit again by λ_2 = dominant delegation.

Now we continue along the arc

$$t \to_{(\mathbf{a}_2,\mathbf{b}_1,\alpha)} t$$

and the arc $t \to_{+(\mathbf{a}_1,\alpha)} s$ is hit by λ_3 = switch. the $+(\mathbf{b}_1,\alpha)$ does not change because it was hit before by λ_2 = dominant delegation and it is now hit by just a switch, which is not dominant.

Now if λ_3 were

λ_3' = dominant revocation

then we would need to decide whether the triple $\{\lambda_2, \lambda_2, \lambda_3'\}$ should end up with + or with -.

This means that in the general case, when we go along a path and trigger various double arrows with labels, we need to calculate using a flattening algorithm Λ, whether any given arc is "+" or "-". We collect all the albels λ_j which hit the arc along the path and let Λ "flatten" it to either "+" or "-".

We also note, see Figure 9.10, that we have the notation to delegate from state t to state r, where r can be anywhere in the system. However the Talmud

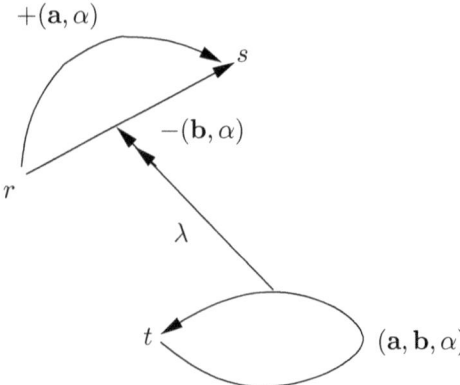

Figure 9.10.

does not allow for delegation for action which is not definite now but will be in the future. We can however put a condition into the precondition of an action but we have to delegate immediately. So I cannot say: when the Euro rate becomes over 1.4 to the Dollar you become my delegate to sell my house, but I can say: I delegate you now to sell my house on the condition that the Euro rate becomes over 1.4 to the Dollar. Thus according to the Talmud, Figure 9.10 cannot arise unless $r = t$.

What we learn from the above examples and discussion is the following:

1. We need to specify an annotated path π of delegation.

2. Final revocation or delegation is according to the last delegation (revocation) action in case of switch double arrows but requires a falttening function Λ if we use labels.

3. The double arrows, through their labels, give us who has power over whom to delegate or revoke.

4. We can constrain the movements along the arcs by the geometry of the arcs.

We are devoting special attention to switch labels because this is the simplest model. An agent **a** at node t who wants to delegate can go the appropriate arc $t \to t$ with the appropriate double arrow emanating from it. To revoke he just goes again through the arc. To cancel the revocation, he goes again, etc.

This is the simplest model.

Option 4: Reactivity model for the *power of attorney* view of Maimonides

Our starting point for modelling this view is Figure 9.7, which we modify for representing the case of power of attorney. We get Figure 9.11.

$\mathbf{a}_1$ can execute action α and move from state t to state s. $\mathbf{b}_1$ cannot do this. In Figure 9.11, the fact that $\mathbf{a}_1$ can go from t to s is represented by the

9. DELEGATION, COUNT AS, AND SECURITY IN TALMUDIC LOGIC

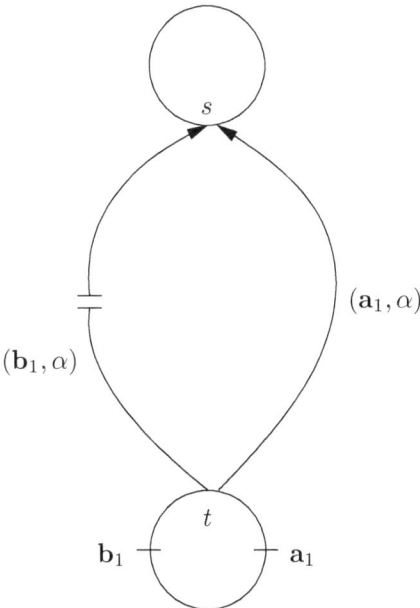

Figure 9.11.

continuous arrow
$$t \to_{(\mathbf{a}_1,\alpha)} s.$$
The fact that $\mathbf{b}_1$ cannot execute action α and go from t to s is represented by the broken arrow
$$t \not\to_{(\mathbf{b}_1,\alpha)} s$$

The big circle around t and the big circle around s are the locations (round tables for t and s respectively) where our agents are sitting ready to delegate and take action. In the *long arm* view, if applied to Figure 9.11, agent $\mathbf{a}_1$ can delegate (long arm) to agent $\mathbf{b}_1$ the action α by sending a double arrow to the gap of agent $\mathbf{b}_1$ and closign the gap for him so $\mathbf{b}_1$ can move from t to s along his own arrow.

Figure 9.12 shows this long arm delegation and it should be compared with the slightly different Figure 9.8.

However, in the case of the *power of attorney* view, $\mathbf{a}_1$ delegates to $\mathbf{b}_1$ by allowing for a double arrow from $\mathbf{b}_1$ to $\mathbf{a}_1$ inside the round talbe circle at t. Figure 9.13 shows what we mean.

In Figure 9.13, agent $\mathbf{b}_1$ does have a way to move from t to s exeuting α. He moves from t to s executing α. He moves along the double arrow $\mathbf{b}_1 \twoheadrightarrow \mathbf{a}_1$ to $\mathbf{a}_1$ position and then moves to s along the $\mathbf{a}_1$ arc
$$t \to_{(\mathbf{a}_1,\alpha)} s.$$
Here we see how $\mathbf{a}_1$ truly sends $\mathbf{b}_1$ along his own arc!

We note that actually there was no need to draw the broken arc $t \not\to_{\mathbf{b}_1,\alpha)} s$ in Figure 9.11. Since $\mathbf{b}_1$ cannot go from t to s by executing α, it is quite

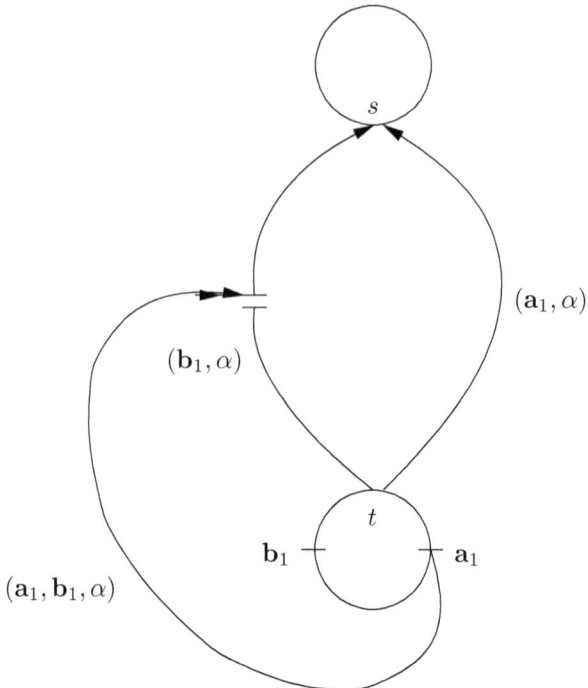

Figure 9.12. Long arm delegation of α from $\mathbf{a}_1$ to $\mathbf{b}_1$

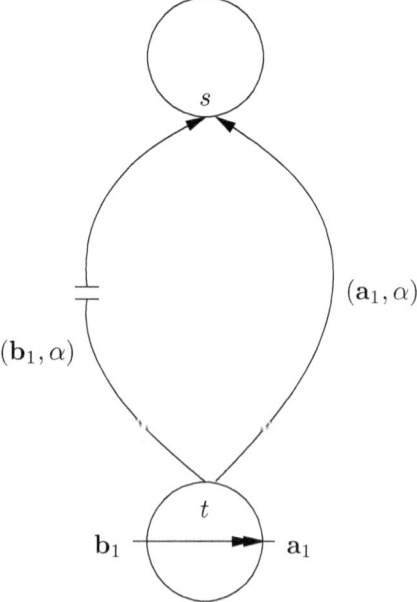

Figure 9.13. Power of attorney delegation of α from $\mathbf{a}_1$ to $\mathbf{b}_1$

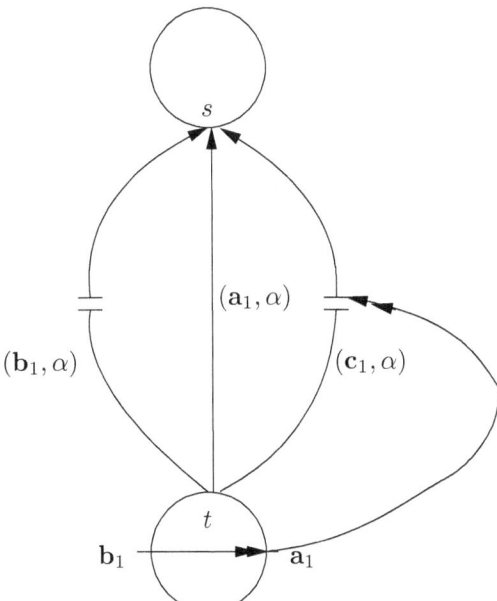

Figure 9.14.

sufficient not to draw an arc for b_1 at all, and the absence of such an arc would indicate that b_1 cannot get to s. However for the sake of comparison, of the *long arm* view with the *power of attorney* view (as shown in Figures 9.12 and 9.13) it is advantageous to draw the broken arc in Figure 9.11.

Note that the Talmudic options for delegation are either the long arm view in all cases, or the *power of attorney* view in all cases. We do not have the mixed option, as in Figure 9.14. In other words, the Talmud has many cases and debates about delegtion. Maimonides takes the view that they are all power of attorney cases and the Tur takes the view that they are all long arm cases.

In Figure 9.14, agent a_1 gives a power of attorney delegation to b_1 to execute α and at the same time gives a long arm delegation to c_1 to execute α.

EXAMPLE 9.6. To show the difference between the *long arm* and *power of attorney* view, consider the following examples.

1. Ruby and Simon delegate to Levy to dig a hole in the road (to access some pipes). An accident happened. A child fell into the hole and died. Ruby panicked and fled the country.

   According to the *long arm* view of delegation, we consider it as if each of Ruby and Simon dug the hole himself. So each is 100% responsible for damages. According to the *power of attorney* view, Levy was their joint agent and so each is 50% responsible for damages.

2. Another example is Simon delegates Levy to go to Sarah and give her a ring of engatement on behalf of himself. Simon has no money to buy the

ring, so Levy (a good friend) buys the ring from his own money and gives it to Sarah.

The Talmudic argumentation for this story goes as follows:

(a) According to the *long arm* view, Levy is the long arm of Simon. So it is as if Simon himself gives the ring to Sarah, which he did not buy with his own money. The law says that the ring must be bought with the money of the person to whom Sarah is to be engaged (i.e. Simon). So the engagement action as performed is not valid. According to the *power of attorney* view, the engagement is valid. Levy has a power of attorney to do a job. Levy is not a long arm of Simon. He does the job with his own money. This is fine.

(b) The Talmud could have argued differently from the above. It could have said that according to the *long arm* view Levy is now Simon and so Levy's money counts as Simon's money, so the engagement is valid. While the *power of attorney* view would say that as an empowered agent, Levy is not Simon, so Levy's money is not Simon's money and so the engagement is not valid.

Our model supports the Talmudic acutal argument (a) and not the alternative argument (b) and thus properly models the Talmud.

In Figure 9.12, it is essentially $\mathbf{a}_1$ which goes through the arc of $\mathbf{b}_1$ to execute α. His long arm $\mathbf{b}_1$ goes for him through the arc

$$t \to_{(\mathbf{b}_1,\alpha)} s$$

which now has no gap.

In Figure 9.13, $\mathbf{b}_1$ goes thorugh the arc

$$t \to_{(\mathbf{a}_1,\alpha)} s$$

and so $\mathbf{b}_1$ is indeed a power of attorney agent for $\mathbf{a}_1$.

The difference between the cases is which arc is traversed by the agent $\mathbf{b}_1$. Is it $t \to_{(\mathbf{b}_1,\alpha)} s$, (long arm case) or is it $t \to_{(\mathbf{a}_1,\alpha)} s$ (power of attorney case)?

3.2 The reactive switch model for the *long arm* view of Tur

We now present formal definitions for the reactive case with switch double arrows.

DEFINITION 9.7. (Reactive delegation action model for switch double arrows) Let $\mathbf{A}$ be a finite set of agents and $\mathcal{A}$ a finite set of actions. Let $\mathbb{L}$ be a predicate language and assume that $\{\mathbf{m}\}$ are models for $\mathbb{L}$. We assume the actions $\alpha \in \mathcal{A}$ have preconditions A_α and postconditions B_α in the language $\mathbb{L}$. By a reactive model we mean a tuple $\mathfrak{M} = (S, \mathbf{R}_a, \mathcal{R}, \mathbb{D}, a, \mathbf{m}_t), t \in S$ where

S is a set of states

$\mathbf{R}_a$ is a function giving values in $\{0, 1\}$ to tuples of the form $(t, \mathbf{a}, \alpha)$ and to tuples of the form $(t, s, \mathbf{a}, \alpha), t, s \in S, \mathbf{a} \in \mathbf{A}, \alpha \in \mathcal{A}$,

9. DELEGATION, COUNT AS, AND SECURITY IN TALMUDIC LOGIC   287

$a \in S$ is the initial state.

$\mathbb{D} \subseteq \mathbf{A} \times \mathcal{A}$ says which agent is a master of which action. Such actions the agent can delegate. We can code $\mathbb{D}$ as part of $\mathbf{R}$ by having

$$\mathbb{D} = \{(\mathbf{a}, \alpha) | \mathbf{R}_a(\mathbf{a}, \alpha) = 1\}.$$

$\mathcal{R}$ is a set of double arrows of the form

$$(t, \mathbf{a}, \mathbf{b}, \alpha) \twoheadrightarrow (u, r, \mathbf{b}, \alpha)$$

or the form

$$(t, \mathbf{a}, \mathbf{b}, \alpha) \twoheadrightarrow (u, \mathbf{b}, \mathbf{c}, \alpha)$$

where $t, u, r \in S, \alpha \in \mathcal{A}, \mathbf{a}, \mathbf{b} \in \mathbf{A}$.
$\mathbf{m}_t$ are models of $\mathbb{L}$.
We assume that if $(t, s, \mathbf{a}, \alpha) \in$ domain $\mathbf{R}_a$ and $(t, s', \mathbf{b}, \alpha) \in$ domain $\mathbf{R}_a$ then $s = s'$.
Note the following:

1. If $\mathbf{R}_a(t, \mathbf{a}, \mathbf{b}, \alpha) = 0$ then at state t, agent $\mathbf{a}$ cannot delegate α as he cannot pass through the arc $t \rightarrow_{(\mathbf{a}, \mathbf{b}, \alpha)} t$.

2. Whenever $(t, \mathbf{a}, \mathbf{b}, \alpha) \twoheadrightarrow (u, r, \mathbf{b}, \alpha)$ (or resp., $(t, \mathbf{a}, \mathbf{b}, \alpha) \twoheadrightarrow (u, \mathbf{b}, \mathbf{c}, \alpha)$) is in $\mathcal{R}$ then agent $\mathbf{a}$ by going through the arc $t \rightarrow_{(\mathbf{a}, \mathbf{b}, \alpha)} t$ (if he is allowed to delegate and other conditions hold) can delegate or revoke the ability of agent $\mathbf{b}$ to execute action α at state u (ending at state v if allowed by other factors), (respectively delegate or revoke the ability of agent $\mathbf{b}$ to delegate or revoke action α at state u to agent $\mathbf{c}$).

DEFINITION 9.8. **(Legitimate path in a model for switch double arrows)** Let $\mathfrak{M} = (S, \mathbf{R}_a, \mathcal{R}, \mathbb{D}, a, \mathbf{m}_t), t \in S$ be a model. We define the notion of legitimate annotated path of the form

$$\pi = (a \rightarrow_{e_1} x_1 \rightarrow_{e_2} x_2 \rightarrow \ldots \rightarrow x_{n-1} \rightarrow_{e_n} x_n)$$

where $x_i \in S$ and e_i are annotation labels of the form

$$e_i = (\mathbf{a}_i, \mathbf{b}_i, \alpha).$$

As part of the definition of legitimate path we associate by induction a function $\mathbf{R}_{\pi_i}$ with the initial path $a \rightarrow_{e_1} x_1 \rightarrow \ldots \rightarrow_{e_i} x_i$.

Step 0 $\pi = (a)$ and $\mathbf{R}_{(a)} = \mathbf{R}_a$.

Step $i+1$ Assume we have $\mathbf{R}_{\pi_i}$.
We define $\mathbf{R}_{\pi_{i+1}}$, where $\pi_{i+1} = \pi_1 \cup \{x_{i+1} \rightarrow_{e_{i+1}} x_{i+1}\}$.

Subcase 1 Delegation. In this case $x_i = x_{i+1}$ and $\mathbf{R}_{\pi_i}(x_i, \mathbf{a}_i, \mathbf{b}_i, \alpha) = 1$ and

$$\mathbf{R}_{\pi_{i+1}}(u, v, \mathbf{b}, \alpha) = \begin{cases} 1 - \mathbf{R}_{\pi_i}(u, v, \mathbf{b}_i, \alpha) \\ \text{if } (t, \mathbf{a}, \mathbf{b}_i, \alpha) \twoheadrightarrow (u, v, \mathbf{b}_i, \alpha) \\ \text{is in } \mathcal{R} \\ \text{and } \mathbf{R}_{\pi_i}(u, v, \mathbf{b}_i, \alpha) \text{ otherwise} \end{cases}$$

Similarly

$$\mathbf{R}_{\pi_{i+1}}(u,\mathbf{b},\alpha) = \begin{cases} 1 - \mathbf{R}_{\pi_i}(u,\mathbf{b}_i,\mathbf{c}_i,\alpha) \text{ if} \\ (t,\mathbf{a},\mathbf{b}_i,\alpha) \twoheadrightarrow (u,\mathbf{b}_i,\mathbf{c}_i,\alpha) \text{ is in } \mathcal{R} \\ \text{and } \mathbf{R}_{\pi_i}(u,\mathbf{b}_i,\mathbf{c}_i,\alpha) \text{ otherwise.} \end{cases}$$

Subcase 2 Action. In this case $x_i \neq x_{i+1}$ and $\mathbf{R}_{\pi_i}(x_i, x_{i+1}, \mathbf{a}_i, \alpha) = 1$ and $\mathbf{m}_{x_i} \vDash A_\alpha$. Let $\mathbf{R}_{\pi_{i+1}} = \mathbf{R}_{\pi_i}$.

Note that if the action α does not change the state x_i, then we still go to $x_{i+1} \neq x_i$, but we will have $\mathbf{m}_{x_i} = \mathbf{m}_{x_{i+1}}$.

REMARK 9.9.

1. Now that we have models, we can use modal operators and define satisfaction for them. The only modal operator of interest is the one having to do with delegation.

2. Note that in this model **a** can delegate to **b** to execute action α from state u. This is not general delegation but a very specific one.

DEFINITION 9.10 (Delegation modalities for switch double arrow). Let us add to the language two modalities $\Diamond$ and $\Diamond_\alpha$, defined as follows in the model $\mathfrak{M}$. $\Diamond$ corresponds to arbitrary legitimate paths. $\Diamond_\alpha$ corresponds to α delegation paths.

1. Let $\pi = a \to_{e_1} x_1 \to \ldots \to_{e_n} x_n$ be an arbitrary legitimate path. Let π' be an extension of π, namely

$$\pi' = a \to_{e_1} x_1 \to \ldots \to_{e_n} x_n \to_{e_{n+1}} y_1 \to \ldots \to_{e_{n+m}} y_m$$

We say

- $\pi \vDash \Diamond A$ iff for some extension π', $\pi' \vDash A$
- $\pi \vDash A$ without modalities, iff $\mathbf{m}_{x_n} \vDash A$.

2. A sequence π is said to be α delegation path if for some t we have $x_i = t$ for all i and $e_i = (t, \mathbf{a}_i, \mathbf{b}_i \alpha)$. We can now define

- $\pi \vDash \Diamond_\alpha A$ iff for some extension π' of π such that $x_n \to_{e_{n+1}} y_1 \to \ldots \to_{e_{n+m}} y_m$ is an α delegation path, we have $\pi' \vDash A$.

3. We can similarly define single modalities for each single connection of the form $t \twoheadrightarrow_{(\mathbf{a},\alpha)} s$. The modality is $\Diamond_{(\mathbf{a},\alpha)}$. Similarly we can define $\Diamond_{(\mathbf{a},\mathbf{b},\alpha)}$.

4 Comparison with modern literature

Let us start with the 2001 survey paper [67] and the 2011 logical implementation paper [14] based on it.

Paper [67] addresses an ownership-based framework for access control. Delegation here takes the form of granting access and administrative rights to other agents thus forming chains of granted accesses. The paper is a comprehensive study of the problem of revoking such rights, and of the impact different revocation schemes may have on the delegation chains. Three main revocation characteristics are identified:

a. the extent of the revocation to other grantees (propagation).

b. the effect on other grants to the same grantee (dominance).

c. the permanence of the negation of rights (resilience).

A classification is devised using these three dimensions. The different schemes thus obtained are described, and compared to other models from the literature of the time (up to 2001).

We begin by comparing this scheme with Delegation in the Talmud. The Talmud deals with a person delegating an action to another, to do the action on his behalf. The situation where a delegate can get instructions from two different people to do the same action as a delegate for each of them cannot arise. For example when delegating the selling of a house, only the owner of the house can delegate. If the ownership is shared, one can delegate selling only his share. We cannot have a situation where two different people delegate the same action to a third party. You may ask, how does the Talmud view the delegation of access control? The Talmud does not consider this as a recognised delegation of Halakhic action.[5] According to the Talmud, one cannot delegate an action which does not affect an actual change in some legally recognised state of affairs[6] Selling property, buying, divorcing, getting engaged, are candidates for delegation in the Talmud; breaking a window, jumping over a fence — are not. So revocation becomes rather simple here. In the *long arm/extended reach* view of Talmudic delegation, the original master can revoke the last link in the delegation chain and reinstate him at will. The other members of the chain are not part of the *long arm/extended reach* at any stage. In the *power of attorney* view each element in the chain can revoke only the next one. So if the master delegates to an agent and the agent delegates to a subagent, theoretically the master can revoke the delegation to the agent alone, and may be too late if the subagent was already delegated by the agent.

---

[5]There are references to access permission, but normally as a peripheral sign of a substantive action — such as giving entrance permission or a key as sign of a finalized sale. Access to information is generally restricted in a ruling named after Rabbeinu Gershom (end of the 10th century), appearing in the Responsa of Meir of Rothenburg (1215 - 1293), IV, Ch. 1000 section 22. The general result is that "...the Halachah insists upon the responsibility of each individual not to put himself into a position where he can pry into his neighbor's personal domain, and this responsibility can be enforced by the courts." (Lamm, Norman, "The Fourth Amendment and it's equivalent in the Halachah", Judaism: a quarterly journal, Volume 16, Number 3, Summer 1967, pp. 300–312, p. 303). In modern information-access scenarios (of passcodes and user access), often the question of access to information databases is deliberated along the lines of the authorities given to someone renting a house (Maimonides Rent Laws, 5,5; Responsa Maimonides , 166) — the possibility of subletting, exceeding the capacity, etc.

[6]Sometimes this is called "words cannot be delegated" (Milei lo Mimseran leShaliach). Cf. Tractate Kiddushin 29a, 42a and the commentators.

There is one exception: although normally delegation does not work when sending an agent to perform an illegal act,[7] there are rare exceptions[8] In cases of great duress (a coerced agent),[9] the act of murder can be considered as delegated — a person can be considered as an assassin-agent with consequent legal blame on the sender. Theoretically, in the case of murdering somebody, you can have an assassin-agent being delegated to murder by several people. In this case revocation policy is simple. If one of the people revokes the other delegations still stand. Note that according to the *long arm/extended reach* view all masters who delegated to the assassin are each individually murdering the victim (because the assassin is their extension) while with the *power of attorney* view, only the agent-assassin is doing the murdering. The second paper, [14], gives a logical model to the first paper, [67]. The implementation is according to Option 1, where the delegation chains only are modelled as an update system. Recently in paper [17] Barker *et al.* offer a reactive model for access control, which is another way of modelling [67] and more.

Other algorithmic papers dealing with chains of delegations and revocation systems are [23; 16; 41; 75; 42; 71; 15; 14].

5 Conclusion and discussion

In this chapter we gave a preliminary study of delegation in the Talmud and compared it with modern delegation theory. In the Talmud the emphasis is more theoretical; the Talmud is concerned more with the nature of delegation and circumstances for its cancellation, death or madness of the people involved and there is not so much emphasis on revocation. Talmudic delegation is more personal, private persons delegate for the purpose of some legal action, divorce, buying and selling, and so revocation is a simple person to person act. Modern delegation is mainly for access control or the endowment of privileges usually involving large institutions and systems and so revocation protocols and the handling of delegation chains is more central. The emphasis is less conceptual and more algorithmic.

---

[7]The reason often quoted is stated in Tractate Bava Metzia as "Who do you listen to — the master or the student?" (*Divrei Harav V'Divrei Hatalmid divrei Me shomin*). This could mean either: a. that the delegation process did not take off, since the agent could not take the word of the sender over that of the Halakhic prohibition (Joshua ben Alexander HaCohen Falk (1555–1614), Sefer Me'irat Enayim, Choshen Mishpat 182(2), 348(20); Tosafot on Tractate Bava Kama 79a, "Natnu"), or b. that the entire concept of delegation in Halakha is an artificial construct, and thus is simply not defined for actions that are illegal (in the words of A. Kircshenbaum: 'The institute of Shlichut is the creation of the law; as an instrument to break the law — it was not created and does not exist', Dinei Israel Vol. 4, 1973, pp. 55–56).

[8]Three cases are listed in Tractate Kiddushin, 13: the sale of stolen livestock, theft from Hekdesh (consecrated property), and the misuse of property given to the sender for safekeeping.

[9]This is extremely rare. Normally there is harsh moral blame on the person hiring an assassin, but not enforceable in a human court (Maimonides, Laws of Murder and Saving Lives, 2(2-4)). The coerced murder delegation status is considered by some as bona fide delegation (R. Mordechai de Boton in his Responsa, p. 127). For example, the case of David and the death of Uriah in battle (David Kimhi (1160–1235), RaDaK on Shmuel II, 12:9). This understanding is hotly debated, and the issue is thoroughly adumbrated by R. Ovadia Hedaya (1889–1969, prominent Israeli Posek of the previous generation), in his Responsa Yaskil Avdi, Yore De'ah Vol. I, section 6(2).

REFERENCES

[1] J. L. Ackrill, (translator). *Aristotle's Categories and De Interpretatione*, Oxford University Press, 1963.
[2] M. Abraham, D. Gabbay and U. Schild. Paper 340 Kal-Vachomer in Hebrew, 112 pages. BDD Journal, Bar Ilan University.
[3] M. Abraham, D. Gabbay and U. Schild. Analysis of the Talmudic Argumentation A Fortiori Inference Rule (Kal-Vachomer) using Matrix Abduction. *Studia Logica*, 92:3, 281–364, 2009.
[4] M. Abraham, D. Gabbay, G. Hazut, Y. Maruvka and U. Schild. *The Textual Inference Rules Klal uPrat* (in Hebrew). College Publicatins, London, 2010. Hebrew paper 369. 200pp. 2009.
[5] M. Abraham, D. Gabbay and U. Schild. Obligations and prohibitions in Talmudic deontic logic. In *DEON 2010*, G. Governatori and G. Sartor, eds., pp. 166–178. LNAI 6181, Springer, 2010.
[6] M. Abraham, D. Gabbay and U. Schild. *Talmudic Deontic Logic*, College Publications, 2010.
[7] M. Abraham, D. Gabbay and U. Schild. *Future Determination of Entitites in Talmudic Logic. Journal of Applied Logic*, 11(1), 63–90, 2013. http://dx.doi.org/10.1016/j.jal.2012.06.001
[8] M. Abraham, D. Gabbay and U. Schild. *Talmudic Temporal Logic*. College Publications, 2011, 600pp.
[9] M. Abraham, D. Gabbay and U. Schild. Obligations and prohibitions in Talmudic deontic logic. In *DEON 2010, LNAI 6181*, G. Governatori and G. Sartor, eds., pp. 166–178, 2010.
[10] M. Abraham, D. M. Gabbay, and U. Schild. The handling of loops in Talmudic logic with application to odd and even loops in argumentation. In *Proceedings of Howard 60*, D. Rydeheard, A. Vronkov and M. Korovina, eds., pp. 1–25, 2011.
[11] M. Abraham, D. Gabbay and U. Schild. *Contrary to Time Conditionals in Talmudic Logic. Journal of AI and Law*. DOI: 10.1007/s10506-012-9123-x.
[12] M. Abraham, G. Hazut, D. Gabbay, Maruvka and U. Schild. Logical Analysis of the Talmudic Rule of General and Specific (Klal-u-Prat). Special issue on Judaic Logic edited by A Schumann, *Journal of the History and Philosophy of Logic*, Vol 32 issue 1, pp 47–62, 2011.
[13] R. von Mises, Probability, Statistics and Truth [Dover, 1957], originally published in German [Springer, 1928].
[14] G. Aucher, S. Barker, G. Boella, V. Genovese and L. van der Torre. Dynamics in Delegation and Revocation Schemes: A Logical Approach. In *Conference on Data and Applications Security and Privacy (DBSec'11)*, Richmond, Virginia USA. July 11-13, 2011

[15] O. Bandmann, M. Dam, and B. S. Firozabadi. Constrained Delegation. In *IEEE Symbposum on Security and Privacy*, pp. 131–140, 2002.
[16] E. Barka and R. Sandhu. Framework for Role-Based Delegation Models,. In *Proceedings of the 16th Annual Computer Security Applications Conference*, May 2000, pp. 168-176.
[17] S. Barker, G. Boella, D. Gabbay and V. Genovese. Reactive Kripke Models and Answer Set Programming Applications to Delegation and Revocation Schemes. To appear in *Journal of Logic and Computation*, 2012. doi: 10.1093/logcom/exs014.
[18] Steve Barker, Guido Boella, Dov M. Gabbay and Valerio Genovese. A Meta-model of Access Control in a Fibred Security Language, *Studia Logica*, 92(3), 437–477, 2009.
[19] P. Baroni and M. Giacomin. Solving semantic problems with odd-length cycles in argumentation. In *Proceedings of the 7th European Conference on Symbolic and Quantitative Approaches to Reasoning with Uncertainty (EC-SQARU 2003)*, pp. 440–451. LNAI 2711, Springer-Verlag, Aalborg, Denmark, 2003.
[20] P. Baroni, M. Giacomi and G. Guida. SCC-recursiveness: a general schema for argumentation semantics. *Artificial Intelligence*, 168 (1-2):162–210, 2005.
[21] H. Barringer, D. Gabbay and J. Woods. Temporal dynamics of argumentation networks. In D. Hutter and W. Stephan, eds., *Mechanising Mathematical Reasoning*, pp. 59–98, LNCS 2605, Springer, 2005.
[22] Moritz Y. Becker, Jason F. Mackay and Blair Dillaway. Abductive Authorization Credential Gathering, *Studia Logica*, this issue.
[23] E. Bertino, S. Jajodia, and P. Samarati. Non-timestamped Authorization Model for Data Management Systems. In *3rd ACM Conference on Computer and Communications Security*, March 1996, pp. 169-178.
[24] P. Besnard and A. B. Hunter. *Elements of Argumentation*, 300pp. MIT Press, 2008.
[25] G. A. Bodanza and F. A. Tohmé. Two approaches to the problems of self-attacking arguments and general odd-length cycles of attack. *Journal of Applied Logic*, 7, 403–420, 2009.
[26] S. J. Brams, D. M. Kilgour, and W. S. Zwicker. The paradox of multiple elections. *Social Choice and Welfare*, 15:211–236, 1998.
[27] M. de Boer, D. Gabbay, X. Parent and M. Slavkova. Two dimensional standard deontic logic. *Synthese*, 187(2), 623–660, 2012. doi: 10.1007/s11229-010-9866-4.
[28] J. Broersen, A. Herzig and N. Troquard. From coalition logic to STIT. *Electronic Notes in Theoretical Computer Science*, 157, 23–35, 2006.
[29] Martin Caminada. A Labelling Approach for Ideal and Stage Semantics. *Argument and Computation*, 2 (1): 1–21, 2011.
[30] M. Caminada. Preferred Semantics as Socratic Discussion, 2011.
[31] M. W. A. Caminada and Y. Wu. On the Limitations of Abstract Argumentation *BNAIC 2011*, Gent.
[32] M. W. A. Caminada and L. Amgoud. On the evaluation of argumentation formalisms, *Artificial Intelligence*, 171 (5–6), 286–310, 2007.

[33] Brian Chellas. *Modal Logic. An Introduction.* Cambridge University Press, 1980.
[34] Maria Luisa Dalla Chiara, Roberto Giuntini and Miklos Rédei. The History of Quantum Logic. In *Handbook of the History of Logic. Volume 8*, pp. 205–283, Dov M. Gabbay and John Woods, eds. Elsevier 2007.
[35] L. Cholvy and C. Garion. An Attempt to Adapt a Logic of Conditional Preferences for Reasoning with Contrary-To-Duties. *Fundamenta Informaticae*, 48, 2-3, 183–204, 2001.
[36] J. Carmo and A. J. I. Jones. Deontic Logic and Contrary-to-Duties. In D. M Gabbayand F. Guenthner, eds. *Handbook of Philosophical Logic*, vol 8, pp. 265-343, Springer, 2002.
[37] H. P. van Ditmarsch, W. van der Hoek and B. P. Kooi. *Dynamic Epistemic Logic*, Volume 337 of *Synthese Library*. Springer, 2007.
[38] Phan Minh Dung. An argumentation theoretic foundation for logic programming. *Journal of Logic Programming*, 22(2), 151–171, 1995.
[39] M. Eilon. *Jewish Law*, 4 volumes. Jewish Publication Society of America. Reprint edition, 1994.
[40] Final Proposed Draft Amendment on Certificate Extensions(v6). Generated from Collaborative ITU and ISO/IEC meeting on the Directory, April 1999. Orlando, Florida, USA.
[41] B. S. Firozabadi, M. Sergot, and O. Bandmann. Using Authority Certificates to Create Management Structures. In *Proceedings of Security Protocols, 9th International Workshop*, Cambridge, UK, pages 134–145. Springer Verlag, 2001.
[42] B. S. Firozabadi and M. Sergot. Revocation Schemes for Delegated Authorities. In *Proceedings of Policy 2002: IEEE 3rd International Workshop on Policies for Distributed Systems and Networks*. IEEE, June 2002.
[43] Menachem Fisch. *Rational Rabbis: Science and Talmudic Culture.* Indiana University Press, Bloomignton, 1997.
[44] D. Gabbay and J. Woods. Resource origins of non-monotonicity. *Studia Logica*, Vol. 88, 2008, pp. 85–112.
[45] D. Gabbay and A. Garcez. Logical modes of attack in argumentation networks. *Studia Logica*, 93(2-3), 199–230, 2009.
[46] D. M. Gabbay. *Labelled Deductive Systems*, OUP, 1996.
[47] D. M. Gabbay and J. Woods. *The Reach of Abduction*, Elsevier, 2005.
[48] T. K. Grabenhorst. *Das Argumentum A Fortiori*. Peter Lang, 1990.
[49] D. M. Gabbay and J. Woods. *Handbook of the History of Logic*, 12 Volumes, Elsevier, 2004–2011.
[50] D. Gabbay. Reactive Kripke semantics and contrary to duties, expanded version. *Journal of Applied Logic*, 11(1), 103–136, 2013.
[51] D. Gabbay and C. Strasser. Reactive Standard Deontic Logic. *Journal of Logic Computation*, 2012. doi: 10.1093/logcom/exs043
[52] D. Basin, M. D'Agostino, D. Gabbay, S. Matthews and L. Vigano, eds. *Labelled Deduction*, Springer, 2000.
[53] D. Gabbay, G. Pigozzi, and J. Woods. Controlled Revision - An Algorithmic Approach for Belief Revision. *Journal of Logic and Computation*, 13(1):15-35, 2003.

[54] D. Gabbay, O. Rodrigues, and A. Russo. *Revision Acceptability and Context*, Springer, 2010.
[55] D. Gabbay. Reactive Kripke semantics and contrary to duty obligations. In *Deon 2008, Deontic Logic in Computer Science*, R. van der Meyden and L. van der Torre, eds., LNAI 5076, pp. 155–173, Springer, 2008.
[56] Dov Gabbay. The declarative past and imperative future: executable temporal logic for the interactive systems. In *Proc. Temporal Logic in Specification, LNCS 398*, pp. 409–448, Springer-Verlag, 1987.
[57] D. M. Gabbay et al. *Temporal Logic: Mathematical Foundations and Computational Aspects, Volume 1*, Oxford University Press, 1994.
[58] D. M. Gabbay et al. *Temporal Logic: Mathematical Foundations and Computational Aspects, Volume 2*, Oxford University Press, 2000.
[59] D. M. Gabbay. Dynamics of practical reasoning: A position paper. In *Advances of Modal Logic, Volume 2*, K. Segerberg, M. Zakhryaschev, M. de Rijke and H. Wansing, eds. pp. 197–242. CSLI Publications, CUP, 2001.
[60] D.M. Gabbay. Introduction to labelled deductive systems. In *Handbook of Philosophical Logic* Volume 17, second edition, 2013.
[61] D. Gabbay. Equational Approach to Argumentation Networks. *Argumentation and Computation*, 3(2-3), 87–142, 2012.
[62] D. Gabbay. Reactive Kripke Semantics and Arc Accessibility. In *Pillars of Computer Science: Essays Dedicated to Boris (Boaz) Trakhtenbrot on the Occasion of His 85th Birthday*, Arnon Avron, Nachum Dershowitz, and Alexander Rabinovich, editors, Lecture Notes in Computer Science, vol. 4800, Springer-Verlag, Berlin, 2008 pp 292-341.
[63] S. A. Gaggl and S. Woltran. Strong Equivalence for Argumentation Semantics Based on Conflict-Free Sets, slides of lecture presented in ECSQARU 2011.
[64] G. Governatori and A. Rotolo. Changing legal systems: legal abrogations and annulments in defeasible logic. *Logic Journal of the IGPL*, 18: 157–194, 2010.
[65] M. Abraham, I. Belfer, D. Gabbay, and U. Schild. *Temporal Logic in the Talmud*, College Publications, 2011.
[66] D. Grossi and A. J. I. Jones Constitutive Norms and Counts-as Conditionals, Handbook of Deontic Logic chapter to appear.
[67] Å. Hagström, S. Jajodia, F. Parisi.Persicce, and D. Wijesekera. Revocation — a Classification. In *Proceeding of the 14th Computer Security Foundation Workshop*. IEEE press, 2001.
[68] J. Hansen, Conflicting imperatives and dyadic deontic logic. *Journal of Applied Logic*, 3, 484–511, 2005.
[69] S. Hartmann, G. Pigozzi and J. Sprenger. Reliable methods of judgement aggregation. Draft, 23 February 2009.
[70] A. Hasan. Analogical reasoning in Islamic jurisprudence, 1986. Republished Adam Publishers, 2007, 486 pp.
[71] A. Herzberg, Y. Mass, J. Mihaeli, D. Naor, and Y. Ravid. Access control meets public key infrastructure, or: Assigning roles to strangers. In *IEEE Symposium on Security and Privacy*, pages 2–14, 2000.

[72] E. Hirsch. Rashi's view of the Open Future: Indeterminateness and Bivalence. In *Oxford Studies in Metaphysics*, Oxford University Press, 2006.
[73] Jese Hughes. The muddy children. A logic for public announcement. Technical University of Eindhoven, February 10, 2007. http://phiwumbda.org/~jesse/slides/MuddlyChildren.handouts.pdf
[74] Louis Jacobs. *Studies in Talmudic Logic and Methodology*. London, Vallentine-Mitchell, 1061. Republished paperback, 2006.
[75] T. Jaeger, A. Edwards, and Xiaolan Zhang. Managing access control policies using access control spaces. In *Proceedings of the seventh ACM symposium on Access control models and technologies*, pages 3–12. ACM Press, 2002.
[76] A. J. I. Jones and M. Sergot. A formal characterization of institutionalised power. *Journal of the IGPL*, 3:427–443, 1996.
[77] M. H. Kamali. *Principles of Islamic Jurisprudence*, Islamic Text Society, 3rd Revised Eition, 2002, 550 pp.
[78] L. Kornhauser and L. Sager. Unpacking the court. *Yale Law Journal*, 96: 82–117, 1986.
[79] L. Kornhauser and L. Sager. The one and the many: adjudication in collegial courts. *California Law Review*, 81: 1–51, 1993.
[80] Arnold Kunst. An overlooked type of inference. *Bulletin of the School of Oriental and African Studies*, X, part 4, pp. 976–991, 1942.
[81] Jacob Neusner. The making of the mind of Judaism;the formative age. *Brown Judaic Studies*, vol 133, Scholars press, Atlanta, 1987.
[82] R. Nozick. *Anarchy, State and Utopia, 84–87*, 1974.
[83] R. Nozick. Coercion. In *Philosophy, Science, and Method: Essays in Hoor of Ernest Nagel*, S. Morgenbesser et al., eds., pp. 440–447, 1969.
[84] G. Pigozzi and L. van der Torre. Premise independence in judgement aggregation. Dagstuhl Seminar 07531, 2007.
[85] H. Prakken and G. Sartor. Argument based extended logic programming with defeasible priorities. *Journal of Applied Non-classical Logics*, 7:25–75, 1997.
[86] H. Prakken and M. Sergot. Contrary to duty obligations. *Studia Logica*, 57:1, 91–115, 1996.
[87] H. Prakken and M. Sergot. Dyadic deontic logic and contrary to duty obligations. In *Defeasible Deontic Logic*, D. Nute, ed., pp. 223-262. Synthese Library, Vol 263. Kluwer, 1997.
[88] H. Prakken. An abstract framework for argumentation with structured arguments *Argument & Computation*, 2010.
[89] E. Rissanen, B. S. Firozabadi, and M. Sergot. Towards a mechanism for discretionary overriding of access control, position paper. Presented at Security Protocols, *12th International Workshop*, Cambridge, UK, 2004.
[90] E. Rissanen, B. S. Firozabadi and M. Sergot. Discretionary Overriding of Access Control in the Privilege Calculus. *IFIP International Federation for Information Processing*, 2005, Volume 173, 219-232, 2005. DOI: 10.1007/0-387-24098-5_16
[91] U. J. Schild. Criminal Sentencing and Intelligent Decision Support, *Artificial Intelligence and Law*, vol. 6, 2-4, 1998.

[92] Erwin Schrödinger. *The Present Situation In Quantum Mechanics*, translator: John D. Trimmer. *Proceedings of the American Philosophical Society*, **124**:323-38. Reprint J. A. Wheeler and W. H. Zurek, eds., *Quantum Theory and Measurement*, Part 1, section I.11, Princeton University Press, New Jersey, 1983. See also article on Schroedinger's cat in *Wikipedia* http://en.wikipedia.org/wiki/Schroedinger's_cat

[93] Adolf Schwarz. *Der Hermeneutische Syllogismus in der Talmudischen*, Ltitteratur, Karlsruhe, 1901.

[94] J. Searle. *Speech Acts. An Essay in the Philosophy of Language*. Cambridge University Press, Cambridge, 1969.

[95] J. Searle. *The Construction of Social Reality*. Free Press, 1995.

[96] V. L. S. Stebbing. *A Modern Introduction to Logic*, London, 1945.

[97] L. van der Torre and Y. H. Tan. Contrary-to-duty reasoning with preference-based dyadic obligations. *Annals of Mathematics and Artificial Intelligence*, 27:1-4, 49–78, 1999.

[98] Bart Verheij. A Labelling approach to to the computation of credulous acceptance in argumentation. In *Proceedings IJCAI'07. Proceedings of the 20th international joint conference on Artifical intelligence*, 623–628. Morgan Kaufmann Publishers Inc. San Francisco, CA, USA, 2007.

[99] T. Wakaki. Preference-based Argumentation Capturing Prioritized Logic Programming, *ArgMAS*, 2010.

www.ingramcontent.com/pod-product-compliance
Lightning Source LLC
Chambersburg PA
CBHW050130170426
43197CB00011B/1777